THE
Palm Springs
DINER'S BIBLE

a,

nat

n

eB'n-Dan

Interesting

hoity

Toity!!

is

And the Compassionate and Just One caused to sprout from the ground every tree that was pleasing to the sight and good for food. (Genesis 2:9)

Every moving thing that lives shall be food for you; like the green herbage, I have given you everything. (Genesis 9:3)

THE
Palm Springs
DINER'S BIBLE

A Restaurant Guide for Palm Springs, Cathedral City,
Rancho Mirage, Palm Desert, Indian Wells, La Quinta,
Bermuda Dunes, Indio, and Desert Hot Springs

PETER OSBALDESTON

PELICAN PUBLISHING COMPANY
GRETNA 2010

To the memory of Julia Child

The word "Pelican" and the depiction of a pelican are trademarks of Pelican Publishing Company, Inc., and are registered in the U.S. Patent and Trademark Office.

Library of Congress Cataloging-in-Publication Data

Osbaldeston, Peter.
  The Palm Springs diner's bible : a restaurant guide for Palm Springs, Cathedral City, Rancho Mirage, Palm Desert, Indian Wells, La Quinta, Bermuda Dunes, Indio, and Desert Hot Springs / Peter Osbaldeston.
    p. cm.
  Includes indexes.
    ISBN 978-1-58980-750-1 (pbk. : alk. paper) 1. Restaurants—California—Palm Springs—Guidebooks. 2. Restaurants—California—Riverside County—Guidebooks. 3. Palm Springs (Calif.)—Guidebooks. 4. Riverside County (Calif.)—Guidebooks. I. Title.
  TX907.3.C22O356 2007
  647.95794'97—dc22
                2007022910

Printed in the United States of America

Published by Pelican Publishing Company, Inc.
1000 Burmaster Street, Gretna, Louisiana 70053

Contents

Introduction

Palm Springs is a city, an area, a resort, and a dreamland. The real Palm Springs is not very well known, but the *idea* of Palm Springs is known to everyone from Mongolian shepherds to the people who affix those little plastic things to the ends of shoelaces. The myth speaks of golf, tennis, and fine dining; sunbathing, swimming pools, and snow-capped mountains; luscious landscapes, abundant flowers, cascading water, and those elegant but oddly ridiculous Royal Palms. The very surrealism of it all feeds the mythology of Palm Springs, inflating it into a universal expression of iconic hedonism.

Is it true? Sure it is, but it is only one chapter—the chapter published aggressively by the Chamber of Commerce. The other chapters have to do with everything not quite so idyllic: taxes, politics, crime. At its core, Palm Springs is a city with a population of about 45,000 permanent residents, a city not very different from many other cities whose livelihoods are tied primarily to tourism.

When most people think of Palm Springs, what they are really thinking of are the nine resort cities of the Coachella Valley. Eight of these cities lie at the base of the Santa Rosa and San Jacinto mountains at the south rim of this low desert valley. From west to east they are Palm Springs, Cathedral City, Rancho Mirage, Palm Desert, Indian Wells, La Quinta, Bermuda Dunes (unincorporated), and Indio. The ninth city, and the only one at the north rim of the valley, is Desert Hot Springs. To outsiders, Palm Springs is the generic term for all these cities. Residents have long ago given up telling people where they live. When asked by an outsider, we simply say, "Palm Springs."

All these resort cities except Desert Hot Springs are connected by Highway 111, a more or less 50-mile-long meandering ribbon hugging the base of the mountains as it carves a path through the south side of the desert before turning right toward the Salton Sea and eventually Mexico. The natives call it Highway One Eleven, not One Hundred and Eleven or One-One-One. It is the fundamental artery of the California desert resort communities, pumping money, golf bags, bathing suits, and tennis rackets throughout the region.

As of fall 2006, there were 124 golf courses. Six years prior to that, there were 99. Yet, the golf courses can be counted. There are approximately 637 restaurants. These come and go so quickly that as soon as they are counted, two have opened and one has closed. No one knows exactly how many there are. The telephone book is out of date the moment it is printed.

The first edition of *The Palm Springs Diner's Bible* was completed early in 2007, which means that most of the research was done in 2006. As I write this, it is January 2010. What this means for you, dear readers, is that the first edition is at least three years old and some of it is older than that. I have deleted 29 restaurants from the first book. They have either closed, been bought out, or have substantially evolved into something else entirely. On the brighter side, an equal number of restaurants have joined the dining options in the Coachella Valley. Of these new additions, several are well worth your time and money. Chef Vince Cultraro has opened the new La Spiga, a magnificent "Italian" villa. Several smaller, more bistro-like restaurants of excellent quality have joined the ranks: Omri Go Med, Lavender Bistro, Zini Café Med, and Le Basil are just four of them.

There is no possible way this book can be accurate in all of its particulars. Prices, menus, and hours of operation change constantly. Three years ago the trend was to close for lunch. In 2009, lunch was all the rage, and many restaurants lowered their prices to reflect more difficult economic times. Other restaurants have undergone minor changes, a menu tweak here, a name change there. Fresh Grill at the Rancho Las Palmas Resort is now BluEmber, and Brissago, at the Miramonte Resort, became Grove Artisan Kitchen although neither restaurant has substantially changed. Minor changes, for the most part, have not resulted in a new review.

Gaps have been filled in as well. Several notable restaurants did not make the first edition simply because I ran out of time. Short shrift especially was given to two notable Japanese establishments. Okura changed chefs just before the deadline for the first edition. That review had to be deleted. Both Okura and No Da Te, fine restaurants, are included here. Some restaurants were closed for major remodeling the last time around, specifically the Riviera's Circa '59 and Colony House's Purple Plum. They are now featured.

Several restaurants with long histories and good reputations have gone out of business: Rattlesnake and Villa Abate, for example. Riccio's Italian Restaurant is now available only for banquets, but a new Riccio's Steak and Seafood is open several blocks south in central Palm Springs. But for all this, there is stability as well. Restaurants, especially at the high end serving great food at prices commensurate with their quality, not only survive, but thrive. Hotel restaurants pose another problem. Many hotel chains offer generic food, staff turnover is high, chefs are rotated, and the parent companies tinker with the menus, searching for exactly the right combination that will sell well in any area. Most hotel restaurants—the Coachella Valley included—cater to what is primarily a captive audience, guests not particularly savvy in the ways of the surrounding area. Without necessarily having access to convenient transportation, perhaps that mediocre $25.00 dinner is acceptable to many a hotel visitor. The Hilton, Wyndham, and Hyatt chains fall into this category. Certain smaller hotels—those increasingly labeled as "boutique"—are attempting to establish themselves as dining destinations distinct from the hotels themselves, including the Parker, Villa Royale, and the Viceroy. Most of the restaurants that are part of hotel chains will not be included in this book unless there is a special feature that makes them particularly desirable. Casinos, too, tend toward the generic with two notable exceptions. Resorts tend to fair better, with three resorts boasting very high-quality dining.

I use a one- to four-star scale to denote quality, but this can often be misleading. While a four-star restaurant is superb in every respect, virtually all the two-star and many of the one-star restaurants have at least something to recommend them. It may be astonishingly inexpensive or may serve one or two dishes that are terrific, but you need to know which ones lest you order from a generally mediocre selection. Inconsistency is the most common problem in any kitchen. Prime steakhouses serve top-quality steaks, but many fall woefully short in the side-dish department. The same is true with the barbecue joints. I personally dislike ethnic food that has been Americanized to the point of blandness. I resent being served insipid Indian, Thai, or Mexican food and may well give such a place one star. But you may prefer your Thai food toned down. That one-star Mexican restaurant may be exactly what you want. The four- and three-star restaurants are cross-referenced in the back of the book, but do not overlook the lesser-rated establishments as you may dismiss a restaurant that suits you better than many of my three-star recommendations. Let the actual text be your final arbiter.

It is a curious fact, but several international chefs of great renown have had an unusually large impact on the finest dining in the Coachella Valley. The inspired cuisines of Paul Bocuse, Roger Vergé, Eric Danko, Jimmy Schmidt, and Eric Rupert have made their ways into the valley by way of their students and sous chefs. Many of these masters' actual dishes have been transplanted to restaurant kitchens here. Jimmy Schmidt is, in fact, chef at the new Morgan's in the Desert at the La Quinta Resort and Club.

Trying to be specific with the cost of dining is difficult as people spend in vastly different ways. I have used a dollar-sign legend to indicate the average cost of an entrée. The reader should use this as a guide, not a rule. It is quite possible to dine inexpensively, especially for nondrinkers, at an expensive restaurant by taking advantage of early-bird specials, bar menus, sharing meals, or summer specials. It is also possible to overspend dramatically—predinner drinks, four-course meals, a bottle of wine, valet parking, and 25 percent gratuity—in a restaurant that has been rated as moderate.

Hundreds of restaurants in the area are not included, such as fast food, chain coffee shops and pizza joints, strip-mall Chinese buffets, taco stands, and sandwich bars. These places do not represent the cuisine of Palm Springs, nor are they in any way unique. Other restaurants will have opened recently, and others will have closed. Some, too, may simply have slipped through the cracks as it were.

The dress code in the desert is almost a misnomer. What dress code really means is, "May I wear shorts?" In virtually all cases, the answer is yes with one caveat. During "season"—November through April—you may do well to avoid shorts in the more upscale venues. The "uniform" of the desert, especially for men, is tennis shoes, shorts, and a pullover shirt. During the summer season, no dress code is enforced—except for the illegal and the blatantly embarrassing. Morton's of Chicago, Firecliff, and Melvyn's have written codes, but they fudge the rules. Cuistot, Le Valauris, Le St. Germain, Azur, Wally's, and a few others at the pinnacle of elegance have an unwritten code, but I would feel comfortable dining in any of these palaces in the off season dressed in the "uniform." One-hundred-and-twenty-degree heat has a way of loosening standards all around.

Since moving to Palm Springs, I have worked as a food writer for three local publications, including one with a huge circulation. It was a constant battle trying to write honest criticism. Local publications depend on advertising. Food writing here is "advertorial" rather than editorial, that is, an advertisement that is written and presented in the style of an article or journalistic report. More than 3.5 million tourists visit the Coachella Valley each year. Most hotel rooms are stocked with a copious supply of publications puffing the area. None of these publications dare discuss quality. Word of mouth supplies the local population with all the information they need, but tourists need help navigating the maze of often-contradictory reports foisted on them by a blizzard of high-gloss promotion.

This guide will not be organized into the usual ethnic divisions. French and Italian culinary techniques are universal. They don't like to mention it, but these archrivals of the culinary art co-opt each other's cuisine whenever they see fit. Such characterizations as Continental, European, Mediterranean, world, international, American, and California Fusion become more meaningless as they become more redundant. Ingredient borrowing is so common that the traditional distinctions mean less all the time. You are almost as likely to find lemongrass and Thai basil in a Mediterranean restaurant as you are to find pasta and pizza in an American restaurant. There are Mexican restaurants here serving sushi! I could deposit everything into the trendy classification, California Fusion, or my favorite, Euro-Cali, but this would leave us with nothing but a huge alphabetized list that is difficult to navigate. I have opted for a different approach, one designed to be more user friendly. Retained are the traditional categories where appropriate: Chinese, Mexican, steakhouse, and barbecue. The majority of restaurants will be organized into the following groups: resort and hotel dining, casino dining, palaces, bistros, trattorie, and other mostly American venues. Other chapters include novelties, kid-friendly places, and even kosher options. Indexes cross relate restaurants into such categories as cheap eats and gay friendly.

It should be noted that many restaurants close for at least a month during the summer. A few years ago everyone closed in August. Now the owners are getting smart and staggering their vacations. However, this is always changing. If you are visiting the Palm Springs area from June 1 through the end of September, it is best to check with the restaurant to find out about closing dates. In addition, the summer months see a rise in the number of dining promotions—usually a three-course dinner at a quite reasonable fixed price. That very expensive restaurant in season may well be in your price range in July.

The most difficult quality for any restaurant to maintain is consistency. Even that four-star chef who cooks every night is subject to illness or exhaustion. Some chefs, having worked 14-hour days for 35 years, are just plain tired. These men (most often), regardless of their greatness in the kitchen, sometimes simply cannot work. Nothing decreases the quality of the food coming out of a kitchen more than an absent head chef, especially in a small restaurant. What can you, the prospective diner, do about it? If you are a tourist and your schedule is not flexible, probably nothing. But if you have the option of dining on a Wednesday rather than a Thursday, call ahead and make sure the chef is going to be present on the night in question. You may be risking a lot of time and a good deal of money—not to mention *my* credibility—on the chance that the chef is playing hooky. A number of chefs are frequently absent even from their own kitchens. If the sous chefs are proficient or even adequate, this may not make a difference, but there are many sous chefs who are incapable of delivering the same quality as the master chefs.

As an interesting and important side note, the chef-owner establishment is more interesting, more consistent, and generally of higher quality than any other configuration. In the back of this book, you will find a list of three- and four-star restaurants. Half of them are chef-owner venues. This is not to say that the majority of chef-owner restaurants are at least three-star establishments, but that chefs own the majority of three-star restaurants. It is in the area of the interesting menu that this is most true. Chefs open restaurants because they have a food vision; they are primarily artists. Entrepreneurs open restaurants because they think of them as good investments. The menu at entrepreneur-operated restaurants is carefully researched to match the lowest common denominator for the demographic that serves as the target patron. There are about 75 restaurants that could switch menus and no one would know the difference. This is not true of the chef-owner operation. La Spiga, Chez Pierre, Cuistot, Johannes, Frankie's Fresh Fish, Copley's, Fireside, Lavender Bistro—these are unique. Here the dining experience is most satisfying and most rewarding.

Restaurants continue to play musical chefs: Beefsteak closed and Chef Wadlund moved to Spencer's; Rattlesnake closed and Chef Schmidt moved to the closed Azur, which has now opened as Morgan's in the Desert; Rattlesnake reopened under the name Ballatrix, under the baton of Chef Greg Monette; Omri came out of retirement to reopen his old restaurant in Palm Desert. Round and round we go.

The year 2009 also saw the unexpected death of Nicholas Klontz, great chef and cofounder of both Zin and sister restaurant, Zini, in Palm Springs. Both restaurants remain open and have maintained the high culinary standards established by Chef Klontz.

I have added two new indexes. Bar menus/happy hours have become increasingly popular, undoubtedly due to harsh economic times. These inexpensive dining options are excellent ways to enjoy food at a fine restaurant without incurring the often outrageous tabs associated with such culinary pleasures. Restaurants with lounges and dance floors, if Hollywood movies have historical credibility, were common in the 1930s and '40s. Well, it seems that they are becoming more common again, at least locally. Indexes have been included for both bar menus and dance floors.

There is also an index of personal favorites. The most common question I get is "Where do you eat?" The answer is not necessarily the answer to the question, "Where should I eat?" I have included this index to both deflect that question and to explain the reasoning behind my personal choices. Just as an example, I prefer to eat early and outside. I also prefer smaller owner/chef bistro-style restaurants with idiosyncratic menus. These preferences will seriously influence my dining decisions but may have no effect whatsoever on yours, nor should they.

There is a special note below to the effect that price has been taken into account in relation to quality. Imagine two restaurants with food of identical quality, say 2½ stars. One of these restaurants is radically overpriced, and the other is downright cheap. A truly objective quality rating without regard to any factor except food will give each restaurant 2½ stars, but the real world does not work like that. Diners at the outrageously expensive restaurant will feel cheated, and diners at the really cheap restaurant may not go at all and miss out on a perfect experience *for them*. I may well adjust the star rating accordingly, awarding three stars to the cheap place and two stars to the overpriced place. In each case, however, this will be noted in the text itself. Likewise, severe discrepancies in ambiance may well effect the quality rating.

Regarding payment, credit cards are almost universally accepted. In the event that a restaurant does not accept credit cards, that fact is noted in the listings. Parking is not a problem here in the desert. The area is not densely populated. Downtown Palm Springs on Thursday evenings is the single exception. There is a street fair on Thursdays. Both street parking and public parking are available, but a walk of a couple of blocks may be necessary.

And a special note about telephone numbers. New for 2009 is the fact that the area code must be dialed for all local calls. All telephone numbers in this book are in the 760 area code.

For your enjoyment and education, here then is my contribution to the aesthetics of dining in the Coachella Valley. This book is not complete, but it does offer a solid foundation for the visitor and local resident alike to begin to decipher this maze. It is also the only book of its kind for this area. I hope you find it entertaining as well as useful.

Bon appétit.

Peter Osbaldeston, January 2010

Legend

★★★★ Outstanding in every respect

★★★ Generally excellent, though probably inconsistent on occasion

★★ Generally of good quality, frequently inconsistent; know the recommended dishes

★ Average to below average but will have something to recommend it, such as very low prices, a special dish, a good piano bar, or exceptional ambiance.

No Stars: Not recommended

Special note: In assigning stars, price is taken into account in relation to quality.

$$$$ Very expensive (entrées $35 and up)

$$$ Expensive (entrées $25-$34)

$$ Moderate (entrées $15-$24)

$ Inexpensive (entrées under $15)

# Indicates that a restaurant has a gay orientation of some kind. See indexes.

Note: All telephone numbers are in the 760 area code.

CHAPTER 1

Resort Dining

A resort is the first destination of most Palm Springs visitors. The definition of the word "resort" is so loose it can mean almost anything, from the Ritz-Carlton to a Motel 6. Here in the Coachella Valley it has come to be identified with something more specific. Our resorts are complete destinations in themselves. Once you set foot on the property of Marriott's Desert Springs, for example, you find all of your dining, sporting, and recreational needs met on the premises. You never need to leave. Virtually all local resorts include multiple swimming pools, tennis courts, gyms, boutique shopping, entertainment, and spa treatments. In addition, the resorts of the Coachella Valley have golf courses—often more than one.

Most of the major resorts boast several dining choices in a range of prices, but visitors who are not experienced with the area may be "trapped" in their resort. Their first option, and certainly the easiest— the resort's own restaurants—may often not satisfy the needs and desires of the discriminating diner. And resort dining generally provides neither the most interesting nor the best-prepared cuisine in the area. Prices are often higher as well, but management is well aware of the limited knowledge of its clientele.

DORAL DESERT PRINCESS
67-967 Vista Chino
Cathedral City
Resort: ★★★

Of the resorts in the Palm Springs area, this is the only one that can be classified as "budget." A room at the Doral can be had for the price of an upscale motel room when negotiated via the Internet. With 27 holes of golf, a large pool with a spectacular view of Mount San Jacinto, tennis, spa treatments, and a lounge with dancing and entertainment, the Doral can fulfill most vacation needs except fine dining. The lone dining option, Fairway Café, adequate at best, has the look and feel of an upscale coffee shop. The resort is located between Rancho Mirage and Palm Springs, where dining choices abound. For tourists who are driving, this is not a problem, but its location off the beaten path leaves tourists who are not driving with few options. The Fairway Café serves breakfast, lunch, and dinner with an American menu, some Italian pastas, and lots of comfort food—a trendy mix and match. Prices are moderate. It is not recommended.

HYATT GRAND CHAMPIONS
44-600 Indian Wells Lane
Indian Wells
Resort: ★★★½

A few years ago the Hyatt was home to the Indian Wells Tennis Tournament, but with the construction of the Tennis Gardens just a mile east, the resort's name has become an anachronism. Still it lingers. The facilities for international tennis competition were removed and the hotel expanded. Since the first edition of this book it has been expanded again, and the restaurant, formerly the Santa Rosa Grill, has been upgraded and renamed Lantana.

The Hyatt shares an entrance with the Renaissance Esmeralda next door (reviewed later in this chapter). Hyatt guests veer left; Esmeralda, right. Golf courses engulf both properties. The Hyatt excels in swimming facilities with seven pools, one with a water slide for the children (well, not *just* for the children). The grounds are more elaborate and intimate than those of its neighbor, the Esmeralda, whose single pool becomes uncomfortably packed with children on major holidays. The building itself is quite beautiful with gorgeous views, especially north and west facing, from the upper floors.

Lantana
★½
$$$
Location: inside the Hyatt Grand Champions, 44-600 Indian Wells Lane, Indian Wells, 674-4165. Food type: California eclectic and pizza; bar menu in the Pianissimo Lounge. Ambiance: (see text). Bar: full. Reservations: suggested. Hours: breakfast, lunch, dinner daily.

The Lantana's patio is quite lovely. Views are of the golf course to the north with rolling hills, palm trees, flowers, and cacti. A stone floor, sun screens overhead, misters and heaters, and earth tones provide a perfect environment for al fresco dining. Inside does not fare as well. One large room is partitioned by a half-wall, allowing for an upholstered bench on either side and tables spotted at regular intervals. Independent tables and chairs occupy the remaining space. The feel is more coffee shop than fine dining.

The food has improved but is still overpriced and uninteresting. This resort is adjacent to the Renaissance Esmeralda with its 4-star-rated Sirocco and across the street from the Miramonte with its 3-star-rated Grove Artisan Kitchen (both reviewed in this chapter). Unless one chooses to sit at the bar (Pianissimo Lounge) to watch a game and nosh on a pizza, one would be better served by taking a short and rather delightful walk. The pizzas are both intriguing and reasonably priced. In addition to the usual "carnivore" and "herbivore" varieties, there are two more creative offerings: the "Lantana" (chicken, beets, goat cheese, tomatoes) and the "Bistro 5th Avenue" (Italian sausage, spinach, ricotta, and oven-dried tomatoes). At $13 and $14 dollars, respectively, these are also reasonable buys.

To those who place a high value on convenience and are unwilling to make the short walk to the highly rated neighboring restaurants, here is a sample of the kitchen's product. It is from the breakfast menu, and it is called "Cactus Cove." My server claimed it was the premier item on the breakfast menu. It is a scramble with lobster, chives, and mascarpone cheese. Its cost is $17, and it sounds much better than it is. The lobster itself is excellent, and it is rather generous. Claw meat is dominant, but there is nothing wrong with that. The cheese, however, is so mild as to be lost in the mix. A stronger cheese would destroy the subtle flavor of the lobster, but the mascarpone contributes nothing. The chives also add nothing but a splash of green color. The eggs simply serve as a carrier for the rest of the ingredients, while the quartered red potatoes, incorrectly advertised as "roasted fingerlings," are heavily sprinkled with what tastes remarkably like Lawry's seasoning salt. This spicy salt was created in 1938 for Lawry's Prime Rib restaurant in Beverly Hills. It was probably a gourmet delight in 1938, but now it tastes quite dated and the potatoes are so heavily seasoned with it that the spice overwhelms the dish. The lobster cannot possibly compete with the seasoning. One is forced to eat the lobster independently of everything else on the plate. A small half-tomato, along with choice of toast, is the only garnish.

Intrinsic quality of the food is good. Preparation is fine. However, the recipes are poorly thought out, and the quantity of food is skimpy. I was not hungry when I left, but I was not satisfied either. Coffee is excellent (Starbucks). My total bill for this breakfast was $25. I could have gone to Sunshine Café (see Chapter 15) twice for $25 and experienced twice the quality and twice the quantity.

LA QUINTA RESORT AND CLUB
49-499 Eisenhower Dr.
La Quinta
Resort: ★★★★

When you first pull into the driveway of the La Quinta Resort and Club you are struck with a certain déjà vu. Perhaps this is a villa in Cannes. You glance around half expecting to see the Mediterranean. The "driveway" is a quarter mile long. Off in the distance you notice some buildings—a Mediterranean estate?

This resort was built in 1926 as a secret getaway—or was it a rendezvous?—for Hollywood celebrities, a mini Hearst Castle without the ostentation. There are no Greek temples, million-gallon lakes, boat taxis, or Babylonian gardens. This is quiet elegance, exploding with bougainvillea, tucked into the craggy foothills of the Santa Rosa Mountains. Nothing is immediately visible. How do they manage to hide three golf courses? Where are the swimming pools—all 43 of them—the tennis courts? Where are the rooms for that matter? Isn't this a hotel? Who knows? The guests of the La Quinta Resort and Club like it that way. Quiet, please. In 1926, the resort was 30 miles east of nowhere and probably required a passport. The resort is part of the Waldorf Astoria Collection.

Morgan's in the Desert
★★★★ (see text)
$$$
Location: 49-499 Eisenhower Dr., La Quinta, 777-4925. *Food type: "elegant American casual dining." Ambiance: upgraded 1926 adobe building with lovely heated and misted patio. Bar: full; extensive wine list. Lounge: piano bar. Reservations: suggested. Hours: dinner nightly. Chef: Jimmy Schmidt. Sommelier: Francois Cinq-Mars.*

Longtime valley residents will recognize the Morgan name. Prior to

2002, the current La Quinta Resort restaurant, Twenty6 (reviewed later in this chapter), operated as Morgan's Steakhouse. Between the exit of the first Morgan's and the emergence of Morgan's in the Desert, the fine-dining and very expensive Azur existed in the new Morgan's venue.

The superb Jimmy Schmidt was brought on board when his four-star restaurant, Rattlesnake, closed in the last month of 2009 (now reopened as Ballatrix; see Chapter 7), as this book was going into final edit. Consequently I have not had a chance to dine at the new Morgan's; however, I am thoroughly familiar with Jimmy Schmidt's cooking. I have made the assumption that the chef's cooking is still of four-star quality. It is, of course, possible that it is not, but all evidence is to the contrary. I am including an excerpt of my review of Rattlesnake at the Classic Club, the aforementioned recent closure, as well as my review of Schmidt's former casino restaurant. This will provide some idea of the culinary skills of the chef.

Schmidt is one of the more renowned chefs in America. He has worked with the likes of Jacques Pepin, Wolfgang Puck, Mark Miller, Alice Waters, and Larry Forgione. He is the winner of the James Beard Award for Best Regional Chef. His originality and range are startling. The chef first came to the desert under contract with the Trump 29 Casino (now called Spotlight 29) in 2002. The restaurant he opened in that casino, called Rattlesnake, as is his flagship restaurant in Detroit, was featured in the first edition of this book. At that time I only gave the restaurant three and a half stars for the simple reason that Mr. Schmidt was not there most of the time. This new restaurant will boast the presence of the great chef most everyday, both lunch and dinner, except summers, when he will return to Detroit. It is arguable that Jimmy Schmidt is the finest chef in the Coachella Valley. There are many first-rate chefs—Omri, Copley, Bacher, Janin, Maddock, Pelech, Lair, Wadlund, Dervieux, Cultraro, and Massignani—but they do not share the hard edge of boundless creativity that Schmidt brings to the culinary art.

At the Classic Club's Rattlesnake, I reviewed two dishes in 2009. As I extolled in my review: "Linguini is actually celery heart shredded to resemble pasta. It looks the part but provides a crunch and deep flavor profile that is entirely different. Fried sage leaves and pieces of roasted butternut squash provide differing textures as well as sweetness to balance the acidity of the celery. Fresh chanterelle mushrooms in a porcini cream sauce tie it all together, providing a depth and earthiness to the sweet/acidic crunch. It is an amazing dish not remotely like anything else in the area. "Deep-sea scallops, seemingly plucked from the ocean only moments ago, are dusted with ground coriander and seared in blisteringly hot oil. The centers are raw and redolent of the salty depths; the surface is a sweet caramelized contrast to the orangey-lemony-peppery tang of coriander bouncing around. These are served with a risotto accented with fennel shavings. A sprinkling of micro greens provides a missing bitterness and the whole thing is gilded with a Parmigiano-Reggiano foam—really quite remarkable!"

The menu at the new Morgan's is considerably less daring and creative than that of the Rattlesnake establishments, and prices are also commensurately lower. Steaks, rack of lamb, duck breast, and seafood ranging from diver scallops and lobster to mahi mahi and ahi tuna form the backbone of the menu. Small plates encompass such things as beet salad, carpaccio, and "seared salt and pepper crusted foie with caramelized Anjou pear and wild mushrooms." Prices are substantially lower than they were at Azur with appetizers now averaging $13, and entrees, $27.

The wine list, emphasizing California, is extensive and covers all bases, but average prices are high. Red wines range from a low of $38 for a 2007 A-Z Pinot Noir to well over $100 for a number of California Cabernets. The mean price is around $80.

(Below is the review I wrote for the casino restaurant in 2004.)

No, this is not an organization for dysfunctional rattlesnakes. And, no, they do not serve filet of rattlesnake on herbed polenta. Master American chef Jimmy Schmidt, winner of the James Beard Award for Best Regional Chef in 1993 and 2000 chairman of the Chef's Collective, of which the likes of Jacques Pepin and Wolfgang Puck are members, founded the original Rattlesnake in Denver in 1985 followed by the one in Detroit 1988. When Spotlight 29 opened, Rattlesnake made its debut in the desert. Schmidt is one of America's great chefs. He received two French culinary diplomas and graduated first in his class from Madeleine Kamman's Modern Gourmet cooking school in Boston. He became executive chef at Detroit's London Chop House in 1977 at the age of 22. This puts him in his 50s now, but with his boyish good looks and charm he appears about 35. However, while Jimmy Schmidt is the founding force behind Rattlesnake and his recipes are served, he is not the chef on a day-to-day basis. On the day I visited Rattlesnake, a special charitable event, Mr. Schmidt was in charge of the kitchen.

Tiny Taste Adventures is an appetizer of choice, amalgams of goat cheese and lobster on crunchy little toasted crackers. A palate pleaser or teaser, you might say. Diver sea scallops, lightly crusted, more like dusted, with mushrooms (flavor not pronounced enough to identify type of mushroom), are served in a garlic custard. Custard is milk thickened with sweetened egg yolks, a mixture most often associated with desserts, but here, infused with a lot of garlic, it becomes a bed upon which the scallops rest. The dulcet crustaceans are flawlessly cooked, nary a hint of dryness. On this garlicky flan you might expect oversweetness, but the ingenious Chef Schmidt sprinkles the little gems with some delicate bitter greens. In addition, this course is served (in a wine-pairing prix fixe) with a grassy young Sauvignon Blanc. The intense grass flavor of the wine and the bitterness of the greens offered the most marvelous counterpoint to the custard and fish. I tasted the wine before tasting the scallops and was startled, especially having just finished a glass of Chardonnay. This was eccentric, even bizarre, but with the scallops all the diverse flavors came together.

Lacquered loin of wild boar on a fresh corn tamale with a Vidalia onion jam is a less successful dish. The wild boar is a mean, tusked, occasionally carnivorous wild pig. It is not as tender as its domestic relative. It can be braised for hours, but then it becomes stringy. Or it can be cooked quickly like a steak, in which case it remains tough. This boar was cooked quickly. Why not use pork tenderloin? The sweet corn tamale proved to be too sweet for the overall dish, especially when coupled with the onion marmalade. As a counterbalance this meat is served with a fascinating sauce. It is tangy, smoky, and tannic. Jimmy Schmidt just happened to be passing by my table, and I asked him about the sauce. He smiled enigmatically and said simply that it was a wine reduction. I smiled enigmatically, too, and gestured for more information. He said, "Strawberries, honey, and chipotle." That explained the smokiness. Outside of this context, I would not criticize this dish, but I expect only the best from a chef of such renown.

A small Prime filet mignon, about four ounces, comes topped with a glorious piece of foie gras. The filet was a perfect medium rare and served with a rosemary-onion potato gratin. A Cabernet reduction was drizzled about the meat. This dish ranks with the scallops in the flawless category.

Many Berry *Financière* Raspberry Sassafras Sorbet is a palate-cleansing respite from the complexity of the previous courses. Chocolate, fresh berries, and the cold sorbet work their magic with a sweet 2002 Moscato. It worked well enough, but I'd have preferred something more aggressive, such as a Botrytis Riesling or an ice wine, but St. Supéry, the vineyard of the evening, does not make these.

The fact that Jimmy Schmidt is not here on a regular basis does not seem to affect the loyalty of the regular customers, who wax ecstatically about both the originality and consistency of the food.

Adobe Grill
★★★
$$$

Location: 49-499 *Eisenhower Dr., La Quinta, 564-5725.* **Food type:** *Mexican fine dining.* **Ambiance:** *second-floor Mexican hacienda; patio; beautiful view; often with live music.* **Bar:** *full, with emphasis on margaritas and Mexican beer; small wine list.* **Reservations:** *suggested.* **Hours:** *dinner nightly.*

Adobe is something one does not encounter very often—a truly high-end Mexican restaurant. There are none of the usual Mexican fast-food offerings many have come to identify as the essence of Mexican food. The ubiquitous taco-enchilada-burrito trio is not available at Adobe. What is served here is a menu you would encounter in an upscale restaurant in Mexico City. For many Americans, it is a revelation to find out that Mexican means so much more than that trio of fast food accompanied by a generic splat of rice and beans.

Not everything served at Adobe is wonderful, but many things are. The cold appetizer *tostaditas de ceviche* is not one of them. Ceviche is raw fish "cooked" in a citric acid, usually lime juice, with peppers and various herbs and spices. Ceviche is touchy. "Cook" it too long and it gets tough. Store it too long and it gets tougher. At Adobe the fish—in this case only halibut—sits in the marinade for eight hours so is tough and a bit stringy. The best ceviches I have tasted have been "cooked" for two hours. Too, halibut is not the fish recommended by most Mexican chefs with whom I have spoken. It takes on lime flavor at the expense of its own flavor. This dish is served on a bed of too-sweet guacamole resting on a crispy corn *tostadita*.

More successful is the way the complex variety of ingredients in the *ensalada tropical* work together. Mixed greens, mostly the mildly bitter and peppery arugula, are tossed with jicama, fresh papaya, toasted pumpkin seeds, slices of mandarin orange, and crumbled ranchera cheese in an orange-shallot dressing. Jicama has almost no flavor, but its texture, like that of a hard, fresh apple, offers the first layer of counterpoint to the arugula. Add to this the papaya—soft and sweet—in contrast to the jicama. Pumpkin seeds bring a nutty and spicy punch to the party. Everything is different. Everything works together. The ranchera cheese is mild, similar to a dry ricotta, and the oranges and dressing bring a subtle acidity and sweetness.

You have to question its "Mexicanness," but the *Halibut Empanisado* is truly a revelation. The fish is crusted with crushed pecans and maple syrup. The flesh retains its juicy tenderness, and surprisingly, the pecan-maple crust works beautifully with and against the fish. Anointing the halibut is a mildly sweet orange-blossom sauce. It is served on a bed of Mexican pasta with a medley of Mexican vegetables—jicama, carrots, zucchini, onions—all blanched. To be really picky, the carrots could have been cooked a little longer, as the jicama and zucchini reach the perfect level of doneness earlier than the carrots.

Camarones Al Estilo Adobe is another entrée that reaches a level of perfection. Jumbo shrimp in a marinade of lime juice, cilantro, and cumin are grilled and served in a unique sauce of garlic, butter, lime juice, cream, pumpkin seeds, and sweet peppers. It is tangy, aggressive, slightly sweet, rich, and garlicky all at the same time. Served with a Mexican version of risotto—less creamy than Italian risotto and redolent of chili powder—this rice manages to be the perfect accompaniment *and* retains its Mexican authenticity at the same time. Less successful is the traditional chicken breast with mole sauce. The *mole negro* (chocolate) is highly Americanized. The use of nuts, raisins, coriander, pumpkin seeds, and dessert spices are unusual enough in savory cooking, but it is bitter chocolate in a brutally hot sauce that makes mole unique. Pasilla chilies, mulato chilies, and ancho chilies are the basis for that heat. This mole has all the complexity that that recipe would indicate, but it is too sweet and does not come close to the level of heat a traditional chocolate mole should have. That fact, however, does not prevent it from having an exceptional flavor. A *mole verde,* also accompanying the chicken breast, is considerably less interesting. If ordering this dish, ask only for the chocolate. Another problem with the dish is its use of chicken breast, one of the most unfortunate trends in American cuisine. Food Network chef Mario Batali calls it the most "overrated food in America." Moles are traditionally served in Mexico with turkey or pork. A tender, rich, juicy turkey thigh would be a vast improvement to the ubiquitous dried-out and over-grilled chicken breast.

In contrast, the Yucatan rack of lamb is a fascinating take on this hugely popular entrée. Lamb, especially the baby ribs, is subtle meat. It usually cannot stand up to an aggressive treatment, and this is very aggressive. A date *reposado* (literally "rested") is used as a marinade for the meat. Annato paste, garlic, cilantro, orange juice, cumin, and fresh, locally grown Deglet Noor dates are the base of this marinade. The rack is then baked and served with a sauce of Ancho chili reduction. It comes with a roasted corn and date tamale. The flavors are exquisite, but they come at the expense of the lamb. The dish is too interesting to pass up, but be sure to order the lamb rare as it is more assertive that way. Chef Leanne Kamekona, who was with the resort for many years, created this prizewinning recipe. Kamekona is currently executive chef at the Rancho Las Palmas Resort, reviewed later in this chapter.

Twenty6
★★★
$$$-$$$$
Location: 49-499 Eisenhower Dr., La Quinta, 564-5720. Food type: American. Ambiance: Mediterranean villa. Bar: full; adequate wine list. Reservations: suggested for dinner. Hours: breakfast, lunch, dinner, and room service daily 6 A.M. to midnight. Chef: Chris Swenson.

Like its companion restaurant upstairs, Twenty 6 delivers several superb entrées but falls short with others. It is difficult to assign stars to these restaurants. Some dishes are easily four stars while others struggle to make two. I give them three, but it is important for the reader to follow the recommendations lest you wind up with one of the two-star offerings.

"Twenty6" refers to the year the resort was built, 1926. See Chapter 15 for more information on Twenty6's breakfast offerings and a bit of background on its chef, Chris Swenson.

In the appetizer department, the Connoisseur crab cake reigns supreme. It is easily one of the three best cakes in the desert. The cake itself is mostly—I would estimate somewhere in the 90 percent range—jumbo lump Maryland crab. You can discern flavors of bell peppers of at least two varieties, a dash of cayenne (too small a dash in my opinion), parsley, onion, and Dijon mustard. A rémoulade of mayonnaise, parsley, chervil, capers, shallots, lemon, and vinegar garnishes. It is reminiscent of a tarter sauce, but don't tell Swenson I said that. This is tart and tangy, so it is counterbalanced with a fascinating tomato jam. (See Chapter 15 for more details.)

The bacon and bean stew is also a winner although perhaps a little heavy as an appetizer. Order a cup not a bowl. This is made with applewood-smoked Nueske bacon, arguably the finest bacon produced in America, in a "stew" with cannellini beans. This little pot is reminiscent of cassoulet.

Spice-of-Life Pork Spare Ribs do not fare as well. Swenson is aiming for an Asian-style rib and winds up in limbo. With a dry rub containing cinnamon and cocoa and a sauce made with apples, tomatoes, and cider vinegar, nothing gels. The ribs, which are parboiled then grilled (the restaurant has no smoker), emerge rather tough as well.

A 14-ounce bone-in, double-rib pork chop is terrific. Glazed with bourbon and maple syrup, it is broiled to form a crust then finished in the oven. The inside is tender and moist. Do not order this well done, or it will be ruined. Pork has been safe to eat rare since 1963. Forget about what your mother said and order it rare to medium-rare. The chop comes with sweet potato fries. Tricky things these are; if they are not hot and crispy send them back for a remake. Tell Chris I said it was O.K.

The cioppino is almost great, but even the chef says it is inconsistent. Swimming in a bath of spicy tomato, garlic, and fish fumet are clams, New Zealand mussels (the big green ones), jumbo shrimp, and half a Maine lobster. Flavors are fantastic, but the shellfish are occasionally overcooked. This is most true and unfortunate concerning the lobster, which is the most delicate. When the cioppino is right, it is *the* four-star dish on the menu. Check with the chef before ordering. It costs $39, so an error will be costly.

A filet mignon, eight ounces of certified Black Angus beef, comes with a rosemary-morel-mushroom cream sauce. The morels pack a punch like a right cross from the reigning heavyweight champ, and the subtle little filet has trouble standing up to it. Perhaps a New York steak would be better, but both the filet and the sauce are superb.

The lobster ravioli comes in with mixed reviews. The ravioli is actually stuffed with a five-cheese medley although ricotta is dominant. These are tossed with a tomato, veggie, white wine, and herbed-lemon broth with chunks of Nova Scotia lobster, but the lobster is overcooked. Among the other offerings the Chilean sea bass, Colorado lamb chops, and 16-ounce rib steak are the best bets.

Dessert is miraculous. Forget the menu, what you want is the lemon cake with sour cream sorbet. I know it sounds weird, but trust me on this one. The cake is in two parts, a light-as-air cake with a lemon custard of sorts on the top. It turns out that this custard is actually created in the cooking process. The cake is a meringue-based poached dumpling. In the poaching process the heavier elements—the lemon juice, sugar, and egg yolks—sink to the bottom and form their own custard. When served, the "dumpling" is flipped so the custard is on the top. To this little wonder two little scoops of sour cream sorbet—sour cream, water, and sugar—churned in an ice cream machine, are added. The taste is like nothing expected. The whole is a tangy lemony air-bomb that dissolves on contact.

RITZ-CARLTON
68-900 Frank Sinatra Dr.
Rancho Mirage
Resort: ★★★★½

As of this writing, the Ritz-Carlton is closed for a complete remodel. It was scheduled to reopen during the fall of 2008, but the economic recession put the entire project on hold. Situated on a panoramic plateau 650 feet above the Coachella Valley, the Ritz-Carlton offers the most spectacular location of any resort in the desert. Two Bunch Palms in Desert Hot Springs (reviewed later in this chapter) is its only competition in the view department. It does not have a golf course.

MARRIOTT'S DESERT SPRINGS RESORT AND SPA
74-855 Country Club Dr.
Palm Desert
Resort: ★★★★

This is the Big Splash of the desert resorts: eight floors, 833 rooms.

This may well be the largest building in the Coachella Valley, with a 30,000-square-foot spa, two championship golf courses, 210,000 square feet of event space including a 25,000-square-foot ballroom, four swimming pools, time-share condos, boutique shopping, ample tennis including a grass court and a sport wall, and even a nightclub. This impressive structure—a 20th-century castle—sits on the crest of a hill encased by a moat. The lush landscaping extends for the better part of a square mile, but nothing prepares the visitor for his first glimpse of the Hanging Gardens of Babylon—the spectacular atrium-cum-lobby. Free water taxis pull into the lobby through automatic hanger-style doors to deliver guests to the restaurant of their choice.

Five restaurants of various types and prices are operated by the Springs, along with the Oasis poolside bar. All the major resorts have poolside bars with snacks, lunch, and bar service, but it has been my experience that these amenities are best avoided. The food quality ranges from bad to passable, and the cost is prohibitive.

Four of the five restaurants are not recommended. The Lakeview serves comfort food at a moderate price; the expensive Sea Grill, steaks, chops, and seafood. The costly Mikado serves Americanized Japanese cuisine. Colibri Grille does Mexican at a moderate price. Ristorante Tuscany is the high-end venue, and it makes a serious attempt at *alta cucina*. It should be better than it is considering its enormous cost.

Ristorante Tuscany
★½
$$$$
Location: 74-855 Country Club Dr., Palm Desert, 311-5828. Food type: northern Italian, alta cucina. Ambiance: formal and elegant, with hints of Vegas kitsch. Bar: full; extensive wine list. Reservations: suggested. Hours: dinner nightly.

The room elicits feelings of a Pompeian mansion, with clever trompe l'oeil murals creating vistas of Roman spender. The interior décor is elegant and expensive with hints of Las Vegas kitsch. The ambiance is formal but not stuffy. Tenor arias from "soft" Italian operas (Puccini and the like) wafting through the space are not going to suit everyone's taste, but volume levels are kept in check. Tuscany serves only the finest seasonal ingredients, and the quality of cooking ranks among the best in the valley. Service and presentation are excellent, but the recipes are frequently irrational. Counterpoint is wonderful in both music and food, but it must function as one. A fugue is not a bunch of tunes played at the same time. It is a single work. The harmony of opposites is just that, a harmony, not a dissonance. At Tuscany, the whole is often less than the sum of its parts.

A confit of Muscovy duck is shredded, sprinkled over tangy goat cheese, and served on a crusty honey bread. The duck is terrific—sweet, flavorful, and rich. But in what way is it a confit? A confit is duck, usually a leg, highly spiced and deep-fried in its own fat. This is simply roasted duck. The cheese is terrific, but it has nothing to do with the duck, succeeding only in smothering its taste. The bread, *farnia crosta,* is ample padding.

Lobster ravioli, with *sambuca rosa* sauce, roasted tomato, and Parmigiano-Reggiano, suffers from the same problem. The pairing of cheese and seafood is problematic as Parmigiano-Reggiano packs a powerhouse punch. The waiter offers the cheese; I had him grate some onto the side of my plate. Since the cheese is listed as part of the dish I felt I should at least taste it once that way. The lobster itself is very small but marvelous. The pasta is tough and chewy, as though made the day before. There is no excuse for this. Tuscan pasta, made of egg and flour kneaded, rolled, cut, and boiled, should be soft enough to dissolve in the mouth. The sauce, redolent of concentrated tomato, obliterated the lobster. I removed the bits of lobster and ate them separately. The cheese went onto everything else.

Again, the problem surfaces with succulent, full-flavored, and perfectly cooked Colorado double lamb chops. The dish is served with cannellini beans. This should be a winner, but these beans are light and slightly acidic (lemon? lime? white-wine vinegar?). They cannot stand up to the lamb and quickly became irrelevant. Some marriages are made in heaven, but the bride and groom should at least have something in common.

Spinach and roasted elephant garlic fare no better in the dish, bringing only an irrelevant bitterness. Roasted red peppers should have been an excellent addition, but these are not hearty in the Florentine manner, sautéed simply in olive oil. This lamb cries out for gutsy rusticity, and it gets delicacy—roasted, marinated, peeled, red pepper julienne. Italian cuisine meets California Nouvelle.

Tiramisu here is simply a version of cheesecake. The mascarpone cheese in a tiramisu has to be whipped with egg yolks and folded with whipped cream and meringue like a mousse. This may be mediocre cheesecake, but it is a violation of the entire concept of tiramisu.

MIRAMONTE RESORT
45-000 Indian Wells Lane
Indian Wells
Resort: ★★★★

From the street, the Miramonte appears rather unassuming, even dull. It has the look of a Renaissance or baroque Tuscan estate, but it is so close to Highway 111 that there is no room to appreciate its timeless beauty. Inside, however, it is gorgeous. Meticulously maintained gardens of roses and bougainvillea season the walkways through lush, vibrant green grass. Villas named after the regions of Italy grace the landscape. Set against the stark rocky grandeur of the Santa Rosas, this lushness, coupled with azure pools and Italian fountains, offers a feast of contrasts for the eye. This resort has recently undergone a $6 million makeover. The air-conditioning system, which has been unreliable in the past, has been replaced.

There is a calm, a serenity, which pervades the environment. Thoughts meander to the luxury of ancient Rome. The Miramonte is not on the scale of its sister resorts across the street—Renaissance Esmeralda and Hyatt Grand Champions—but it achieves an intimacy and seclusion of which those two mega-resorts cannot even dream.

There is no house golf course, but the three courses at the Golf Resort at Indian Wells are adjacent, and Miramonte guests have priority there. Several package deals provide for a round of golf. The other usual resort amenities are present.

Grove Artisan Kitchen
★★★
$$-$$$
Location: 45-000 Indian Wells Lane, Indian Wells, 341-2200. Food type: Italian/Mediterranean. Ambiance: rather ordinary interior; beautiful patio with views of lush grounds and mountains. Bar: full; adequate wine list. Reservations: suggested for dinner. Hours: breakfast, lunch, dinner; room and pool service daily; Sunday brunch. Chef: Robert Nyerick.

When cost and food quality are averaged, the Miramonte offers one of the better values in the desert. The BluEmber at Las Palmas Resort in Rancho Mirage, a similar style of resort, provides for a slightly better dining experience but at a higher cost.

The Miramonte's restaurant changed its name from Brissago and underwent extensive remodeling in 2009, but the advertised emphasis on fresh local and organic produce is mostly cosmetic. The menu is still mixed Mediterranean. That is to say, a variety of dishes are offered from the Mediterranean rim with the emphasis on Italy and Spain.

Lobster bisque with mascarpone cheese and chive oil may emphasize its tomato base at the expense of the lobster, but it is certainly full-flavored and satisfying. Seared sea scallops are just this side of perfect, garnished with an oven-dried tomato and baby frisée. The menu claims diver scallops, which they are not, but they are excellent nevertheless. The surface is caramelized, and the interior moist and rare. Carpaccio is Prime filet with caper berries and shaved Parmigiano-Reggiano. This is one instance where a lower grade of beef would work better. Prime filet mignon has so much marbling, the flavor of the meat is reduced. Choice or even Select filets are certainly not lacking in tenderness, and the corresponding increase in flavor would better serve this dish. A thin coating of Dijon mustard does not contribute either; its uncut flavor is too potent.

The Miramonte paella is superb. More of a Cuban paella than the traditional Valencia style, this one brings shrimp, scallops, mussels, and clams to a powerful saffron-infused Arborio rice. This creamy short-grain Italian rice, usually the foundation of risotto, is an excellent substitute for the more exotic Valencia rices. Flavors here are balanced, and none of the seafood is dried out or overcooked—something not easy to pull off. The addition of shaved Parmigiano-Reggiano is not exactly Spanish, but so what! At $19 for lunch and $26 for dinner, it is also a good value.

Chef Nyerick does thick slices of Kurobuta pork tenderloin Saltimboca with wilted organic baby spinach and a grilled polenta cake. This is another winner from the entrée list. The supremely tender and flavorful Kurobuta pork (ask for it rare or medium rare) is paired beautifully with the polenta and spinach. Again, at $24 it is good buy.

A 12-ounce Black Angus New York steak ($26) or an eight-ounce center cut filet mignon ($28) that actually includes potatoes and winter vegetables beats the overrated steakhouse prices by half.

Wild-mushroom risotto with truffle essence cannot be faulted, but the molten chocolate cake with fresh berries certainly can be. The berries, strawberry coulis, and molten chocolate are terrific, but the cake itself tastes strictly out of a box.

The new restaurant offers something quite fascinating and unique for this area—a honey lavender ice cream. Lavender is a decidedly savory herb, like thyme or basil. Its flavor profile is tart and acidic. Marrying this to ice cream is wildly unexpected. It is a bit startling at first, but is irresistible by the third taste.

Even the pool menu offers more quality than is usually offered at such venues, including a half-pound Angus burger with Gorgonzola, Greek salad, calamari, and a panini with grilled seasonal veggies.

MIRACLE SPRINGS RESORT AND SPA
10-625 Palm Dr.
Desert Hot Springs
Resort: ★★½

The resorts of the south valley are designed around golf; the resorts of Desert Hot Springs are designed around water—natural hot mineral water that bubbles up from the earth at 170 degrees. These resorts do not have golf, and tennis is minimal or nonexistent. With one exception— Two Bunch Palms—they do not have gourmet restaurants. For the most part these resorts are rather decrepit affairs, and food is most decidedly an afterthought. (There is a place called Doc's Diner located within the Agua Caliente Hotel, 14-500 Palm Dr. Avoid both it and the hotel like the plague.) With the exception of Two Bunch Palms, Miracle Springs is the nicest resort and the only one with tolerable food.

There are eight natural hot-water pools, massage, and various spa treatments. Guests are also treated to views not available from "the other side." Desert Hot Springs sits at the foothills of Joshua Tree National Park. Its elevation is 1,100 feet above sea level. Across the valley, elevations are near zero, with below-sea-level numbers existing from Indio east to the Salton Sea. This elevation gives Miracle Springs a spectacular view across the desert floor as well as the snowcapped north face of Mount San Jacinto. For a review, see the section on Chuckwalla in Chapter 15.

RANCHO LAS PALMAS RESORT
41-000 Bob Hope Dr.
Rancho Mirage
Resort: ★★★★

This is a resort for the person inclined toward a slower, less frenetic vacation. The hotel is older. With its Spanish architecture of high ceilings, extensive use of wood, and Saltillo and ceramic tile, there is an air of European old-world elegance not found in the newer resorts. Even the La Quinta Resort, built in 1926, does not share in this grandness as it is not really a hotel but a series of separated casitas.

Ironically, Las Palmas, built on 249 acres of lushly landscaped grounds, is located in central Rancho Mirage directly across the street from the trendy shopping venue known as The River and a few blocks from the Rodeo Drive of the desert, El Paseo. Rancho Las Palmas is within walking distance to scores of restaurants, theaters, and fancy shopping boutiques, yet it manages to maintain a quiet sense of isolation. Twenty-seven holes of golf and all the expected amenities are also hidden away in this low-profile resort.

Having recently shed its connection with Marriott and been acquired by the KSL Resorts Collection, the entire property is undergoing an extensive remodeling. This change is physical to be sure, but it is also centered in the very heart of the kitchen. Executive Chef Leanne Kamekona, with years of experience both as chef de cuisine and executive chef at the La Quinta Resort and Club, joined Las Palmas and was charged with the task of redesigning the menu from the ground up. The result is a startling improvement in Las Palmas's dining room. Sous chef under the great chef emeritus Sarah Bowman at the Miramonte, Todd Claytor has joined Kamekona at Las Palmas. The result is a marriage made in heaven

BluEmber
★★★½
$$$

Location: 41-000 Bob Hope Dr., Rancho Mirage, 568-2727. Food type: California Fusion (Southwestern). Ambiance: mansion on the Spanish Riviera. Bar: full; small but adequate wine list. Reservations: suggested.

Hours: lunch and dinner daily. *Chefs: Leanne Kamekona (executive), Todd Claytor (cuisine).*

The food at BluEmber under the capable and creative direction of the Kamekona/Claytor team is terrific. It is four-star quality, and the only reason I haven't given them four stars is because it lacks the originality and perfection of a Jimmy Schmidt at Rattlesnake (see Chapter 4) or Vince Cultraro or Livio Massignani at Morgan's (this chapter) and Sirocco, respectively (this chapter).

Chilled tomato and crab soup is served cold and presented as a relative of gazpacho, but its takes that venerable Spanish staple to a whole new place. Crab or lobster claws float gently in what appears to be a red-pepper bisque rather than a tomato-vegetable purée. When you first venture a taste of the bisque, the cold is a pleasant surprise. The flavor profile follows. This is decidedly *not* a vegetable purée, nor is it based on red bell pepper. This bisque boasts of fresh tomatoes, but there are other tantalizing lines of counterpoint—garlic certainly, but fennel and coriander are harder to discern. It is spiked with a little cayenne and a drizzle of chive oil. This is a superb soup; everything works together with the crustacean as focal point.

A roasted tomato and mozzarella tart doesn't look like something special on the menu. It doesn't say, for example, that the tart is a wonderfully sweet and light puff pastry. It doesn't say that the sweetness comes from caramelizing the tomatoes or reducing the 10-year-old balsamic vinegar by 70 percent. Nowhere does it say that the soft earthiness of the melted cheese, the light crunch of the pastry, and the acidic bite of the tomatoes are expertly foiled by the use of bitter micro greens.

Want a sandwich? Sandwiches are the foundation of almost every lunch menu in the valley. Tell you what: forget about all of them and ask for the El Cubano at Rancho Las Palmas. This is braised pork shoulder that has been shredded. It is unbelievably tender and full flavored. It is stacked onto a telera, a Spanish roll similar to a ciabatta. Paper thin slices of Black Forest ham are layered on top of Swiss cheese. When garnished with dill pickle and stone-ground mustard, this is an unusual sandwich that sandwich fans will immediately label as "to die for."

Chef Claytor cures Scottish salmon in Grand Marnier and brandy. The result is sweeter—because of the orange liqueur—and fatter—because it is Scottish salmon—than the usual vodka-cured gravlax. With frisée, thick slices of tart Granny Smith apple, juniper berries, and fennel, another masterful appetizer is created.

Both the grilled swordfish salad and the shellfish pasta are superb choices, but it is the Kurobuta pork that garners the greatest accolades. I can say without risk of being proved wrong that this pork entrée is the finest in all the valley. It begins with Kurobuta pork, developed in Japan from the Black Berkshire hog as a companion to Kobe beef. The Black Berkshire is bred for a very high fat content in the manner of beef, and the meat is marbled like Prime steak. Kurobuta pork is also red, not white, and should be eaten medium rare. It is available at Jensen's grocery for $15 a pound. Expensive? Yes, but it is so rich that eight ounces is plenty for a normal appetite. In a magazine column I wrote in 2003, I explained the purpose and use of this amazing pork. At that time, no restaurant in the desert was serving it. It has slowly moved into a couple of them, but this is its best use. It is a large rib chop weighing approximately 10 ounces. The meat is everything you always dreamed of in a pork chop: tender as filet mignon, flavorful as a slab of shoulder. The chop is covered with ground cumin and coriander seed, seared, and finished in the oven. A risotto flavored with poblano chilies, shallots, garlic, and cayenne—to bump the heat without interfering with the flavor—is made with cream and white wine instead of the traditional chicken stock. The result is a big creamy risotto equal to the task of accompanying the pork, its Southwestern flavors perfectly compatible with the cumin and coriander on the meat. Roasted asparagus, a notoriously difficult partner, has no trouble sliding right into this context. With appropriate attention to detail, these stringy stems are nicely peeled.

One new menu item that must be noted is the pork shank in puttanesca sauce. This is hugely satisfying. It is both physically big (the pig's ankle bone being larger than that of the lamb), but big in the flavor department as well. The puttanesca sauce is a little disconcerting at first. One doesn't expect olives, anchovies, and capers with a shank bone, but it certainly isn't bad.

This is a terrific restaurant in a terrific space. Dine in the atrium or outside on the magnificent new patio off the pool. Except for the lack of the Mediterranean Sea, this could be the hills of Barcelona or the Amalfi Coast.

THE RENAISSANCE ESMERALDA
44-400 Indian Wells Lane
Indian Wells
Resort: ★★★★

This is one of three resort destinations tucked away in the wealthy little enclave of Indian Wells. With a population of less than 4,000 people and a median family income of $134,237, Indian Wells is the wealthiest city in Riverside County and in the 98th percentile in the nation. Not as splashy as Marriott's Desert Springs, the Esmeralda pursues a lower profile though it is no less elegant.

Architecture is 1980s-style postmodern: pink, turquoise, and overly ornate. It does, however, get the job done gracefully and efficiently, and the grand staircase, although stylistically at odds with the general theme, is gorgeous. Sirocco, serving *alta cucina,* is a four-star restaurant. Chef Livio Massignani, with credentials a mile long, is a genius in the kitchen.

Sirocco
★★★★
$$$-$$$$
Location: 44-400 Indian Wells Lane, Indian Wells, 773-4666. **Food type:** *northern Italian,* alta cucina. **Ambiance:** *formal and elegant; view of fountains, lake, and golf course.* **Bar:** *full; excellent wine list.* **Reservations:** *suggested.* **Hours:** *dinner nightly.* **Chef:** *Livio Massignani. Note: If Massignani is not present, quality is inconsistent.*

"Everything in life—whether you are a tenor, pianist, race car driver, or chef—is a gift from God, a manifestation of his will. We must make ourselves fluent in order to bring these gifts to life in the best possible way. I am compelled to give the best possible food to my customers. I work within a tradition of culinary greatness that dates back to the eleventh century."—Livio Massignani

A sirocco is a hot and muscular wind that blows across the Mediterranean into Italy from the Sahara. Sirocco is also the name of a marvelous restaurant in another desert. At its helm is Livio Massignani. This is not a good restaurant where, if you order carefully, you may well have a fine meal. Sirocco is a great restaurant. You may order whatever you like from a substantial and creative menu with complete confidence. Massignani serves only the finest quality ingredients, prepared with enormous skill and artistry.

Venetian born, Chef Massignani is broadly and deeply educated, speaking four languages and having extensive knowledge of economics and the fine arts. A graduate of the prestigious Instituto Rossi di Vicenza, he has served as chef to kings as well as some of the finest hotels and restaurants in the world.

With 120-degree views—lake, golf course, fountains—Sirocco also offers a beautiful dining environment. Italian opera, played at an unobtrusive level, manages to sway your soul in the direction of the fifth muse.

House-made rosemary bread sticks, a sun-dried tomato butter, and peppery Tuscan olive oil are delivered to your table. Massignani himself serves an *amuse bouche,* or an amusement for the mouth—a raviolo made with beet pasta, stuffed with spinach and ricotta cheese, and immersed in a sauce of heavy cream sprinkled with shaved four-year-old Parmigiano-Reggiano. The intensity of the cheese merges with the subtlety of the beets and spinach and conspires with the cream. How can something this "simple" be this good?

Reading the menu is addictive. This is not a menu designed by poll takers or focus groups; this is the creative passion of a master chef, a genuine artist. *Vellutata d'Aragosta* (lobster bisque) breaks all taste barriers. The word is flavor—huge, gigantic, all-encompassing mountains of flavor saturating the taste buds. Massignani, if time allows, visits with his customers. "Reduction, reduction, reduction," he says. The cream does not go in until the very end. Chardonnay, brandy, tomato, a mirepoix, oregano, parsley, basil, and lobster (including all the shells and coral) are simmered forever and reduced by more than 75 percent. Then the cream is added, and it is reduced again. The final product is strained and fresh pieces of lobster and shrimp are added. Truly, an amazing bisque!

Melanzane grigliate con caprino caldo (eggplant grilled and topped with caramelized onions and served with pan-seared goat cheese) is an unlikely combination of tastes. First the eggplant is salted to leach out liquid. This intensifies the flavor. It is then grilled. The onions, which are now sweet and soft, bring a different texture and flavor to the party. Goat cheese offers a creamy pungency. A trio of diverse flavors and textures, all of which complement and foil one another, is born.

If Livio Massignani has a first love, it is the mushroom. He is a vast library of knowledge concerning the miraculous fungi, and wherever practical, they make their way into his cooking. The magnificent porcini is packed into his wild mushroom risotto. This big, soft, earthy mushroom is simmered with Arborio rice, herbs, chicken stock, white wine, and more Parmigiano-Reggiano until it gives birth to a dense, powerfully flavored risotto. Finally, it is anointed with truffle oil.

Lombatina di vitello Valdostana (stuffed veal chop) is dry-aged for 58 days—compared with 35 days at the best of the Prime steakhouses—which gives it a nutty taste and renders it unbelievably tender. It is stuffed with prosciutto di Parma and Fontina Val d'Aosta cheese. Consider the super-tender, slightly perfumed baby calf rib with a pocket of potent "ham" and "cheese." But wait! The sauce! The sauce is actually a fondue rather than a sauce. Imagine this: a prime stuffed double-thick veal chop resting in a thick liquid. You taste the liquid. This is not meat-stock reduction. In its stead is a reduction of Prosecco (Italian sparkling wine), cream, melted Parmigiano-Reggiano, and morels. Along with chanterelles and porcini, morels are among the world's best wild mushrooms.

Sirocco is a "must go" restaurant, even if only for special occasions. Entrée prices are high—an average of $35—but the appetizers, soups, salads, and desserts are all lower than those of comparable quality around town. The wine list, too, has a substantial number of bottles in the $30 range. Entrées are large and eminently splitable.

RIVIERA RESORT AND SPA
1600 N. Indian Canyon Dr.
Palm Springs
Resort: ★★★

Built in 1958, this is the only standing resort of the golden age of Palm Springs. The Riviera has been substantially rebuilt, refurbished, updated, and upgraded, and the phantasmagoria of Frank, Dean, Sammy, and even Elvis, once deeply embedded in the pores of the building—especially the showroom—are gone. In fact, even the showroom is gone. In their stead is a stunningly beautiful new main building all done in a luscious charcoal gray (with a most subtle brown back note), a brilliant red orange, and the neutrals of natural woods and stone. This is a 1950s-style desert resort built when land was cheap. It is spread out with wings of two-story bungalows extending from a central core. Here the rebuilding is not as complete. Many of these distant wings still show their age. However, the architecture elicits feelings of nostalgia for those of a certain age, which is hardly a bad thing. This is not a negative nostalgia by any means.

Amenities are thin by contemporary standards: two pools and Jacuzzi spa. There are three golf courses within a 10-minute drive, but none on premises. Size is the limiting factor. Many of the big resorts have many times the acreage of the Riviera.

A new restaurant with the amusing appellation Circa '59 is part of the new Riviera.

Circa '59
★★
$$$-$$$$
Location: 1600 N. Indian Canyon Dr., Palm Springs. Food type: American. Ambiance: Several beautiful rooms, indoor/outdoor cabana-style rooms, and large outdoor patio, all with views of the clover-shaped pool. Reservations: suggested: Hours: breakfast, lunch, and dinner daily.

Like its neighbor down the street, Purple Plum, annoying music is piped aggressively throughout both the adjacent pool area and outdoor dining patio of Circa '59. For a full description of those sounds see Purple Plum at the Colony Palms Hotel in Chapter 2.

When is service too good? When it is fawning. My flatware was changed three times before my entrée even arrived. Every time I touched my knife or fork, somebody switched it for a new one. The moment I took a sip of water, somebody was there to refill the glass. Even my napkin was changed once I unfolded it. Throughout my dinner I must have been asked 20 times if everything was all right and/or did I want anything, and not just by my server, but by the maitre d' and bus staff as well.

It is common practice for me to request that the chef choose my order, usually from two or three menu options. With a chef I know and love, I often tell him to just feed me. Pelech at Chez Pierre (see Chapter 5), for example, falls into this category. At Circa '59 the waiter decides. Isn't that nice? Saves so much time.

The *amuse bouche* is a little tiny cup of lobster bisque "with cognac foam." It has a huge lobster flavor. The intensity of the lobster ranks right up there with the master, Livio Massignani at Sirocco (this chapter). It is, however, laced with so much heavy cream that it becomes cloying. The menu says "light cream," which is an oxymoron. The term "light" is used but it may not mean what you think it means. Whole milk is 4 percent butterfat. Half-and-half ranges up to 18 percent; "light" cream, up to 30 percent; whipping cream, up to 36 percent; heavy cream, to 40 percent; and manufacturer's cream is anything over 40 percent. Butter is 90 percent. So even if the chef is using "light" cream, we are still talking about a liquid that is almost one-third butter fat. After the second spoonful the soup is so rich it coats the mouth with an unpleasant greasiness. By contrast Livio Massignani at Sirocco reduces his lobster stock base until it becomes thick by evaporation. Cognac foam? Oh, that must be that little white line across the top.

The crab cake is advertised as coming with "lemongrass lobster sauce and tomato jam." The "lemongrass lobster sauce" is the lobster bisque! What lemongrass? The crab cake is mostly crab; in other words, it is not really a crab "cake." There is very little binder, which generally comes in the form of mayonnaise. Mustard, Old Bay seasoning, parsley, onion, maybe some bell pepper—none of these traditional crab cake ingredients has a presence. Nor is it coated with crumbs and fried. In other words, it is not really a crab cake in any traditional sense of the word. The flavor of the crab is also overwhelmed by the intense lobster bisque, and the butterfat content is off the charts. To further complicate matters there is the overpoweringly sweet tomato jam. Cris Swensen at Twenty6 (Chapter 15) does a tomato jam that functions as a foil between Humboldt Fog goat cheese and an omelet. His is moderately sweet and flavored with cardamom and shallots. This one could substitute for any red jam slathered on a peanut butter sandwich. There is no acidity here to break up the already sweet bisque and crab. The jam doesn't work at all.

One of my rules for dining out is never to order chicken. The rule was ironclad until I ordered it here. Why am I breaking it now? Two reasons: I think I should order it once in a while—chicken, after all, is one of a restaurant's staples—and this one also looks particularly interesting. The hype reads, "Organic Chicken sea salt roasted, wild mushrooms, midnight tomatoes, goat cheese dumplings, Madeira cream." Interesting that the menu puts the "sea salt roasted" after the organic chicken. It makes more sense to write "sea-salt-roasted organic chicken," but I suppose they wanted the primary ingredient listed first. It makes no difference whether this chicken is roasted in a hardened block of salt or not. There is no taste residue either way. This cooking technique is generally used for prime rib, where it creates a controlled, even cooking temperature all around the meat. A thigh and half a breast arrive. The plate is attractive. The skin is wonderfully crisp. The thigh meat is cooked well but is as uninteresting as a chicken thigh can possibly be. The breast is overcooked and dried out. The Madeira cream sauce with wild mushrooms is once again loaded up with cream. While adding clarified butter, cream, or bits of cold butter to a sauce is standard practice in classical French cooking, it works best when the meat for which the sauce is intended is particularly lean. Venison and rabbit come to mind. The "wild" mushrooms are shitake. Shitake mushrooms have been cultivated since 1940, so they really can't be called "wild" any more. This aside, they do work well with both the Madeira base and the chicken meat.

"Goat cheese dumplings" is one dumpling-shaped piece of mashed potato. (I know my grammar is mixing up singular and plural, but that's what happens when a menu says "dumplings" and you get only one.) Anyway, the thing on my plate is not a dumpling (in the dim sum sense or the gnocchi sense, where a piece of dough is filled with something then boiled.) This is a batch of mashed potatoes mixed with some goat cheese. Two tablespoons were used to form a quenelle shape, which was then baked or pan-fried. As mashed potatoes, it tastes fine. As a goat cheese dumpling, it is a huge disappointment.

Midnight tomatoes? I have no idea what that means. There is a slice of fried tomato on my plate.

At an adjacent table this dish is left half-eaten. I did not eat the breast.

Dessert is Circa '59's take on the banana split. This is clever and successful. Half a banana is coated with sugar, which is then burned in the manner of a crème brûlée. The sweet/bitter flavors work nicely with the banana. An éclair is split open and filled with three little scoops of ice cream in the classic flavors. The whole thing is drizzled with chocolate. The best thing about it is the fact that it is not some enormous sickeningly sweet concoction fit only for the rapacious appetite of a teenage boy.

There is a peculiar arbitrary quality to this restaurant. The menu is terribly safe: something for everyone, nothing to offend, but nothing to inspire either. At the same time, classic recipes and sauces are changed for no apparent reason. What, for example, is a jalapeño pesto? Is it an Italian pesto—basil, garlic, pine nuts, olive oil, and Parmesan—with a jalapeño chili added? This is completely incompatible with the other ingredients. Perhaps it is a bunch of jalapeño peppers substituting for the basil. This will render a blistering hot condiment only a Thai or Indian could appreciate. This "pesto" is served atop the wild salmon. A woman at an adjacent table took one bite and pushed it aside.

Purple Plum (Chapter 2) at Colony Palms Hotel is just up the street. Have a pleasant walk.

TWO BUNCH PALMS RESORT AND SPA
67-425 Two Bunch Palms Trail
Desert Hot Springs
Resort:★ or ★★★★★, depending on your perspective

Visit Two Bunch Palms for a true schizoid experience. Independent Web sites call Two Bunch Palms a three-star hotel. After all, three is the average on a five-star scale. People either adore it or detest it. There is no golf, minimal tennis, and one restaurant. The emphasis here is on tranquility, a stunningly beautiful environment, and spa treatments—no fewer than 52 of them. No one under 18 is allowed. There is a hot springs grotto, several areas set aside for nude sunbathing, and a yoga pavilion.

Fans call the rooms "shabby chic"; detractors call them dreadful. Prices are off the charts—a low of $185 to a high of $675 per night! This does not include a single spa treatment. On the favorable side, the readers of both *Travel & Leisure* and *Condé Nast Traveler* magazines rate Two Bunch Palms as one of their "top 10 favorite spas in the United States and the world."

This is a secret place—difficult to find and heavily guarded—into which one does not walk off the street. Even the name of the resort is not posted out front. Entry is past a stone guardhouse. Reservations are mandatory. There are no exceptions. Huge tamarisk trees, radically bent by six decades of high winds, grow up and out of every available space. A meandering stream, several lakes, and a yoga pavilion are things not found at your local Hyatt. With only 44 rooms, casitas, suites, and villas on a property of about 250 acres, this resort is more about space, solitude, and Zen-like relaxation than it is about fun in the sun. It is an uncomfortable mixture of health farm, 1970s-style commune, and hedonistic hideaway.

Desert Hot Springs offers virtually no shopping or fine-dining options. Unless Two Bunch Palms guests are willing to commute the 15-odd miles to downtown Palm Springs, they are truly isolated. Rumors abound that Two Bunch Palms was originally built by Al Capone as a getaway for himself and his gang. Whether true or not is irrelevant. The restaurant is called The Casino, which is what it allegedly was when Capone was in charge. Capone's house still stands, and girlfriend Gladys Walton's car, a bulletproof 1929 Duesenberg, is parked in front of the office.

Casino Dining Room
★★★

$$$

Location: 67-425 Two Bunch Palms Trail, Desert Hot Springs, 329-8791. Food type: California Fusion. Ambiance: seems to have been designed by a relaxation therapist. Bar: full, but wine is the drink of choice. Reservations: mandatory if not staying at the resort. Hours: breakfast, lunch, and dinner daily. Chef: Michael Hutcheons.

The dining room is almost round, with a wall of glass facing the San Jacinto Mountains to the south and west. The veranda is perfectly situated to toast the sun as it gradually withdraws behind 10,000-foot snow-capped peaks. The crackling fireplace surrounded by deep-pile love seats and armchairs is often the only sound heard in the dining room. Silence is mandatory; signs saying so are everywhere. The owner of a ringing cell phone is subject to flagellation. A nice touch, though not exactly consistent with the overall tone, is the presence of several original Hurrell-signed photographs of the luminaries of Hollywood's golden age.

The food ranges from astonishingly good to oddly inconsistent. Crab cakes, seared on the surface, tender and moist on the inside, are dressed in a lime cream sauce. Unusually and successfully made with pimentos and sweet onion—easy on the filler, thank you—and garnished with fresh corn, the whole package is quite delightful. The lime-cream reduction (without a starchy thickening) is especially welcome as a change from so many complex and often heavy sauces.

Scallops crusted with sweet macadamia nuts do not fare as well. The nuts, in a syrupy base, are so sweet that the natural sweetness of the scallops is lost in a sucrose fog. The reason scallops do so well with Asian treatments is that the use of citrus, soy, or rice vinegar provides an opposite or complementary taste rather than an analogous one. To make matters worse, Chef Hutcheons garnishes with a mound of couscous and yellow tomato coulis. Couscous adds nothing except an additional texture to no purpose, and the tomato flavor is too intense to provide an acidic balance. The scallop, the primary ingredient, is lost in a blizzard of flavors.

Three double-rib lamb chops—called a rack on the menu—are cut from the rack and completely trimmed. Grilled hot and served rare, these are exquisite. There are both advantages and disadvantages to serving a "rack" like this. The downside is that the core of the meat cannot be cooked to a uniform state. This is why many people prefer prime rib to a rib steak. They want that uniform level of doneness. The upside is what makes a rib steak the choice of many over prime rib. They like the caramelized surface and the rare interior. The fact is that both can be excellent, but these are more correctly called double rib chops rather than a rack. The meat here is butter tender, wonderfully flavored, and the seared surface in no way detracts from the rare interior. With a simple pan juice reduction and a half-head of baked garlic, this is a most welcome treatment. It seems that half the chefs in town are trying to outdo each other with increasingly complex toppings, rubs, sauces, and fruit compotes for the ever-popular rack of lamb.

Again, Hutcheons shows a measure of insensitivity by serving, thankfully on the side, a cold and very sweet Dijon mustard sauce. Dijon mustard is a classic with lamb, but the degree of sweetness here smothers the subtlety of the meat. Simple garden vegetables garnish: red potatoes (slightly undercooked), Italian yellow squash, broccoli, and a carrot.

Redemption arrives with a superb sauce for the half duck. The various fig concoctions appearing at a number of upscale establishments are interesting, and often satisfying, but this one is a gem combining two successful traditions. Several restaurants are using Chinese plum-ginger sauce as a base for their duck sauces. Johannes Bacher at Johannes (see Chapter 7) adds honey, Chinese chili paste, mirin, and star anise. At Casino, Chef Hutcheons begins with hoisin sauce—that other famous Chinese duck accompaniment—and combines it with orange and port reductions. This is at once sweet, sour, bitter, and acidic, providing the tongue with all the taste elements. Tremendous depth comes from the port wine.

Desserts are strictly routine: crème brûlée, berries, sorbet, and chocolate cake.

Considering the cost of a stay at Two Bunch Palms, one is pleasantly surprised that the cost of dining there is reasonable (relatively speaking). All the dinner entrées are between $18 and $30, with the majority at $26. The markups on the wine are acceptable. Bottles range from a low of $22 to a high of $110. A moderate corkage fee of $15 is printed in large letters on both sides of the menu. This means the practice of bringing your own wine is encouraged.

A superb dinner for two could easily be had for under a C-note, all inclusive with sensitive ordering. Order the scallops, a salad, and the duck, bring your own wine, and share everything. Total cost including tax and 15 percent tip? About $80.

WESTIN MISSION HILLS RESORT AND SPA
Dinah Shore and Bob Hope Dr.
Rancho Mirage
Resort: ★★★★

The Westin was built in the mid-1980s, but it assaults the senses like a medieval Moorish fortress in Spain. With massive arches, Doric columns, and the look and feel of stone, it doesn't matter that this is really a postmodern building. Actually, to be more exact, postmodernism has a self-consciousness that is not present here. There is no parody or ironic commentary as there is at the Renaissance Esmeralda or the Spotlight 29 Casino. With its uniform deep burnished red color, the effect is imposing rather than friendly. But soon the mind adjusts and begins to appreciate its compelling beauty.

The Westin is spread out. Its "rooms" are a series of two-story quadruplexes. Architectural integrity is maintained throughout. There is little splash and flash, favoring a sense of privacy and quiet. The two golf courses are gorgeous and provide stunning views of both the Santa Rosa and San Jacinto mountain ranges. Three pools (the largest with an impressive water slide), tennis, basketball, soccer, biking, and spa services round out the amenities.

The restaurant, Bella Vista, has come up with a new name for its generic fine-dining menu. It is called (ready?) Euro-Cali.

Bella Vista
★★
$$$-$$$$
Location: Dinah Shore and Bob Hope Dr., Rancho Mirage, 770-2150. **Food type:** *Euro-Cali (in reality, California with Italian influence).* **Ambiance:** *infinite golf-course views, fountains.* **Bar:** *full; mediocre wine list.* **Reservations:** *suggested for dinner.* **Hours:** *breakfast, lunch, and dinner daily.*

The Bella Vista name is certainly accurate. The décor is blond wood with blue linens. The southerly view from the patio is wonderful. Golf courses extend into the mist of the Santa Rosa Mountains. The noise of the fountains is a little disconcerting but certainly not offensive. Unfortunately, the food does not live up to the splendid environment. A watery martini set the tone. The tab for this liquid libation? $11.50. It was made from Bombay Sapphire but *please!*

The menu isn't bad; it's just safe. Oven-baked lobster pot as a first course seemed to offer at least a bit of creativity. Advertised as lobster with truffled mascarpone with penne, tomato, and parsley, it appeared to be one of the more interesting offerings. The "lobster pot" is a pasta pot with a few tiny pieces of lobster. This is not to say that it is not good. It is, but it is a huge disappointment. Minimal truffle oil is present but dissipates after the first bite. The mascarpone all but obliterates what lobster flavor exists. The creamy cheese and layers of flavor produce a pasta dish that is both satisfying and flavorful but decidedly not that which is advertised.

Entrées are divided into two groups, pizzas and entrées. In the latter category, nine dishes cling desperately to the safe: steak, chicken breast, halibut, veal, pasta, salmon, and roasted tofu (for the health conscious). Side dishes of Yukon mashers, cauliflower mashers, and a lox risotto comprise the list. There is nothing here to excite an adventurous taste bud.

Pizzas are more interesting. From the classic Margherita to a squash, mozzarella, garlic, Gorgonzola, mint, and parsley concoction, this sextuplet of Italian pies proves to be the menu's best feature. A pizza made with a spicy lamb sausage, portobello mushrooms, grilled zucchini, and goat cheese is probably the most interesting. The sausage has a perfect kick redolent of anise and chili flakes but also packed with flavor. Think of hot-sweet Italian sausage made with lamb instead of pork. Zucchini brings the crunch factor usually supplied by green bell peppers, and portobello mushrooms deliver a soft earthiness not found in the standard white button mushroom. These three toppings on a bed of melted mozzarella form the basis of a truly fine pizza. The goat cheese manages to interfere with everything except the sausage. Its soft texture and tangy acidic flavor work in opposition to the basic idea of a cheese pizza. The hot melted mozzarella is so different from the cold soft goat cheese that they damage the flavors of each other.

As a whole, Bella Vista has some merit. It is certainly overpriced, and the menu is dull. But the basic quality, both of food and preparation, is there, and the service is excellent.

CHAPTER 2

Hotel Dining

"Hotels" is a catch-all category, including boutique stays as well as hotels that could not be considered resorts in the same sense as those in Chapter 1. The Ingleside, Viceroy, Colony Palms, and Villa Royale are the only true boutique hotels on the list—expensive, small, and one of a kind—with a significant dining room. They may be quirky, luxurious, or intimate. Emphasis is on service and seclusion. All have 30 or so rooms and were built circa the 1930s. The dining rooms range from good to very good. The *ne plus ultra* boutique hotel is Willows in Palm Springs. Adjacent to renowned French restaurant Le Vallauris (see Chapter 4), this superb hotel exemplifies the very essence of "boutique," but Le Vallauris provides for its dining needs.

The other hotels on this list range from the Holiday Inn to the quirky and outrageous Parker and the time-share condo complex Palm Springs Tennis Club. The Tennis Club has a fine restaurant and the Parker has an "interesting" one, both of which are reviewed in this chapter. The Embassy, Hilton, Hyatt Regency, Wyndham, and Zoso are large hotels but do not achieve resort status. The Indian Wells Resort, despite its name, does not have the amenities to be a self-contained resort. The Embassy, Hyatt Regency, Indian Wells Resort, and Wyndham do not have dining rooms that I can recommend.

COLONY PALMS HOTEL
572 N. Indian Canyon Dr.
Palm Springs
Hotel: ★★★

I have not stayed at this hotel. The star rating is an average based on an accumulation of reviews from several sources as well as relative ratings of other local boutique hotels. Some people love it and give it five. Just as frequently some individuals hate it and rate it one or two. This is clearly personal taste speaking.

Colony Palms was built in 1936 as a mobster-owned (Al Wertheimer) getaway replete with underground speakeasy and brothel. It changed hands in the late 1940s and became a haven for Hollywood celebrities for the next 25 years. It was closed after the turn of the millennium for extensive remodeling and reopened in 2007 in its current form. It is really quite beautiful. No attempt has been made to mask its history, unlike the Riviera, whose main building no longer suggests its storied past since undergoing renovations in 2008. The architecture is Spanish Colonial with extensive use of wood, verandahs, and intricately patterned ceramic tile. Built in a rectangular shape with pool and grounds in the center, the hotel has allowed its restaurant the entire east side of the rectangle. Cabanas and casita-style guest rooms provide additional privacy.

Purple Palm
★★★
$$$-$$$$
Location: 572 N. Indian Canyon Dr., Palm Springs, 969-1800. **Food type:** *California.* **Ambiance:** *poolside dining unique in the desert.* **Bar:** *full:* **Reservations:** *suggested.* **Hours:** *breakfast, lunch, and dinner daily; Sunday brunch.* **Chef:** *Erykka Fide.*

Purple Palm is built, excluding the actual deck, right up to the pool. Patio dining and the bar open directly to the pool. What this means in practice is that the people sitting next to you at the bar may well be wearing bathing suits. It also means that the general ambiance is extremely informal, at least on the patio. This attitude is not as pervasive inside, but it cannot help but carry over, as more often than not the inside is open to the outside by way of huge sliding-glass doors.

Purple, teal, and chocolate-brown wood dominate the color scheme. Intricately patterned ceramic tiles popular in Spanish architecture a century ago echo those colors.

The menu bills the food as Mediterranean "without any gratuitous fusion flourishes." The "gratuitous" part is true, but the "fusion flourishes" part is not. Everything on the eclectic menu is contemporary California cuisine from its Japanese-influenced tuna tartare to its grilled hanger steak and roasted saddle of Colorado lamb to its California goat cheese with honey and local dates.

Food is surprisingly good. Actually, the food taken out of context is worth 3½ stars. Rough edges, sloppiness, excessive prices, and the world's second-most annoying music mar the total experience. I don't know what they call this music, but it is probably some kind of aggressive New Age techno. Pick any one of a number of infinitely repetitive beats from a drum machine in ¼ time. Add washes of synthesized harmonies all stuck on the same tonality—static. Add a voice, usually grating, moving through some pentatonic modal scale and getting nowhere. This drones on forever. Okura (Chapter 10) has irritating Japanese techno-pop, but this is worse. At Okura one can also get away from the sound on the patio, but here it is piped all over the entire pool area.

Tuna tartare appetizer is spectacular. This is a common dish in these parts, but this one has something that magically transforms it to another level. Small dice of sashimi-grade tuna are mixed with bits of avocado and yellow tomato and formed into a mound. The mound is placed on a bed of butter lettuce, which is then placed on a ring of elegantly arranged slices of very thin cucumber. So what is so spectacular, you have a perfect right to ask. I left out the spectacular ingredient—white grapefruit. Grapefruit provides everything the tuna/avocado lack. It is bitter and astringent. The bite of critic acid marries perfectly and wonderfully with the soft, fat, meaty, earthiness of the tuna/avocado. Each brings out flavors in the other that were masked without this catalyst, and together another entirely new taste is born. This is an inspired combination. The slight downside is only one of quantity, proportionally too much lettuce and cucumber.

Seared scallops are another dish found all over town, but served over a bed of saffron-infused risotto with a *sauce Américaine,* this dish also transcends the norm. Parisian chef Pierre Fraisse invented *sauce Américaine* in 1860 as a quick way to prepare shellfish, especially lobster. The sauce is based on a lobster stock to which tomatoes, white wine, tarragon, chervil, cognac, and heavy cream have been added. Here the chef substitutes Pernod for cognac and tomato paste for fresh tomatoes, but the result is the same—terrific! Over a seared scallop, the inherently aggressive sauce draws out the subtleties of the marine bivalve. Where one might expect it to mask the flavors, it does the opposite. The family relationship of base flavors (lobster and scallop) intensify one another. The potent herbs add counterpoint, but a backnote counterpoint. I do not taste the Pernod. On top of a bed of thick, creamy, saffron-infused risotto, this dish is a masterpiece. It is probably an anomaly, but my serving was slightly oversalted.

The chef responsible for these two remarkable dishes is equally unexpected. For food like this, one tends to automatically think of some old expatriate Frenchman, right? At least a middle-aged American male who graduated from a major culinary school 25 years ago and worked his way up the ladder as sous chef in eight or 10 fine restaurants around the world. Surprise! Executive chef Erykka Fide, a young chef from Hollywood with cursory training and minimal experience but a fertile imagination and a tremendously sensitive palate, created and executed both of these dishes. She has a great future ahead of her.

Dessert is strawberry shortcake courtesy of pastry chef Lorissa Burton. I had to wait for the shortcake to finish baking. I did not mind. This is actually a good sign. When it finally arrives, it is superb, buttery and crisp with a dollop of Tahitian vanilla ice cream. The strawberries, however, do not measure up. They have been marinating too long and have lost their sprightly essence and fresh crunch.

I request a late-harvest Riesling or Ice wine to accompany the dessert and am rewarded with a blank stare. The waiter speaks to the bartender, who then serves me a regular Riesling. What is going on here? As it turns out, neither the bartender nor the waiter has any knowledge of late-harvest wines. Most peculiar for a restaurant of this type and a first in my experience.

Other appetizers that look promising are a salad of braised leeks with Roquefort, dates, celery, and walnuts in sherry vinaigrette. A couscous salad with shrimp, English peas, and red peppers with red wine vinaigrette also looks enticing.

By comparison, the remainder of the small entrée list is tame: chicken, hanger steak, salmon, lamb.

HILTON PALM SPRINGS
400 E. Tahquitz Canyon Way
Palm Springs
Hotel: ★★★

The Hilton is a nice hotel. It is also relatively inexpensive. Situated on seven acres of lush landscaping, the hotel feels like an isolated retreat although it lies in the heart of downtown Palm Springs. The pool area is large and comfortable. Most rooms have balconies overlooking the pool and/or beautiful mountain views. Service merits mixed reviews.

Terrace
★½
$ ($$ without two-for-one coupon)
Location: 400 E. Tahquitz Way, Palm Springs, 320-6868, Ext. 470. Food type: American with a few popular Italian dishes. Ambiance: coffee shop. Bar: full. Reservations: suggested. Hours: 6:30 A.M. to 10:00 P.M. daily.

The Terrace can supply a respectable dining experience at a very low cost if you have a two-for-one coupon. This is offered year round and is a regular rather than special-event deal. The coupons are available every Wednesday in the food section of the local newspaper, *The Desert Sun*. Ambiance at the Terrace is that of an upscale coffee shop. The menu is basic American, but it is extensive, and prices, moderate without the coupon, are downright cheap with it. The coupon is good for dinner only, everyday except holidays.

The entrée list includes several fish dishes, three steaks, surf and turf, lamb, and a chicken or two—something for everybody, uninspired, but adequately prepared.

INGLESIDE INN
200 W. Ramon Rd.
Palm Springs
Boutique hotel: ★★★

This is one of the oldest buildings in Palm Springs. It was built in 1925 as a private residence and converted into an exclusive inn in 1935. With 30 luxurious rooms with every conceivable amenity—fireplaces, bathrobes, whirlpool tubs, stocked bars, DVD players—this famous but low-profile and totally secluded getaway has been the haunt of many a Hollywood celebrity since its inception. Greta Garbo was perhaps its most notorious guest. Mel Haber bought the place in 1975 and completely restored it in 1994. The restaurant, called Melvyn's (after its owner), bills itself as having Continental cuisine.

The Casablanca Lounge, adjoining, has the look and feel of the 1930s, with mirrored walls and black and white paintings of the usual big name stars of Hollywood's golden age. With an elegant and sexy staff, Casablanca Lounge maintains an image that is genuine. This is not faux 1935; it is genuine 1935. There is a dress code, but it is pretty loose, and people tend to dress up here anyway. Replete with décolletage and dinner jackets, Casablanca Lounge is the Sunset Strip of the '30s without working at it.

A generally accomplished pianist presides over the lounge, providing an appropriate repertoire from the American songbook (with a little Beatles thrown in) for your dancing pleasure.

Melvyn's
★★½
$$-$$$$

Location: 200 W. Ramon Rd., Palm Springs, 325-0046. Food type: "Continental." Ambiance: 1930s nightclub and Régence or Louis XVI-style dining room. Bar: full; extensive wine list. Reservations: suggested. Dress code: A posted sign states, "Appropriate Attire Please." They probably won't throw you out, but this is a dress-up place, and you will feel a little uncomfortable in shorts and a T-shirt. In the desert "appropriate attire" does not mean suits and dresses. Virtually nobody wears a tie. Hours: lunch and dinner daily.

Interior décor at Melvyn's may be just to your liking or thoroughly off-putting. It is in the highly ornate style known as French *Régence,* characterized by curved lines, silk upholstery, lots of gold, and excessive and self-conscious elegance. Goyaesque portraits hang on the walls. Far too many servers, all ensconced in the traditional black tuxedo, hover about.

Melvyn's is the frequent haunt of many celebrities. From the past, you find the names Andre Kostelanetz, Salvador Dali, Lili Pons, Greer Garson, Marlon Brando, and the elusive Garbo. Patrons still point to a table and say, "That's where the Chairman of the Board used to sit." More recently, John Travolta, David Hasselhoff, Cyndi Lauper, Cher, and Goldie Hawn have made appearances. I find it all a bit strange, but "different strokes" as the saying goes.

The appellation "Continental" does not mean anything. Does it mean Hungarian, Polish, German, Spanish? Does it mean that both French and Italian food are served? Do they have prime rib? Is it one of those catch-all words designed to provide cachet without offending anyone? In truth, the food served here could be served at any one of a hundred other restaurants that call themselves everything from California Fusion to Euro-Cali to contemporary American.

Most entrée prices hover around $25, with a few beef dishes kissing the mid-$30s. Soup or salad is included, so the entrées are only moderately expensive. However, Melvyn's more than makes up for these relatively modest prices with a wine list with a mean price of about $60 for a California Cabernet and a hefty tab for cocktails. A four-course prix fixe dinner can be had for just under $30 but it takes a disciplined diner to hold it there.

The menu is stiffly old fashioned, as though nothing has happened in the world of food preparation since 1965. Mushroom soup is an intense reduction of puréed white cultivated mushrooms. Perhaps a crimini or shiitake or two are thrown in for good measure, but I doubt it. There are no mushrooms of the porcini or chanterelle variety. However, this soup, though completely traditional, has a good solid flavor in a traditional stock/cream base.

Spinach salad is assembled tableside in spectacular flaming bacon fat but nevertheless delivers old-fashioned spinach salad taste—warm wilted spinach, bacon bits, bacon drippings, and chopped egg—belying its spectacular origins.

The house salad is not an afterthought, which is so often the case when soup or salad is included with the price of the entrée. Julienne of beets, cherry tomatoes, and mushrooms in a generous serving of fresh crunchy romaine is the foundation. The house dressing—announced as Italian by the waiter—is ranch or ranch with a little Roquefort added. I have no idea where the Italian comes from. When I asked, nobody knew.

Veal Oscar is a classic recipe combining veal cutlets, asparagus, crab meat, and béarnaise sauce. There is no question that Melvyn's management buys only high-quality ingredients. This veal is tender, white, and flavorful. The crab is fresh and full bodied; the asparagus are young, fresh, and crunchy. Likewise, everything is cooked properly. The problem is in the béarnaise. It is not the usual problem, which is a lack of tarragon or too runny a texture. This has the texture of mayonnaise, which is correct, and the tarragon is prominent. This béarnaise tastes metallic. The only thing that could explain this is the wine or champagne vinegar used in its preparation or, and I hate to bring it up, a commercial preparation. The filet of sole picatta is simply done but quite good nevertheless. A high-quality fresh fish sautéed with a splash of Chardonnay and lemon juice, cooked perfectly, and garnished with a few capers makes for a successful though not exactly original or exciting dish.

The chicken Pommeroy with jumbo shrimp is another recipe with fine ingredients that falls short in preparation. First, let me say Pommeroy (or Pommery) is French whole-grain mustard. The shrimp is superb. Who can say whether this is an accident of the little critter itself or Melvyn's has a secret supplier who delivers shrimp with monster flavors, but this one ranked with the finest in my experience. The chicken, on the other hand, is the usual dried-out chicken breast. I know people actually like chicken breast, but I have to agree with Mario Batali. This is the most overrated food in America. Sautéed and served with a Chardonnay suprême, this dish has the possibility of being something better if the chicken were treated with much more care. A sauce suprême is a basic cream sauce with a fish fumet or stock to which mushrooms have been added.

A small filet mignon is served with escargots in a garlic-butter sauce, an interesting idea, but only moderately successful. This, in fact, is the only original idea coming out of this kitchen. The escargots add a layer to the beef that increases its depth of flavor and its resulting effectiveness on the tongue. The only negative is that the snails themselves are absorbed into the nimbus. There are precious few recipes involving escargots. Their flavor characteristics are so neutral that they manage to be assimilated into almost everything except butter and garlic.

Melvyn's serves a whole Colorado rack of lamb for two for $69. While the Colorado rack is larger than an Australian rack and of sufficient size for two, this is still an excessive hit for eight little ribs. It is promoted as "nestling in an herb crust, carved tableside with a bouquetiere of fresh vegetables." I failed to detect an herb crust and had to smile to myself when asked, "Would you like some mint jelly with that?" This was the final confirmation that Melvyn's is indeed two generations behind the times.

Routine scalloped potatoes—russets not quite cooked, probably to ensure a nice presentation—accompany most entrées. They, too, somehow manage to take on a slight metallic taste. A tomato stuffed with almost raw peas and corn kernels was the vegetable du jour on the evening of my visit; nothing quite worked.

In summary, I would say that Melvyn's is probably worth a visit. The food is good enough, although certainly not great. The atmosphere is unique and should be experienced at least once. The music and dancing begin at 8:30 P.M. Keep the drinking to a minimum and stay with the soup/salad/entrée limit, and costs will be reasonable.

PALM SPRINGS TENNIS CLUB
701 W. Baristo Rd.
Palm Springs
Club: ★★★

The Palm Springs Tennis Club is one of the oldest of Palm Springs' landmarks. It is nestled into the rock face that begins Mount San Jacinto's two-mile vertical ascent. The Tennis Club is now a time-share and vacation condos. Check online for availability. Spencer's is the name of the attached restaurant. It is part of the same complex of buildings, but it is independent from the Tennis Club itself. Spencer's has the dubious distinction of spending truckloads of cash on advertising

Spencer's Restaurant at the Mountain
★★★½-★★★★
$$$-$$$$
Location: 701 W. Baristo Rd., Palm Springs, 327-3446. Food type: California/Pan-Pacific Fusion, French technique. Ambiance: Zen-like; one of the most serenely beautiful patios in the desert; piano bar in the interior dining room. Bar: full; excellent wine list. Reservations: suggested. Hours: breakfast and lunch Monday through Saturday; dinner daily; Sunday brunch. Chef: Eric Wadlund.

Spencer's finally has it right. They have been trying for years, but with the hiring of Chef Eric Wadlund after working their way through two others in the last seven years, it has all come together. Chef Wadlund has impressive credentials here in the desert. From Rattlesnake when it was part of the Trump 19 Casino to Azur (part of the La Quinta Resort and Club now reopened as Morgan's) and finally opening his own superb but awkwardly placed four-star restaurant, Beefsteak, which closed in 2008, Wadlund has found his home.

In 2004, Spencer's went through extensive remodeling, and the resultant product is Mies meets Noguchi, a fascinating fusion of modernist truth to materials and Japanese minimalism. Here is a Zen-like sense of repose. The garden space is all neutral colors. Trees rise up within the space itself. It is encircled with "walls" of windows, open unless the weather intrudes. Natural blond wood frames these windows. The extensive use of misters is part of the interior design, refracting sunlight throughout. The floor is gray stone; the linens are black; the chairs, gray. Glassware and silverware sparkle. The only color? Yellow. Plant life just outside the windows bursts forth with a blast of yellow—flowers mostly. And an intense azure sky unifies the total experience. Spencer's is unique and quite special. Cooling has been improved upon with the addition of an unobtrusive black evaporative cooling duct encircling the entire room. This, plus the misters, can reduce the temperature of the patio by 19 degrees, all *without* the use of air conditioning.

The food is best described as California/Pan-Pacific Fusion with French technique. The list of 14 appetizers runs the gamut from kung pao calamari and lobster pot stickers to pan-seared Sonoma *foie gras*. The ahi tartare, a holdover from the previous chef, consists of small dice of raw sashimi-grade yellowfin tuna commingled with minced red onion, cucumber, and Tobiko caviar. It is served on a bed of avocado; chiffonade of beet, carrot, and something green; and a gorgeous white and violet nasturtium—Monet in a steel martini glass. It is beautiful, but its multiple and complex flavors tend to cancel each other out. By the way, nasturtiums, while edible, are really meant to be looked at. They have virtually no taste.

Chef Wadlund has added a number of spectacular new appetizers, among them the braised "Wellington" sandwich and the crisp fried oysters. Most people have never really tasted oysters. I don't mean that they have never eaten one or rather swallowed one. I mean the statement literally. They do not know exactly what oysters taste like. When an oyster is served freezing cold with a squirt of lemon and a dash of Tabasco, and the "diner" slides it down his/her throat, no actual taste is available. Oh, the lemon will get through, and the Tabasco will burn, but I defy anyone to describe the actual taste of the mollusk. These people are pretending to eat oysters, perhaps because they like tossing back shots of zero degree vodka. Then there is the other group—people who order oysters Rockefeller. I like oysters Rockefeller, but the oyster taste is so clouded by the presence of everything else, one cannot claim to have tasted an oyster.

Butter, onion, Pernod, spinach, parsley, celery, breadcrumbs, lemon, Tabasco, watercress, bacon, garlic, even cheese (!) will conspire to mask anything, especially the subtle and delicate flavor of an oyster. Fear no more. At last the actual taste of the oyster is available at Spencer's. Chef Wadlund lightly dips the little critters in something or other and flash-fries them. The surface is crispy and the inside is raw but warm, intensifying the flavor. The flavor is most like an undercooked large New Zealand mussel. It is briny and redolent of offal. The texture is soft, almost dissolving in the mouth. There is a certain "weirdness"; think of the first time you experienced sweetbreads. The surface, spritzed with lemon, is crunchy, and the interior explodes with the magic of true oyster flavor. Cilantro, frissée, and pea shoots bring complementary flavors, textures, and a touch of bitterness. Chef Wadlund calls his sauce a "gribiche" sauce although others may call it a rémoulade, and the ferociously unpretentious among us will call it tarter sauce. All are correct although tarter sauce conjures images of a generic bottled product containing pickles and mayonnaise with back notes of cardboard and kerosene. Chef Wadlund's sauce is a marvel of ingredients containing capers, mustard, cornichons, shallots, mayonnaise, and parsley. The subtle and delicate oysters are set off perfectly by everything on this plate. It is a perfect dish.

Another Chef Wadlund creation is the "chopped tomato tartare." This is a kind of chef's joke, a play on the concept of steak tartar with the same herbs and spices but a different primary ingredient. Here it is the tomato rather than raw filet mignon that takes center stage. Tiny dice of red and yellow tomato—peeled and seeded—are formed into something and dressed in a most amazing manner. An extremely light "Doc Umbra" olive oil anoints the tomato mixture. This is how it is printed on the menu, but it is in error. "Doc" seems like an Americanism, short for doctor. It actually refers to *Denominazione d'Origine Controllata* and refers to controlled quality. "Umbra" is a typo. It should be Umbria, referring to the region southeast of Tuscany in central Italy. The magic of this dish, which distinguishes it from a tomato salad, is the periodic "hit" of truffle and licorice/anise. The interesting thing is that these unique and powerful flavors are tasted only sometimes. Chef Wadlund has sparingly dropped small sprigs of tarragon sprinkled with truffle oil atop a dollop of ricotta cheese that rests on the tomatoes. One has to combine the truffled tarragon and tomato in order to get the "hit."

Continuing the twists on classical cuisine is the Wellington sandwich. This is either the best roast-beef sandwich the world has ever seen or a disappointing reference to beef Wellington. In essence, the dish is sliced braised short ribs on a Brioche roll with mushrooms and a wine sauce. Chef Wadlund should have stopped there and presented it as the world's finest sandwich. He adds a superb piece of pâté atop the meat to reference the "Wellingtonness" of the dish. The problem is that the spice rub and braising liquid for the short ribs disguise the taste of the pâté. The Wellington quality never comes through. (I removed the pâté from my sandwich and ate it on the side, thus having both a superb piece of pâté *and* the world's greatest beef sandwich at the same time.) Perfect (and truffle-flavored) shoestring French fries accompany the Wellington. Forget about the "Wellington" part and order the world's greatest roast-beef sandwich for only $13.

A Lake Superior whitefish of exceptional quality, done simply with a crispy skin and soft, gloriously cooked interior is presented about 48 hours after being removed from the depths of the great lake. A gratin of local Indio corn and Yukon Gold potatoes accompanies, along with some fine-shaved fried onion.

Slices of rare duck breast are prepared with quinoa. Quinoa is an ancient grain (or pseudo-grain) indigenous to both the Andes and the Himalayas, namely Peru and Pakistan. It has a nutty flavor and works as a more healthful substitute for couscous, served with slices of figs with cilantro, rosemary, and red bell pepper, apple syrup holding the flavors together. Chef Wadlund offers an interesting and satisfying alternative to what has been, in the past decade, an overused recipe.

Wild mushroom pasta, which has since mutated to ravioli, boasts flavors big and bold. Made with a vodka cream sauce and currently with portobellos, its initial impact is one of a rich earthiness. Velvety and redolent of that strange woodsy quality associated with spring dampness and forests, this pasta is hugely effective, but the palate grows weary before long.

Center-cut veal chop, rack of lamb, center-cut pork chop, halibut, swordfish, sea bass, salmon, and a couple of chickens round out this extensive and generally very well-prepared menu.

Spencer's is actually less expensive that it used to be. This may have to do with the addition of several lower-priced items and the elimination of some of the more outrageously expensive surf and turf combinations. On the present menu the filet mignon and Australian lobster tail comes in at $55. Most entrées are in the $20 and $30 range.

Spencer's finally has it right!

THE PARKER HOTEL (a.k.a. LE PARKER MERIDIEN)
4200 E. Palm Canyon Dr.
Palm Springs
Hotel rating: see text

I have never stayed at this hotel so what I am about to relate to you is hearsay. A check on the Internet will render a full spectrum of anecdotal experience concerning this rather notorious establishment. The grounds are unique and spectacular with fire pits, hammocks, meandering pathways, and flowerbeds. Of this, everyone agrees. Another subject upon which there seems to be no disagreement is that the Parker is ridiculously overpriced. Tales concerning service and accommodations run the gamut from fabulous to terrible. Theoretically, it is a five-star hotel. It is not. At best, it is a four, at worst a two.

Mr. Parker
★★
$$$$
Location: 4200 E. Palm Canyon Dr., Palm Springs, 770-5000. Food type: Euro-Cali and pseudo-French. Ambiance: kinky, dark, New York-style supper club. Bar: full; interesting wine list. Reservations: suggested. Hours: dinner Wednesday through Sunday. Chef: Shannon Cummins.

"A deconstructed formal hangout for fops, flâneurs and assorted cronies." That's how they describe themselves, honest! It's all over their Web site and on the menu. By the way, a "flâneur" is a loafer or stroller, someone who walks the streets.

Mr. Parker is without a doubt the most pretentious establishment in the Coachella Valley, as well as the most expensive. There is an outré ambiance at Mr. Parker. A marriage of New York supper club and gay cabaret, but it is neither. Augmenting the eccentric quality is aggressive background music: alternative jazz and bizarre covers of classic rock 'n' roll. There is a cover of the Stones' "Satisfaction" by some French group that is both more abrasive and kinkier than the original! Or this, a wildly over-arranged cover of the Beatles' "I Wanna Hold Your Hand," only it comes out "I want to hold your hand." Yes, with perfect diction. The darkness of the dining room with black or almost-black violets, greens, and grays and ceiling mirrors sets the tone. The bulk of the light comes from tiny candles on each table. The black walls are covered with elaborately framed art of the surreal, pop, and soft-core-porn genres. A "devil" cartoon, much like the Playboy Bunny logo, appears on everything: napkins, plates, even the little piece of waxed paper on top of the butter. As a total package, the room is more like Blame It on Midnight (Chapter 8) than any other place in the valley.

Of the 29 menu listings, about six are genuinely French. Another handful *might* be French depending on ingredients and/or technique. The majority are Italian, American, or Japanese although the entire menu is written in French. Prices are off the charts, with the mean carte entrée listing at $46. The 18-rib steak is $65, and the roast chicken, at the lower end, is $31. With a drink, appetizer, salad, entrée, dessert, an inexpensive bottle of wine, tax, and tip, the total tab for two could exceed $400. Are these prices justified? The answer is an emphatic no. The food at Mr. Parker's is not bad. Some of it is pretty good, some of it is disturbing, and none of it is worth the money. Both the restaurant and the prices are absurd.

Chef Rosio Varela—Puerto Rican-born, French-trained, and an accomplished Caribbean chef has been replaced twice since the first edition of this book. The current man at the helm is Shannon Cummins. The menu is essentially the same except for some minor tweaking, but subtle changes abound.

A steak tartare is a beautifully prepared and presented appetizer. It is a healthy serving of finely chopped filet mignon, as much as eight ounces, served in a mound the size of two stacked hockey pucks. A handful of frisée adorns the top along with four triangular-shaped "toast points" of ordinary white bread with crusts removed. Many an establishment oddly shun this dish. I say "oddly" because the Italian version, carpaccio, and the hundreds of Japanese versions with raw tuna saturate the market. Chef Cummins does his tartare with an inordinate amount of Worcestershire sauce in addition to the usual capers, chives, shallots, and Dijon mustard. Under Chef Varela there was a healthy dose of truffle oil. Here that has been eliminated. One has to wonder why, because the lack of balance caused by the excessive use of Worcestershire sauce also makes the tartare a little too salty. Fortunately, not unpleasantly so. The "toast points" are silly. The superb mini-loaf of San Francisco-style sourdough at each table is better by a logarithmic factor. At $18, this is one of the better buys on the menu.

A beet salad with shaved "Parmesan" is actually an arugula salad with three little slices of yellow and red beets each. Beets with an aggressive cheese are a terrific combination, but this is nothing more than false advertising and certainly not worth anything like the $14 asking price. There is a bit of good quality shaved "Parmesan" on the top, but it is not Parmigiano-Reggiano. Genuine beet salads are common this year. Johannes (Chapter 5) has a good one, as does Lavender Bistro (Chapter 5).

Salad frisée is more amusing than satisfying. It is a parody of breakfast as a dinner salad. This is bacon and eggs, only the bacon is lardon, little dice of rendered applewood-smoked fatback. The flavor is bacon, but much more intense. The eggs are quail eggs, and a bed of frisée dressed in walnut oil vinaigrette holds everything. Yes, it is fun and tasty, but it is not worth the $16 tab.

The deciding factor is a major house special and a genuine French signature dish, bouillabaisse. Expectations are high. I look first at the broth. It is opaque! Why is that? Bouillabaisse is a clear soup/stew, the base of which is primarily water, white wine, and clam juice, none of which is opaque. I smell it. Aromas of shellfish permeate the environment. I taste a bit of the liquid. Superb flavor—huge, redolent of crushed lobster and crab shell—but it is creamy, even greasy (?). This is a bisque liquid, not a bouillabaisse liquid. Has Chef Cummins added heavy cream or butter to the base? It would seem so. With increased fat content, the first bite becomes more satisfying, but one tires quickly. Think of eating five scoops of French vanilla ice cream. The first bite of the butter- and egg-laden ice cream is heavenly, but five scoops later you are ill. It is the same here. One cannot finish this bouillabaisse because it is not a fish stew; it is a complex bisque served in an unnatural quantity.

I tested this thesis and took some home with me. After a night in the refrigerator, a quarter inch of fat solidified over the plate. It took three degreasings to purge this dish of its fat. There must be a quarter pound of butter in each serving. This is not a French bouillabaisse.

To be sure, the flavor of the bisque liquid is potent and the entire stew is laden with fish, well, at least shellfish. The fish are hard to locate, however. In fact, I find very few pieces of fish. According to the traditions of Marseilles, where this dish was born, a bouillabaisse should contain at least five different kinds of fish. In Marseilles, seven is the norm. Recommended are the flounder, haddock, cod, perch, white fish, whiting, porgies, bluefish, and bass. This particular bouillabaisse is, however, packed with shellfish: lobster, shrimp, crab, scallops, mussels, and clams. There is something else here too. Something not found in any French bouillabaisse: Spanish chorizo. What is this hard Spanish/Portuguese sausage doing in a French fish stew? This kind of spicy smoked paprika pork flavor is at odds with the flavors of bouillabaisse.

The bisque broth is complex; fennel, tomato, leeks, and saffron are prominent. Other flavors are more a part of the back note and overall texture: garlic, orange, cloves, thyme, red bell pepper. In Marseilles the stew is spooned over a piece of crusty French bread and served with a sauce *rouille,* a spicy-hot garlicky saffron mayonnaise. Chef Pelech at Chez Pierre (Chapter 5) does one with this *soupe de poisson. Formidable!* There is no such nod to France at this "French" restaurant. (The butter and salt levels here are also a health concern.)

It comes in at $42 and is a most disturbing dish.

The wine list is divided into a triptych: crazy, sexy, and cool. That translates into really expensive, moderately expensive, and not too expensive.

So is Mr. Parker worth even two stars? Probably, if judged strictly on food quality alone. On the other hand, ya gotta see this place to believe it. Spend $11 for a martini and have a look around, or better still order the tartare and go somewhere else for your entrée. Oceans (Chapter 8) is just a few minutes up the street (make a left on Highway 111). Order a simple grilled fish, salmon, or sand dabs, and you'll be fine and will have saved a hundred bucks or so.

VICEROY
415 S. Belardo Rd.
Palm Springs
Boutique hotel: ★½

This is a fascinating property. It was built in 1938 and fully refurbished in 2000 in an aggressively moderne/art deco style self-proclaimed as "Hollywood Regency." Hollywood Regency is a neologism probably derived from the writings and interior designs of Dorothy Draper (1889-1969) from the 1920s. Kelly Wearstler, who did the makeover, is the author of a book called *Modern Glamour: The Art of Unexpected Style,* wherein the term is promoted. The cover of Wearstler's book uses an identical visual aesthetic and color scheme to the hotel. Viceroy is dominated virtually in its entirety and down to the smallest detail by black, white, gray, and screaming primary yellow—even such minute details as pool towels and white vases with lemons in them. The effect is startling, especially in the rooms and villas, where everything is a pristine white, including the marble floors, all the furniture, and the appliances, punctuated by brilliant yellow bedspreads. One room may be completely covered in a black and white leaf-patterned wallpaper. The yellow theme is consistent throughout all the public areas: spa, pools, restaurant, bar, and even the menus. Its initial effect is startling but beautiful. Some may find it sterile, but others endlessly fascinating. Personally, the main dining room leaves me uncomfortable as a fine-dining venue, but the patio is wonderful with its silhouette of the huge Mount San Jacinto rising straight up from the back of the hotel.

Rooms and villas are expensive ($200 to $700 in season, $100 to $500 off-season), but many perks are provided.

Citron
★★★½
$$$-$$$$
*Location: 415 S. Belardo Rd., Palm Springs, 320-4117. **Food type:** California Fusion. **Ambiance:** hard moderne in so-called Hollywood Regency style; black, white, and yellow exclusively. **Bar:** full; mojitos based on fruits grown on premises; carefully chosen wine list. **Reservations:** suggested. **Hours:** breakfast, lunch, dinner, room service, and Sunday brunch. **Chef:** Stephen Belie.*

Mojitos are all the rage now. That refreshing rum-lime-mint-soda concoction has been altered here with the use of ruby red grapefruit grown on the premises. These are truly wonderful as a poolside libation with a relatively low alcohol content. The soda and grapefruit juice provide delicious and much-needed hydration. Raspberry, grape, and watermelon are also available depending on season.

Twenty-six-year-old Stephen Belie does remarkable things in the kitchen. An assorted charcuterie with artichokes, grape tomatoes, olives, deli meats, cheeses, and pâté proffered a remarkable assortment of tastes and textures. The top-of-the-line cheeses—Morbier, Humboldt Fog Goat, and Saint-André—fulfill the need for tough, aggressive dairy flavors, but the pâté is neither here nor there, not the rustic variety, nor the creamy/dissolve-in-your-mouth variety. Vegetation is uniformly excellent.

A huge prawn (no more than a U8) is served with true Spanish chorizo and a mango tempura with a drizzle of vanilla bean-lobster reduction. This imaginative appetizer provides for all the taste groups, with the mango tempura being the most interesting. The cold fruit adds a clean, refreshing, moderately sweet and slightly acidic counterpoint to the richness of the crustaceans. Tempura batter is as light as the air (and egg white) from which it is made. Spanish chorizo is nothing like its Mexican namesake. This chorizo is a hard and spicy sausage resembling linguiça.

A flawlessly poached dayboat fluke is served over truffled spaetzle. Elevating comfort food, in this case Austrian macaroni, to the realm of gourmet cuisine is currently popular with California chefs. In this case, black truffle, thyme, and rosemary do the elevating.

A magnificent slice of foie gras is garnished twice. The first and more successful accompaniment is that of peaches poached in a sugar syrup. The sweetness of the syrup, the acidity of the fruit, and its natural crunch all combine superbly with the foie gras. I do, however, have to question the pairing of foie gras with anything at all. This is an expert choice, but even the most perfect pairing results in a diminishment of the unique qualities of foie gras. That caveat most certainly does not apply to the simultaneous ingestion of a wickedly sweet late-harvest Riesling. The second choice does not fare nearly as well. It is cornbread stuffing more at home inside a Thanksgiving turkey than alongside a piece of foie gras. This resulting mixture merely turns the stuffing into giblet-based stuffing—a decided waste of a magnificent piece of foie gras.

Stephen Belie's take on the French classic cassoulet is made with turkey confit, lamb sirloin, and several varieties of sausage, including the aforementioned Spanish chorizo. The lamb, sausage, beans, and rich meat sauce are all superb. The turkey seemed a little stringy; perhaps this is why confit is usually made with either duck or goose. Belie does not use the traditional layer of breadcrumbs on the top of his cassoulet. The purpose of the breadcrumbs is the formation of a crunchy layer, which is repeatedly cut into the cassoulet as a whole. The downside of using crumbs is that it soaks up the sauce, leaving the dish dry. This is an excellent cassoulet, but it is not as good as the one at Chez Pierre (see Chapter 5)

A chocolate mousse is decidedly uncompromised. This is the real thing in all its light and airy glory. So many lesser establishments are passing off some version of chocolate pudding as mousse that the word is losing it meaning. A mousse must be made with both whipped cream and meringue in order to be worthy of the name. Both of these ingredients are 90 percent air when at their peaks, and it is through these that a mousse is truly defined.

Citron serves a Sunday brunch that surpasses everything in town. The cost is $35, which includes bottomless champagne or mimosas, but locals should join the My Very Viceroy Club, which allows the member and up to nine guests a 25 percent discount on everything Sundays through Thursdays. This includes bar service, wines, all meals, and even spa services. With the discount, the cost of the Sunday brunch drops to $26, and it is worth every penny.

Citron boasts approximately 50 percent local business. This is astonishing for a hotel dining room. The La Quinta Club and Resort is extremely high at 40 percent, but 50 percent is unheard of.

VILLA ROYALE INN
1620 Indian Trail
Palm Springs
Boutique hotel: ★★½

Villa Royale began life in the 1930s. Palm Springs' apocrypha has it as actress Sonja Henie's hideaway. Low ceilings, ornate rounded doors, and eclectic ornaments speak of ancient building codes. It opened as Villa Royale Inn in 1947, a small local inn and hideaway. The place oozes charm, avoiding the precious only because it is absolutely genuine. Whatever its history, it is an irresistible romantic getaway replete with fountains, fireplaces, and all sorts of little nooks, crannies, and patios in which to hide.

Europa
★★½
$$$
Location: 1620 Indian Trail, Palm Springs, 327-2314. Food type: California

*Fusion (French). **Ambiance:** small French country house; utterly and completely charming; 1932 building reminiscent of Provence. **Reservations:** required. **Bar:** full; adequate wine list. **Hours:** dinner Tuesday through Sunday.*

Europa has been voted "most romantic" in any number of dining polls throughout the years, and indeed it is. A series of intimate rooms can effectively isolate a couple or a large party from the hustle and bustle of a crowded restaurant. Soft, muted light and a fireplace will further enhance the environment.

Crab cakes on a spicy red-pepper coulis are not remarkable. The ratio of crab to filler is adequate, but the flavors are ordinary. Huntsman country pâté is one of those dissolve-in-your-mouth rustic pork pâtés with pistachios, garlic, and fresh herbs you find in the country inns of Provence. Served on toast wedges layered with Parmigiano-Reggiano, gherkins, scallions, and baby field greens, this is a terrific starter. Little cups shaped from green and yellow zucchini filled with a brandied orange-cranberry sauce and a rouille complete the presentation. The cranberries are incompatible, but everything else works well. I am confused by the use of the word "rouille" here. A rouille is a fiery-flavored, rust-colored sauce of hot chilies, garlic, fresh breadcrumbs, and olive oil pounded into a paste. Rouille literally means "rust." Nevertheless, this rouille is a mayonnaise redolent of saffron and garlic. Ordinarily I would simply chalk this up to sloppy use of French, but the term is also used to describe a similar mayonnaise-based condiment at Chez Pierre (see Chapter 5), where a mistake like this would be unheard of. Regardless of terminology, the sauce did act as an efficient catalyst for all the diverse flavors.

The duck confit is amazing. A confit is duck or goose preserved in its own fat. Prepared with a dry rub—bay, basil, juniper, and peppercorns—it is cooked in the oven at 250 degrees for four hours (!) in a bath of duck fat. At this point it can be stored in the refrigerator indefinitely as long as it is completely covered with fat. When ready to serve, the duck is removed from the fat and placed under a hot broiler until crispy. The result of this process is incredibly tender and flavorful meat. This duck is served with a bigarade. Orange sauce is more or less obsolete these days, but this had a powerful shot of Grand Marnier and managed just the right balance of bitter, acidic, and sweet. Wild rice works perfectly as an accompaniment for duck; unfortunately this is a wild rice/white rice combo. On the evening that I dined, it was much too salty. Probably an accident, but this is the kind of accident that should not happen.

The rack of lamb is one of those dishes with marvelous ingredients whose total effect misses the mark. The lamb itself—six chops—is perfectly cooked, perfectly flavorful, perfectly presented. The sauce is perfect as well—a rich lamb-stock-based demi-glace with hints of lavender and Madeira. The problem? While no damage was done, neither the sauce nor the meat benefited from juxtaposition with the other. The chef eschews the traditional mint/rosemary/mustard escorts in favor of lavender, but it did not gel. A cold Mediterranean "salsa" of pine nuts, black olives, tomatoes, and shallots dressed with balsamic vinaigrette and luxuriant mashed potatoes provides all the contrasting flavors and textures the lamb lacks.

The attraction of the place itself is a big part of the dining experience at Europa. The food is certainly satisfactory although not exceptional. It is not overpriced and specials and discounts are frequently available. Those attracted to its quiet intimacy will find it most satisfying on all counts.

HOTEL ZOSO
150 S. Indian Canyon Dr.
Palm Springs
Hotel: ★★★ (Rooms: ★★★★★)

This is a complete rebuild of a preexisting hotel in Palm Springs. The change has been so profound it can actually be stated that Hotel Zoso (the sign out front has it as one word, HotelZoso) is a new hotel entirely. Its style is unique for this area and demanding. It is Bauhaus by way of Mies van der Rohe, Philip Johnson, and Le Corbusier—uncompromising high modernism. The color is brown with the richness removed. Imagine a gallon of paint 60 percent of which is dark gray and 40 percent chocolate brown. That is the color. Truth to materials, reduction to geometric abstractions, no ornamentation—the vocabulary of high modernism is fully integrated throughout, but more so on the outside. Triangles, cones, pyramids, cubes, spheres, and half-spheres govern all visible surfaces. All furniture, from end tables to lamp shades and even showerheads and ashtrays, are consistent with the overall aesthetic. Inside, gray is the dominant color with accents of black and white. For the most part natural materials—metal, slate, marble, and onyx—are left untouched. A sleek and elegant gray motorcycle, a Kawasaki ZX-10R, rests outside the huge sliding-glass doors, a mute metaphor for the entire structure. Landscaping is 100 percent desert natural: rock, cacti, and various species of palm. There is no color except for the neutralized brown and a bit of green. It is pure. It is clean. It is elegant, striking, imposing, and perfect.

Rooms and suites are utterly gorgeous. Red is introduced as an accent when you enter the security-protected hallways and rooms. The austerity of high modernism is slightly modified in the rooms with the use of muted lighting, carpeting, and red accents. Still, high technology reigns supreme with 42-inch plasma televisions and wireless Internet access in every room.

EAT
★★½
$$-$$$
#

Location: 150 S. Indian Canyon Dr., Palm Springs, 325-9676. **Food type:** California Fusion. **Ambiance:** sterile, frigid, Bauhaus-style coffee shop. **Reservations:** not needed. **Bar:** full. Hours: breakfast, lunch, and dinner daily. **Chef:** Juan León.

The restaurant is EAT, and this level of architectural purity in a dining room translates into sterility. The ambiance of the room does not lend itself to comfortable dining, and perhaps this is why EAT is totally empty for dinner. This is an austere coffee shop with a long brown counter with 50 chairs and place settings lined up in perfect order. Breakfast and lunch do a good business, but customers are rare for dinner.

Considering the fact that EAT does virtually no dinner business, the food is surprisingly good although it does suffer from inconsistency. Chef Juan León, whose training can be traced most recently to work with the Patina Group under Joachim Splichal, first as sous chef and then as executive chef for eight years, is more than competent in the kitchen. He does an interesting take on the basic desert salad of cheese, nuts, and fruit. In this case, it is manchego cheese, pistachio nuts, and apples or dried apricots, thus increasing the complexity of the fruit component. This dish is O.K.; only the cheese is at fault. On the particular evening that I tasted this salad, the cheese used was mild Gouda. It didn't exactly work. The texture was wrong—too firm—and the flavor not sufficiently potent to function as the third strain of this trio. The most successful versions of this salad use Gorgonzola, candied pecans, and pears, but numerous combinations work as long as the trio of tastes is sufficiently different. I can't speak to the use of manchego, but I suspect the results would not be that different from the Gouda. Arugula with bits of frisée is a good choice of lettuce.

Grilled tuna on a wonton crisp with ponzu and shiitake mushrooms is Chef León's version of the now ubiquitous tuna carpaccio. This one is a bit odd. To begin with, why is he cooking the fish at all? It is only slightly seared around the edges. A customer who wants the tuna cooked will be dissatisfied with it, as it is virtually raw. A customer who wants it raw will wonder why the edges were ruined. The wonton crisps are called *mille-feuille,* which translates as "a thousand leaves," as in a thousand sheets of pastry. This was a simple wonton, not a puff pastry. Puff pastry would be a disaster here. His ponzu sauce is, likewise, not much more than soy sauce. Genuine ponzu is made with lemon juice or rice vinegar, soy, mirin and/or sake, kombu (a type of seaweed), and dried bonito flakes.

Seared sea scallops on a bed of preserved lemon risotto and sweet-pea purée are a winner. The textural contrasts of the three ingredients all work together to generate what we in the food writing biz call "the harmony of opposites." The rice is grainy with a slight crunch, the purée is soft and creamy, and the fish is smooth and tender with only a slight resistance. The flavors complement one another—the acid of the lemon, the earthiness of the peas, and the intense flavor of almost raw shellfish.

Kurobuta pork chop with watercress, aged Vermont white-cheddar macaroni and cheese, and truffle oil is a major hit of an entrée. Kurobuta pork is the pork equivalent of Kobe beef. It is as tender and well marbled as a filet mignon. Forget about that dried-out "other white meat" promotion that has been going on now since the 1970s. This is genuine, full-flavored, tender, juicy pork tasting more as though it came from a pork shoulder roast from a kitchen circa 1955 than a rib from this era of cooking. Special note: This meat tastes best when cooked like a steak—very hot and medium rare. If you do not order it like this, it will come to you cooked medium. All that stuff you heard as a kid about rare pork is a half-century out of date. Forget about it. León does this pork with a sauce made from the meat juices and laced with bacon. It is superb all the way around. In an inspired twist on "comfort food," mac and cheese is served to accompany this meat, and what an interesting twist. The chef uses the highest quality Vermont sharp white cheddar with the bitterest of greens, watercress, splashed with truffle oil. The watercress is really needed as without it the dish is too rich. The fat of the meat combined with the fat of the cheese conspires to weigh it down.

Chef León does a creditable job of wine pairing as well. He pours an excellent Rutherford Sauvignon Blanc with the scallops and an equally appropriate Rutherford Cabernet with the pork. Other pairings are not as inspired.

EAT has a relatively small menu with eight house specialties. Wild Scottish salmon with shallot purée, roasted root vegetables, and cinnamon foam certainly seems like something worth trying, as do the sun-dried tomato and goat cheese ravioli with smoked chicken and pesto.

Zoso is an interesting, comfortable, and architecturally fascinating hotel. Dining is good even as the environment is awkward. However, guests of the hotel have three excellent alternatives within easy walking distance: Johannes (Chapter 7) is right next door, and both Zin and Zini (Chapter 5) are a block away.

CHAPTER 3

Casino Dining

There are four casinos in the general resort area. Various local Indian tribes operate all of them: Spa in Palm Springs, Agua Caliente in Rancho Mirage, Fantasy Springs in Indio, and Spotlight 29 in the city of Coachella. Perhaps the most lavish casino is the Morongo, located 20 miles northwest of downtown Palm Springs in an unincorporated area known as Cabazon. This is a sprawling megaresort in the Vegas tradition. Information on its dining options is listed below but not reviewed as it is so far outside the resort area.

The much smaller Augustine Casino is in Thermal, an unincorporated area northeast of Indio. This is mostly a slot-machine venue. There is a small coffee shop but no serious dining options. Of the four casinos within the resort cities, only Spotlight 29 has no hotel.

Nowhere is food quality less consistent than in a casino. Prices can be ludicrously high and food quite abysmal. Spa and Agua Caliente casinos hold the record for the most absurd prices: $85 for a 24-ounce lobster and $75 for the surf and turf combo. Vegas-style buffets are also found at Fantasy Springs, Agua Caliente, Spa, and Morongo, but forget about the "all you can eat for $2.99." Now it is all you can eat for $20 or so.

AGUA CALIENTE CASINO
32-250 Bob Hope Dr.
Rancho Mirage
Hotel: ★★★★

A lavish new resort hotel matches the style and elegance of this beautiful casino. Dining options include The Steakhouse, Waters Café, Poker Deli, and Grand Palms Buffet. Waters Café is a coffee shop; Poker Deli is burgers, sandwiches, and snacks. Neither are reviewed here. There is also Java Caliente for coffee and pastries. The buffet does a whole roast turkey and serves a variety of popular cuisines. Thursdays are all-you-can-eat-crab nights. At $20, this is a good buy. The Steakhouse holds the premier position, but something is peculiar here. In bold and boasting letters, the Web site announces, "The best steakhouse in Rancho Mirage." The hype is not odd; what is odd is the fact that in Rancho Mirage, The Steakhouse's only competition is Fleming's (see Chapter 9), which is both considerably better and less expensive.

The Steakhouse
Not recommended
$$$$
Location: inside the Agua Caliente Casino, 32-250 Bob Hope Dr., Rancho Mirage, 888-999-1995. **Food type:** *Prime steakhouse.* **Ambiance:** *dark, quiet, high tech, claustrophobic, 1960s-style modern jazz.* **Bar:** *full; huge wine list; inflated prices.* **Reservations:** *suggested.* **Hours:** *dinner nightly. Note: Must be 21 to enter.*

The menu is posted outside the door, whose thick glass panes make it difficult to discern much inside the restaurant. You look at the menu. The fare is typical of any steakhouse in the area; the prices are higher than LG's (see Chapter 9), which is to say they are astronomical, and in a few instances, they are bizarre. The surf and turf combination is $75; a 24-ounce lobster is $85! By comparison, the surf and turf (Prime filet also) at Spencer's, which has the reputation of being overpriced, is a bargain at $55. It is true that Spencer's (see Chapter 2) delivers only (?) a pound of meat for that price, whereas Agua Caliente presents its patron with 22 ounces, but what are we talking about here? Spencer's includes a broiled herbed tomato and braised endive. All sides at The Steakhouse are six dollars more, which would bring that surf and turf to a total of $87. This is for one person! Spencer's serves two eight-ounce lobsters with two sides for $49. That is identical to the quantity served at The Steakhouse for $97. We have entered a completely surreal world. If The Steakhouse were serving truly great food for these prices there might be some justification, but this food is mediocre at best.

The Steakhouse advertises Prime meat specially aged 21 days. All steaks are aged 21 days before they are shipped to market. LG's, for example, dry ages their steaks another two weeks before serving it. Boasting about 21 days is meaningless. The Steakhouse also advertises its special award-winning dry rub. What is this about? Barbecue masters developed dry rubs for ribs. Putting a spicy dry rub on steak does nothing but mask the flavor of the steak, and depending on how the steak is cooked, it may have other detrimental effects.

I ordered a 16-ounce New York steak cooked black and blue. The waitress assured me that black and blue was no problem. She was wrong. The restaurant does not use an overfired high-tech broiler but an under-fired grill. (See Chapter 9 for a full explanation of "black and blue" and cooking techniques.) Cooking black and blue requires an overfired broiler attaining temperatures as high as 2,000 degrees. Attempting to achieve this level of doneness on a grill results in carbonized meat. Caramelized crispy goodness from the application of intense heat above the meat is an absolute good; carcinogenic carbonization from actually incinerating the flesh of the steak with flame is an absolute evil. The burning of dripping fat by a live flame is death to the steak. This is what happened here. This burning is aggravated by the dry rub if there is sugar in it. I had to cut off at least four ounces of my 16-ounce steak to remove this carbonization.

Five sauces are available (at no cost yet!): béarnaise, bordelaise, Dijonaise, au poivre, and wild mushroom. The béarnaise is an accurate rendition of the classic French sauce. It has the consistency of mayonnaise, to which it is directly related, and the right amount of tarragon, its defining ingredient. The other sauces all taste as if they are made from those packages of dried stuff where you simply add water. Raw starch and wine are the primary ingredients. The "bordelaise" here is completely unrelated to true bordelaise. The defining ingredient of bordelaise is poached marrow. The foundation of the traditional sauce is demi-glace and red wine. Shallots and parsley provide counterpoint. The au poivre (literally "with pepper") is equally ridiculous. Steak au poivre requires that the meat be heavily crusted with a variety of cracked peppercorns before cooking. None of this happens here. In addition, all these sauces are compromised by the dry rub already on the steak. The wild mushroom sauce at least had pieces of mushroom in it, even if the type of mushroom is impossible to identify.

The kitchen does manage to turn out a simple baked potato that is actually baked in an oven. Unlike so many other places, foil and microwaves are not found here. A sage butter arrives with the bread. It is free with your $50 steak dinner. Nice, too, but not worth $50.

FANTASY SPRINGS RESORT AND CASINO
84-245 Indio Springs Parkway
Indio
Hotel: ★★★-★★★★

Travelocity rates this venue generously at four stars. The new hotel is certainly in the four-star category, and the entire resort is in the process of undergoing massive improvements. A golf course is planned as well as another hotel tower. The pool is 1,103 feet long and features a beach volleyball court. These are the only amenities other than a bowling alley. The casino itself is the old building. It is crowded, noisy, and a little unpleasant.

Players is the high-end restaurant. That it is a steakhouse should come as no surprise. The Bistro is next, featuring a fine-dining menu with eclectic Asian influences. POM is the coffee shop open for breakfast, lunch, and dinner, and the usual buffet spread called Fresh Grill dominates the lower end of Fantasy Springs' dining options. The dinner cost is $18. At the top of the hotel is a nightclub with bar, dance floor, DJ, room for a live band, and spectacular views.

The Bistro
★★½
$$$
Location: inside Fantasy Springs Casino, 84-245 Indio Springs Parkway, Indio, 342-5000, Ext. 84919. Food type: California Fusion. Ambiance: second-floor colonnade, beautiful view, terrace, comfortable, casual. Bar: full; wine list is small but adequate. Reservations: not accepted. Hours: dinner nightly. Chef: Josalito Asisitio.

The Bistro is off the colonnade, the long transition between the new hotel and the old casino. The floor is slate for a luxurious look and feel. The south wall is all glass for a view overlooking the pool area and the Santa Rosa Mountains in the distance. The Bistro itself is at the end of the colonnade before descending via escalator to the ground-floor casino. In beige, gold, red, and ample use of wood, it is comfortable and casual. A large square bar ties the foyer and dining room together. The sights and sounds of an open kitchen, with its attendant aromas, remind patrons that this is real food prepared by real men (as is usually the case). The chef is Josalito Asisitio, a native of Guam.

The *amusée,* or *amuse-bouche,* is a French tradition rarely practiced in America. There is only one other chef in this area who indulges his customers with the quaint and delightful custom, Livio Massignani at Sirocco (see Chapter 1). An *amusée* is an "amusement" or "amusement for the mouth" (*amuse-bouche*). It is a little tidbit of startling and/ or delectable quality, a teaser, the oral equivalent of the first flash of forbidden flesh from an exotic dancer. Chef Asisitio's *amusée* on my last visit was a thin slice of raw albacore rolled onto a toothpick and dressed with pea shoots, aïoli-wasabi sauce, and Tobiko caviar. A mouth amusement indeed! Never look a gift horse in the mouth, but the aïoli could have used more punch.

Wild mushroom soup is a thick, potent explosion of mushroom flavors. Cream and sherry-based stock are the foundation. The dominant mushroom is the crimini, which can hardly be considered a wild mushroom. Chef Asisitio puts pieces of chicken and shavings of some highly flavorful ham, like prosciutto di Parma, in the soup. This is a gilding of the lily that serves only to detract from the singular qualities of the mushroom. It is akin to decorating a rare and spectacular orchid with tinsel. Truffle oil, maybe; chicken, no.

The Mediterranean salad is like salad niçoise without the tuna and potatoes: green beans, cucumber, egg, tomatoes, red onion, and kalamata olives. This refreshing summer repast is dressed in a light balsamic vinaigrette. The veggies are all freshly chopped to retain maximum flavor, texture, and color.

A grilled veal chop served with a peanut sauce is one of the more interesting treatments of this perennial favorite. Chef Asisitio picked up this recipe while in the Philippines. The use of peanut butter in savory dishes is common throughout that region, especially in Thailand and Indonesia, but as a garnish for freshly grilled veal is a first for me. The sauce itself is thickened with toasted and ground rice kernels for a smooth body without the addition of fat or the starchy taste of flour or corn starch. Shallots, demi-glace, and ancho chilies form the body of the sauce and drive it with some acidic sting and a sweet touch of fire. It is quite fascinating when paired with veal, a meat more than willing to take on the tastes around it. It is just that we are so accustomed to veal with Italian treatments—Madeira, white wine, capers, lemon, cheese, mushrooms—that anything this exotic needs a little getting used to. It is served with jasmine rice and a medley of Asian vegetables, including the wonderfully bitter bok choy.

Mushroom-dusted scallops over lobster risotto is another highly recommended dish. The Arborio rice, sticky and swollen with lobster stock, is the perfect accompaniment for its briny delights. The two shellfish flavors complement and enhance one another in full harmonic balance, while the rice provides a strong textural contrast. Asisitio does a roasted red pepper sauce, but I find this too mild. It really needed something like a chipotle cream to provide a more aggressive counterpoint.

There are countless variations on the pasta theme out there in dining land. The possibilities seem to be infinite. Baked ziti with pieces of leg of lamb in a demi-glace-based sauce with fresh peas, pine nuts, and small white beans seems interesting enough left at that, but covered with goat cheese and broiled, a whole new experience opens up. The mildly gamey taste of lamb marries beautifully with the rich, tangy goat cheese. Each provides what the other lacks. With the pasta, beans, and pine nuts establishing a neutral background of textures against which the central players can contend, this is probably the most interesting dish on the menu. Personally, I would use either braised lamb shank or shoulder rather than the leg portion. The leg, especially the upper leg, does not need to be cooked this long; it becomes stringy. A perfect garnish of a sprig of sage functions as zesty punctuation.

Try the chilled fresh fruit "soup" for dessert. The use of the word "soup" in the name of this dessert is a trifle misleading. It is not a soup but simply seasonal fresh fruit in a sweet puréed fruit sauce with a scoop of vanilla bean ice cream. The *coup de grâce* here is the champagne that is poured over the whole thing. It is like a float with champagne instead of root beer. The sizzle of the carbonation mixed with the dryness of the wine against the sweet ice cream is really quite lovely.

Players Steakhouse
Steak: see text
Everything else: see text
$$$$
*Location: inside Fantasy Springs Casino, 84-245 Indio Springs Parkway, Indio, 342-5000, Ext. 84919. **Food type:** Prime steakhouse. **Ambiance:** dark and windowless but elegant and plush. **Bar:** full; extensive wine list. **Reservations:** suggested. **Hours:** dinner Friday through Sunday.*

I have not dined at Players since the 2007 edition of this book. Since then there have been some significant changes. On the negative side, management has abandoned the superb Creekstone Prime Angus beef in favor of (presumably) generic USDA Choice grade. This cannot help but reduce the steakhouse experience per se. On the positive side the rest of the menu has been completely revamped with a more sophisticated, and presumably better prepared, variety of sides and alternate entrées. Gone, for example, is the poorly thought-out and executed escargot *Chablisienne,* replaced with the traditional but still excellent escargot Provençale (puff pastry, spinach, tomatoes, roasted garlic-lemon butter). Non-steak entrées include a mushroom-stuffed chicken with white cheddar bread pudding and tarragon *a jus,* a bacon-wrapped white marble pork tenderloin with a fig chutney, and a miso-glazed Chilean sea bass. The rest of the menu does not deviate far from the expected.

Before its was revamped, Players offered what was arguably the finest steak in the valley. It served Certified Angus Prime beef from Creekstone Farms exclusively, thus guaranteeing meat of the highest quality in the world as well as consistency. Although the meat now served is Choice, the use of a Montague Radiglo overfired broiler capable of searing, without burning or carbonizing, a steak at 1,800 degrees is still the standard at Players. The high-tech broiler delivers the power necessary to insure a true black and blue steak—hot, seared, caramelized, salty on the surface and cold, luscious, butter tender at the center. Only Morton's of Chicago (see Chapter 9) is able to do this as well. An 18-ounce bone-in New York, 16-ounce boneless New York, 24-ounce porterhouse, bone-in rib-eye (the real thing trimmed of everything but the eye), and filet mignon in two sizes are available. Prices are competitive, sometimes even a few dollars less than the norm.

Side dishes have been refined, but my review reflects the quality in 2007 of those dishes management chose to keep. As of my tasting, lobster bisque lacked the punch of true concentrated lobster. Creamed spinach had good flavor—garlic and cheese—but was thin and a little runny. Mac and cheese is silly but not bad if that is your bent. A nice sharp cheddar was the driving force.

This is just a guess on my part, but I would estimate Players at an all-around three stars. It is too expensive for what is delivered, but this is the norm for casino dining. Fantasy Springs is well off the beaten path so unless you are driving your choices are limited to the casino. Guests of the hotel who have wheels might try El Campanario (Chapter 12), the fine Mexican restaurant in Indio, Frankie's Fresh Fish (Chapter 7) for an entirely "other" experience, or drive all the way to the La Quinta Cove for a whole series of fine dining options, Lavender Bistro (Chapter 5) being my first choice.

POM

Not reviewed

$-$$

Location: inside Fantasy Springs Casino, 84-245 Indio Springs Parkway, Indio, 342-5000. Food type: American coffee shop. Ambiance: spacious upscale coffee shop open to the resort grounds. Bar: full. Reservations: no. Hours: breakfast, lunch, and dinner daily; late-night dining on weekends. Thursday night is Italian Feast Night for $14.95.

POM fills in the dining blanks between the buffet and the Bistro. It is inexpensive and the environment is very pleasant (with real windows!), especially considering the fact that it is housed in a casino. POM serves all meals, all the time, including late-night dining.

MORONGO CASINO, RESORT & SPA

49-500 Seminole Dr.

Cabazon

Tourists staying at the Morongo Casino have virtually no other dining options except the casino itself unless they wish to commute to Palm Springs. Locally, only a coffee shop and fast food are available. Casino options include the high-end Cielo restaurant located atop the hotel tower. The view is magnificent. The cuisine is California Fusion with an Italian accent and steaks. It is very expensive, but there is a happy hour from 4 P.M. to 6 P.M. called six-for-six, when appetizers, wines by the glass, and well drinks sell for six bucks a pop.

The buffet is called Potrero Canyon. There is seafood on Fridays and brunch on Saturdays and Sundays. This is an expensive buffet with prices ranging from a low of $13.95 for lunch to $25.95 for dinner Thursdays through Saturdays.

In between is Serrano, open 24 hours a day. It is essentially a prime rib house specializing in surf and turf. Costs are moderate relative to the cost of everything else at this casino, with the prime rib and lobster going for a nickel short of $30.

SPOTLIGHT 29
Interstate 10 at Dillon Rd.
Coachella

There is no hotel here, but the casino's 1950s-style architecture, reminiscent of the Frontier in Las Vegas, creates an attractive venue for the wagering set. Major Vegas headliners appear regularly at The Spotlight showroom.

Jem Steakhouse
Not reviewed
$$$-$$$$
Location: inside Spotlight 29, Interstate 10 at Dillon Rd., Coachella, 775-2880.
Food type: *steakhouse.* **Ambiance:** *nicely appointed single room, claustrophobic.*
Bar: *full; extensive and expensive wine collection.* **Reservations:** *suggested.* **Hours:** *dinner Thursday through Sunday only; happy hour/bar menu 4 P.M.-8 P.M.*

I have not eaten here (perhaps for the third edition?), but word of mouth and reviews have been mixed. Prices are medium high with the most expensive offering coming in at $49 for a 29-ounce rib steak. The menu is straightforward American with an emphasis on steak. Chicken, fish, and lamb are also available. They advertise Angus beef, which generally means Choice. If it were Prime they would not hesitate to post it everywhere. Except for the 29-ounce rib, steaks are in the 12-ounce range—certainly small by steakhouse standards.

The space has no windows as it is contained completely within the casino. The bar area is more open than the dining room.

Café Capitata
Not recommended
$-$$
Location: inside Spotlight 29, Interstate 10 at Dillon Rd., Coachella, 775-2880. **Food type:** *American coffee shop, five-station buffet.* **Ambiance:** *rather cute, built on a spiral ramp, postmodern 1950s appropriation.* **Bar:** *no.* **Reservations:** *not accepted.* **Hours:** *open 24 hours.*

Do not dine at Café Capitata. If you are stuck in Coachella and need a place for breakfast or lunch and do not want to drive very far, may I suggest El Campanario (see Chapter 12). It is a fine restaurant serving three-star

Mexican food and the only decent eatery anywhere near Spotlight 29. Take a cab if you have to.

SPA RESORT CASINO
Hotel: 100 N. Indian Canyon, Palm Springs
Casino: 401 E. Amado Rd., Palm Springs

Unlike its sister casino, Agua Caliente, Spa was not designed and built as a single entity. A half-century ago Spa Hotel operated without any associated gambling. The hotel building in use in 1965 is the same building that houses the hotel today. When gambling first entered the picture some time in the 1990s, a big tent was added to the hotel site. This was the casino. In 2004, a new casino was built a block away; hence, the two addresses. The architecture is the prevailing Spanish Mediterranean seen throughout the valley. While both casinos are new and fully appointed, Agua Caliente is more Vegas-like in its ambiance. Spa actually has windows, which lends a more open, spacious feeling to the gambling environment.

Spa Steakhouse
Not recommended
$$$$
Location: inside Spa Hotel, 100 N. Indian Canyon, Palm Springs, 888-999-1995.

See the review for The Steakhouse at Agua Caliente discussed earlier in this chapter. The Spa Steakhouse is identical—same menu, same prices, same recipes—as The Steakhouse at Agua Caliente. Naturally, there are different chefs, but they perform the same operations.

Agua Bar and Grill
Not recommended
$-$$$
Location: inside Spa Hotel, 100 N. Indian Canyon, Palm Springs, 888-999-1995. Food type: casual dining. Ambiance: comfortable indoor/outdoor space, attractive. Bar: full. Reservations: suggested. Hours: 7 A.M. to 10 P.M.

Basic coffee-shop fare of mediocre quality is offered for double what you would pay elsewhere ($11 for a basic plate of sausage, eggs, and hash browns). The coffee shop at the sister casino, the Agua Caliente in Rancho Mirage, offers more or less the same fare but at a more reasonable cost.

CHAPTER 4

Palaces

Palaces—big, beautiful, frequently intimidating, fine-dining establishments—often appear to be something they are not. Most are expensive; some are very expensive. Most actually *are* fine-dining establishments. A few have the trappings of palaces but are quite ordinary. The building and the environment define a palace more than the quality of the food or its cost. The final bill at a palace can easily exceed $250 for two people. This total includes tax, gratuity, and valet parking, but so what? For a vacationing couple even on a generous budget, $250 is a hefty hit. Dining at this type of a palace should be one of the high points of your vacation. When you pay $250 for dinner and the food is mediocre, the feeling of being cheated is exacerbated.

But there is another side. For many people the food may not be the most important consideration when dining at a palace. The evening out in a spectacular environment may well be more important, and a restaurant's larger-than-life reputation may grant boasting rights. "My dear, you simply must dine at Wally's!" Or, perhaps expressed in the negative thus: "I don't want to say anything negative about Wally's, but, my dear, let's just say we won't be dining there again."

The best of the palaces have been built by their chefs who started out in the 1980s on a shoestring and, with skill and hard work, eventually built their own palace. Other palaces try to maintain a reputation even as their chefs come and go and their quality emerges as inconsistent. The generally acknowledged premier palaces are Wally's, Cuistot, and La Spiga. Until recently, Omri & Boni also qualified, but that venerable institution is no more, having been sold and replaced by Amore. Omri alone has since reopened as a superb little bistro (Chapter 5).

Amore
★★★
$$$-$$$$

Location: 47-474 Washington St., La Quinta, 777-1315. *Food type:* *nonregion-specific* alta cucina. *Ambiance: uncompromising original architecture;*

gorgeous view; fascinating décor; entirely comfortable. **Bar:** *full; extensive wine list.* **Reservations:** *suggested.* **Hours:** *dinner nightly.*

Amore replaced the four-star valley legend Omri & Boni. Chef-owner Omri Siklai built this palace in 2001. The architect incorporated many of Siklai's ideas into the building. Siklai sold the building and retired in 2006 but has reopened as a bistro (Omri Go Med, Chapter 5). The new owners have toned down the postmodern exterior by eliminating the audacious use of color and replacing it with a simple beige, but the interior remains the same.

The building is amazing. It is a big, tough, postmodern objet d'art designed by Kevin Leonhard with references to Palm Springs modern, especially Albert Frey in its use of the slanted roof line, and the high modern concept of truth to materials. For readers unfamiliar with Frey, he was a Swiss-born architect and one of the more important founders of the style called Palm Springs modern from the mid-20th century. Many Frey buildings still stand, preserved as historically significant. Cement, aluminum, steel, glass, wood, slate, granite, and the lowly concrete block all speak for themselves: unpainted, unvarnished, untreated. The building is as drop-dead gorgeous as it is uncompromising. Attention to detail is so complete that you cannot help but smile in appreciation.

Views are west facing the foot of the Santa Rosa Mountains. At sunset, it can be unbearably beautiful. Huge slabs of slate define a misted al fresco patio. The Postmodern color accents of brick, burnished gold, and blue seem odd at first, but when you see interior echoes of the same colors everything comes together. The new owners have altered this, reducing its aggressiveness, but also its coherence. From the intimate, comfortable, friendly bar to the arboreal and concrete-block wine station, the interior space is, at least to these semi-educated architectural eyes, flawless.

Amore's menu is huge, much too large to manage quality control. There are 96 items on the menu excluding various pasta sauces. Still, Amore manages to serve both interesting and well-prepared *alta cucina,* albeit at excessive prices. This is not a region-specific restaurant. The food is not Tuscan or representative of any one of the other Italian regions. The food draws from the general Italian tradition in both preparation and ingredients but jumps around all over the place. Many of the dishes are undoubtedly created right here.

Take, for example, the rather peculiar appetizer seven-spice-crusted baby lamb chops with fig essence, dates, and almonds. This somewhat irrational attempt at California cuisine introduces to the lamb a complex spice mixture dominated by cumin. The combination of cumin and lamb seems to be a recent phenomenon. I understand that it started in Morocco, found its way to Provence, then jumped the pond. Lamb does not hold up well to this aggressive spice. Undressed bitter greens actually serve the lamb quite well by themselves, cutting through the billows of cumin with their fresh, raw tastes. A thick date-almond paste rather like a filling for some exotic Moroccan pastry skews whatever balance there is well over to the sweet end of the spectrum. To make matters worse, there are droplets of fig and cherry essences. With everything combined, the Moroccan dessert theme is complete; the lamb is irrelevant, and the greens are bizarre.

Things improve dramatically with tomato-rosemary soup. The tomatoes are roasted in a wood-burning oven and roughly puréed with a powerful essence of rosemary. The rosemary leaves, thankfully, are strained out. A drizzle of crème fraîche adds a subtle sweetness and little pieces of panchetta or guanciale (pig cheeks) floating in the center bring that earthy, cured Italian bacon taste to the party. This is a big, rustic soup, and whatever the source, it carries with it a powerhouse of Italian flavors.

From a seemingly endless list of various pasta combinations, the Michelangelo is one of the best. It is a creamy fettuccine with mushrooms—crimini, shiitake, porcini, and white button—providing copious amounts of earthy umami flavors. Curiously, the server raved particularly about the use of champignon mushrooms, which he pronounced correctly in the French manner. The champignon is simply a cultivated white button, the most common and least flavorful mushroom in the world. With panchetta and the addition of a few peas, this pasta is delicious; with a generous sprinkling of cheese it is wonderful. The cream sauce is made with tangy Asiago, but the sprinkling is a combination of Parmigiano-Reggiano and Pecorino. All three of these cheeses form a triumvirate delivering monster flavors.

It would take months to eat your way through the menu. Quite possibly, these four dishes only give a tiny picture of the whole, but they are probably representative—although I certainly cannot be sure. Fish, chicken, veal, lamb, pork, and steak are all interpreted here along with nine desserts.

Arnold Palmer's
See text.

$$$$

Location: 78-164 Avenue 52, La Quinta, 771-4653. *Food type: American comfort and California steakhouse.* **Ambiance:** *sports bar and nightclub married to a Midwestern mansion, plus a putting green.* **Bar:** *full.* **Reservations:** *suggested.* **Hours:** *dinner nightly; bar opens at 3 P.M.; happy 4 P.M. to 7 P.M. daily.* **Chef:** *Brett Maddock.*

Arnold Palmer's is a shrine to its namesake. It is a mansion of the kind that you might find in Oak Park, Illinois, an early Frank Lloyd Wright design perhaps. What is that lush landscaping? Why, it is a golf course. It's not 18 holes, of course, but there are sand traps and greens. Anyone who wants to play simply has to ask at the reception desk. Putters and balls are provided at no cost.

The ample foyer houses display cases filled with Palmer's trophies. The walls are filled, even cluttered, with pictures of Palmer on the cover of *Life,* playing golf, schmoozing with celebrities. The building itself boasts wood and stone as the primary materials. If lounge entertainment and dancing are an important part of your evening out, Arnold Palmer's arguably serves up the best in town. Kevin Henry is currently in the lounge. With a repertoire of more than 600 songs ranging from the major standards of the 1930s to current hits, Henry is entertainer nonpareil. He is also willing to accommodate most any listener if he can—and he usually can, whether it is raucous rock 'n' roll or a mellow Gershwin tune.

Prices here are out of sight. Most entrées are between $25 and $35, with 11 ounces of lobster going for $58! But these prices do not seem to have any effect on the popularity of the restaurant. It is one of the most popular in the Coachella Valley. During season, they routinely serve more than 500 people every night. There are, essentially, two menus. One is American comfort food, and the other is something like a California steakhouse expanded to include a large number of eclectic favorites. The chef is Brett Maddock, a man with impressive credentials.

Rating this restaurant is difficult. I should begin by stating, unequivocally, that Brett Maddock is a superb chef. That being said, the food at Arnold Palmer's is unworthy of his considerable talent. This, of course, is not his fault. Maddock was hired to produce this food, and he has, in many cases, transcended the inherent limitations of the food itself. But let's face facts. Meat loaf and pot roast, regardless of how well they are prepared, can never achieve the level of four-star dining. What is the humble meat loaf? Meats ground together; bound with egg, some vegetables for increased flavor, maybe some filler; baked in a loaf pan; and smothered with gravy. It is cheap, nutritious, satisfying, and can actually taste pretty good. What are the downsides of mom's meat loaf? It is often greasy. The gravy is mostly flour and milk or, worse, ketchup. Maddock has taken this humble American concoction and elevated it to a standard about as high as it can go. The meats are beef and pork sausage ground to the smoothness of country pâté. With onions, carrots, celery, and green bell pepper, it is tender, moist, flavorful, and not the least bit greasy. The gravy is not so much gravy as demi-glace *tomatée,* a stock-based, French-style sauce with tomato sauce added. It is clean and slightly sweet, with layers of meat and tomato flavors. The loaf is served with simple mashed potatoes and steamed broccoli. The broccoli is cooked to a perfect al dente, and the potatoes are creamy without being puréed. They perfectly complement the best meat loaf in town, but they are boring.

Pot roast, even more so than the meat loaf, is elevated to uncharted territory. And, once again, it is a sauce of such sophistication and complexity that it is almost shocking to find such a thing on this meat. The meat is Prime eye of chuck. Chuck is the inexpensive shoulder cut usually used for hamburger. The "eye" is the tenderest center of the chuck roast. When I was poor in my youth, just out of college, this was what I made when I wanted steak. I could get it for about 79¢ a pound in 1970. Chef Maddock braises it in wine, a bouquet garni (herbs tied in cheesecloth so they can be removed), and aromatic vegetables. A couple hours later, after simmering until tender, the liquid is degreased, the bouquet garni removed, and the vegetables puréed into the braising liquid. The result is a glorious sauce the likes of which mom never even dreamed unless she was trained at the Cordon Bleu. But the overall result is schizoid. Pot roast is like a mediocre beef stew—inexpensive meat cooked to the point of stringiness—but covered with a glorious, sophisticated French sauce.

Potatoes here are wedges of russets brushed with melted duck fat and baked. The duck fat, as opposed to olive oil, imparts a somewhat sweetmeat flavor to the potatoes as it forms a crispy surface over the soft inner core. This is, again, an excellent and sophisticated solution to an ordinary problem. Thin slices of carrot and celery blanched or steamed just this side of raw accompany.

Beef medallions Palmer style is the second most popular item on this huge menu. It consists of medallions of filet mignon smothered in blue cheese and broiled. These are served with a medley of fresh vegetables—caramelized onions, mushrooms, and julienne of red and green bell pepper—in a bordelaise sauce. This dish is a huge moneymaker so it is ridiculous to alter it, but the blue cheese overwhelms the delicate nature of filet mignon. With a more flavorful steak, like New York, and less cheese, the appropriate balance could be achieved. This is just too much of a good thing. The sauce and vegetables are both excellent although I had trouble identifying the signature ingredient—beef marrow—of the bordelaise.

Chicken pot pie transcends the genre. Who ever heard of putting puff pastry on the lowly meat pie? The English, for whom the meat pie is a staple, do not even know what puff pastry is. Maddock has produced a pastry as light and buttery as a fine croissant. The traditional cream sauce—milk, flour, and maybe some chicken broth—has been replaced by a sauce suprême, a velouté made with cream, meat jelly, chicken, and veal stock. Layers of intense meat flavors resonate within this sauce. The actual chicken, along with the peas, carrots, onion, pimento, and green bell pepper, almost becomes irrelevant, swimming as it does in this splendid juice.

Side orders include a sweet potato brûlée (purée of sweet potatoes with torched sugar on the top), mac 'n' cheese (with Parmesan torched under the broiler), and creamed yellow corn. These have no real affinity for any of the entrées that I noticed. Maddock told me people order them to share. Nostalgia has long tentacles.

I have not sampled anything from the "other menu," but the skill of Chef Maddock is going to carry through the entire menu. Look for "Arnie's Favorites." These are comfort foods. Beef stroganoff, sand dabs, spit-roasted chicken, and even a cheeseburger grace this part of the menu in addition to the dishes reviewed.

Bangkok 5
★★★
$$

See full review in Chapter 11.

Bing Crosby's Restaurant and Piano Lounge
★★
$$$$

Location: 71-743 A Highway 111, Rancho Mirage, 674-5764. Food type: American. Ambiance: nightclub with a 1930s retro feel. Bar: full. Reservations: suggested. Hours: dinner Tuesday through Saturday.

There are three of these establishments. The other two are in San Diego and Walnut Creek.

You've just stepped into a postmodern appropriation, a time warp circa 1937. Unlike, say Cunard's (Chapter 8), which really is an anachronism, Bing Crosby's is a deliberate attempt to evoke the illusion of a "better time." It is, of course, a Hollywood illusion completely overlooking the fact that 1937 was the worst year of the Great Depression and about 20 cosmic minutes away from Hitler's invasion of Poland. This illusion is specifically based on Cole Porter's musical version of Phillip Barry's Broadway hit play and subsequent movie *The Philadelphia Story,* starring Cary Grant, Katharine Hepburn, and James Stewart. The play dates from 1939, the Cukor movie from 1940. The musical version from 1956 stars Bing Crosby, Frank Sinatra, and Grace Kelly. Louis Armstrong plays himself. A huge black and white photographic mural featuring all four of these luminaries ornaments the front of the building.

The architecture is postmodern palatial nightclub with at least one semicircular wall per room. High-backed circular banquettes echo the circular architecture. Tables are bare wood on dark brown, with the color scheme completed by a muted teal. The lack of linens contributes to an already uncomfortable noise level. Track lighting illuminates scores of photographs featuring Bing Crosby with everyone Bing Crosby ever worked with or even knew casually and, of course, Bing Crosby on the golf course. The bar/lounge area features an aggressive pianist/singer who realizes mostly swing music of the era. A makeshift dance floor provides space for would-be terpsichoreans.

Bing Crosby's atmosphere is better than the food, which is officially billed as "Innovative Country Club Cuisine." It is essentially a steakhouse with an assortment of a few old-fashioned high-end American dishes like Waldorf salad, crab Louie, and oysters Rockefeller, along with trendy California Fusion.

Prices are off the charts with the surf and turf (eight-ounce filet and six-ounce lobster) coming in at $58. A 24-ounce porterhouse is $45 a la carte, but add a couple of sides, and you are at $60. Consider a first course ($15), dessert ($11), a couple of drinks ($22) or an inexpensive bottle of wine ($35), tax, and tip and you are in the neighborhood of $125 for *one* person. Bing is selling an illusory atmosphere and doing it very well. Make no mistake about it, you are not paying so much for the food as you are paying for the game. Pretension is my first thought, but upon consideration, that is not the case. It is more surreal than pretentious.

Tuna three ways is my appetizer selection. The first is a little mound of "spicy chopped tuna." Remaining in my proximate imagination is Erykka Fide's (Purple Plum, Chapter 2) wonderful spicy tuna tartare with its kick of grapefruit. This mound was definitely chopped tuna, and a good tuna at that, but it is bland and boring. Maybe, just maybe, there is a hint of soy sauce on it. The second mound is a cubic inch or so of tuna upon which rests a cubic inch or so of watermelon and a few pea shoots. The watermelon is sweet and watery. The tuna is bland and boring, the bitter pea shoots carry the day. Mound number three is a little bit of tuna wrapped in nori seaweed on a bed of pickled ginger. At least the ginger has flavor.

I leave my entrée selection to the chef. He chooses for me the shrimp with angel hair on a bed of spinach. I am surprised because I gave him the option of the house signature dish, the filet with "black truffle demi-glace, braised *haricot vert* [green beans], spinach, and crispy potato cannellonis," or the "panko crusted Loch Duart Salmon, with mushroom *spaetzle,* rainbow chard, mustard vinaigrette, and fig balsamic reduction." I consider his selection to be the least likely option. Obviously, the chef thought the shrimp offering was the best of the three. When the hyperbole is removed from the menu descriptions what we are left with is a small filet with green beans, spinach, and a small cannelloni stuffed with mashed potatoes. Demi-glace is not a finished sauce, but a sauce base. This makes no sense even if a few drops of truffle oil are added. Loch Duart is a farmed salmon, but it is a farmed wild salmon from Scotland, specifically from the Loch Duart. Sprinkled with breadcrumbs and dressed with a vinaigrette, this dish is not likely to impress. So, the chef chose the shrimp.

The shrimp themselves are of first-rate quality. They are very large, I'd guess in the U12 range. They are also seriously overcooked; they are not only tough but also almost flavorless. The pasta is dressed with very nice garlic, butter, white wine, clam juice liquid. The spinach is also bland. Kalamata olives are added in great quantity. These potent vinegar- and salt-brined Greek olives dominate all other flavors. They are ruining the entire dish, and there is no reason to actually eat them. I push them aside.

A molten chocolate cake with a side of vanilla ice cream and a couple of raspberries rounds out the meal. The flourless chocolate cake shell appears soft and delicious on the plate. By the time it actually hits the mouth, it has cooled; it has also hardened as though it is has just come out of the microwave. Two raspberries and a mint leaf are not enough to save it.

I think of Franz Kafka. I have a sudden urge to escape. As I get up to leave, I wonder if the doors will open. I think of the final scene in the Kubrick/King movie *The Shining* where the ghosts of a bygone era cavort in a long-deceased nightclub.

There ought to be a dress code here: formalwear only, tuxedos and long gowns. They could not actually do it, of course, but you know, to maintain the illusion . . .

Cheesecake Factory

$$-$$$

Location: at The River at Rancho Mirage, 404-1400. **Food type:** *eclectic American; something for everybody.* **Ambiance:** *Babylonian movie set.* **Bar:** *full.* **Reservations:** *before 6 P.M. only.* **Hours:** *lunch and dinner daily.*

For some, eating is a religious experience (a Shabbat dinner in a Jewish household). It can be a celebration, as it is at a wedding or Thanksgiving. For others it is only healthful sustenance (a tofu taco at Native Foods) or the alleviation of hunger while on the run (a burger at Jack-in-the-

Box). Others relish the nostalgia of comfort food. For many readers of this book it is an aesthetic experience (five courses of haute cuisine with wine pairings). But for the patrons of Cheesecake Factory, it has to be food as an arcade game. There are some 120 of these behemoths nationwide. Everything is larger than life. The interior looks like a movie set for a DeMille extravaganza set in ancient Egypt. With massive murals, Corinthian columns going nowhere, masses of bent copper tubing, custom lighting in every conceivable size and shape, and upholstery resembling animal hides, this place has more kitsch packed into a single square inch than does a Las Vegas casino.

The menu, replete with advertising, is immense, a spiral-bound tome more suited for the Vatican library than a restaurant. Everything an American could possibly think of to eat is listed. Much of the food is in the fast-food/casual-dining category, and portions are enormous. Every cheesecake ever conceived—30 different varieties, some verging on the absurd—is displayed in the gargantuan pastry counter. Preparation is reasonably competent, but there is nothing here to excite the taste buds. Patrons really do not come here to dine, but to experience the environment.

This spectacle does not come cheap either. Prices range from the more or less reasonable ($14 for many pasta dishes) to the ridiculous ($28 for a small filet with French fries and onion rings). With the obvious exception of the more excessive cheesecakes, everything on the menu can be had elsewhere better prepared and at less cost. Children like it here.

Wait times can be brutal, and the hustle, bustle, and ruckus could disturb the sleep of a vampire. Oh, lest I forget, this Cheesecake Factory is in the middle of a faux river—a faux moat for a faux palace.

The Cliffhouse

$$-$$$

*Location: 78-250 Highway 111, La Quinta, 360-5991. **Food type:** American.* ***Bar:** full. **Ambiance:** spectacular; built into the side of a rock face with views all across the desert floor. **Reservations:** suggested. **Hours:** dinner nightly.*

The Cliffhouse is part of the TS Restaurants chain of 12 establishments in California and Hawaii. Its Web site touts its unique cuisine, but the menu is mundane. The following is also an excerpt from the Web site: "Perched on historic Point Happy, the restaurant captures the area's ranch heritage and architecture of the early 1900s. So successful is its ambiance, it won the American Society of Interior Designers first place award in Restaurant Design." This is accurate. The Cliffhouse has one of the most beautiful views and is certainly the most interesting setting of any restaurant in the valley. It is only a pity that the food does not measure up. It has early-bird and summer specials, significant wine discounts, and a children's menu. It has also recently begun serving Prime steak, albeit rather small ones. It is just that none of it is very good. The one star is for value and view.

Cuistot
★★★½
$$$$
Location: 72-595 El Paseo Dr., Palm Desert, 340-1000. **Food type:** *French haute cuisine.* **Reservations:** *recommended.* **Ambiance:** *elegant and formal French country inn.* **Bar:** *full; extensive wine list.* **Hours:** *lunch and dinner daily.* **Chef-owner:** *Bernard Dervieux.*

In 1987, Chef Bernard Dervieux, a student of French master chefs Paul Bocuse and Roger Vergé, brought haute cuisine to the desert and reigned unchallenged for at least a decade. His place in the desert's aristocracy of great chefs remains unchallenged. He is the man most responsible for raising the bar for fine dining in the Coachella Valley. From 1987 until 2003, Dervieux held court in a not-so-modest storefront on trendy and exclusive El Paseo Drive in Palm Desert. It was there that his reputation was made. It was there that Dervieux earned his stripes and paid his dues. In 2003, he built his palace.

The old Cuistot was so formal that it verged on sterility. In the fall of 2003, the new Cuistot opened about half a mile away, a custom-designed re-creation of a French farmhouse dominating the entire southwest corner of El Paseo and Highway 111. Whether you find this kind of displaced architecture awkward in the California desert is a matter of personal taste, but there is no denying that Bernard Dervieux has poured his heart and soul into establishing the finest restaurant money and human creativity can unleash. The new Cuistot is still formal, but the sterility is gone. With extensive use of rock façades both inside and out, a high-pitched roof (to shed the snow of the French Alps), massive open beams, wood, fireplaces, and appointments in copper, burgundy, and gold, Cuistot is rich, serious, and comfortable.

The spectacular open kitchen occupies the entire eastern third of the building. Islands are arranged to eliminate any crossing of the chefs. Separate stations exist for all preparations. Burners are tiered—rear burners higher than front burners—to decrease the chance of seared fingers. There is also an herb garden of rosemary, thyme, borage, chervil, parsley, basil, marjoram, mint, and sage. (Why is my herb garden so scrawny?)

That the food at Cuistot is magnificent is a given. The issues are those of cost and ambiance. It is important that a diner know what to expect before making the decision to wander into one of the premier restaurants in the desert. The food is classical French haute cuisine with a California twist. The menu is not a clone of other popular establishments: scallops and lobster in filo dough, a tower of tomatoes with smoked trout fillet, rabbit in Dijon mustard with tarragon, Chilean sea bass over steamed baby bok choy.

The garden vegetable salad is simple yet perfect: peas and little dice of blanched carrots and potatoes on a bed of butter lettuce and radicchio. Bernard's Secret Dressing, a citrus vinaigrette with a touch of sweetness, unifies and brings to life the contrasting flavors.

Sole-wrapped lobster in a chervil sauce served with wonderful potatoes dauphinoise (cream, Gruyère cheese, butter, egg, and nutmeg) is a marriage made in heaven. A quartet of fresh vegetables is along for the ride, but what a ride! Whole pea pods, baby carrots, *haricots vert,* and beets. The lowly beet steels the show. I don't mean the vegetable show, I mean the whole show. These are more interesting than the lobster. Forget the past: healthful and hideous beets out of a can from 1957. Most of us wish to purge these memories from even the most distant recesses of our brains. Dervieux's beets are glorious. They are just tender and infused with the most wonderful something while retaining the pure essence of the beet. "More!" I demand, fists pounding the table.

The sole/lobster roll is poached until just cooked and butter tender. A sauce of fish fumet and cream laden with chervil serves to support this most subtle and delectable of aquatic life. Chervil, a.k.a. French parsley, has a flavor falling somewhere between Italian parsley and anise. Hints of coriander and lavender wander through it as well. Its subtlety gives it a special affinity with fish. Ironically, it is the lobster that has trouble contributing its fair share.

Salmon Paul Bocuse is a cold slice of raw salmon "cooked" in citric acid—lemon juice with shallots and acting as counterpoint—like a ceviche. This tangy and unique concoction most resembles gravlax. The fish is luscious, soft, sweet, and oily, reminiscent of sea foam. The lemon acts as a balance, sour and acidic. The two contrasting forces—the harmony of opposites—work with and against one another to produce something wondrous, then comes the catalyst in the form of the crisp, crunchy shallot.

More complex and much more expensive are the diver scallops and Maine lobster layered in filo dough over a garlic-tomato coulis with thyme essence. This is an explosion of tastes and textures. Whereas the salmon is a relatively simple dish, this one is a riot of interaction. The shellfish are the first tastes. When they are good, they are amazing, and these are amazing. The fish are soft and sweet, with big but illusive flavors. They are served on a coulis of some orange stuff. Traditionally, a coulis is a thin meat or crustacean purée, but more recently, the term has come to denote fruit or vegetable purées. The menu says garlic-tomato, but the mouth says carrot. The second impression is butternut squash. Next, there is something curious: paper-thin rounds of deep-fried filo dough adding a crunch to the textures but no new taste. A potent counterbalance of flavor is needed to make this fugue come together. It comes in the form of basil oil and parsley. The menu says thyme oil; I taste basil. Is my mouth playing tricks on me? Did Devereux change it? In any case, the pungent herb slices through the sweetness of the fish and squash. Fantastic! My only complaint? Not enough of it.

Fresh rabbit in a Dijon mustard sauce with tarragon and rabbit liver *feuilletée* with braised leeks fills the bill with a much-needed and too oft-missing entrée, rabbit. The critical ingredient in this dish is tarragon. When I was a child, I did not like tarragon. Boy, was I wrong! Sauce béarnaise was the proximate cause of my enlightenment. I have never had rabbit dressed with tarragon before, and it was a revelation. The sauce itself is probably made from rabbit stock reduction, butter, and Dijon mustard with essence of tarragon. Rabbit, like venison, is very lean and needs a buttery sauce to give it a fat/lean balance. The sauce is reduced to the consistency of light syrup. Accompanying the rabbit was a *feuilletée,* the definition of which seems to be a bit of a moving target. Traditionally the word seems to be *feuilleton,* and it was a small round composed of thin slices of veal or pork alternating with layers of minced mushrooms wrapped in fat and braised. A *feuilletée* in current cooking vocabulary is a small round of puff pastry stuffed with something. Devereux's *feuilletée* is a small round of braised leeks with small pieces of rabbit liver. There is no puff pastry. It is delicious; so why be picky?

An array of beautifully prepared vegetables graces the plate—a baby carrot, some fresh peas with pods included, baby green beans—blanched and finished in butter with just a hint of crunch. Too much al dente does not result in a full-flavored vegetable. A round of the crispiest potatoes completes the dish. How does he manage to get all the little potato slices crunchy and still have them stick together?

My first dessert is a layered gateau: chocolate, a crispy/crunchy bit of pastry, hazelnut mousse, chocolate mocha mousse, whipping cream, a crispy/crunchy bit of pastry, and chocolate in a hazelnut-chocolate sauce. With a bottle of very dry, full-bodied Concannon Chardonnay for only $27, this is a true feast in the classical Alsatian tradition. The wine is fruity, clean, and sprightly, not oaked and buttery.

A thin slice of flourless chocolate cake piled high with chocolate mousse, garnished with fresh raspberries, and served on a coulis of *crème anglaise* is the featured dessert of the day. I requested that a half shot of brandy be poured over the mousse. This was done willingly and at no charge. The mousse was a real mousse, that is to say, melted bittersweet chocolate with folded meringue and chantilly cream. Some lesser establishments have been known to pass off chocolate pudding as mousse, a shameful ruse.

If there is a criticism to be applied to Devereux, it is the fact that he really hasn't grown much in the last few years. It is true that in the mid-1990s Cuistot was the only game in town, the only restaurant that dared serve haute cuisine. Nevertheless, more recently younger chefs have opened restaurants with larger perspectives questioning the nature and limits of great food. There is, however, no question that Dervieux is a great chef, firmly planted in and fully facile with the great traditions of high French cuisine. Among valley foodies, Cuistot has garnered a reputation of being overrated. I think this has more to do with the fact of his continued popularity and longevity than a decline in food quality.

The wine list is not huge but it is both broad and deep, with ample selections from both France and California covering all tastes and wallet sizes.

Desert Sage
★★★

$$$-$$$$

Location: 78-085 *Avenida La Fonda, La Quinta,* 564-8744. *Food type: California eclectic. Ambiance: exquisite postmodern refurbishing of an old house. Bar: full; extensive and first-rate wine list ranging from several bottles under $30 to a 2003 Screaming Eagle Cabernet for $4,000. Virtually all are from California. Reservations: suggested. Hours: dinner Tuesday through Sunday, happy hour and bar menu 4 P.M. to 7:30 P.M. Chef: Keith Otter (executive), Yves de Bard (pastry chef).*

Desert Sage has undergone three metamorphoses in the last eight years. It debuted with Chef Jeffrey Russell, a nationally acknowledged master recognized by the James Beard Foundation. Food quality was superb, but astronomical prices forced it to close and its owners to rethink the entire project. In its first reincarnation, Aaron Barnet, sous chef to San Francisco superstar Gary Danko, was placed at the helm. Prices were brought down marginally and the four-star rating held, but that version also failed. Desert Sage has risen yet again, this time with Keith Otter as captain of the ship. Graduate of CIA San Francisco, mentored by Julian Serrano of Masa's in San Francisco and Joachim Splichal of Patina in Los Angeles, he has not the credential depth of Barnett, and his food is impressive but flawed.

A bar menu at happy hour, 4 to 7:30 all week, has been added with consumer-friendly half-priced appetizers and $3 well drinks. A jazz pianist of some renown is present to provide background sounds of a pleasing nature. There is also a dance floor (see the back of the book for a new index of restaurants providing live music and a dance floor).

Desert Sage is a stunning building. It began life as a private home and was completely remodeled as a restaurant in 2000. The color palette is copper, from gold, yellow, and orange to burnt umber, raw sienna, and everything in between. Muted shades of these warm tones enliven the total environment. Most original are the walls, which have been painted as a kind of Picasso-like *papier collé.* With textures of wood, sometimes rough, sometimes smooth, the viewer is confronted by what appears to be a huge flat pastiche of various wallpapers with iconic desert images sprinkled here and there. The colors on the walls are all at the lighter end of the copper spectrum. The floor is a rough stone tile incorporating the darker tones. Actual copper facings appear above the fireplace and the reception desk. A mass of twisted hand-torched wrought iron functions as a railing for the staircase. The bar consists of two layers of laminated glass with pieces of screen pressed between them. The elegance and beauty, not to mention originality, of Desert Sage has to be experienced to be believed. An outdoor courtyard and glass-enclosed atrium complete the dining areas. The atrium is all weather, heated and cooled, with flowers and the aroma of fresh-growing herbs suffusing the air.

It is difficult to know exactly how to rate this establishment. It has so much going for it yet there are inconsistencies that were not present in the past. Take, for example, the Tortellini Pasta. The ringed pasta is stuffed with a nondescript filling and served in a sauce of creamy Gorgonzola cheese. The sauce is excellent! The pungent blue cheese in its velvety bath perfectly complements the bland pasta. Moving the flavor profile in another direction are chunks of pancetta, that wonderful Italian bacon. The addition of radicchio, however, delivers a blast of bitterness disturbing both the balance and the context. This first course is also so heavy it alone can seriously dull the appetite.

Crab cakes also start out beautifully but are ultimately flawed. Dungeness crab and rock shrimp (which have a lobster-type flavor) are merged. Typically, crab cakes are about 60 percent crabmeat mixed with mayonnaise, breadcrumbs, parsley, Old Bay seasoning, and an egg for a good bind. They are either pan-fried or deep-fried. Good ones have a lot of explosive crab flavor and an often spicy cream sauce. Chipotle peppers make a good heat source. These, while apparently containing less filler than the norm, have less flavor as well. The inclusion of bits of yellow bell pepper further masks the crab taste. One can only conclude that it was the fault of the crab and shrimp. The sauce, too, was bland, made from a puree of red bell peppers. On the other hand, a light mazuna (usually spelled "mizuna," Japanese mustard greens very much like arugula but not as peppery) and green apple salad with its fresh acidity is the perfect foil for the heavier fried crab cake. With a simple vinaigrette this side is interesting, creative, and unusual.

The French dip is a bar menu item, happy hour only, but it is terrific. The menu says brioche roll. It is not. I had simple French bread, but no matter. The meat was thin sliced prime rib, butter tender and flavorful.

This is slathered with Gruyère cheese, melted under a broiler, and served with a big, aggressive beef broth. The dip is neither greasy nor oversalted, a rarity in French dip land. A pungent and vinegary horseradish also accompanies. Bar menu items are inexpensive, and this French dip for $7.50 and a beer or bourbon and soda ($3) can provide a tasty early dinner for the cost of a Tyler's burger and fries (Chapter 8).

Calamari is a beautifully prepared appetizer containing both rings and bay tentacles. The tentacles are light and crunchy; the rings are inevitably more chewy. I do not know the nature of the batter used here but I would guess it is egg white based as opposed to the heavier buttermilk/flour combinations. This is Southwest or Thai style rather than the more usual Italian style with a tomato sauce. The large bowl of calamari is dressed with a medium spicy East Asian sweet-chili-garlic sauce. With a squeeze of lemon, the mouth experiences a tart, acidic, sweet, spicy-hot, heat-hot, garlicky, crunchy fish taste. To gild the lily even further, an even hotter chipotle mayonnaise is served on the side. Nice!

Dinner entrées are expensive (from $24 for a lemon chicken to $45 for a rib-eye steak) and not the least bit original or daring, but the standards for both quality of ingredients and preparation are high. Chilean sea bass with garlic potatoes, asparagus, capers, fava beans, and dill in a butter sauce and rack of lamb with vegetable-barley risotto, asparagus, and a red wine, rosemary, roasted garlic sauce are particularly desirable.

Dink's

½

$$

#

Location: 2080 N. Palm Canyon Dr., Palm Springs, 327-7676. *Food type: everything. Ambiance: big, open, noisy nightclub, west-facing wall of tinted glass, indoor-outdoor lounges. Bar: full. Reservations: required on weekends. Hours: lunch and dinner daily; Sunday brunch; happy hour 5 P.M. to 8 P.M. daily. Dress Code: "desert casual attire is appropriate."*

"DINK" is an acronym for "Double Income, No Kids." It refers to the most affluent demographic in America, the gay male couple. Yet there is something odd happening here. Dink's, a kind of pseudo-gay restaurant and "ultra" lounge, is afraid to capitalize on this obvious gay reference. They have raised the ire of the very demographic they court by banning men dressed in drag (presumably even if the drag ware qualifies as "desert casual").

This indecisiveness is carried throughout: menu, service, architecture, everything. A lot of money was spent here. This is an original building with over 10,000 square feet. There are indoor and outdoor lounges with sofas and matching armchairs. Terry-cloth robes are provided for those wishing to experience the outdoor patio on cooler nights. Both outdoor patio and restaurant feature cabana-style curtained-off booths. The inside cabanas are so awkwardly placed as to be jarring. For true privacy, Shame on the Moon (Chapter 8) is the place to be. The ceiling is made of hardwood flooring. It looks like mahogany. This is at the very least odd, as well as expensive. The tables and chairs also appear to be mahogany. The deep red color is contrasted with a muted green and pale gold to complete the color scheme. Anecdotal but consistent information indicates that both service and drinks are erratic, even bizarre. The menu is irrational. There is no focus whatsoever: pizzas, sushi, tapas, sandwiches, burgers, satay, crab and avocado quesadilla, Southwestern chili, rubbed steak, Cobb salad, prime rib, paella, seafood fettuccine, peaches Melba, and "Elvis' Famous Red Velvet Chocolate Cake." This is something for everybody, but something for no one. It is Italian, Mexican, American, and Asian fusion all at the same time.

I elect to sample from the extremes: sushi and paella. Both are disappointments. A sampler of salmon and shrimp sushi arrives at my table. The salmon is tiny, perhaps a square inch, on a mound of rice. The shrimp is maybe a U20, two and a half inches long including tail. The salmon is gloriously soft but almost flavorless. The rice is extremely sticky and underdone. Combine these two and both are damaged. The shrimp has substantially more flavor than the salmon, but here, too, the rice only damages the experience. Horseradish passing itself off as wasabi overwhelms.

A side of peas, soy, and lima beans accompanies. A shiso leaf rests beneath. (Shiso has a flavor somewhat between mint and basil.) A tiny sprinkling of tobiko caviar sits on top. The trio of beans is interesting enough. Each bean has an independent flavor, yet all are related, shifting the focus in the mouth but never interfering with one another. The caviar is completely lost in the more dominant beans. Tobiko is not potent anyway, so its presence here is just for looks. Eat it separately. Shiso is always interesting even as its rough texture is reminiscent of something caught in a lawnmower. As a condiment this is primarily something to add bulk at a low cost to the stingy serving of fish.

Good paella is not that difficult to make. Paella is fundamentally a rice dish flavored with saffron. The rice should be short grain, preferably the premium Spanish rice called Bomba, but Arborio makes a good substitute. Paella Valenciana, the original, was made from snails, rabbit, and chicken thigh meat. Cuban paella was first to integrate seafood (shrimp, lobster, mussels, and clams), and somewhere along the line, the spicy Spanish chorizo sausage became an optional addition. As long as the chef realizes that the primary ingredient is saffron-flavored rice, he is more or less free to manipulate the meats. The paellas at both Oceans (Chapter 8) and Artisan Grove (Chapter 1) are excellent. This one, along with many others around town, is not.

The chef at Dink's first does not recognize that paella is a rice dish. The rice is a nondescript medium-grain varietal. It could be the same sticky rice as used for the sushi. Saffron, if any, is lost in a blizzard of competing notions. Five tiny and tasteless mussels (I mean really tiny, somewhere in half-inch-long territory) and four equally tasteless clams are stuck into the surface rice. Two of the mussel shells are empty, well, empty of the mussel that is. Two decent shrimp (the same as the shrimp of the sushi) decorate the top, but the paella has no taste of shellfish at all. Chunks of chicken breast abound, but they, too, have little flavor. There is only one taste and it overwhelms everything. And what is that taste? It is something in the family of Hillshire Farms sausage. This paella is flooded with it. I left about half a cup of Hillshire Farms Polish kielbasa pieces on my plate. This paella is nothing more than a sausage dish with some chicken and shellfish for decoration with a side of rice.

So why do I give Dink's even a half star? For the environment. The building is beautiful. Both outdoor and indoor lounges are unique. The entertainment is often loud and raucous, but that may appeal to many. If one's culinary discrimination is secondary to the environment, Dink's may be just the ticket for a fun evening.

Jillian's
Not recommended
$$$$
*Location: 74-155 El Paseo Dr., Palm Desert, 776-8242. **Food type:** faux*

French. **Ambiance:** *beautiful converted old house with open courtyard, Roman villa style.* **Bar:** *full.* **Reservations:** *suggested.* **Hours:** *dinner Monday through Saturday.* **Chef:** *Jay Turbee.*

Special note to the owners and fans of Jillian's: At the request of the owners, and as a result of the level of dissent I received regarding my rating of the restaurant in the first edition, I agreed to do a second review for this edition. When I attempted a second review in late spring, the restaurant was closed for the season. Jillian's old review stands until a third edition.

Jillian's is the most overrated restaurant in the desert. To be sure, the building is beautiful, with an open courtyard in the style of an Italian villa, but ambiance does not make a restaurant. Recipes are irrational; quality is inconsistent. A rack of lamb ordered rare arrives medium well. Pastas are sticky. Desserts are cloying.

The era of vertical food is exemplified by a tower of Dungeness crab stacked on a bed of avocado, which is stacked on a bed of diced fresh tomatoes, which is placed on a round of crispy toasted brioche. All of this is pressed into a conical ring mold and released onto a lemon/dill mayonnaise. Fussy, yes, but not unsuccessful. The balance of acid and sweet, soft and crunchy, the herbal twinge of the dill all come together for a favorable outcome.

Salad of Two Hearts (palm and artichoke) does not add up to much of anything. Again, the dish shows a penchant for fussiness: lettuce, artichoke, hearts of palm, and julienne of red and yellow bell peppers. Only a few kalamata olives deliver any kind of distinctive flavor. The whole is less than the sum of the parts. The harmony of contrasts needed to produce interest is not present. The dressing, billed as roasted red pepper vinaigrette, is virtually nonexistent.

A double-cut pork rib chop lined with sausage, apple, and date stuffing, grilled moist and graced with a vintage port wine demi-glace is how it appears on the menu. The meat itself is excellent: full of flavor and as tender as pork is these days since the genetic engineers have managed to remove all the fat from its tissues. The stuffing has notes of Thanksgiving—sweet and mushy with dominant apples and dates. The pork is complemented well by the stuffing. But the dish does not arrive with the sauce as defined on the menu. What does is chipotle-chili based and does not work at all. The smoky-sweet chili might work with the pork with an entirely different flavor profile, but with the apples and dates it is a disaster. What this dish needs is a heavy dose of acidity: lemon, vinegar, white wine, or best yet Calvados (apple brandy). The sudden introduction of Mexican flavors into this mostly French context works against itself. It is served with an array of vegetables: beets, corn, carrots, and broccoli. Is it possible that the corn and beets are canned? The broccoli and carrots are blanched but unfinished. They are essentially raw. With an entirely different sauce—flamed Calvados, shallot, veal demi-glace, or green peppercorns—served with crunchy caramelized pearl onions and butter-soaked yam, this could be a fine dish, but this is not the case.

Jillian's remains one of the premier palaces in the desert. "Why?" he asks. Don't ask me; I'm just the piano player.

La Spiga Ristorante Italiano
★★★★
$$$½
Location: *72-557 Highway 111, Palm Desert, 340-9318.* **Food type:** alta cucina. **Ambiance:** *spectacular Italian villa.* **Bar:** *full; excellent wine list, mostly Italian and Californian.* **Reservations:** *required; reserve well in advance.* **Hours:** *dinner Tuesday through Saturday.* **Chef-owner:** *Vince Cultraro.*

There are several spectacular restaurants in the Coachella Valley. Wally's, Cuistot, Sirocco, and Le Vallauris, all in this chapter, come immediately to mind. But none have the grounds of La Spiga. This is a case where the quality of the food and the quality of the environment are fully balanced: both are marvelous. The Italian villa—think of a hilltop villa outside of Florence or Sienna surrounded by vineyards and olive trees, something like the Villa San Andrea—was built in 2007 to the needs and specifications of the chef-owner. The grounds appear to be about two acres walled and enclose olive trees, a vegetable garden, and an herb garden. The grounds and the gazebo with functional fireplace, kitchen, and bar make for a spectacular location for a large party, wedding reception, or anniversary. The architectural success seems to be based on the fact that La Spiga is at once expansive and intimate. Everything from valet parking to main dining room, from foyer to bar and the massive kitchens is completely successful. The dining rooms and outdoor patio look southward toward the gardens and the Santa Rosa Mountains rather than northward toward the street, as does adjacent sister palace Cuistot.

Chef-owner Vince Cultraro is one of a handful of the valley's master chefs. Originally from Sicily, he received his training in classical technique in Milan, focusing on the specialties of the northern regions of Piedmont, Lombardy, Tuscany, and Emilia-Romagna. With his charming and beautiful wife, Connie, who hails from Calabria, he opened a wildly successful restaurant in Edmonton, Alberta, Canada. La Spiga, Alberta, is the favorite restaurant of former Canadian prime minister Jean Chrétien, who regularly flew across the country to sample its culinary delights. Vince and Connie sold the Alberta restaurant, thus assuring us that this master chef is fully in charge of his kitchen night after night. In other words, he belongs to us.

When I suggested that the fundamental inspiration for the cold potato-zucchini soup was vichyssoise, Cultraro looked a little surprised and a bit insulted. The rivalry between the world's two premier cuisines remains amusing to Americans, but for the French and Italians, the roots of the antagonism go all the way back to the Italian Renaissance. In 1553, Catherine de Medici, a Florentine, married Henry II of France. It was she who introduced the concept of cooking as high art to the French court. The French will never forgive the Italians for being the foundation of their cuisine, and the Italians will never forgive the French for actually improving, albeit only occasionally, on their classical techniques. French high cuisine tends to be elaborate and subtle; that of Italy is bold, simple, and direct.

The base of this pottage is cream and potatoes—starchy potatoes like Russets, boiled and puréed. The result is a thick, satiny-textured wonder with little flavor. Vichyssoise uses the leek, a member of the onion family, to supply the flavor. Chef Cultraro substitutes Italian squash, zucchini, for the leek. He also interjects subtle notes of fennel, tweaking it in curious directions. Finished with a splash of cream, a dollop of extra-virgin olive oil, and a ribbon of Parmigiano-Reggiano this is a superb opening, even if it does have its origins in vichyssoise.

Carpaccio de manzo is an appetizer consisting of paper-thin slices of raw filet mignon. It is unique and fascinating. The acid from a shallot and a creamy, powerfully flavored bite from herbed Dijon mustard move into the sphere of influence. A complex counterpoint begins to form. Then cheese. It is the pungent sting of Asiago catalyzing the entire experience. A whole emerges, original and perfectly balanced.

Cultraro does a wonderful fennel salad. American palates tend not to appreciate fennel as they should. It is a bit tart, has decided notes of licorice, and is crunchy and bracing. When combined with the soft, bitter greens of arugula in a light vinaigrette, the flavor-texture opposition results in a salad with unique and astonishingly refreshing properties.

There is a little fruit called a dwarf peach that grows in the Piedmont area of northern Italy. This weird little thing is the size and shape of a large green olive. I don't have any idea what it tastes like in its unadorned state because the two I ate had been macerating in white truffle oil. The peach takes on the taste of truffle. It retains its crunchiness but has no peach flavor whatsoever. The perfume of the white truffle is both stunning and startling, like some bizarre, earthy, pungent wild mushroom. Upon tasting it, I react physically, as though being pushed backwards. Could it be that this dwarf peach with apparently no taste of its own served to intensify the taste of the truffle? This is not even a truffle; it is truffle oil! Slices of this dwarf peach and white truffle oil top an eight-ounce Prime filet mignon seared for a few moments and served with a green peppercorn demi-glace wine reduction. Served with blanched baby vegetables and a deep-fried croquette of risotto, this entrée has to rank with the finest anywhere.

Salsiccia di casa is an appetizer of fresh house-made pork sausage— lean pork packed with flavor. Where is the balance? Anise, and lots of it, charges the meat with the combined tastes of sweet and licorice. A counterpoint is established, but now comes a heavy dose of chili flakes. The last taste to hit is heat, which washes away the meat and the anise for a harmony of opposites.

Pappardelle al bosco is wide noodles (dry, soft, mild) in a cream sauce (wet, fat, mild) with shaved white truffles (earthy, dense, potent) and Asiago cheese (tangy, sour). The interplay of these diverse tastes works together, and Chef Cultraro's innate understanding of these factors results in the finest of creations.

Cervo al funchi di bosco—venison with wild mushrooms—is the equivalent of a rib chop from a lamb. One venison rib has about four times the meat of one lamb rib, and the entrée comes with two chops, the equivalent of a whole rack of lamb. It looks like filet mignon, has the texture of leg of lamb, and tastes like deer. Do not order this dish cooked more than medium rare, as it will be dried out. At first bite, it resembles lean New York steak. Then its uniqueness, a blast of smokiness, a subtle gamey quality, hits at the back of the mouth. At first taste, it is odd, then interesting, then good, and finally wonderful. The key element that must be worked with, as with rabbit, is the lack of fat in the meat. The solution is a most elegant sauce borrowed from the F country (France), a reduction of a red wine and veal demi-glace infused with rosemary and crushed green peppercorns. The pungent herb and the sweet-hot peppercorns charge the sauce, as do the white truffles in the pasta. The sauce is then strained and clarified, but it is not over. Chef Cultraro still hasn't solved the problem of the lean meat. Borrowing once again from the French, he whips sweet butter into his sauce. It is then reduced to the consistency of light syrup before serving. Complementing the venison is a cornucopia of blanched and sautéed vegetables—asparagus, green beans, carrots, stuffed zucchini, eggplant, and mushrooms—finished in butter and served al dente. The venison is an on-again-off-again menu item. Order it when making your reservations.

Lemon granita, the likes of which I have not had since 1990 in a little *gelateria* in Florence, overwhelms the taste buds with an assault of lemon flavor. It is bold, aggressive, and almost unbearably intense.

Chef Cultraro is consistent and he is there every night. Virtually everything I have tasted has been exceptional: bruschetta, *salsiccia di casa, pappardelle al bosco, insalata bocconcini, agnello arrosto alla grappa* (rack of lamb marinated in grappa), calamari, mussels, tiramisu, dark chocolate terrine.

Prices are high as one would expect for this kind of quality, but they are not absurdly so. One can spend a lot more for quality considerably beneath that of La Spiga. Lunch is available for parties of 40 or more. Reservations are a *must*. During peak season (November through March) two weeks' advance notice is necessary, although last-minute diners can be placed on a waiting list hoping for a cancellation.

Le St. Germain
★★★
$$$$
Location: 74-985 Highway 111, Indian Wells, 773-6511. **Food type:**

Euro-Cali (French). **Ambiance:** *formal but not pretentious; beautiful patio with fireplace.* **Reservations:** *suggested.* **Bar:** *full; large, comprehensive wine list, France and California dominate.* **Hours:** *dinner nightly; Sunday brunch.*

Le St. Germain in Indian Wells has evolved from the celebrated Le St. Germain restaurant of the same name in Hollywood, which had a serious run for some 17 years, from 1971 through 1988. This one opened in 1995. Are they the same? No. Chefs come and go, yet through the years the owners have remained the same.

Divided into six rooms, including salons and galleries, this restaurant attempts to create the feeling that it is smaller and more intimate than it is. With a total capacity of 384 diners and 140 people in the cocktail lounge, this is a huge space, but the main dining room and bar area both feel quite intimate. The building has elements of the French Provincial and French Normandy styles, but with the ubiquitous Spanish tile roof found on almost everything in this area. The interior is elegant in an understated way, with lots of wood, recessed lighting, muted colors, and a wall of windows. The climate-controlled patio surrounded by bougainvillea and with its own fireplace is quite stunning

An oddity controls the menus at both this restaurant and its sister in Palm Springs, Le Vallauris (featured later in this chapter). The clientele of both establishments are largely retired people with money and sufficient influence to demand and get a very conservative menu. This can be frustrating for the chefs, but it is a fact of life, the inevitable clash of art and business.

Food at both restaurants is "California-ized" French. Ads appear stating that the menu is classical French. It is not. Even during high season, only a handful of dishes—escargots, veal tenderloin, filet mignon with Roquefort and *au poivre* reduction—can be said to be in the classical tradition. On the other side of the coin, it seems that everybody in California is doing a tuna tartare with ginger and shallots. I wonder if they are doing that in Aix or Avignon.

There is a twist here on the basic desert salad: baby greens, nuts, Gorgonzola, and pear. Variations of these four ingredients are found everywhere. Here the pear is poached, the Gorgonzola is feta, and the nuts are candied pecans. The salad suffers from the poaching of the pear. Part of the success of this combination is the contrast between the rich, soft ripe cheese and the crunch of fresh fruit. Poaching turns the pear soft, resulting in a loss of this textural contrast. A tangy port-balsamic glaze on the cheese does not make up for it.

A crab tower with avocado, cucumber, and salmon caviar in a rice-wine-based sauce of ginger, sesame, and pink peppercorns is a little too complicated to allow the crab to "speak" but is quite delicious nevertheless. The French tendency to remake the primary ingredient into an entirely new creation is at play here, but I cannot help but wonder where all the crabmeat went. By the way, this dish is terrific when paired with the Bancrott Sauvignon Blanc, an inexpensive, crisp, dry New Zealand white with some serious honeydew overtones.

Black cod on a bed of niçoise vegetables, while sharing some of the complexity of the crab tower, emerges successfully. The cod itself is flavorful and cooked perfectly, and the niçoise mixture surprisingly does not interfere. A seemingly arbitrary assemblage of black and green olives, tomatoes, artichoke hearts, and fava beans delivers a battery of contrasting flavors and textures.

Salmon on a bed of spinach is a house favorite. The spinach manages to be both blanched and cooked through but not water logged or heavy. (Wish I could do that!) The combination works on every level. The duo of tomato relishes—puréed red and yellow—is not so successful with the salmon, but, again, the total dish works.

Sautéed maple duck breast over tabbouleh is definitely over the top. This is so confusing to the palate you tend to give up entirely and eat the individual elements independently. The current habit of serving rare duck breast has run its course in my opinion. The glory of a well-cooked, falling-off-the-bone-tender bird with a crackling, sweet-glazed skin is totally lost with this trendy practice. In contrast with most meats, duck develops flavor with cooking. Sautéeing for a few minutes delivers little taste. To make up for this lack of serious duck flavor, sauses overwhelm the dish; condiments and relishes, all of which are excellent when taken independently, are gratuitous together. An apricot-date relish, for example, atop the duck would offer all the traditional sweetness and fruit flavors of the more traditional orange or cherry accompaniments but bring something new and exciting to the party. Or a sauce of a fig-orange reduction with ginger and a pinch of sugar would satisfy any traditional duck lover's fancy. Together this is enough to cause considerable palate confusion, but with the addition of tabbouleh, the dish is incomprehensible. The Middle Eastern entrée heavy with mint and parsley just doesn't work here. In its favor, a couscous-based tabbouleh is lightened by reducing the ratio of mint and parsley to grain. Minced cucumber and tomato are added. It is a fine tabbouleh, but it does not belong here.

Rack of lamb is a monster. Marinated Australian lamb is crusted with garlic and pistachio nuts then grilled. Big deal, you say! Everybody does that. This one is superb in its simplicity. It is pure lamb stock reduced to the consistency of light syrup. There is an infusion of fresh mint, but the real taste marvel is a kind of crème brûlée-style burnt sugar. This subtle bitterness, apparently a result of caramelized sugar, enhances the flavors of the lamb. And the sauce base itself is nothing but lamb flavor. Superb all the way around!

The wine list is substantial and prices reasonable. French and California labels predominate, and several interesting dessert wines are also featured.

Oh! Just thought you'd like to know, Le St. Germain has the most outrageous doggie bags in the world. High-tech black things that appear to be made of lead, vessels for plutonium or possibly kryptonite. Way cool!

Le Vallauris
★★★½
$$$$

Location: 385 W. Tahquitz Canyon Way, Palm Springs, 325-5059. **Food type:** *Euro-Cali (French).* **Ambiance:** *Spanish/Mediterranean Revival-style converted house with Flemish tapestries and Louis XV furniture; gorgeous patio.* **Reservations:** *suggested, especially for the patio.* **Bar:** *full; very expensive wine list, with a few wines by the glass; $30 corkage fee.* **Hours:** *lunch and dinner daily; Sunday brunch.* **Chef:** *Jean Paul Lair.*

For the geographically curious, the original Vallauris is a small town near the French Riviera three and a half miles north of Cannes.

This beautiful restaurant was built as a private home in the Mediterranean Revival style in 1927. In 1973, Paul Bruggemans and Camille Bardet, owners of the famous Le St. Germain in Hollywood, decided to open a restaurant in Palm Springs and fell in love with the house. Great care was taken to maintain the house's original layout, and it opened as Le Vallauris a year later. As an interesting sidebar, the Hollywood Le St. Germain closed in 1988 and a restaurant of the same name and same corporate lineage opened in Indian Wells in 1995 (featured earlier in this chapter).

Perhaps the nicest thing about the environment at Le Vallauris is its stunning courtyard. Seven old gnarly ficus trees growing right up through the tiled floor form a shaded canopy over the patio. It compares favorably with the patio at Spencer's (Chapter 2). Inside, you get the feeling of dining in someone's home.

There is an odd but rather serious defect in this restaurant and it has to do with wine. The restaurant greatly needs a sommelier, and it needs a decent list of wines by the glass to give that sommelier something to do. The wine list is huge, but it is outrageously expensive with the average bottle selling for around $200 and several vintages going for between $2,000 and $3,000. Even the corkage fee is expensive at $30. I tested the wine-pairing abilities of both the chef and a rather pretentious but ill-informed waiter. Both failed badly. The dish in question was a cumin-glazed rack of lamb. More on this later, but a dish this smoky and oddly spiced cries out for something like a peppery Shiraz. First came an extremely acidic Cab from Chile that was undrinkable in this context. It was replaced by a Pinot Noir that was not offensive but did nothing for the meat. Le Vallauris is an extremely successful restaurant, the premier restaurant of old Palm Springs, so there is no serious economic reason to alter its wine policy, but from an aesthetic gastronomic standpoint this is a serious lack. There is also the question of the integrity of a fine restaurant.

Kitchen skills are another story altogether. Chef Lair has created a menu that reflects California Fusion techniques, often including the desert's own produce, while maintaining a legitimate connection with classical French cuisine. This connection is more pronounced and successful than that of sister restaurant Le St. Germain across town.

An exotic lobster cocktail is the only dish of six that even comes close to being too complex. With papaya, mango, rice-wine-blanched onion, and avocado as a condiment, the lobster is nicely enhanced with a not-too-sweet cold garnish that brings a bright and refreshing sparkle to the venerable shellfish. A topping of Tobiko caviar augments the brininess natural to the lobster, and a coulis of passion fruit with a slight mustard tang completes the ensemble. Too much? No. The diverse elements all work either together or in concert to harmonize one another. By using papaya and mango rather than, say, peach and pear, Chef Lair does not introduce too much sweetness.

The porcini tart is perfect. Slices of the powerful wild mushroom rest on a thin piece of puff pastry. This is cooked like a pizza. The pastry puffs, and the mushrooms soften and release their earthy aromas. Lair places a mound of bright and peppery arugula atop the tart and drizzles truffle oil. The result is magical. This is the definition of umami, at least in my lexicon: an intense, savory, earthy-based aroma that seems to build in the mouth. With the bitter green as foil, this tart generates an uncanny mouth feel. The effect of the truffle oil on the roof of the mouth is addictive.

Of course, there is the ubiquitous tuna tartare, the signature trendy dish of recent years. On the other hand, the escargots here are arguably the best in town. Lair sticks with the classic French recipe, using only the biggest, fattest, freshest snails, and broiling them until just cooked through. And let us not forget the basic desert salad of Gorgonzola, walnuts, and pear with baby greens. The version here features Stilton cheese, pear, and Belgian endive.

Lake Superior whitefish has been on the menu since 1995. Lair is tired of making it, but his customers refuse to let it go. Any attempt to remove it is met with a storm of protest. The succulent, perfectly sautéed fish rests on a bed of shiitake mushrooms and blanched spinach. This is dressed in a *beurre blanc* probably with cream added. Lair, in an amusing touch, has given new meaning to onion rings. He makes a julienne of onion. These spindly threads of onion are then deep-fried. The result looks like confetti. They have little taste but look terrific and add a nice textual contrast to the otherwise soft ingredients. Little wedges of something that looks like peach or papaya garnishes. In actuality, this is turmeric-colored potato wedges. This looks good on the plate, but neither the texture nor the starchy flavor does anything for the fish at all.

The rack of lamb served at Le Vallauris is unique. It is drenched with cumin, as mentioned above, with a drizzle of something that, at first taste, elicits thoughts of mild chipotle in adobo sauce. Mild chipotle is an oxymoron, so I move on to an olive tapenade. This isn't right either. The flavors are intense and mildly spicy, but perhaps that is all that cumin speaking. The drizzle is caramelized tomato. It takes a few minutes to work these unusual (with lamb) flavors around in my mouth, but eventually everything comes together in harmony. The cumin is a shock, however; be alert to it before ordering. Lamb with cumin apparently started in Morocco. It was picked up by a handful of chefs in Provence.

The Sunday brunch, which includes a half bottle of red, white, or champagne, at $47.50 is easily the least expensive way to dine at this restaurant. The food served at this brunch is drawn directly from the dinner menu. It is not your usual upscale breakfast. An appetizer, an entrée, dessert, and coffee/tea are served.

Lord Fletcher's

$$

Location: 70-385 Highway 111, Rancho Mirage, 328 1161. **Food type:** *American, but claims to be English.* **Ambiance:** *old English country house and pub.* **Bar:** *full.* **Reservations:** *strongly suggested.* **Hours:** *dinner Tuesday through Sunday.*

Ring-a-ding-ding! The Chairman of the Board dined here when it opened in 1966. For almost three decades Lord Fletcher's was one of Frank Sinatra's haunts. He celebrated his 70th birthday here. "He would usually have the pot roast and potato pancakes," says owner Michael Fletcher, who waited on Sinatra for 13 years. Jack Daniel's on the rocks, Tanqueray martinis, and Château Lafite Rothschild—if you had Sinatra's income Chateau Lafite would be in your budget too—were his libations of choice. I don't know for sure whether Lord Fletcher's has changed since Sinatra was a regular, but I do know that the dining world has. Lord Fletcher's may have been the premier dining spot of 1966, but the British monarchy is in serious decline today. In all likelihood, Lord Fletcher's now is exactly the same as it was in the 1970s; that is the problem. Nevertheless, the building is still beautiful, the parking lot is full, the attendants line up the Jaguars (Anglophiles, no doubt) all in a row, and guests pack the place every night.

The dark woods favored by the English nobility rule the day. Carpeting in reds, stained-glass windows, and the noise and ambiance of an English pub define the environment. Paintings and tchotchkes galore line the walls.

Objectively, I would probably have rated this restaurant with one star, but there are millions of people out there in dining land who really appreciate this kind of simple, well-prepared, easy-to-understand cuisine.

Who am I to question that taste? Thanksgiving dinner seems to be the model. It's American comfort food passing itself off as representative of the British nobility. Take, for example, the "roast chycken" dinner. A half chicken stuffed with traditional bread, onion, and sage turkey dressing arrives with glazed sweet potatoes, string beans, potatoes, cranberry sauce, and turkey gravy. This is Thanksgiving with chicken rather than turkey. The flavors are basic; the food is unadorned. Everything is plainly cooked and served. The gravy is chicken broth and a roux (sautéed flour and butter). There is no attempt to transform plain gravy into a more interesting sauce. Everything follows the same philosophy. Cranberry sauce, for example, is vastly improved by the addition of some form of critic acid, usually grated lemon or orange peal. This is cranberries cooked with water and sugar.

All entrées come with soup or salad, and the pattern remains true. Lentil soup is characteristic of north African cooking. In Moroccan cuisine, lentil soup is a spicy, complex dish kicked up with harissa. At Lord Fletcher's, the only taste is lentils cooked in water until tender. It even lacks salt and pepper. It isn't cooked badly; on the contrary, everything here is cooked well. It is just that there isn't any recipe.

Nightly specials include barbecued beef ribs, fresh Atlantic salmon, roast beef, and prime rib in several sizes. Those with "Sweete Toothes" should sample the rice pudding served with raspberries or cinnamon and whipped cream or the Royal Brandy Ice, an after-dinner ice cream drink.

One significant reason for the popularity of this restaurant is the cost. Nightly specials are in the $18 range, and almost nothing on the menu exceeds $29. There is no appetizer list, and the kitchen prepares one soup and one salad. These come with the entrées, so decision making is relatively easy.

I wonder why Lord Fletcher's does not actually serve some more traditional English cuisine, like steak and kidney pie, fish and chips, bangers and mash, bubble and squeak, shepherd's pie, mutton, game, or Cornish pasty. It does serve Yorkshire pudding with the prime rib, but otherwise, Lord Fletcher's is English only in name and ambiance.

Lyons English Grill
Not recommended
$-$$$
Location: 233 E. Palm Canyon Dr., Palm Springs, 327-1551. **Food type:**

American pretending to be English. **Ambiance:** *old, dark, and showing it; stained-glass windows.* **Bar:** *full; poor wine list.* **Reservations:** *suggested.* **Hours:** *dinner Wednesday through Monday.*

Amidst the stained glass representing Ye Old England, banners, shields, orange lighting, and portraits of the queen, a man sings Elvis songs to prerecorded tapes. What are we to make of this place? An aging palace, past glories withered away.

It certainly looks like an English restaurant. Even the menu is designed with bold Gothic script engineered to give patrons the impression that the Magna Carta has just been signed. Yet the menu features such items as teriyaki steak kabobs, chicken piccata, scampi, barbecued beef ribs, shrimp tempura, Chinese chicken salad, and matzo ball soup. What kind of a restaurant is this? It is essentially an American steakhouse filled with English trappings. Two cuts of prime rib and no fewer than seven steaks dominate the menu in addition to the above-mentioned oddities. Unlike Lord Fletcher's (reviewed earlier in this chapter), its venerable neighbor in Rancho Mirage, Lyons serves two dishes that are actually British: steak and kidney pie and fish and chips. There is something called chicken Kensington—chicken breast in a sherry wine sauce with mushrooms—but the Kensington appellation is meaningless. When Mr. Google and Ms. Yahoo have no record of such a recipe, it probably means it does not exist outside of this restaurant.

This is a simple menu of grilled meats and fish, so you can understand my surprise and trepidation upon reading that beef Wellington was a frequent special. Wellington is one of the world's most complex dishes and, in the form we know it, is a French recipe called *filet de boeuf en croute.* The English had a habit of wrapping any number of meats in a pie crust in the early 19th century, but that is the extent of their contribution. Pâté de foie gras, duxelles, truffles, puff pastry, and Madeira sauce—the defining tastes of the dish—are all French. Upon learning and sampling that the pâté de foie gras-duxelles-truffles topping for the filet was actually a vegetable pâté cut with minced mushrooms, I quickly dismissed the dish entirely.

Steak and kidney pie is the defining English dish on this menu. Everything else is available at hundreds of other restaurants. Kidneys are not a staple on the American diet, so they will come as a shock to the American palate. Their texture is that of overcooked beef liver or chicken gizzard. Their flavor is similar to pork liver with a hint of urine. Kidneys are baked or braised with pieces of steak, usually top sirloin, and mushrooms in a thick brown gravy. The mixture is then put into an individual skillet, covered with pastry dough, and baked. I cannot speak to the relative quality of this pie as my experience with this dish is negligible. I can tell you that the gravy is unconscionably greasy and the underside of the pastry is soggy, but I cannot tell you whether this is a fine British example of steak and kidney pie. When I am in England, I consume bangers, sweet, and a pint (sausage, puréed rutabagas, and dark ale).

All entrées come with soup or salad. Soup is chicken noodle. Salad is basic 1970s-style iceberg, shredded carrot, tomato, red onion, and shredded red cabbage. My red onion was stale so that the cysteine-based amino acid generated that infamous sulfurous odor with which we are all too familiar. An accompanying vinaigrette is watery probably because the greens are not dried properly.

Yorkshire pudding is not served even with the prime rib, but popovers come instead of bread. The ingredients for each are the same—eggs, milk, flour—with the exception that Yorkshire pudding has a quarter cup of bacon fat per serving.

Entrées come with wedges of nicely sautéed and seasoned russet potatoes and green beans with a decidedly commercial taste. There are early-bird specials for $12.95, including beef ribs, ground sirloin, chicken, and sole, and the atmosphere and prime rib may well be a draw for some.

Bananaz
Not reviewed
$-$$$
Location: 69-934 Highway 111, Rancho Mirage, 770-7772. Food type: American with an Asian/Hawaiian emphasis. Ambiance: stunning; reminiscent of Frank Lloyd Wright's Taliesin West. Bar: full. Reservations: suggested. Hours: dinner nightly; happy hour from 4:30 P.M.

This restaurant has endured several reincarnations since it was part of the Charthouse chain a decade ago. In the intervening years it was Haleiwa Joe's, then Oceans 111. A Palm Desert nightclub called Bananaz Beach House burned down in 2004. That marque is now resurrected on this location.

The building, from 1978, is a stunning but largely plagiarized version of Frank Lloyd Wright's masterpiece of idiosyncratic modernism, Taliesin West, dating from 1937. Most of it is underground and built into the side of a hill. What shows above ground is a long, sloping roof resembling a wing perhaps three feet off the ground. Pools of water encircle the front and move in and out of the building itself. Construction materials are wood, rock, glass, and water, in that order. The architect was Kendrick Bangs Kellogg, an eccentric visionary from San Diego who claimed to live in a country called "Oceanus." The interior is similarly radical. The ceiling is a huge wooden arc braced by wooden beams and, of all things, sawed-off telephone poles. Windows circle the structure but comprise, perforce, only the top three feet of wall space. A translucent plastic skylight runs the length of the dining room. The building is large with seating for upwards of 250 at both tables and booths. The lounge area is separate; a copper-surfaced bar acts as focal point between the lounge and dining room.

Remarkably, the new Bananaz has kept much of the same menu as both Haleiwa Joe's *and* Oceans 111. I will not venture a guess as to what that means, leaving it to the legal imaginations of my readers, but I have retained any reviews of identical dishes from past incarnations.

The business model seems to be something-for-everyone-at-a-reasonable-price kind of establishment. The menu is huge. It features everything from a fish monger soup ($6.50) to crab legs and lobster at the market price with just about every American staple in between, from poke, coconut shrimp, pork sliders, and calamari to baby back ribs, chicken, steak, pasta, and prime rib.

The fish monger soup is a holdover from both Haleiwa Joe's and Oceans 111. This soup is essentially a tomato-vegetable melange. Chunks of tomato with the dominating influence of green bell pepper is the basic taste. Celery and onion are in evidence. My bowl had about a cubic inch, one piece, of undefined fish. The fish is tender, which would indicate that it is placed at the last minute, else it would be tough and stringy. I can not identify the fish. It is not salmon or halibut. This is a tomato-vegetable soup with a piece of fish in it, not a fish soup. The bell pepper overwhelms everything.

"Sticky Kalbi Ribs" (also held over) the menu calls baby backs "slow roasted Hawaiian style." They are charbroiled, not smoked in the way of mainland barbecue, neither are they cooked enough. The meat still clings tenaciously to the bone. It is not that they are undercooked, but one has to work a little harder than one would like. The sauce is good.

Hawaiian sauce differs from the many mainland sauces by its addition of pineapple juice, ginger, and soy or teriyaki sauce to the tomato-sugar (honey, molasses, corn syrup, brown sugar?) base. They arrive on a bed of shredded fresh cabbage (at least they used to). The fresh crunch works well with the meat. Think coleslaw in the Texas barbecue tradition. The sushi for the day could not have been less interesting. These are wheels an inch thick, and an inch and a half in diameter, but consisting almost entirely of rice. Sheets of nori, a small piece of avocado, and a tiny piece of tuna—this is the sushi special? The ubiquitous California roll is a marvel of pizzazz by comparison. (This is the Oceans 111 sushi; the Bananaz sushi rolls may be quite different.)

Calamari seems to have been updated with a Thai dipping sauce (peanuts?).

The Oceans 111 Poke was just good enough. It is now Emma's Poke, but the recipe seems to be the same. Here is what I wrote before: "Good-sized chunks of ahi tuna are presented with some sesame seeds and soy sauce on a bed of the same shredded cabbage as the baby backs. Jicama and bean sprouts are added to the cabbage. It all works, but once again nothing is particularly noteworthy. For noteworthy turn to Chapter 7 and look up Frankie's Fresh Fish. Read about his 'Poki.' This is the difference between a chef who loves food and is a serious artist and somebody with a job.

The best way to describe Oceans 111 was that it was good enough. Whether or not Bananaz can transcend this tepid compliment has yet to be determined. The menu is essentially the same, as is their entire presentation.

Roy's
★★★
$$$

Location: 71-959 Highway 111, Rancho Mirage, 340-9044. *Food type:* Hawaiian Fusion. *Ambiance:* palace with dark wood, bamboo, and high-tech lighting. *Bar:* full, with Polynesian specialty drinks; extensive wine list. *Reservations:* required during season, suggested otherwise. *Hours:* dinner nightly.

The name of the corporation is OSI Restaurant Partners Inc. It is a huge, multinational conglomerate based in Tampa, Florida. OSI owns outright or by joint venture operates Outback Steakhouse, Carrabba's Italian Grill,

Lee Roy Selmon's, Cheeseburger in Paradise, Bonefish Grill, and Fleming's Prime Steakhouse & Wine Bar. It also has a joint-venture development relationship with Roy Yamaguchi, the chef and creator of Roy's Restaurants in Hawaii, mainland United States, and Japan. This is one of the largest restaurant chains in the world; think of it as the McDonald's of sit-down dining. Roy's is also one of the most successful restaurants in the Coachella Valley. Reservations are mandatory during season.

Roy Yamaguchi was born in Tokyo and trained at the Culinary Institute in New York. He apprenticed in Los Angeles at L'Escoffier and L'Ermitage under the late master French chef Jean Bertanou. This eclectic training combined with his obvious entrepreneurial skills eventually led to the creation of Roy's in Hawaii in 1988. Since then, he has opened 29 restaurants in the United States in addition to international venues in Guam, Hong Kong, and Japan. Most of the restaurants are located in resort areas. Given this kind of corporate history you might expect the restaurant to fall into the cookie-cutter mold: bland, routine, ordinary. Surprisingly, this is not the case.

Let's start with the term "Hawaiian Fusion." What does it mean? At its core it means that Roy Yamaguchi was born and raised with Japanese and later Polynesian cooking methods and ingredients. Upon graduating high school, he immediately enrolled at a cooking school that teaches French techniques. He then worked at French restaurants and apprenticed with a master French chef. On his own, Roy combines the two. It is an old story, but the late 20th century has seen more radical marriages than in the past.

A case in point is the roasted macadamia mahi mahi. Here is a fish native to the Hawaiian waters. It is sweet, its flavors are subtle, and it is delicate. When cooked, it flakes like halibut. In a typical Hawaiian-style recipe you might find soy sauce, pineapple, ginger, green and red peppers, and curry powder. Macadamia nuts are consistent with Hawaiian cooking. But how does Yamaguchi deliver his fish? It is served over a combination of garlic mashed potatoes and slices of simple boiled red potatoes. A lobster-based butter-cognac sauce dresses it. This is Hawaiian Fusion. Everything is just right. The nuts are golden and crunchy. The fish is delicate and flaky. (Order it medium rare or medium. Medium rare is not for everyone as the interior of the meat is still translucent. But because this fish is grilled, it can overcook easily and become dried out. Your waiter will warn you of this.)

The use of butter and brandy take the dish in an entirely different direction, imbuing it with French flavors. I requested a bit of Hawaiian sea salt as my fish was just slightly undersalted, and I wished to test that particular salt in its natural habitat. It is fascinating stuff—red from the natural volcanic baked clay but also highly metallic. I cannot possibly tell you what metals I taste, but I can tell you that this salt is absolutely nothing like the stuff that comes in the blue box. A few baby asparagus spears did not work. The jolt of bitterness into this otherwise delicate and sweet combination is disruptive of its balance.

Appetizers are likewise interesting fusions of East and West. Baby back ribs are entirely successful. They arrive without a slather of ketchup and corn syrup. They are smoky, but there is no myoglobin-caused pink smoke ring just beneath the surface. A discussion with the chef reveals the truth here. The pork is par-braised in veal stock. As a general principle, I am opposed to the braising of pork ribs. It can remove all the fat and connective tissue and rob the meat of flavor. These ribs, however, do not suffer from this. The braising is done at a very low temperature, and the ribs are only partially cooked. They are removed and placed in a smoker to finish. Unlike the 15- to 20-hour smoking that ribs undergo in a Texas-style barbecue, these are only smoked a few hours as they are mostly cooked already. This is not enough time for the pink ring to develop but plenty of time to impart a deep smoky taste. At this point, a Texas-style rib would be served smothered in a pungent and spicy sauce. Yamaguchi dips his ribs in a Szechuan sauce and grills them for a light char before serving. Szechuan barbecue sauce is a chicken-stock-based sauce with vinegar, sugar, soy, sesame oil, and Chinese five-spice powder (star anise, Szechuan peppercorns, fennel, cloves, and cinnamon). This glazes the meat but no sauce is served with the meat. It doesn't need it. The layers of flavor inherent in its preparation render it complete as is.

Seared tiger shrimp with a wasabi cocktail sauce is considerably less interesting. The shrimp is fine, first quality and not overcooked, but the sauce is a boring tomato ketchup, horseradish, and lemon juice mixture found in every free shrimp cocktail in Las Vegas. Even with wasabi substituting for horseradish (highly doubtful since virtually all American wasabi *is* horseradish) there is little or no heat.

Lobster pot stickers also fail to measure up to the high standards set by the ribs. The dough is crispy in places but soggy in others. The lobster meat is probably cut. Its flavors are quite excellent but are not the flavors of pure lobster. The sauce, advertised as spicy togarashi miso butter, tastes only of miso and butter. Togarashi is a mixture of sesame seeds, sansho (peppery berry), dried laver (seaweed), tangerine peel, chili powder, and poppy seeds. None of these sapidities are noticeable. Fish is the most serious ingredient at Roy's, dominating both the appetizer and entrée lists. Gorgonzola-broiled swordfish and saffron-infused scallops with mushrooms, gnocchi, and basil balsamic are two that reflect the fusion aspect of his cooking in a most obvious and exciting manner. Meat dishes seem to be on the menu primarily to satisfy the nonfish eaters. With a couple of steaks and a pork chop, the true creativity in this restaurant clearly lies with the fish.

Service is perhaps too hovering, and the waiters try hard to push the alcoholic side of the menu. The building is indeed a palace, done in dark woods with recessed and muted lighting, an open kitchen, and lots of glass. The judicious use of bamboo hints of the islands.

While not overpriced on the surface, it is easy to run up a vastly inflated bill by ordering a couple of mai tais and a bottle of wine. Appetizers are at the high end of the price spectrum for this kind of restaurant.

Sammy G's Tuscan Grill
★★½
$$-$$$
Location: 265 S. Palm Canyon Dr., Palm Springs, 320-8041. Food type: mixed Italian although claims to be Tuscan. Ambiance: gorgeous building in Santa Fe style; dancing. Bar: full. Reservations: suggested. Hours: dinner nightly, happy hour/bar menu.

This "palace" is located in The Vineyard, a small enclave of boutique shopping in downtown Palm Springs. It is to the south and behind LG's Palm Springs (Chapter 9) and across the street from Las Casuelas Terraza (Chapter 12). The colors and the layout of the restaurant suggest the southwestern United States, especially Sante Fe and Tesuque, New Mexico. The look is adobe, but it is all dry-wall façade. Doorways are archways. Corners are rounded; ceilings are beams. There are several rooms of various sizes as well as an elevated patio laid out in different dining styles: small tables, banquettes, banquet tables, isolated tables for that romantic couple, large tables for that family dinner. The patio is beautiful, elevated and with a low wall, roof, and misters and heaters. Since the restaurant is set back from the street there is no immediate intrusion of traffic either visually or aurally.

The bar area, traditionally the hub of this restaurant during its long life as St. James at the Vineyard, was torn down and is to be completely redesigned and rebuilt, commencing in July 2009. The wall behind the old bar, which was the east wall of the wine room, is slated to be removed and the wine room eliminated. The north wall is to be pushed out and indoor/outdoor tables expanded to seat about 20. The extra space will incorporate a stage for live music and a significantly larger bar. The former intimacy will be lost, but Sammy G's exchanges that for a functional nightclub.

Food is safe Italian, a step up from the neighborhood Italian diner. It looks impressive at first glance with everything printed in Italian, but when the actual translations are stripped of their hyperbole and gloss, neighborhood diner emerges. Pizzas (tomatoes, basil, mushrooms, prosciutto, red onion, chicken), pastas (meatballs, sausage and peppers, Alfredo, Primavera, Bolognese, carbonara), chicken breast (picatta, paillard, Milanese, Parmigiana, carbonara), fish (salmon, shrimp, sand dabs, sole), a few routine appetizers and salads, the usual veal and a couple of steaks—we have seen it all before, countless times.

Safe menu aside, a black olive tapenade of considerable merit is delivered with some fresh slices of Italian bread, quality olive oil, and aggressively sweet balsamic vinegar. The use of black olives reduces the acidic bite of the more common kalamata or green olive tapenades. I did not perceive the usual anchovy or caper additions, but as a simple black olive spread it fulfilled its function quite adequately.

Sammy G's has been known to serve frozen fish rather than seasonal fresh fish. This shows a distinct lack of respect for the customer. If halibut is out of season, serve black bass or another appropriate substitute. We can all go to Trader Joe's for a perfectly frozen fish filet.

I sampled the classic Neapolitan pizza, the venerable Margherita: mozzarella, tomato, and basil leaves. After the soup, which is really very good, I expected much more of the pizza than was delivered. The classic Margherita should be constructed on a robust, chewy, fresh piece of pizza dough prepared that very afternoon. The classic Margherita should be made with well-drained fresh tomatoes or canned and drained San Marzano tomatoes although a freshly made flavorful tomato sauce is acceptable. The classic Margherita should have thick slices of mozzarella cheese interspersed with large pieces of torn bail leaves. Part of the idea is to represent the red/green/white of the Italian flag. In many ways, the Margherita is the perfect pizza. Each of the four elements provides a different aspect of taste and texture: pastry, acidic fruit, pungent herb, and cheese. My pizza has a light and cakey dough with little or no crust. It has just a hint of nondescript tomato sauce, hardly enough to impart any tomato flavor. Cheese covers the entire surface, and basil is limited to a sparse chiffonade, tiny bits of "confetti." This "Italian flag" resembles more the flag of surrender than a call to arms. I manage to wake up the whole affair by spreading the black olive tapenade and dousing it with the fruity herb-infused olive oil.

The bar pours a nice house Cabernet (generous too, possibly seven ounces) for the happy hour price of $5.

Once the bar area is converted into a nightclub, perhaps this level of food may well be the correct marketing decision. However, for foodies with Italian cravings, may I suggest the following alternatives: La Spiga (this chapter), Sirocco (Chapter 1), La Bella Vita (Chapter 6), even Amici (Chapter 6).

Vicky's of Santa Fe
Not recommended

$$$-$$$$

*Location: 45-100 Club Dr., Indian Wells, 345-9770. **Food type:** American. **Ambiance:** faux Santa Fe-style adobe house; good lounge, piano bar, and dancing. **Bar:** full. **Reservations:** not accepted. **Hours:** dinner nightly.*

I hesitate to call Vicky's a palace as it has little in common with the true palaces—Wally's and Cuistot—except its appearance and location. It is a large, stand-alone Santa Fe-style building in a premium location in Indian Wells. Other than that, Vicky's is a rather mundane American restaurant featuring steaks, chops, seafood, and "comfort" food. Cooking is plain, and prices are deceptively low, as everything is a la carte. Pork chops, for example, are $18, but if potatoes and a vegetable are desired, the tab goes to the $27. How about an appetizer? $9. And a salad? $6. Dessert is $7 more. Your total is now $49 without bar service, tax, or tip. A couple dining out at Vicky's could accumulate a final check close to that of Cuistot (reviewed earlier in this chapter) for half the quality.

Ah, but there is a piano bar with dancing, quite a nice one if you like your music free of prerecorded tracks and electronic manipulations. The featured pianist is Juilliard-trained Doug Montgomery. Have dinner across the street at Sirocco (see Chapter 1 under Renaissance Esmeralda) and come here for dancing.

Wally's Desert Turtle
★★★½
$$$$

Location: 71-775 Highway 111, Rancho Mirage, 568-9321. **Food type:** *California Fusion (French).* **Ambiance:** *Palace at Versailles meets art nouveau.* **Reservations:** *suggested.* **Bar:** *full; comprehensive wine list.* **Hours:** *dinner nightly.* **Chef:** *Pascal Lallemand.*

Wally's Desert Turtle is *the* dining palace of the desert. Competition in the palatial category goes to Cuistot, La Spiga, and Amore (reviewed earlier in this chapter), but Wally's is the winner. Not because it is better—it isn't—but because it is more excessive. In the flashy department nothing can compete with these mirrored columns, atrium, split levels, murals, Peruvian artifacts, and marble and granite surfaces. Even the tables are padded. The Hall of Mirrors from the Palace at Versailles comes to mind upon entering. But it is also fussier, eliciting thoughts of Victor Horta and Belgian art nouveau. Is it comfortable? Perhaps not for everyone. Service personnel in tuxedos hover everywhere, although discretely. An ever-so-light-of-touch pianist persuades the instrument to deliver Gershwin songs from the 1930s. Wally's is formal, elegant, very expensive, and just a bit intimidating.

Wally's has been advertising itself as the best restaurant in the desert probably since some local publication affixed that tag a generation ago. Although the chef is French born and French trained, he has been in this country since 1982 and has absorbed California Fusion's use of Pacific Rim style and ingredients. There are a handful of welcome deviations, such as venison and roasted pheasant breast, but what really stands out are the prices: liver and onions for $32.75, farmed Atlantic salmon at $34, braised short ribs for $34.50, and $42.75 for veal scallopine served with caper sauce. Most beef and lamb entrées at Wally's are in the $45 range. Is this a joke? On the other hand, it costs a fortune to operate a palace such as this. Someone has to polish all those mirrors. Much of the cost has nothing to do with the food; it goes to pay for the astonishing environment. Is it overpriced? Hard to say, really. The food is certainly overpriced, but what is this kind of ambiance worth to you personally? The food should be four-star quality. It is not. It is close, but the cigars go to a handful of restaurants east of Wally's. The gazpacho is flawless. Made with golden tomatoes, cucumbers, garlic, and onions, a perfect balance of sweet and sour and acid is achieved. The vegetables are uniformly puréed but stop short of becoming V8 juice. The addition of bay shrimp, finely minced shallots, and parsley to the top of the cold soup is original and coherent.

Ahi tartare does not fare as well. Chef Lallemand's single apparent flaw is revealed here. He gives the mouth too many flavors to deal with at the same time. There is a limit to the capacity with which the mind can separate and process complex information. Lallemand begins with a sashimi-grade tuna. It rests on a bed of avocado. There is a horseradish (wasabi) sauce to the left of the tuna tower. An aïoli made with tomato, garlic, and olive oil is on the right. The two sauces are incompatible. Tobiko caviar mounds are sprinkled around the plate, their pungent fishiness tending to overwhelm the subtleties of the tuna. Pickled ginger draws the mind back to the sashimi roots of this dish, but it is wildly out of place with the French origins of the aïoli. A few bitter greens dot the top, adding another layer of taste to an already cluttered palate. Is it any good? Yes, it is delicious, but the tuna, which is what this dish is about, is overwhelmed.

A salad of red and yellow heirloom tomatoes is all but perfect. Here Chef Lallemand allows the inherent qualities of the tomatoes to shine. With radicchio and frisée and the most wonderful and sweet Provençal olives everything comes together brilliantly. The addition of little balls of mozzarella is irrelevant but not damaging.

With the carpaccio the same problem surfaces—too much complexity. Chef Lallemand applies a drizzle of Dijon laced with a distinctive and brutally hot English dry mustard. Capers, shallots, cherry tomatoes, lemon juice, peppery arugula, and bitter radicchio contribute six more lines of counterpoint to this presentation. Shavings of powerful Parmigiano-Reggiano finish the dish. Lallemand's carpaccio is so complex the intrinsic flavor of the filet mignon, the foundation of the dish itself, is lost.

Sea bass also leans in the direction of too much complexity but stops short of damage. Chef Lallemand slightly overcooked my fish, but that is undoubtedly an anomaly. A spectacular sauce graces this prized fish: cream, lobster broth, fennel, and saffron. Roll those flavors around in your imagination. The lobster enhances the bass flavors, the cream brings richness to the otherwise lean meat as well as supplying a luscious mouth feel, the fennel adds an ever so slight licorice hint, and what can I say about saffron? Saffron, the world's most expensive food at nearly $3,000 a pound for 100 percent red threads, this elixir of love, the slightest pinch of which will transform any dish, finds a true home in this sensuous sauce. A fascinating yin-yang of puréed carrots and broccoli provides contrast. (I wonder how he managed to get these two purées in the yin-yang shape.) Both vegetables are intensely flavored. Chef Lallemand may well have stopped here, but he serves this fish over a bed of artichoke hearts, sautéed onions, and shiitake mushrooms. Too much? No, but close.

Roasted pork tenderloin on a warm, German-style potato salad with shiitake mushrooms and radicchio is one of a trio of entrée salads unique to Wally's. This dish is completely successful—well, almost. The pork is served medium rare, as it should be. Chef Lallemand, when complimented on this, said that most customers do not ask to have it cooked to a higher temperature. This speaks highly of Wally's customers. The slices of meat are dressed with a slightly sweet, cider-based vinaigrette. Kurobuta pork would bring more tenderness to the party, but other than that this dish is perfect.

Light-as-air soufflés are the most interesting of the desserts. Grand Marnier, raspberry, lemon, chocolate, piña colada—take your choice. They are all masterful examples of the soufflé maker's art. The pineapple-coconut version is, surprisingly, the most interesting.

The menu at Wally's is quite large—especially during season—with pasta, duck, lamb, veal, game, and beef offerings sufficient to tempt any palate.

Yard House

$$-$$$
Location: at The River at Rancho Mirage, 71-800 Highway 111, Rancho Mirage, 779-1415. Food type: eclectic American, something for everybody. Ambiance: huge high-tech sports bar/video arcade without the actual games. Bar: full; every beer in the world on tap. Reservations: parties of 10 or more Sunday through Thursday only. Hours: lunch and dinner daily.

Beer, beer, beer, beer, beer, beer, and still more beer. This is the Cheesecake Factory (reviewed earlier in this chapter) with beer instead of cheesecake. The huge, eclectic menu is more or less the same as that of the Cheesecake Factory with something for everybody, adequately prepared though not much else. The building is equally excessive, though in a different way, and prices are almost identical. One thing it does have that the Cheesecake Factory does not is a kids' menu. It has all the usual things on it for $6.50 each.

Yard House has approximately 159 beers on tap. I say approximately as they have house picks, blends, and nonalcoholic brews and are continuously adding labels to the selections. The restaurant gets its name from the half-yard glass used to serve beer. This is a 15-inch-tall glass tapering in the middle and expanding near the top. It comes with its own wooden stand and holds 23 ounces. If you order one of these, you have to pay $10 up front in case you break the glass. The restaurant also more or less doubles as a sports bar. The general ambiance is like being locked inside a multimedia convention center.

CHAPTER 5

Bistros, French and Otherwise

Small chef-owned bistros are where the magic lies. There are many of these little restaurants. A few of them are superb, with food as good or better than the palaces and at significantly less cost. These are my hidden treasures. Unlike the palaces, the bistros do not bombard the tourist scene with advertising, and they are frequently difficult to find. Accordingly I have provided directions for the more difficult.

Many restaurants call themselves bistros, but they only co-opt the word to effect credibility. A bistro is a small, informal, and inexpensive French restaurant, usually family run, serving *vin de maison,* or house wine. In France, the clientele of a bistro would be almost entirely local. Demanding? Yes. Pretentious? No. Children—in France, even pets!—can be found in bistros. A French bistro, in rural areas especially, might also be a little noisy. I use the term "bistro" tentatively, as most restaurants in this chapter are not true bistros; most are not even French. I have seen Italian bistros, in actuality, a trattoria. I have even seen a Chinese bistro! There is only one authentic French bistro in the entire Coachella Valley, and that is Chez Pierre in Palm Desert. However, the term does have a certain usefulness in describing small and informal restaurants that usually have only a beer and wine license. Most bistros are chef-owner establishments, where the chef has a direct relationship with the success of the business. He or she is cooking, more often than not, every night.

Café des Beaux-Arts
★★
$$-$$$
Location: 73-640 El Paseo Dr., Palm Desert, 346-0669. *Food type: California-ized French bistro.* *Ambiance: charming French sidewalk café.* *Reservations: suggested. Bar: full. Hours: breakfast Saturday and Sunday; lunch and dinner daily.*

One could not ask for a spot more charming than this one. Located

125

on the northeast corner of El Paseo and Larkspur, Café des Beaux-Arts manages both the look and feel of a genuine Parisian sidewalk café. And the food isn't bad, it's just rather mediocre. More's the pity, too, because having lunch in this little bistro on a gorgeous winter afternoon bathed in the warm sunlight is a truly luscious experience. I have eaten here many times. Why? Because I love rabbit Dijonnaise, even mediocre rabbit Dijonnaise served with a plain pasta and inconsequential vegetable du jour. Unfortunately, the rabbit is no longer on the menu.

The food here is best described as faux-French, American in French translation. I've had a number of salads and soups, a few desserts, the rack of lamb (six chops), and scallops. The lamb is quite good, and the scallops, fair. Everything else is poorly prepared (especially the soups), poorly finished, and without concern for texture or proper balance. If ambiance trumps taste for you, this may well meet all of your desires.

Café Scandia
★★½
$
#

Location: 356 S. Indian Canyon Dr., Palm Springs, 320-0427. *Food type: Eastern European and the usual American favorites.* **Ambiance:** *one square room, comfortable and nicely designed.* **Bar:** *full.* **Reservations:** *required.* **Hours:** *dinner daily.* **Chef-owners:** *Sven, Reiner, and Anka.*

Chefs Sven and Reiner are in the kitchen; hostess-manager Anka takes care of the customers and a good time is had by all. Café Scandia boasts the best cheap menu in the desert. All the usual suspects are covered—prime rib, duck with orange, lamb shank, rack of lamb, Lake Superior whitefish, and salmon—augmented with a bounty of Eastern European and Scandinavian specialties: schnitzel, Rouladen, Swedish meatballs, and goulash.

Café Scandia is tucked into the far corner of a workaday strip mall. The walls are an elegant dark red; lighting is warm and subdued. Prices are astonishingly low, considering the quality of the food. Three-course meals are available for $14.95 with a 5 percent reduction for payment in cash.

Polish beet soup is based on a duck stock, which gives it an unexpected depth and richness. Into this base are added primarily beets, but also carrots, celery, tomato, and green bell pepper. Surprisingly, each retains a slight crunch. The dinner salad is dressed with dill in a light ranch. The characteristic Scandinavian herb gives this melange of lettuce, tomato, and cucumber a new twist. Creamed spinach with nutmeg, horseradish, and curry powder is unexpected, innovative, and surprisingly effective. *Roulade* means "to roll up." For the Rouladen, a piece of top round is pounded until it is a quarter inch thick. Dill pickle, bacon, onion, mustard, and parsley are spread on the meat, which is then rolled and braised. The unexpected tangy bite of sour pickle is the defining taste. While beef Rouladen may be home-style German food, it is not smothered it in the generic brown gravy that Mother used to make. This is a demi-glace-based sauce—richly flavored, velvety smooth, butter enriched.

Pork is the meat of choice in much of northern Europe, forming the basis of so many sausages and schnitzels. Pork loin is stuffed with a combination of passion fruit, apricots, prunes, cranberries, and freshly grated ginger in a slightly sweet demi-glace. Fruit and pork are natural comrades, but the loin is dry as usual, as genetic engineers have managed to remove all the fat from the tissues of the venerable pig. Perhaps if this dish were made with the less lean shoulder cut it would be moister.

This restaurant provides a much better inexpensive experience than does its closest rival, John Henry (Chapter 8), a couple of miles to the north. Do not expect startling quality, but where else can you dine like this for $15? Reservations are mandatory.

Chef George
★★½
$$

Location: *40-100 Washington St., Bermuda Dunes, 200-1768.* **Food type:** *Hungarian/Yugoslavian/Italian.* **Ambiance:** *Vegas camp in one small room.* **Reservations:** *required.* **Bar:** *beer and wine; adequate wine list; corkage fee of $8.* **Hours:** *dinner Tuesday through Saturday.* **Chef-owner:** *George Ristich.*

George Ristich, executive chef emeritus for the entire chain of the now-defunct Los Angeles-based Velvet Turtle restaurants, resurrected that venerable marque under his own name in a small but astonishing establishment in Bermuda Dunes. In 2006 the name was changed to Chef George. I know nothing of the legalities involved, but from the diner's point of view, who cares? This restaurant is hard to find. There is a big shopping center on the southeast corner of Washington and Country Club. Park there and ask somebody. It is found in an archway between buildings. The first thing that strikes the unwary diner in this quirky rendezvous is the extreme décor. Vegas-like in its excess, it somehow manages to remain marginally tasteful. The walls are inlaid with tapestries and glass blocks. The carpet is black. Table linens are maroon on pink. The walls above and below the tapestries mirror these colors exactly. Chairs are black-burnished aluminum with red and green accents. A dark green wall panel echoes this green. Plants, faux Tiffany lamps, and overhead fans abound. But the *pièce de résistance* is the artwork. At least eight paintings in the soft-core rococo style of François Boucher—like *The Birth of Venus* and *Diana Resting after Her Bath*—adorn the tapestries, either amusing, arousing, or annoying the unsuspecting. All of this is packed into a room seating only 47, and all 47 of them were there by 6:45 on the Tuesday I chose to sample the menu. And all of them seemed to be intimately familiar with everybody and everything: food, menu, wait staff, hostess, chef, and each other.

At first glance, the menu appears completely unremarkable, even boring: soups, salads, chicken, pasta, fish, stuffed cabbage, Hungarian goulash. Here are 47 apparently blissfully happy diners, and here is a menu that appears to lack any sort of charm whatsoever. Forty-seven people packed into a tiny little restaurant on a Tuesday evening waxing poetic about a plate of spaghetti in marinara sauce! Something does not add up.

But it does add up. This food is put together with such taste and refinement as to render the most mundane plate of spaghetti a work of art. Everything from acid balance and flavor to textural contrasts and presentation is done with the utmost care and precision.

Mushroom soup abounds with heavy cream, sherry, and explosions of mushroom flavor. Pea soup is made not with dried split peas, but from peas shucked by hand from the pod and mashed into a purée. If your pea soup experience is limited to the other stuff—as it is for most of us, including me—put this on your must-try list.

Hungarian goulash is no big deal, right? Beef stew with vegetables and paprika. Rethink that stereotype. The meat itself is braised to perfection, tender without being dried out or stringy. But this goulash is all about the sauce, with its hints of bacon, tomato, red bell pepper, and onion. All of these gave up their flavor to the braising liquid, which is undoubtedly a stock, not water, and is finally strained out. The liquid is then reduced to concentrate the flavors, charged with hot, sweet Hungarian paprika, and served with a dollop of sour cream.

Everything on the plate is prepared with the same artistry, including velvet-smooth, rosemary-garlic mashed potatoes. Mash them too much and they become rubbery; mash them too little and they are lumpy. These are perfect, as is the balance of garlic and rosemary. Pickled red cabbage and broccoli flowers, blanched and finished in butter, complete this platter. Should you choose to share a dinner, do not ask the kitchen to split it for you. Ristich adamantly refuses to destroy his presentation.

Cajun salmon à la Raymond comes topped with tomatoes *concassé,* mushrooms, and scallions. *Concassé* means peeled, seeded, and chopped. This mixture is part of a sauce every bit as sophisticated as that on the goulash. Notable was the perfect acid balance: lemon, vinegar, and white wine. Whatever the exact ingredients, the effect on the fish is that of a flawless counterpoint. Chef Ristich did overcook the fish, however.

The corkage fee here is $8, and bringing your own wine is apparently a regular practice. While entrée prices are reasonable and servings large, everything is a la carte. Don't even try to get in without a reservation.

Chez Pierre
★★★½
$$$

Location: 44-250 Town Center Way (in the southeast corner), Palm Desert, 346-1818. Food type: French bistro. Ambiance: happy, informal, fun, and energetic; flowers vines and an herb garden; seating mostly outside (heated and cooled). Reservations: suggested. Bar: full; small but adequate wine list. Hours: dinner Monday through Saturday. Chef-owner: Pierre Pelech.

This restaurant, one of my personal favorites, is tricky to find. The Town Center Shopping Center covers a square block on the southeast corner of Town Center Way and Fred Waring. Chez Pierre is located in the extreme southeast corner of the complex, around the corner, and partially hidden by vines and flowers.

Seating at Pierre's is almost entirely al fresco, so happy, boisterous conversation dissipates into the warm evening air. Chez Pierre is a genuine addition to the desert dining scene, an almost authentic French bistro, not just a place calling itself a bistro because somebody thought the word had cachet. The only reason Chez Pierre is not fully authentic is because the government will not allow it to serve house wine from a barrel with pitchers on the tables. The food is authentic French country cooking. Chez Pierre has only one style of wineglass, unfortunately the white-wine type. You don't get three iced forks. There is no sommelier. Waiters do not hover, relentlessly brushing crumbs from 1,500-thread-count Egyptian cotton linens. Your food is not assembled to reincarnate Pisa towers. Your waitress affects neither haughtiness nor accent. What you *do* get is wonderful food, beautifully prepared, at fair prices, a relaxed atmosphere, inexpensive *vin rouge,* fun, friendly, and knowledgeable service, and the Gallic sparkle and charm of your maestro. Background music is Parisian street music—concertina sounds from the *fin de siècle.*

Servings are large, but you will want to sample more than one course. Here's a little hint: Chez Pierre leftovers make for a terrific breakfast the next morning. Pelech is restless. His menu is as flexible as a politician's core beliefs. Specials, which dominate the menu, change with the seasons. Specials appear whenever something fresh and interesting comes to market—a tomato, a whiff of mint, an unusual fish.

A ramekin of pâté appears with bread and butter. What is this? A house-made pâté to smear liberally on the French bread! This pâté is duck liver with sherry, a *mirepoix* of aromatic vegetables, butter, and heavy cream processed to a heavenly smoothness. Could this be for real? It is free, served automatically with the bread and butter.

As an appetizer, the *soupe de poisson,* or fish soup, is something about which I cannot speak highly enough. Reminiscent of a Marseilles bouillabaisse with saffron and the essence of Mediterranean crustaceans, it is served with a *rouille,* a garlic-saffron mayonnaise, and grated Gruyère cheese. A veritable feast! With a glass of wine and some bread, along with Pelech's free pâté, this alone could be one of the great lunches in the desert. Oh darn! Pelech stopped serving lunch in 2004. Harass him; maybe he will reopen.

Cassoulet is a fall special. Pelech's cassoulet is the finest within my experience. In the early 19th century, every household in every small village—at least those defining the three great cassoulet traditions, Toulouse, Carcassonne, and Castelnaudary—had its own earthenware pot called a *cassole.* Each *cassole* had its own design etched into the pottery. This design functioned as a brand or coat of arms identifying the owner. Each family would prepare its own *cassole* and bring it to the baker, the most esteemed man in the town as he had the only oven capable of overnight controlled-temperature baking. The baker would bake everyone's *cassole*. The owner would return in the morning for their completed dish, the cassoulet.

In case you are not familiar with this classic French country dish, it consists of a base of garlic and herb-infused white beans to which various meats have been added. Together these bake in a thick stock for hours, days, or weeks. Rumor has it that a restaurant in Provence has been simmering the same cassoulet pot since 1942! Traditionally the meats are *confit d'oie* or *confit de canard* (preserved leg of goose or duck; Pelech uses duck), chunks of lamb, pork, and garlic sausage, but cassoulet is one of those dishes that evolves with the house leftovers. Leg of mutton, spicy Portuguese sausage, ham, bacon, even partridge have all found their way into this concoction. After a sprinkling of breadcrumbs—Pelech uses panko—and herbs and baking forever, a crust forms. The crust is broken and cut into the pot, and the process begins anew. Pelech's cassoulet Toulousian is large enough to serve two or three if you order appetizers. I have the dubious distinction of being one of two people who have finished an entire order. Like its related dishes from Spain (paella) and Italy (cioppino), the flavors of the inferior versions tend to meld and become tiresome. Not so with Pelech's cassoulet. This one never gets boring; everywhere throughout the dish is a new taste experience.

Pappardelle (a wide flat noodle) with wild mushrooms and quail in a light cream sauce is another winner. The wild mushroom is fresh, not reconstituted, shiitake. Its soft, spongy, earthy power and passion kick the creamy noodles from here to eternity. The quail, frequently tough and stringy in lesser restaurants, sits atop a sprinkling of sun-dried tomatoes resting on the mushroom and cream-infused pappardelle. This quail is fat and tender and oozes flavor. For those not familiar with quail, think of it as a cross between duck and frog's legs—slightly gamey with a spicy sort of twist.

In the Moroccan-style lamb shank you find the Arabic proclivity to employ sweet spices like cinnamon, nutmeg, and allspice in savory dishes. The shank is bathed in honey before serving. Julienne of baby carrots and *haricots vert,* set off by cumin and ginger, marry the vegetables to the other Moroccan flavors. Finally, reconstituted prunes are added to the luscious reduced braising liquid, further complementing the unique and wonderful Moroccan treatment.

Coquilles St. Jacques is a bistro classic traditionally made with scallops. Pelech also uses pieces of halibut. The fish is seared in butter. White wine, shallots, herbs, and mushrooms go into the mix. The liquid is reduced, combined with a thick béchamel, and poured over the fish into a large shell. This is then topped with Gruyère cheese, dotted with butter, and broiled until bubbly and golden. Imagine cheese, scallops, and mushrooms in a pungent tarragon-infused cream sauce.

Organ meats are a staple of bistro cooking, and Pelech does not eschew them. In fact, Chez Pierre's is the only restaurant in the valley routinely serving offal. Everything from brains to tripe will show up on one of Pelech's menus during the year. Sweetbreads (veal thymus) are the king of organ meats. These tender morsels, thoroughly cleaned of membranes, sautéed until crispy, flamed in sherry, and served with a pan sauce of mushrooms, garlic, shallots, demi-glace, and baby artichoke hearts, are focused, balanced, and superb. Few restaurants serve them.

Chez Pierre is not always consistent, especially with its seasonal specials. In addition to the aforementioned organ meats, Pelech is the only valley chef routinely featuring unusual fish and game, but these occasionally do not measure up to the standards set by so many of his other dishes.

Double venison chops are marinated for three weeks in wine and herbs in order to attempt duplication of the taste of wild deer. Farmed venison has less flavor than the animal that forages on wild herbs and berries. Served rare with juniper berries in a rich wine sauce, this is one of the more unique tastes of the desert. Red cabbage with Belgian bacon accompanies.

Try the upside-down chocolate soufflé for dessert. Cut into this trifle and luxuriate in the luscious molten chocolate as it spills across your plate. Alternatively, have apple tart Tatin with chantilly cream. Order it with a three-ounce glass of Botrytis-infected late-harvest Riesling and luxuriate in every crumb.

Jake's Ready-To-Eat
★★★ (potentially at least)
$$
Location: 664 N. Palm Canyon Dr., Palm Springs, 327-4400. **Food type:** *American with decidedly French accent.* **Ambiance:** *Funky little courtyard,*

minimal interior, plastic furniture. **Bar:** *full.* **Reservations:** *accepted but generally not necessary.* **Hours:** *lunch and dinner Tuesday through Saturday, Sunday brunch, happy hour (5 P.M. to 7 P.M.).* **Chef-owner:** *Christopher Malm.*

The first thing you need to get over is the name; "Jake's Ready-To-Eat" suggests a fast food stand in Arkansas where Bill Clinton and Mike Huckabee could have hung out as teenagers. It most decidedly does not suggest a rather sophisticated quasi-French bistro in uptown Palm Springs. I almost didn't bother with this place, so put off was I by the name. A look at the menu, however, gave pause.

The restaurant is easily overlooked. Not only is it several blocks north of the well-trod path, it looks like nothing more than a small real estate officer held together by a rather tenuous economic thread. Only a little sign with a fork on it—a sandwich board with nobody in it, propped up on the sidewalk—indicates the presence of food at all.

Jake's is very much like a bistro on the fringes of some small French village, down an alley and around the back. One enters though a walkway between two nondescript buildings and into a small courtyard. It will hold exactly 42 people if all tables are stuffed and the bar is full. The bar is outside under an awning. Tables and chairs are plastic, there are no linens, and umbrellas along with some assorted greenery provide shade. Nevertheless, flatware and stemware are real and appropriate. The interior is an afterthought, mostly deli counter. There are a few tables at the far end, but outside, weather permitting, is far nicer, even if in a shabby-chic sort of way. The bar is in white ceramic tile and the television set does not play the basketball game but the Food Channel. Background music is largely classic rock (Cher sings the "Shoop" song). The kitchen is the size of a large postage stamp.

Out of this postage stamp comes some surprisingly sophisticated food. It is mostly American and nothing particularly original or daring, but it is well done and, considering the competition, really cheap. Appetizers are in the single digits; entrées, in the teens; and wines, in the low $20s. Three-course meals are the norm for $24. You can have a pork chop with apple confit and sauce Robert for $15.95, rack of lamb for $17.50, or roasted salmon on braised fennel with blood orange sauce and fingerling potatoes for $15.95

A sparkling *amuse bouche* is placed before me: diced heirloom tomato

> type

macerated in balsamic vinegar and served on a toast point with a chiffonade of basil. There is nothing unusual about this, but it is prepared with more care and sensitivity to ingredients than any of the last four such presentations in my experience, all four of which were three times the cost. Tomato flavor is huge, the balsamic is not cheap caramelized vinegar, and the basil adds an unexpectedly potent punch.

I opted for the $24 three-course prix-fixe dinner special. Seared scallops on a bed of root vegetables opened. Three scallops with beautiful, deep caramelization appear on a mound of fine white dice in a cream sauce. It is often difficult, even impossible, to get a good sear on scallops. They are frequently water logged and/or treated with a preservative that keeps them water logged. Chef Malm sends them back to his supplier if they come this way. For a good sear, scallops must be dry or they simply steam and become rubbery and overcooked. These are hot, crunchy, and sweet on the surface, warm, full flavored, and rare in the center. Celery heart and potato are cut into fine dice. A béchamel sauce, probably with some white cheddar, binds the dice together. Minced scallion provides an acidic contrast as an excellent appetizer comes together.

My entrée is the lamb rack: five frenched rib chops in a bordelaise sauce with roasted garlic cloves. The lamb is a perfect rare/medium rare (well, not exactly perfect. To be perfect it would have to be Colorado lamb instead of New Zealand, but then it would cost double). It is unbelievably tender and the perfume of baby lamb permeates the environment. It is the sauce that surprises me. Lamb sauces are difficult. The majority overwhelm the subtlety of the meat. Most of the rest are neutral. Creating a sauce that enhances lamb flavor without overwhelming it is tricky. I have experienced many a failure at two, even three times this cost. This one is superb. To do this well the chef must know when to back off. This one is a bordelaise, but it is a very quiet bordelaise: veal or lamb stock, a hint of tarragon, and a pinot noir reduction. On a steak, this bordelaise would have bone marrow; the wine would be a Cab or a zin; the stock would be a demi-glace; it would be accented heavily with tarragon and peppercorns, laced with butter, and reduced to a syrup. With that kind of over-the-top bordelaise, the lamb may well be left in the kitchen for all the taste it would have. The roasted garlic cloves—roasting removes all traces of bitterness and leaves them sweet—provide an appropriate "spiciness."

Red potatoes are cut into olive shapes with a melon ball cutter. This is a labor-intensive French practice done for presentation purposes. They are perfect (but there are not enough of them; next time I want more!): crispy and golden on the surface, soft and light on the inside. Three perfectly peeled, blanched, and butter-finished asparagus spears complete the dish. The asparagus is too bitter for the lamb, interfering with the overall balance. Baby carrots or pearl onions would be better. A sprig of tarragon would provide a green color as well as introduce a flavor echo.

Chef Malm is into cakes. Dessert is about six different kinds of cake from chocolate to coconut cream. I had the latter. It was big, sweet, moist, luscious, and full of coconut, but I'm not a cake fan. I enjoyed half of it.

My entire bill for this meal, including tax and tip, is $31.18! (No wine.)

I have not tried the pork chop (my next order), but it is served with a sauce Robert (ROH-bare). I have not seen this locally. Robert is a demi-glace to which minced shallot, a white wine reduction, Italian parsley, and Dijon mustard have been added. It is one of the sauces most often recommended by French culinary tradition as appropriate for pork.

Were I the owner of this restaurant, I would push the menu further into the French quarter, deleting most of the American offerings and substituting more French bistro cuisine: coquilles St. Jacques, cassoulet, a braised rabbit, sweetbreads, etc. Then I'd change the name to, perhaps, Petit Maison, Maison Jacques, or Chez Jacques. I'd spice up the décor with Toulouse-Lautrec posters and pipe old-fashioned French popular music all around (Chavalier and Piaf), and maybe even get rid of the plastic furniture, at least inside. I would also serve a decent quality but inexpensive *vin ordinaire* by the carafe. Lunch would be a smaller mirror of the dinner. But then I'm not in the restaurant business, I'm in the eating business.

La Quinta Baking Company
★★½
$-$$
Location: 78-395 Highway 111 (in the Von's shopping center), La Quinta, 777-1699. Food type: French bistro. Ambiance: bakery/coffee shop but quaint with a nice patio. Bar: beer and wine. Reservations: suggested during season. Hours: breakfast, lunch, and dinner daily.

It's a darn shame! This place is halfway to being the foodie's dream spot. What it is, is a cute little café-bakery in an attractive shopping center. There is a fountain in the center of its charming patio. It pretends to be a French bistro, and in some respects, it actually is a French bistro, but it is largely only Gallic façade and too many corners are cut, many needlessly, to keep the prices low.

The café rests comfortably in the corner of the eastern end of the Von's shopping center at the intersection of Washington and Highway 111. It is one of the most heavily traveled intersections in the valley, yet this little bakery manages to find peace and calm without even a view of the traffic. Sitting around the fountain in the winter sun is an absolute delight. Inside is less attractive, a light and bright bakery space with tables and chairs and windows all around. Colors are all in the beige family except for the blue linens, and even those are covered with white paper.

The dinner menu has 23 listings subdivided into the usual categories. Of those 23, only nine can arguably be called "French," led by escargot and onion soup. Italian diner favorites and a handful of American clichés dominate the remainder. Many of these are translated into French in order to maintain the illusion.

Little *bruschetti* are served as *amuse bouche*. The French dinner opens with the ubiquitous Italian appetizer. The chopped tomatoes and basil rest precariously on small toast points, only it isn't toast. It is soft white bread. *Bruschetta* is made by rubbing toast with cut garlic and smearing it with a thin coat of olive oil. This prevents the juices of the tomato from sinking into the bread. These *bruschetti* are soggy seconds after they are delivered.

Onion soup has a strong reputation here. It is a large serving arriving in a bowl six inches in diameter. A massive serving of beautifully melted mozzarella cheese covers the surface. The onion-impregnated beef stock is rich and sweet. For $8, could one ask for more? Unfortunately, the answer is yes. First, the ratio of onion broth to cheese bread is 1:2, whereas it should be closer to 3:1. Far too many small slices stacked into the broth make the dish more about cheese and bread than it is about the onion. Second, the bread is the same soft, fresh variety as used for the *bruschetti*. One piece of well-toasted French bread is all that is called for. Here the soft, fresh bread soaks up half the broth. The third problem is the cheese. Onion soup should be made with Gruyère cheese, not mozzarella. Gruyère cheese is sweet and salty, assertive, earthy, and complex. Mozzarella is creamy, bland, and melts well. There is also about three times too much of it. It is also true that Gruyère is about three times the cost of mozzarella, but the quantity should be reduced by 65 percent, thus coming in at par. On the bright side, a bowl of this stuff is a meal in itself. It does taste good if you are not expecting or don't know French onion soup.

There is a niçoise salad, but the rest of the appetizers are standard American fare.

Three of the four bistro specialties offer light meals from the genuine French repertoire: a stuffed seafood crepe (this I have not tasted but most assuredly shall), a quiche du jour, and a chicken-mushroom crepe. All of these are in the $12 range. The seafood crepe is described as follows: "Shrimp, scallops, and clams in a seafood sauce atop a hand-made crepe ["Hand-made"? I certainly hope so]. Served with sautéed vegetables and gratin dauphinois potatoes." If this is half as good as it sounds, with a bottle of Sauvignon Blanc and some real French bread, a fine time should be had by all.

One of the better buys in the desert is called the "peasant supper": soup and salad, a glass of wine, all the bread you can eat, and a dessert of choice, all for $14.95. The onion soup may be substituted for an extra dollar and a half.

"Grilled Specialties" are mostly Italian: chicken piccata, veal Marsala, linguini with shrimp, linguini with clams, and lobster ravioli. There is a rib steak, rack of lamb, hamburger, pork chop, and salmon. There are, however, sole meunière and chicken cordon bleu. All of these dishes, as well as the quiche and crepes, come with the dauphinois potatoes and sautéed vegetables. While this would be a legitimate criticism in a bigger and more expensive restaurant, it is acceptable in a small, inexpensive bistro as it results in considerable savings. Pastas begin at $12.95; the lamb and steak are the most expensive at $21.95.

I opted for the lamb rack. After the negative experience with the onion soup, I was not prepared for the quality of the rack. Five chops, separated, arrive with a light wine/stock reduction atop a dollop of Dijon mustard. The chops are New Zealand/Australian (naturally). I asked for rare, and I got rare. The mustard is a cliché, but with the wine sauce, it is perfectly successful. The sauce itself is gentle enough not to interfere with the subtle flavor of the lamb. Potatoes are superb. These are difficult to pull off correctly. Getting the potatoes perfectly cooked without burning the cream-cheese-egg mixture is challenging. There should be a light crust (there was), the egg should be amalgamated into the cheese and cream sufficiently so as not to scramble (they were), and the cheese should not get tough (it didn't). There is also the perfect hint of nutmeg. Vegetables are carrots, broccoli, asparagus, and zucchini. They, unfortunately, all seem to have been cooked together as the zucchini is overcooked and the carrots are undercooked. They did, however, provide for a medley of complementary flavors. A variety of flavors always keeps things interesting.

The La Quinta Baking Company is a bakery, so I asked the chef for his pastry selection. He choose a fruit tart: kiwi, raspberry, strawberry, and peach in a light syrup over a custard in a pastry shell. The peach has no flavor; the other fruits have moderate flavors. The custard is routine. The pastry shell is a little tough, but a hit of marzipan both surprised and delighted me.

Corkage is only $6, thus further reducing the cost.

This could be such a wonderful addition to the east valley's dining scene. Just imagine a real French bistro serving such traditional bistro fare as cassoulet, braised rabbit, sweetbreads, coquilles St. Jacque, and bouillabaisse. None of those dishes is expensive. Granted, they are significantly more labor intensive, but this place could be a three-and-a-half-star dream come true with the right menu and fewer corners cut. This could be a kind of cross-town version of Jake's Ready-To-Eat (this chapter).

Breakfast and lunch are not as good a deal as dinner. Breakfast is actually more expensive than a good American coffee shop like Sunshine Café (Chapter 15). There are, however, crepes and quiches on the menu for around $10. Lunch is almost bereft of French dishes. It is an ordinary mix of salads and sandwiches with prices all around $11.

McGowan's Irish Inn
★½
$-$$
Location: 73-340 Highway 111, Palm Desert, 346-6032. *Food type: American. Ambiance: European-looking country-hotel dining room. Reservations: suggested. Bar: full; adequate wine list; Guinness on tap. Hours: lunch and dinner Monday through Saturday.*

There is, of course, such a thing as Irish food. Colcannon and boxty cakes come to mind, along with black pudding (with a quart of fresh pig's blood), Irish bangers, spiced beef, Dublin coddle, rarebit, crubeens, various savory pies, and mackerel rolls. Most Irish dishes are based on the potato and/or some inexpensive cut of pork. Other than the potato, leeks, onions, cabbage, turnips, parsnips, and carrots are the most often used vegetables. Irish food is not likely to sell well in the Southern California desert resort cities; it therefore follows that a restaurant cannot survive by making the attempt. However, it seems somewhat absurd for a restaurant to call itself Irish and offer virtually no Irish food. McGowan's serves standard American fare: hamburgers, hot dogs, baby back ribs, steak, prime rib, country-fried steak, crab cakes, and New England clam chowder. Fish and chips are on the menu, but those are English. Five different pastas are offered, but we all know the source of pasta, and it ain't Ireland. Beef stew is served at dinner, but the Irish version is made with mutton, onions, potatoes, bacon, and carrots. Gin, Guinness stout, and hard cider also find their way into many an Irish recipe, but not at McGowan's.

Corned beef and cabbage, the dish that most Americans identify as the Irish signature, is really an Irish-American dish. Traditionally, the cow was only eaten when it was too old to milk or was accidentally killed. Pork and lamb are the meats of choice in Ireland. Nevertheless, the ever popular corned beef and cabbage is the sole representative of Irish cooking on McGowan's menu, regardless of authenticity.

So how is the corned beef and cabbage? The corned beef is excellent. Cut thick across the grain, it is as wonderfully tender as a well-cured brisket should be. Its flavor is deep and layered with the brine and aromatics of the braising liquid. Red potatoes are quartered, boiled, and served plain. Half a cabbage head is simmered with the corned beef for the last hour or so and served plain. This cabbage is not cooked past the outer leaves, as the core is not removed and the simmering water can not get to it. A prepared horseradish garnishes, no mustard. The server suggests a pint of Guinness on tap, but that enormous stout will overwhelm the simple dish. Opt instead for a Harp's lager in a bottle.

Fish and chips are a winning dish. The fish is simply battered and deep-fried, but it is crispy, not at all greasy, fully cooked, tender, and moist. Chips (fries) are likewise nicely crisp with nary a hint of too much fat. They come with tarter sauce, but a malt vinegar is on the table. The British use malt vinegar not tarter sauce, which is nothing more than a simplified American corruption of the French condiment rémoulade.

The space itself is cute, with its French windows covered with lacy this and flowery that. Dark reds and the usual green lend a homey touch. Baskets hang in clusters from the ceiling and pictures of notable Irish celebrities decorate the walls. The popular bar holds a prominent position just inside the front doors, dominating the entire right-hand side of the building. The price is right here, especially at lunch where $11 will get you just about everything on the menu worth eating.

Miro's

$$

Location: 1555 S. Palm Canyon Dr., Palm Springs, 323-5199. Food type: Eastern European, primarily Balkan, home-style cooking. Ambiance: Spanish old-world feel; comfortable and friendly. Reservations: accepted for dinner only, but probably not necessary. Bar: full. Hours: lunch and dinner daily.

Many restaurants are inconsistent. Miro's is one of them. I like Miro's. I like being there. The patio is delightful. Even the view—smack up against Mount San Jacinto—contributes to the overall experience. Miro's is not the least bit pretentious, the prices are reasonable, and the service is excellent. Its home-style cooking is an eclectic mix of generic Mediterranean and central European samplings: Spanish, Italian, Greek, and Austro-Hungarian. The ambiance is old Palm Springs circa 1930, and the background music ranges from Tony Bennett to Italian folk songs.

House-baked bread—a white and a whole wheat—arrives as soon are you are seated. It is good, thick, rich, cakey, and flavorful. Loaves are available for sale.

The prosciutto plate is not di Parma, and occasionally it is garnished with something truly incongruous like an orange, but it is both flavorful and satisfying. Served with feta cheese, kalamata olives, and ajvar, it need not, nor should it, be compared with the classic Italian appetizer prosciutto di Parma-wrapped melon. Ajvar is a Serbian condiment made from roasted paprika, garlic, olive oil, and some combination of red peppers, eggplant, and/or tomatoes. Paprika and eggplant are the dominant flavors. With a little heat, this relish is quite fascinating on the unsuspecting tongue.

All entrées come with soup or salad. Order the Caesar. No, it is not a real Caesar salad. LG's Prime Steakhouse (see Chapter 8) has a real Caesar, and it costs $20. The dressing is bottled, the croutons are probably from a box, and the cheese is most definitely not Parmigiano-Reggiano. On the other hand, the romaine is fresh and crispy, and with the addition of two or three anchovies (for which you have to ask), it is more than adequate as a pre-entrée salad. Just don't think of it as Caesar. The tomato-basil soup, on the other hand, has a decidedly commercial taste.

A winner from the entrée list is the pork medallions, which are, unfortunately, no longer a standard menu item. Three medallions cut from the pork tenderloin—wrapped in bacon and sautéed—are served with a mushroom sauce. The sauce is basic, but it contributes well to the overall taste and adds a contrasting texture. Here we have a reduced chicken stock and white-wine base with button mushrooms. This is served with a medley of blanched vegetables—broccoli flowers, carrots, celery, and cauliflower—finished in butter and served al dente. The flavors are big, compatible, and very fresh.

Entrées come with either mashed potatoes or rice, but Miro's also makes an Austrian potato salad, listed as an appetizer. This is not the warm German potato salad with bacon drippings with which we are all familiar. This is cold with thin slices of a waxy potato, egg, and onion. If you order it as an appetizer, you will ruin your appetite. However, you may exchange the mashed potatoes or rice, which are not interesting, for the Austrian potato salad, which is. Make sure to tell your server that you also want the vegetables. The cold, acidic crunch of the potato salad completes the battery of tastes, and this dish is now excellent.

Orange roughy, stuffed cabbage, and various schnitzels round out the menu. None is particularly good. One has to look a little askance at a restaurant that features "osso buco in marinara sauce" and is still serving rack of lamb with mint jelly.

For dessert, the apple strudel comes with a scoop of French vanilla ice cream. The pastry is not as flaky as it should be, but it is loaded with apples and raisins.

Omri Go Med
★★★½
$ (lunch), $$-$$$$ (dinner)
Location: 73-675 Highway 111, Palm Desert, 341-7004. **Food type:** *Mediterranean rim.* **Ambiance:** *bistro.* **Reservations:** *suggested.* **Bar:** *full.*

Hours: breakfast (see Chapter 15), lunch, and dinner; closed Tuesday. **Chef-owner:** *Omri Siklai*

Chef Omri Siklai is back in business—and back in his old restaurant—after a two-year "retirement." A history lesson is not necessary; the bottom line is Omri's food is better than ever.

The location itself is nothing special: a triangular shaped building surrounded by what is essentially a parking lot. But by the judicious use of trellises and bougainvillea, it has been attractively isolated from its mundane surroundings. There is even a charming one-table patio (please do not request this table on Wednesdays for lunch as that is *my* table). Omri's architectural sensibilities are much like his cooking: big, bold, and assertive. Tables are metal; paintings (his) are in the same expressionistic vein. Cameras monitor the action in the kitchen and relay the activity to flat-screen television monitors positioned throughout the space.

The best word to describe Omri's food is "aggressive." If you like subtlety or worse, blandness, go elsewhere. The power of his food is first evident when you sit down and your server delivers a metal bowl of rolls to your table. Did I say "rolls"? Well, yes, it is bread. Ping-pong ball-sized rounds of bread baked to a golden brown, rolled in olive oil, and sprinkled liberally with minced fresh, raw garlic. If you do not like garlic, you will hate these. If you do, you will love them. There is no in-between with Omri. It is best to share, as this quantity of raw garlic will permeate your life for the next 16 hours.

Omri, like Pierre Pelach at Chez Pierre (this chapter), is restless and inexhaustibly creative. His regular customers don't even ask for a menu. They come in and immediately ask, "What's new?" before even being seated. Specials often outnumber the menu offerings. The menu is dominated by Middle Eastern (Israeli—as Omri is Israeli—Greek, Turkish, Lebanese) North African (Moroccan, Algerian, Tunisian), and Italian. French and Spanish also make frequent appearances, but anything can show up on Omri's specials list. Nothing should surprise you here. Almost everything is superb, but some things transcend even that accolade. Omri is self-taught for the most part, but his technique is French. His use of ingredients is guided by his own unique and daring sense of taste.

Soups range from mushroom barley, borscht, cucumber yogurt,

and the astonishing fish. The fish soup is clams, mussels, shrimp, and, presumably, whatever fish is left over in a seriously potent tomato-basil garlic (think Naples) base. It does not happen very often and is a money loser at $4, but if it is a special when you are there, order it.

Then there is the unique cold grapefruit/date soup. Omri uses the gold grapefruit, which is big flavored and has a texture that does not break down. There are many different kind of dates grown locally, but none compares with the medjool. The most popular, the deglet noor, accounts for about 75 percent of local production, is moderately sweet, and has a firm texture. The medjool, on the other hand, is soft, creamy, and incredibly sweet, as though soaked in honey. This date, the medjool, is paired with the bitter and tart grapefruit. The result is related to the traditional sweet-and-sour sauce served with countless fried shrimp in Chinese takeouts. That sauce, however, is created with the condiments vinegar and sugar. This sweet and sour is not a sauce but the essence of the dish itself. Its impact cannot really be described except to say that the intensity of opposite flavors creates balance. In one sense the result in not sour, bitter, or sweet but both a balance and a melange of all three. A word of warning: if by any chance you end up ordering a bottle of red wine to go with your entrée, do not drink any of it with this soup. The combination is truly hideous. The bitterness and acidity of the soup destroys everything in the wine. Champagne is best here, or a tart and fruity Sauvignon Blanc. This soup is also seriously at odds with the garlic rolls.

Salads and appetizers include stuffed grape leaves with yogurt tzatziki; labane (homemade yogurt cheese, avocado salad, and sweet potato chips); a scallop, tuna, and caviar carpaccio dish; and a mixed Mediterranean plate of hummus, baba ghanoush, tabouleh, olives, and grilled pita. Not on the menu, but almost guaranteed when up to Omri's demanding standards, are mussels and/or clams in various sauces or with some form of pasta. Mussels are huge and tender; sauces are big and bold. These should be compared with the mussels at Zin American Bistro (this chapter). Which are better? Who knows? Who cares. Just go back and forth; that's what I do.

Lunch entrees on the menu include homemade sausage carretierre, moussaka, tuna (fresh) *shishlik* (on a skewer), half a roasted chicken with fresh herbs, a shawarma plate, peppercorn-encrusted prime rib steak with a port glaze, and scampi Provençale on risotto. This last is my favorite although the steak is astonishing, especially for the money.

The *pescatore* is magnificent: mussels, shrimp, clams, calamari, and fish over linguini with a spicy pomodoro sauce. The most astonishing and most original dish is the pork shoulder. This is pounded to about half an inch, then stuffed, rolled, and braised Rouladen style. The stuffing consists of slices of pork sausage, bread, caramelized onions, apples, garlic, parsley, cilantro, and dill. The whole thing is braised, but only for an hour at 350 degrees, in chicken stock. The pork shoulder is not a tough piece of meat. The three-hour braise at a low temperature is not necessary as it would be for a lamb shank or osso bucco. Omri prepares a sauce for this meat unlike anything you've ever experienced. The surface of the meat is seared in duck fat and glazed with fresh pineapple. A sauce of cilantro, jalapeño, tarragon, apples, rosemary, juniper berries, thyme, sage, and triple sec (orange liqueur), in a reduced duck stock. Omri uses duck stock rather than pork stock because it holds up to all the flavors better. The final touch is Maplewood sap. No, not maple syrup, but the unclarified sap that is the actual extract of the maple tree from which the syrup is made. This is not as sweet as the syrup but brings the power of the maple flavor.

Omri serves this dish with Jerusalem couscous (the little "peas" of pasta popular in Israel and usually available in the kosher section of the supermarket) and a medley of root vegetables dominated by beets. Omri loves beets, which he roasts, rather than boils, as roasting generally enhances flavor rather than dissipating it.

You will not believe what I paid for this dish at lunch. $14! It is a special and extremely labor intensive, so it is unlikely to find its way onto the lunch menu on a consistent basis. If there is any criticism that can be made of Omri's cooking, it is that there is a certain flavor resemblance from dish to dish. He likes a certain flavor profile and may be inclined to overdo it.

At lunch, Omri, along with Zin, serves the best food for the money in the Coachella Valley. This is astonishing quality for an often absurdly low price.

Omri Go Med has been criticized in the past for being significantly overpriced at dinner. This is no longer the case. About 80 percent of the dinner entrée prices have been cut by about 40 percent. They are now in the high teens and low twenties. A few of the higher end items—rack of lamb, veal chop, lobster—are still expensive, but a superb dinner can be had for less than $20.

Omri is now open for breakfast. See Chapter 15 for a review.

Palmie

$$$

Location: *44-491 Town Center Way, Suite G, Palm Desert, 341-3200.* **Food type:** *pseudo French bistro with a strong California influence.* **Ambiance:** *country French hotel dining room; cozy and intimate, with Lautrec posters.* **Reservations:** *suggested.* **Bar:** *beer and wine.* **Hours:** *dinner Monday through Saturday.* **Chef-owner:** *Alain Clerc.*

This is one of those sad instances where a restaurant that should be good just isn't. Palmie has a long history, having been established in Palm Springs some time in the early 1990s. In 2003, it moved to Palm Desert roughly one block due west of Chez Pierre (reviewed earlier in this chapter). Alain Clerc is the chef-owner, and he has a substantial following. Palmie's appears at first glance to be a genuine French bistro serving bistro fare, but there is something wrong. The problems are subtle, but I think they can be identified as follows: Chef Clerc has attempted to over-California-ize basic bistro cuisine, and some of his recipes are irrational. Rustic peasant food like duck and cassoulet have been simplified and lightened to the point where they are no longer French rustic but California nouvelle.

I have visited twice and sampled six dishes. The recipes are consistently unsatisfactory. Flavors are placed in a context with other flavors and textures that do not complement one another. Perhaps the worst offender is the *magret de canard roti,* Muscovy duck breast with pear slices in red wine. A purée of celery root works with the duck but not with the pear. The red wine poaching liquid conflicts with the orange sauce, and the spiced pear clashes with the duck meat. The whole is decidedly less than the sum of its parts.

The cassoulet is almost precious. This is supposed to be a peasant dish. The flavors must be big and bold: garlic sausage and duck confit with white beans in a pungent sauce of herbs, wine, and stock. Here the cassoulet is again transformed into California nouvelle. It is thin instead of robust, delicate instead of aggressive. It is the same with the fish stew. The flavors are good, but the butter-cream broth is thin and the whole dish is skimpy with respect to both quality and quantity.

Pomme Frites

$$$

Location: 256 S. Palm Canyon Dr., Palm Springs, 778-3727. *Food type:*
French, Belgian. **Ambiance:** *European-style sidewalk café.* **Bar:** *beer and wine;*
liquor license pending. **Reservations:** *suggested.* **Hours:** *lunch Friday through*
Sunday; dinner Tuesday through Sunday. **Chef-owner:** *Jean-Claude Constant.*

This, along with Café des Beaux-Arts (this chapter), is perhaps the
sidewalk bistro with the most ambient feel of a genuine Parisian sidewalk
café. It does not have the kitsch look of something constructed to
resemble a Parisian café. It has also survived the brutal local restaurant
scene of downtown Palm Springs since 1999, undoubtedly due, in large
part, to its look and feel. The patio is misted and heated with ample
use of overhead fans, the interior is plastered with French and Belgian
commercial posters, and the walls are cleverly covered with the wooden
tops of wine cases. The whole place is quite small, seating maybe 40
people both inside and out. I am, in fact, giving Pomme Frites one of its
stars because it is just so darn cute.

The Internet is bombarded with complaints about the service here.
One must, for example, plead with the server for bread (I did). Arguments
between both staff and customers and management and staff are common
if these complaints are to be believed, and there are simply too many of
them to dismiss. Incorrect bills are another common grievance. Customers
do not get an itemized bill, just a total, leaving the customer to do the
math for himself.

Food preparation is competent, but many corners are cut. On one
occasion I ordered the house specialty, two pounds of mussels served in one
of seven different ways: "Marinière" (white wine, leeks, shallots, and celery),
"Provençale" (white wine, tomatoes, garlic, onions, and bell pepper), saffron
and lemon grass, garlic and cream, mustard and cream, blue cheese and
cream, or endive and cream. I had the "Marinière." Readers of this book
will be well aware that I love mussels, but these mussels rapidly became
boring, followed shortly by irritating. The relentless acidity of the leek-
shallot-wine bath all but destroyed the depth and brininess of the mussels
over time. Perhaps the Provençale version is better.

The signature dish is *pomme frites,* a.k.a. French fries. They are frozen!

This sad fact has actually been verified by the owner, one Jean-Claude Constant. These are the same fries one gets at any fast food outlet: uniformly cut, blanched, chemically treated, dried, flash frozen, and packed for every McDonald's within a 1,000-mile radius. On making fries from actual potatoes Constant says, "No one does that anymore." I have news for M. Constant. Stroll over to Spencer's (Chapter 2) for a taste of Chef Wadlund's fries—house-made shoestrings with truffle oil. Now those are *pomme frites!*

Constant's fries come with three sauces: mayonnaise, catsup, and a mixture of the two. By contrast compare this with the three sauces served with the fries at Zin just down the street (this chapter): mayonnaise, roasted red pepper, and garlic.

Onion soup is not difficult to make, yet I have had onion soups ranging from mediocre to terrible all over town. One must first seriously caramelize in butter many sliced onions. Several different varieties are desirable. To this, a degreased beef broth of great depth is added. The soup in poured into individual terrines. Just before serving a large crouton of dried-out and toasted French bread is placed on top with a modicum of grated Gruyère cheese. The terrine is then placed under the broiler until the cheese is melted and the soup is hot. Since this is not difficult, why are so many onion soups so poorly made? I suspect it is because restaurants find they can save considerable money by not using Gruyère cheese—mozzarella is half the cost (La Quinta Bakery, this chapter)—or skip the crouton and add a sprinkling of pre-grated Parmesan (Oceans, Chapter 8). In its worst manifestation, my wife once noted onion soup made with a slice of American cheese. (Fortunately, that place is no more.) Another common error is the use of either too much bread or fresh bread. Both errors are disastrous. The bread soaks up all the liquid and becomes a soggy mess, sort of an onion-flavored bread pudding. This is the big error here at Pomme Frites. Other soups are simply made by a lazy chef who can't be bothered making a good beef stock or who uses broth out of a box or worse, chicken broth. Or he does not caramelize the onions sufficiently. Here at Pomme Frites the broth is both greasy and has a strange, sour aftertaste.

Quiche Lorraine is another easy recipe that is given short shrift. In essence an omelet pie made with bacon bits, Swiss cheese, and minced onion, a Lorraine is baked in a pie crust and cut into wedges. What is difficult? The pie crust? For a French chef? I don't think so: cup of flour, three tablespoons of lard, pinch of salt, and enough ice water to bring it together. If not overworked, it is light and flaky. This crust is heavy and tough. Instead of bacon, the omelet is overwhelmed with some kind of sausage. It is served with some basic greens from a package and lightly dressed. Does not one have the right to expect more for $12?

Chicken *vol au vent* ($18) is a French version of the chicken pot pie. This is supposed to a beautiful and elegant presentation done as only the French can. A shell, like a cup, is created with puff pastry. It is brushed with egg wash to seal and facilitate browning, then baked. Into this shell is poured the chicken mixture: diced chicken, carrots, leeks, onions, thyme, bay leaf, all in a thick cream sauce. At Pomme Frites it is a bowl of light cream sauce with some overcooked chicken breast and a few white button mushrooms. A round of puff pastry is placed in the center of the sauce. It promptly becomes soggy. Does it taste bad? No. Just uninteresting, bland, and overpriced.

The menu is quite large and includes a number of specials: orange duck, rack of lamb, bouillabaisse, pork tenderloin stuffed with prunes, Flemish-style beef stew, *coq au vin,* various steaks, and fish presentations. Desserts include a *baba au rhum,* something I have not seen on a local menu. I am not returning to this restaurant, but if anyone is still interested, try the entrée special for the day and the *baba* for dessert, and write a review online (www.tripadvisor is a good choice). I'll read it.

Wolfgang's Bistro
★½
$-$$
Location: 77-932 Country Club Dr., Palm Desert, 360-7775. Food type: rustic German with nods to France and Italy. Ambiance: nondescript storefront with a nice patio. Reservations: accepted but not usually necessary. Bar: full, but table service only. Hours: dinner Monday through Saturday. Executive chef-owner: Wolfgang Schumann. Chef: son, Michael Schumann.

It is a pity that Wolfgang's is not better than it is because this little restaurant fills a much-needed niche. German food is a rarity in the valley, and inexpensive little bistros are as scarce as overcoats. But this one?

Located in large street mall with its back to Country Club Drive, Wolfgang's is not easy to find. Turn into the mall just west of Washington Street and look for it.

A beige and gold color scheme organizes the space. The east wall is upholstered entirely in flowered brocade like one long half-booth. It looks uncomfortable but isn't. Linens are cream colored; suspended lamps with brick-colored shades hang above each table. It is simple but charming. The patio is the place to be, weather permitting.

The "Late Lunch" early-bird special, offered 4 P.M. to 5:30 P.M. daily, slides easily into the cheap eats category with nothing over $12.95. Even the regular menu features many entrées under $15.

The chicken noodle soup is indistinguishable from the stuff in the red and white can. The house salad is chopped romaine with a few slices of raw white mushrooms. The dressing has papaya seeds in it. As far as I can tell, this does nothing for the taste. A very nice veal bratwurst, tender and flavorful, rests upon a bed of sauerkraut and pickled red cabbage. The sauerkraut is a bit better than the norm, with apples and bacon added to the otherwise commercial preparation. The bottom line is you could do this at home for about two dollars. Unless you are a tourist, why bother?

Hunter-style schnitzel is served over a homemade spaetzle. Spaetzle is German egg pasta usually with a hint of nutmeg. This one is sweet, which makes it taste almost like boiled strips of pancake batter. The spaetzle is sautéed after it is boiled, bringing a little caramelization to the party, but the sweetness is counterproductive. Very nicely cooked—not at all overdone—slices of pork tenderloin are placed over the spaetzle and dressed with a mushroom-Burgundy sauce. The sauce tastes of the starch of uncooked flour and of wine without all the alcohol burned off.

Vienna-style schnitzel fares better. This dish features the pork tenderloin lightly breaded with capers and lemon. It comes with home-fried potatoes and red cabbage, a better option than the spaetzle.

On the non-German side of the menu, there is a duckling *à l'orange* and a Hungarian goulash. With fascinating versions of duckling happening all over town, a basic orange sauce seems at best an anachronism. This one has good "orangeness," but no depth. Made with Grand Marnier and obviously fresh orange juice and zest, a big orange flavor is extracted. What it lacks is a base of gelatinous duck stock to provide richness and depth of flavor. If the desire for goulash resides in your soul, this one should not be ordered. It is also based on the pork tenderloin, and once again the sauce is superficial. Tomato soup dominates the taste. As with the orange sauce, there is no depth of flavor.

Pâte brisée is the preferred pastry for an apple strudel. This is simple pie dough made with flour, ice water, butter, a pinch of sugar, and salt. The final product after baking is light, buttery, flaky, and crisp. It tends to crumble in the mouth. Phyllo dough can substitute, but it is difficult to work with. Puff pastry should not be used because the filling is too heavy for the pastry, and the layers—the marvelous, airy pastry characteristic of a perfect French croissant—compress and lose their puffiness. The strudel at Wolfgang's is made with puff pastry and is served with a spray of canned whipped cream.

Zin American Bistro
★★★½
$$
#

Location: 198 S. Palm Canyon Dr., Palm Springs, 322-6300. Food type: billed as American, but rotates between French, Italian, Spanish, and American. Ambiance: corner storefront in the heart of downtown Palm Springs; comfortable people-watching venue. Reservations: suggested; required on weekends in season. Bar: beer and wine; large, comprehensive wine list; not too expensive; 22 Zinfandels; half-price wine specials are common. Hours: lunch and dinner daily. Owner/pastry chef/sommelier: Mindy Reed.

Special note: Chef Nicholas Klontz, the creative force behind Zin and Zini restaurants, suddenly and unexpectedly passed away in the summer of 2009 shortly after the opening of Zini. With the exception of a couple of more complex recipes both restaurants have been able to maintain the quality of the cooking with the sous chefs and the very capable management of Mindy Reed. Requiescat in Pace.

Zin is now open for lunch! This is wonderful news for those of us who prefer to dine midday. Mindy Reed and the late Nicholas Klontz put together a restaurant that quite possibly serves the finest food for the money in the Coachella Valley.

Unlike at its most serious competition, Omri Go Med, the lunch menu here is not an edited version of the dinner menu although there is some crossover. Soups include French onion and wild mushroom-truffle cream. Prince Edward Island mussels in any of three ways (Thai, wild tomato-basil, and garlic white wine), tuna or filet mignon tartare, oysters, and a cheese/charcuterie plate comprise the list of appetizers. The Angus beef stew in Belgian beer and a half-pound Kobe sirloin burger with caramelized sweet onions, cheddar cheese, fries, smoked bacon, and or/avocado are two excellent lunch options. Veal and ricotta meatballs, broiled salmon, or even buttermilk-fried chicken are also viable choices, along with several salads and open-faced sandwiches.

Management allows me to order from the dinner menu for lunch. This does not mean you can, but all they can say is no. There is something new on this menu—the finest preparation of sweetbreads within my experience. Here the "king of organ meats" is seared in butter after being soaked, blanched, and peeled. Fresh chanterelle mushrooms and minced shallots are sautéed with thyme, tarragon, chicken stock, white wine, and lemon juice. After a 50 percent reduction, heavy cream is added. Bits of cold butter are whipped into the sauce for thickening and the whole thing is served on a bed of, and topped with, puff pastry. This dish is $15 for a small plate and $26 for a large one. The sweetbreads do reflect the loss of Chef Klontz, but as a shared appetizer it will set your taste buds aflame.

The menu is always changing, rotating dishes to represent different European cuisines. Klontz was Belgian, and he trained with some of the finest chefs in Europe, including Roger Verge. He was a master at what he did, and his restaurant still does it for considerably less money than the competition.

The environment is not quite as spiffy as its rivals, but for my taste, it is more comfortable. The ceiling is black acoustic tile with embedded spotlights. The floor is concrete painted the color of a rich Zinfandel. The walls are golden; the linens, white. Large paintings in a style of a toned-down Eric Fischl adorn the walls and are for sale. A series of windows join the tables along the front and side walls directly to the hustle and bustle of Palm Canyon Drive. Largely because of the location, the majority of patrons are gay men, but the restaurant has no gay orientation. There are little money-saving devices built into this restaurant. Paper, for example, covers the top of the linens. Do you really care? This meal will cost you double elsewhere.

Crab and avocado is Zin's take on the ubiquitous crab cake: pure Dungeness crab topped with a little diced tomato and pea shoots. It builds to a terrific mouthful with its contrasting textures. The oiliness of the avocado, acidity of the tomatoes, and bitterness of the pea shoots all act as foils for the briny density of the crab. Take a sip of Reed's wine selection, a Spanish Verdejo.

Something weird happens. The wine, which is a relatively simple, crisp, and fruity mix, suddenly causes your lips to burn. What is going on here? Try it again. The avocado seems to trigger the effect. Take a bigger bite and drink more wine at the same time. A rush of capsicum burn floods the mouth. How is that possible? It's a trick. There is a very small quantity of minced jalapeño in the avocado, a sort of Spanish guacamole. The taste is not detectable until the wine reacts with the chemical, releasing the burn effect on the tongue and especially the lips. Quite startling! Quite wonderful!

Fried shrimp Parmesan cakes are served on a bed of deep-fried Italian parsley. Small shrimp are minced and mixed with Parmesan cheese and a béchamel sauce. They are deep-fried, which forms a crunchy surface without affecting the creamy interior. The final product is dusted with smoked paprika. This is similar to a chipotle pepper but not as hot. A squeeze of fresh lemon sets off the flavors. Reed pours the great wine of the evening, an Albariño Rias Baixas. This is a Spanish white that is not too fruity—apple stands out—but is powerful with a deep, dense, mouth-puckering dryness. It is so crisp it verges on metallic, the perfect accompaniment for the soft, creamy shrimp cake. This wine, by the way, is one of the most expensive on the menu at $41.

A Spanish version of vichyssoise with *crème fraîche,* croutons, chervil, and chives arrives at your table. There is something else, something that removes it from the French version of this classic soup. Your mouth moves it around testing different taste buds. You taste it only on exhale. It is nutmeg.

Monkfish wrapped in prosciutto or *jamón* Serrano (Spanish ham the quality of prosciutto) is the "poor man's lobster"—at least that is what many people call this fish. For me it is a misnomer. Monkfish may not have the complexity and the almost toxic charge of a great lobster, but it is much more consistent, and an ordinary monkfish is better than an ordinary lobster. Served with a wild mushroom sauce (morels, yet!), elbow pasta, English peas, broccoli, and diced tomatoes, this is one of the best and most fully realized entrées on the menu. A sauce of fish fumet and cream with hints of thyme, tarragon, and shallots integrates everything into the totality of the creation. A sprinkling of pea shoots brings a tinge of bitterness to the party, completing the round of five taste sensations: sweet (fish), sour (tomato), salt (prosciutto), bitter (pea shoots), and umami (mushrooms).

Reed pours a Caracol Serrano Tinto Jumilla Cabernet with this fish. A

Cab! Are you horrified? This Cab is blended with Monastrell and Syrah and does not have the tannins associated with a full-bodied Cab. Reed knows what she is doing. A rabbit appears on each of the regional menus. This one is braised in a white wine with a bouquet garni of cloves, bay leaf, and rosemary. Strips of fire-roasted red and yellow bell peppers and Spanish onion accompany. It is served with French fries dusted with that same smoked paprika found on the shrimp cake. This is a fine dish but probably not as satisfying as the French version, lapin Dijonnaise, found on the French menu. Like the sweetbreads, this dish reflects the loss of Klontz in the kitchen, but it still makes a fine meal.

An Australian lamb rack boasts one of the few successful sauce-lamb pairings in Palm Springs. Tomatoes and oranges are dried in the oven and then cuts into a lamb stock. When this is puréed, strained, and reduced, a sauce that is not too sweet but which carries the distinct aromas and acids of tomato and orange finds a perfect home on the tender baby lamb. Reed pours the Zinfandel of the day with the lamb, a Limerick Lane delivering scents and tastes of raspberry, plum, and a light whiff of pepper in a style that can only be called elegant.

I generally do not have dessert. By the time it is traditionally served I usually do not want anything else, but this one was forced on my poor, overworked stomach. Of all the desserts in the world, cheesecake ranks near the bottom for me. It is just too heavy. But Reed has created something quite special, a goat-cheese-based cake. The cheese is whipped and sweetened. This cheesecake is mildly tangy and much lighter than those made with cream cheese. With an anointing of very old balsamic vinegar and a few fresh berries, this cheesecake becomes magical. Reed pours an Inniskillin ice wine, Canada's most significant export, for a perfect finish. This stuff costs a small fortune, and with flavors and aromas of dried apricot, blood orange, and mint and residual sugars potent enough to induce a diabetic coma, this is the monster of all monsters when it comes to dessert wines, possibly even surpassing Château d'Yquem. (Nah!)

Zini Café Med
★★★½
$$
Location: 140 S. Palm Canyon Dr., Palm Springs, 325-9474. Food type:

Mediterranean rim. **Ambiance:** *much like Zin (see above) but with cute sidewalk seating.* **Bar:** *full.* **Reservations:** *suggested.* **Hours:** *lunch and dinner daily.* **Owner/sommelier:** *Mindy Reed.*

Special note: Chef Nicholas Klontz, the creative force behind Zini and Zin restaurants, suddenly and unexpectedly passed away in the summer of 2009 shortly after the opening of Zini. Both restaurants have been able to maintain the quality of the cooking with the well-trained sous chefs and the capable management of Mindy Reed. Zini has actually added a delightful tapas menu.

Can you really have too much of a good thing? The restaurant with the best food for the money in the Coachella Valley has just doubled itself half a block down the street. Not a clone, this is not a second restaurant in a chain, but an entirely new establishment with a new menu. There is a little crossover, as the ricotta-stuffed veal meatballs, the hanger steak, and the salmon filet appear on both menus, but it retains what is best—the sommelier/manager, the quality, the prices—and gives us a whole range of new choices. It is billed as Mediterranean, but it is mostly Italian with a little Spanish. Only a couscous lamb stew comes from the other side of that venerable sea in the middle of the planet, but that will change as the restaurant fully establishes its menu. The only other genuine Mediterranean restaurant in the area is the superb Omri Go Med (this chapter), but that is 15 miles east in Palm Desert. Omri is more representative of the Mediterranean rim in its entirety, but I would be happy to dine at either place for the rest of my life.

The other Zin is on the corner. There the windows slide back, opening the inside to the outside, weather permitting. Here there is sidewalk seating. It is the same view—people-watching on the main drag in downtown Palm Springs. It is the same no-frills environment (keeping costs low is important at both Zins), but this restaurants is inherited from the recently closed Enzo's, where richer materials were in evidence. The floor is Italian tile. The bar is black marble (or ceramic tile), while tables and chairs are dark wood upholstered in deep reds. Paintings are of flamenco dancers and Italian or Greek landscapes.

From the Italian side of the show comes first a pappardelle (a big wide noodle) with braised rabbit, tomatoes, roasted red peppers, smoked paprika, olives, and capers. For pasta lovers the addition of rabbit offers something a little offbeat, a terrific but unexpected flavor not generally found in ordinary establishments. Many people are unfamiliar with the subtle goodness of rabbit and others tend to avoid the meat as it elicits images of cuddly little white Easter bunnies. May I remind these readers that almost all baby animals are cute (alligators excepted), and certainly lamb has to rank right up there with Easter bunnies. Others have been told that rabbit tastes just like chicken. These people are lying to you. If comparisons must be made, rabbit tastes more like an ever-so-slightly gamy pork tenderloin. It is also almost fat free so it requires a rich environment like, say, a pasta. The complementary flavors of tomato, capers, and roasted peppers all serve the final dish. For my taste the olives, San Remos, are a bit too pungent for use here. San Remo olives, much like kalamata olives, are a secondary ingredient of this well-respected rabbit dish, appropriately called *coniglio alla sanremasca* or "rabbit San Remo style." Perhaps it is the presence of the other full-flavored ingredients—tomatoes, capers, peppers—that interfere, or perhaps it is just a personal quirk. A powerful and tangy Grana Padano (a Parmigiano-Reggiano-style cheese) anoints the whole. This is one of the best and most interesting pasta dishes in town. Mindy pours a complex dry Italian red, a Montepulciano, with this, and all is right with the world. At $15 it is also a terrific value.

I continue by ordering the *zuppa de pesce* (fish soup). Mindy thought I wanted the previous listing on the menu, the *cozze,* which is mussels in a tomato, white wine, and fennel broth with tomatoes, red onion, and garlic. The fish soup is more or less the same broth, but it has salmon, shrimp, clams, and calamari as well as mussels. The *cozze* is terrific—big, tender, flavorful black mussels in the pungent tomato-garlic broth—but my mouth wanted something to compare with Omri Go Med's (this chapter) magnificent fish soup. It was not going to happen; no room left, sorry, tummy full.

From the Iberian Peninsula to the west, Spain, comes paella. As readers of this book well know I am a huge fan of paella, which also makes me exceptionally critical of poorly made ones. Paella is primarily a rice dish. Paella Valenciana, the original and most authentic, is not a seafood paella but contains chicken, rabbit, and snails. Eel, wild duck, and frog are also sometimes included. The seafood paella is primarily a Cuban influence, but this variety is the more common in this country. Since rice is the primary ingredient, it is important that the "correct" rice be used. This would be either Bomba or Calasparra short-grain rices grown in Valencia. However, the Italian Arborio rice makes a fine substitute and is more readily available.

This paella is *meloso,* or "juicy" as they say in Valencia. I like it this way, but purists will argue that paella should be *seco.* Saffron is in perfect balance. Clam and mussels are redolent of the sea as are the perfectly cooked shrimp. Sausage is the hot Italian-style pregnant with anise. Chicken and calamari play a minor role. Mindy pours a bold red wine from the Toro region of western Spain, only 25 miles from the Portuguese border. It is big, bold, and dry but, as it is based on the Tempranillo grape, it is not as complex as the Montepulciano, which I prefer.

This is one of the better paellas in town. The one at Oceans (Chapter 8), is also superb, as is the one at Grove Artisan Kitchen at the Miramonte (Chapter 1).

From across the Mediterranean comes the best dish I have tried so far, a marvelous lamb couscous. I'm not here as an advocate of colonialism, but certainly from a culinary standpoint the ex-colonies of France in North Africa cross-pollinated with their "oppressors," resulting in some fine and most original cuisine. In Morocco, Algeria, and Tunisia we find the use of sweet spices, nuts, and dried fruit in savory dishes. Couscous replaces pasta and potatoes. Cinnamon, nutmeg, and cumin replace thyme, basil, and tarragon. Not since the unfortunate demise of terrific little Hedi's Café Paris in 2006 have we had been exposed to the heady aromas of Moroccan cuisine at this level. Pierre Pelach at Chez Pierre (this chapter) does a wonderful Moroccan lamb shank, but Chef Hedi Hamrouni specialized in North African cuisine.

Braised lamb shoulder is served on a base of couscous and chickpeas. Sweet grilled eggplant and zucchini crisscross the top. (Almonds, dates, and dried apricots might be nice . . . just at thought.) But it is the Arabic spices, cinnamon especially and cumin, that give the dish its distinctive Moroccan flavor. Harissa, a hot chili paste, from the "colonies" is another distinctive addition. The use of Mergez sausage is a terrific touch, one that Hedi did not use. Mergez is a hot, dry, densely packed lamb sausage from Algeria and Tunisia. It is popular also in France and Israel. That's the dish: full of kick, powerful, satisfying, even challenging those who do not know what to expect.

Pairing a wine with a dish this spicy is difficult. The easy way out is to serve a big, dark beer, which has an automatic affinity for spicy foods. But if the right wine can be found, it is even better. Mindy finds it. It is called Wolftrap, and is from Franschhoek in South Africa's Western Cape. It is an inexpensive wine (Zini sells it for $25), but it is probably one of the few wines in the world that will tie all these flavors together without getting in the way of the spiciness. Wolftrap is made from Syrah, mourvèdre, and viognier grapes. The Syrah is extremely peppery and is what makes it work with the harissa. The wine has a big nose and oozes sweet fruits—blackberries, cherries, plums, even cocoa from the mourvèdre—but seems to shift back and forth between sweet and savory. This is a tricky match, but this is why we all need a sommelier at times.

Tiramisu is soft and creamy. It is also the lightest tiramisu I've ever tasted. Mascarpone, whipping cream, egg yolks, and sugar are whipped full of air. Ladyfingers are soaked with coffee and rum. A layer of chocolate is added. Chill until it doesn't fall apart. Throw in a few raspberries and a mint leaf. What could be better? I like it when the ladyfingers retain some of their crunch. If they soak too long they fall apart. Here they are completely absorbed into the overall texture. Is that bad? Just a quibble. Vince Cultraro's is better, but the four-star La Spiga (Chapter 4) is the gold standard of Italian restaurants.

Zin and Zini are not the best restaurants in town, but they certainly provide the best food for the money. They are also consistent and always interesting. Service is always more than satisfactory; it is never cloying or intrusive. Ambiance is fun and relaxed. Zini is a Parisian-style sidewalk café; Zin offers as close to al fresco dining as you can get without actually being outside. And Mindy is a fine sommelier. These restaurants remain at the top of my personal favorites list for both lunch and dinner.

CHAPTER 6

Trattorie and Ristoranti

Next to steakhouses, Italian restaurants of one kind or another are the most popular in the desert. There are more Italian restaurants here than there are steakhouses, but they collectively do not generate as much revenue. Many of these can simply be considered diners—pizza houses and pasta and sandwich shops located in strip malls everywhere. Most of these are chains, and many are not included in this book. One such place, Fontana's—an exceptional example—*is* listed. There is a great deal of redundancy among Italian restaurants. Many entrepreneurs are well aware of the money-generating potential of an Italian restaurant so they proceed to hire a chef and duplicate the menu of every successful Italian restaurant in town. Where this is the case, I have, somewhat arbitrarily, not included the more obvious examples.

A trattoria is the Italian version of the French bistro, although both designations have all but lost their meaning in this country. Any restaurant called a trattoria will most likely be Italian although it may not really be a trattoria. Strictly defined a trattoria is small, family run, and serves robust and rustic Italian fare along with a copious supply of good house wine. A ristorante, on the other hand, is a larger upscale establishment whose food may range all the way up through *alta cucina,* or high cuisine. Many places calling themselves trattorie are actually ristoranti and vice versa.

Amici
★★½
$-$$
Location: 71-380 Highway 111, Rancho Mirage, 341-0738. Food type: rustic Italian. Ambiance: genuine trattoria; small, simple, quaint. Bar: full; adequate wine list; free corkage on Sundays. Reservations: suggested, dinner only. Hours: lunch Monday through Friday; dinner nightly; Sunday brunch.

Except for the full bar, Amici is the quintessence of a trattoria. Food like this—hearty, robust, unpretentious, honest, homemade, no fuss, and no frills—can be found throughout Italy in the smaller towns and villages. There is nothing wimpy or compromised about the flavors. At Amici, if you order pasta puttanesca you get pasta puttanesca—red pepper flakes, capers, anchovies, black olives, and garlic—not some aborted California-ized concoction with kalamata olives, chicken breast, and goat cheese.

The building is small and comfortable. In no way does it resemble a coffee shop, but rather an old country restaurant somewhere in Calabria. A full bar is a surprise in a restaurant of this type, where you would expect wine to dominate the libations department. Trees and a wrought-iron fence surround a quaint patio, nicely misted for comfort during the hotter months. The floor consists of wooden planks and concrete once painted in the Italian colors, now faded to just this side of oblivion. Tables, tall stools, umbrellas, and chairs are mix and match. Inside there are white linens, but "formality" is a word unknown in these parts.

Fresh trout, pork loin, and veal are the *secondi* entrées of choice. There is a *bistecca del giorno* (steak of the day) and a *pollo arrosto alla romana* (roasted half-chicken), but reliance on chicken breast done six different ways and a battery of steaks is notably absent.

A *penne al pastore* in a creamy homemade tomato sauce with sun-dried tomatoes, shredded basil, and a generous supply of Italian sausage redolent of anise is typical of the bold pastas served at Amici. It arrives from the kitchen already awash with a potent Parmesan cheese. It is not Parmigiano-Reggiano, but at $11 (lunch price) you could hardly expect that. There is an interesting Italian take on Spanish gazpacho. It is much chunkier than the classical Spanish version, and with the addition of shrimp, calamari, scallops, and a few of those tiny octopuses, this more resembles a cold cioppino than a gazpacho.

For lunch, Amici falls into the cheap-eats category. At dinner, everything is reasonably priced, with most entrées under $20.

Back Street Bistro
★★
$$

Location: 72-820 El Paseo Dr., Palm Desert, 346-6393. **Food type:** *mostly Italian trattoria food.* **Ambiance:** *back street sidewalk café; faces rear parking lot but with mountain views and attractive landscaping.* **Bar:** *full.* **Reservations:** *suggested.* **Hours:** *lunch and dinner daily.*

The sign says "bistro," but it's a trattoria. Go figure. The patio is charming, perhaps because of, rather than in spite of, its unusual location. It faces an entire block of parking lot but provides an unobstructed view of the Santa Rosa Mountains. Umbrellas and nice landscaping insulate the immediate environment from the mundane.

Food is ordinary but adequately prepared trattoria cuisine: pastas, chicken, veal, a little bruschetta, a *pasta e fagioli,* and a Caesar salad. Everybody serves this cuisine. During lunch, the Italianate menu is dropped in favor of American sandwiches and salads.

Four paragraphs back from what you are reading now is a review of *penne al pastore* as served at Amici for $11. Here this dish is called *penne al Nona.* The difference is that this one is bland, and at Amici it is robust and full flavored. Think of it as the physical difference between Audrey Hepburn and Sophia Loren.

New England clam chowder (not very Italian, huh?) has a terrific ratio of clam to potatoes, probably three to one, and an interesting celery back note, but the cream base tastes oddly commercial. Calamari are done well, deep-fried in a paper-thin, light-as-a-feather, egg-white-based batter. The fish is tender and moderately flavorful. A commercial-tasting cocktail sauce is adequate but provides no zing.

Peroni beer reminds one of that special week spent in Rome, but the wine list is mediocre at best. It will provide for your needs, but do not order the house wine. It is Delicato. In this case, cheap is *not* adequate.

Bellini
★★½

$$$

Location: 73-111 El Paseo Dr., Palm Desert, 341-2626. **Food type:** *Sicilian ristorante.* **Ambiance:** *formal in its look and feel, but the effervescent personality of hostess/co-owner Marylena Pisano more than compensates.* **Bar:** *full; excellent Italian wine list.* **Hours:** *dinner Monday through Saturday from 6 P.M.* **Chef-owner:** *Carlo Pisano.*

With more than half the entrées and pasta dishes using tomato sauce and cheese, the emphasis here is on the southern regions of Italy, namely Naples and Sicily. Bellini is most accurately described as an "osteria" (like the French equivalent, the brasserie), a word not used in the desert. An osteria lies somewhere between the rustic food of the trattoria and the *alta cucina* of the ristorante.

Bellini, the restaurant, is named for Vincenzo Bellini, the composer, and the Bellini cocktail created in the composer's honor by Harry's Bar in Venice, Italy, in 1948. The cocktail, made with peach nectar and Prosecco spumante (Italian sparkling wine) is now the signature drink at Bellini, the restaurant. Got that? The peach is the trademark of the restaurant, finding its way into not only the cocktail, but also a number of other dishes, occasionally to their detriment.

Here the carpaccio is "cooked" in lemon juice, like ceviche. The cheese is shaved Parmigiano-Reggiano. The final presentation is very good, but the acidity of the lemon diminishes the meat's flavor.

A salad of organic baby greens, Belgian endive, Gorgonzola, cherry tomatoes, peaches, walnuts, and balsamic vinaigrette is California cuisine, not Italian. The combination is exceedingly popular. In some form it is served all over town, usually with pears. For most of the year, peaches are either not available or mealy and flavorless. In July, a full-flavored, firm organic peach can be fabulous, but in an effort to maintain the peach signature, quality is lost the rest of the year. The core Italian culinary principle is seasonal, fresh, and local, not frozen.

Rigatoni Norma (*Norma* is Vincenzo Bellini's most famous opera) is a pasta whose defining ingredient is eggplant. When I was a teenager, eggplant Parmesan was the cheap substitute for veal Parmesan. I never really liked it; it was squishy and bland. I have news for you: eggplant, when prepared properly, which means primarily that the excess liquid has been leached out, is an extremely flavorful element in its own right. It's tough to explain the taste. It is delicate and a little acidic, with characteristics more reminiscent of a fruit than a vegetable. Only in Indian cuisine should it be mushy. The Rigatoni Norma allows perfectly prepared eggplant to speak. Dressed with garlic, basil, tomato sauce, and shaved dry-aged ricotta, this is a first-rate pasta dish.

Polenta is still rather uncommon in these parts. Chef Pisano's polenta is creamy and smooth. The natural graininess of the corn flour is gone. With Italian sausage, roasted red bell peppers, mushrooms, shallots, kalamata olives, tomato sauce, and Parmigiano-Reggiano, this is a terrific substitute for a pasta course.

A large veal chop is pounded to a quarter-inch thickness, washed in egg, breaded, and sautéed. It is served bone in. The chop when flattened somewhat resembles an eight-inch-diameter pancake. It can be ordered either parmigiana style (sautéed in olive oil with cheese and tomato sauce) or Milanese (sautéed in butter with prosciutto, cheese, and a truffle shaving). What is unique and wonderful about this offering is the tenderness of the veal, which in lesser venues is overcooked and tough.

Desserts are a major attraction at Bellini. The *cannoli al limoncello* features sweet ricotta cheese whipped to a silky smooth consistency and flavored with Limoncello. *Millefoglie* Bellini is more original but less successful, again because of the peaches. It's layers of puff pastry—buttery, flaky, and light as a feather with *crème anglaise,* peaches, and a raspberry coulis. With a good, ripe, fresh peach, this dessert could be a monster.

Capri Italian Restaurant
(See Capri Steakhouse, Chapter 9.)
Not recommended
$$
Location: 12-260 Palm Dr., Desert Hot Springs, 329-6833. Food type: Italian and steaks. Ambiance: throwback to 1960; nice bar area; oppressive and claustrophobic dining room. Bar: full; adequate wine list. Reservations: suggested; required for bar area. Hours: dinner Tuesday through Sunday.

Capri is actually two restaurants in one. The Italian side of this venerable Desert Hot Springs landmark is the inferior of the two. The steakhouse is both surprisingly good and one of the desert's best buys.

The osso buco is stringy and tasteless in a watery sauce. Manicotti is made with crêpes rather than pasta. The tomato sauce has a metallic taste as though from a can. The pasta alio olio with lots of chopped garlic, olive oil, and anchovies is good. I recommend it as a side dish with a steak. All entrées come with soup or salad and garlic bread; steaks come with a side of pasta or baked potato for an extra charge.

The usual soup is minestrone, or at least claims to be minestrone. Classic Italian minestrone is a vegetable melange including cannellini or borlotti beans in a vegetable stock, usually without meat but sometimes with bacon or salt pork, and finished with a generous grating of Parmesan cheese. The minestrone at Capri is a tomato broth with a little celery, onion, and carrots.

The house salad fares better: fresh, crunchy romaine and iceberg with chickpeas, kidney beans, and a beet slice (from the can). House-made blue cheese dressing is acceptable although the cheese is mediocre. House-made vinaigrette is a simple vinegar and oil—not emulsified properly—but full flavored and compatible with the salad's flavors.

Castelli's
★★★
$$$
Location: 73-098 Highway 111, Palm Desert, 773-3365. *Food type: Italian, almost* alta cucina. *Ambiance: high-energy, busy lounge with entertainment. Bar: full; extensive wine list, mostly Italian and Californian.* **Reservations:** *suggested.* **Hours:** *dinner nightly.*

If you are looking for a quiet, romantic environment, Castelli's is not the place for you. The place is crowded, even on a hot September weeknight. Celebrity photos, trompe l'oeil murals, stone walls, an enclosed patio (Italian/French style), a large active bar, and all the hustle and bustle of lots of people having lots of fun defines Castelli's environment. *Palm Springs Life* proclaims, "Enter the doors of Castelli's and you'll believe you have just stepped into a small bistro in romantic Tuscany. Soft lighting, lace curtains, dark, warm woods, an abundance of fresh flowers and greenery set the tone for a wonderful dining experience." Forget about it. It is not small, and it is not a bistro but a ristorante. It is not romantic, but it is fun. And the food is generally excellent.

The menu says tenderloin beef spiedini. *Spiedini* is Italian for "skewered," like a kabob. A beef spiedini is a filet mignon pounded to a quarter inch thick and rolled with sautéed onions, Parmesan, Romano, and mozzarella cheese; rolled in egg and flour; and broiled or grilled. The dish labeled as spiedini at Castelli's does not even remotely resemble the spiedini I just described. This dish resembles a *filetto al Marsala*, a charbroiled filet topped with a Marsala wine sauce. Both the filet and the sauce are beautifully prepared. The level of acidity in the sauce is exactly right for a perfect complement.

Vitello alla Piccatina does not fare as well. This is essentially veal milanese, or pounded veal sautéed in olive oil with lemon, white wine, capers, and mushrooms. The lemon, which includes a "confetti" of lemon zest, obliterates the subtle flavors of the veal, and the mushrooms have no flavor at all. They are quartered white buttons, which cannot be expected to hold their own in a dish like this. Capers and lemon may well have been served by themselves. *Scampi della casa* are terrific. The shrimp are large and have that bizarre and wonderful "toxic" effect, a drying at the back of the throat much loved by true aficionados of crustaceans. Aside from the fact that my shrimp were overcooked, their flavors were terrific, and the sauce of butter, garlic, and white wine brought out all that is magical about big shrimp.

A side of pasta comes with all entrées, but only one way. It is a penne with Castelli's own full-bodied tomato sauce filled with large chunks of tomatoes. It is an excellent sauce. Unfortunately, it does not complement every entrée. For example, it is terrible with the shrimp scampi, mediocre with the veal dishes, and good with the beef dishes. Any request for pasta other than this one results in a higher cost, but it seems hard to believe that a simple pasta with oil and garlic or butter sauce would incur an additional tariff.

The menu is large and covers all the bases. The quality of raw materials is very high, and preparation ranges from excellent to inconsistent. The wine list is extensive, with Italian wines organized according to region. Prices cover the gamut from inexpensive to very expensive.

Chapelli's
★★
$$
Location: 50-949 Washington St. (Ralph's shopping center), La Quinta, 564-9835. Food type: rustic Italian. Ambiance: trattoria. Bar: full; lower-end wine list. Reservations: suggested. Hours: dinner nightly.

"It's that little Italian place next to the dry cleaners!" Yes it is, and that is just how Chapelli's bills itself. For the not-too-demanding local diner without deep pockets, Chapelli's may be just the ticket. The owners have done remarkable things with this little pedestrian storefront "next to the dry cleaners." With walls textured in a faux plaster in a muted golden brown to resemble a Renaissance home, candles, tiny overhead spots, and bar lamps bouncing light of the same color, Chapelli's takes on a warm, intimate glow. A rose on each table (also faux), the voices of

Dino and Frank, and the aromas of garlic and oregano create a thoroughly enjoyable ambiance reminiscent of a private party. Intimate, relaxed, and completely unpretentious, Chapelli's beckons in an uncanny way.

The antipasto plate is a nice opening: shaved Parmesan, prosciutto, spicy salami, pepperoncini, a delightfully crispy mini loaf of crusty bread, olive oil, and balsamic vinegar. None of these things are first quality, but if they were, prices would jump dramatically. Chapelli's is not that kind of restaurant.

The house salad, included with all entrées except pizza, is not a throwaway as is so often the case where it is included. Yes, it is iceberg (sorry, no arugula), but the addition of a potent Maytag blue cheese, seasonal veggies (cucumbers, shredded carrots, red cabbage, and tomatoes), and a chiffonade of hard salami raises an otherwise mundane house salad to the next level. Replacing the iceberg with *anything* would raise it still further.

The lowly spaghetti and meatballs is almost a signature dish. The reason is a remarkable meatball. A medley of ground meats, breadcrumbs, egg for a smooth texture, and a hint of anise results in a meatball of terrific texture and flavor. Pastas are uniformly al dente.

Another recommended dish is sand dabs meunière. *Meunière* is French for "miller's wife" and refers to the cooking technique of dredging in flour and sautéing in butter. It is not Italian, but the dish fills a welcome niche in a menu replete with all the usual Italian suspects. A meunière sauce—butter, lemon, garlic, parsley, capers, and cream—is reduced to the consistency of syrup and is a perfect complement for the delicate fish.

Rice pilaf has a prepackaged taste. I asked the waiter to ask the chef what kind of rice he was using. It had a basmati texture without the distinctive basmati flavor. The waiter came back and said, "Near East." Near East is a brand name, not a type of rice. This is Near East brand rice pilaf, which is about 50 percent orzo, flavored with onions and garlic, colored with turmeric, and spiked with pine nuts. It is compatible enough, but the commercial packaged taste is obvious.

Overly garlicky and overly salted sautéed spinach rounds out the ensemble. The spinach overwhelms the sand dabs. On the other hand, the same spinach served with the veal piccata is just fine. Small restaurants are frequently not equipped to prepare different side dishes for each entrée, and this is a case where that particular cut corner matters. Milk-fed veal *scaloppine* pounded to a quarter-inch thick, sautéed, and served over thick spaghetti noodles is actually more successful than the sand dabs as well as being a dollar cheaper. The same sauce is used on both to no ill effect. Dessert is included in the price of an entrée as well: bread pudding, spumoni, New York cheesecake, or cappuccino ice cream. Have the spumoni.

Devane's Italian Kitchen

$-$$

Locations: 40-101 Monterey Ave., #E5, Rancho Mirage, 342-5330; 78-065 Main St., La Quinta, 771-5330. Food type: pseudo-Italian diner. Ambiance: coffee shop. Bar: beer and inexpensive wines. Reservations: not accepted. Hours: lunch and dinner daily.

There is a new Devane's. In the new Old Town in La Quinta next to Hog's Breath Inn (Chapter 8), it is much more attractive than the "coffee shop" in the strip mall on Monterey. In the new location there is a beautiful heated and misted patio. Here the menu is more upscale but still conservative. Prices remain reasonable but a few of the more expensive entrées will cross the $30 benchmark.

Devane's aspires to be Chapelli's (reviewed earlier in this chapter) and fails. The first thing you notice about Chapelli's is how very Italianate the environment is—music, aroma, lighting, colors. The first thing you notice about Devane's is the fact that it screams, "Hello! I'm a coffee shop." There is nary an aroma anywhere except the vague hint of bleach.

The food at Devane's is not bad; it is just that it is not what it pretends to be. Stracciatella, for example, tastes more like Chinese egg drop soup or chicken soup with eggs in it than the Italian staple. Missing are the defining ingredients of nutmeg, Parmesan cheese, semolina, and Italian parsley. In their stead are chicken pieces and spinach. I am not one to insist on steadfast adherence to a recipe, but when a dish claims to be one thing and resembles something else entirely, I am not pleased.

The pasta alla puttanesca is even guiltier of misrepresentation than the soup. Puttanesca is one of my favorite pastas. I prepare it at home a couple of times a month. Also known as "whore's pasta," this hearty and aggressively spiced pasta dish originated in the brothels of Naples and was placed in the windows to entice men to shop for the even more exciting wares within. The defining ingredients are garlic in copious quantities, a large kick of chili flakes, anchovies, tomatoes, parsley, cheese, capers, and olives. Devane's will never be accused of violating vice laws. Its puttanesca is spaghetti with olives and capers. It is as bland and soulless as . . . Well, never mind. Let's not go there. This book is rated PG-13.

Shrimp scampi is equally bland. The shrimp are two-inchers—possibly two and a half—and swimming in a lemony sauce heavy on the grease.

Ironically, when considered without the cumulative baggage of a thousand years of culinary art behind it, Devane's is not a bad coffee shop. The prices are downright cheap, and everything tastes pretty good outside of the Italian context. The usual pastas and baked dishes, pizzas, panini, salads, chicken, and veal round out a large menu. A kids' menu for $5 is also available.

Kalura Trattoria Italiana
★★½
$$
*Location: 124 S. Palm Canyon Dr., Palm Springs, 323-4748. **Food type:** trattoria. **Ambiance:** people-watching in the heart of Palm Springs. **Bar:** full; excellent Italian wine list categorized by region. **Reservations:** suggested, especially for a street-side table. **Hours:** lunch and dinner daily; open till 1 A.M.*

Kalura is the Sicilian word for heat. Kalura Trattoria Italiana is located under the Blue Guitar and next to the Plaza Theatre (home of *The Fabulous Palm Springs Follies*) in downtown Palm Springs. The ambiance is all about people-watching. Energy flows around and through this restaurant. With music, dancing, and laughter all about, Kalura takes on the flavor of the local scene. It is fun, active, noisy, busy, and hot. Kalura is also one of the valley's few places open for late-night dining.

The designation "trattoria" here is reasonably accurate. Kalura serves pizza and spaghetti alla Bolognese. The menu designates its wines by region: Piedmont, Veneto, Tuscany, etc. This is an excellent policy, as it allows the customer to pair a regional wine with a regional dish, a highly respected practice in Italian circles.

Caesar salad comes with calamari and generous shavings of pecorino Romano on fresh crunchy romaine leaves. The calamari is peculiar. Slices a quarter-inch thick are grilled and placed around the salad. They are bland, and their soft texture does nothing to complement the salad. Where are the anchovies?

The pizza, a *quattro stagioni,* is an Italian division. Four toppings—cheese, mushrooms, Italian ham, and artichokes—are placed individually on each quarter of the pizza. The effect is four mini pizzas, each with its own distinctive taste. This is a particularly Italianate concept. Here the ingredients are overlapped in the center, which becomes mushy and undercooked, but the concept is a good one. The pizza is thin crust and boasts big flavors. The ham is especially notable; the menu specified Italian ham, but it is not prosciutto di Parma.

Risotto porcini e salsiccia is a fine risotto. The first taste to hit the palate here is white truffle oil—a blast of umami—rich, pungent, earthy, and wild. The second blast is of the porcini, in my opinion the pinnacle of wild-mushroom flavors. The other flavors begin to work their way through the texture—cream, some wine (Pinot Grigio), a *salumi* (cured pork like pancetta or Italian sausage), demi-glace, and brandy—a swirling mass of powerful, weaving flavors and textures.

A rack of tiny veal chops no larger than those found on a lamb is the dish I recommend most. This rack has seven chops served in a wild-mushroom sauce. Veal, like other extremely lean meats such as rabbit and venison, needs something to compensate for its leanness. Many Italian veal dishes are finished with some kind of cheese. Here chefs Ignazio Battaglia and Enzo Amodeo finish their veal rack in heavy cream and wild mushrooms. The neutrality of the veal with its gentle, perfumed loveliness gives it the capacity to absorb the surrounding tastes. Served with wedges of baked and sautéed russet potatoes and some simple spinach probably sautéed briefly in garlic and olive oil, this ranks close to a perfect dish. Your party will fight over the spinach but likely shun the potatoes in favor of the risotto.

Have a lemon *sorbetto* for dessert. Made with Limoncello, a native of the Amalfi coast and a potent lemon liqueur, this is an Italian ice worthy of a long memory.

La Bella Cucina

$-$$

Location: 72-355 Highway 111 at Desert Crossing, Palm Desert, 836-3280. Food type: trattoria. Ambiance: nondescript storefront with sidewalk dining. Bar: beer and wine. Reservations: taken only for parties of six or more. Hours: lunch and dinner daily.

There is little indoor seating, and the patio has no climate control, but it does have a lovely view of the parking lot. La Bella Cucina does a substantial takeout business, especially for its deli platters. Traditional trattoria fare is found on the menu: fried zucchini, bruschetta, minestrone, panini, pizzas, pastas, and the usual chicken and shellfish. Quality ranges from fair to poor depending on what is ordered. Steamed mussels swim in a traditional but quite lovely white wine, garlic, and parsley bath. The bread is fresh and hot. The dipping oil is a light olive oil spiked with peppercorns, garlic, red serrano chilies, and fennel seeds. The fennel seeds do some fascinating things to the little condiment, but the mussels themselves are tiny and woefully lacking in flavor.

Cannelloni stuffed with assorted meats and topped with *besciamella* cream sauce are dreadful. I will walk you through this experience one step at a time. Before ordering this dish I asked the waiter to allow a space of a few minutes between courses. Not only did he not wait, the cannelloni arrived well before I had finished the mussels. The waiter returned it to the kitchen where it undoubtedly sat under hot lights for 20 minutes. When it came back, it was lukewarm. It was not stuffed with assorted meats, as the menu states. It was stuffed with mystery meat. It reminded me of what a friend who visited the Soviet Union during the 1980s said of the tour food: "What *is* this stuff?" It was a funny gray color and had the texture of finely shredded eggplant. It had no taste at all. Rather than being covered with *besciamella* sauce (the Italian version of the French béchamel), it was drenched in a very commercial-tasting tomato sauce, all tomato, with a metallic back note. That's it: an ordinary pasta stuffed with tasteless mystery meat and drenched in bottled tomato sauce.

Stay away from the pastas, shellfish, and chicken dishes. The pizzas and sandwiches are O.K. The deli plates are good. It is also inexpensive.

La Bella Vita
★★★
$$-$$$$
Location: 74-970 Country Club Dr., Palm Desert, 776-7500. *Food type:* alta cucina. *Ambiance:* trattoria. *Bar:* full, wine list small but adequate. *Reservations:* accepted. *Hours:* late lunch and dinner daily.

What we have here is something of an anomaly: a restaurant serving expensive, high-end food along the lines of La Spiga (Chapter 4) in a strip mall space along the lines of Chapelli's (this chapter). The strip mall in question is Desert Springs Marketplace, also home to Morton's (Chapter 9), Corktree (Chapter 7), and City Wok (Chapter 10). All four restaurants are worthy in varying degrees; all four are directly across the street from the Marriott Desert Springs (Chapter 1), which, although a spectacular resort, has five restaurants unworthy in almost every respect.

The space is a small but pleasant trattoria with burnished faux-textured gold paint and brick façades, dark wood, and cream-colored linens. Aromas wafting from the kitchen immediately spark the appetite. Amusing stills from Italian movies (I think) depicting various personages gluttonously enjoying huge mounds of pasta grace the walls. Background music ranges from *The Godfather* score to MUZAK-style arrangements of Verdi arias. The outside patio is somewhat masked from the parking lot, but a parking lot is still a parking lot even if it is more likely to house Jaguars than Fords.

If you are satisfied with an excellent pasta and a glass of adequate Chianti, you can dine here for little more than $25. If you want osso bucco, braised rabbit, or the veal chop with appetizer and desert and lean toward a bottle of decent Cabernet, you are looking at over a $100.

There is no bar per se, but La Bella Vita does possess a liquor license. Basic cocktails are available from your server. The wine list leans toward the California product, odd for a restaurant so unabashedly Italian, but Napa is more than sufficient to complement the menu.

An excellent crusty Italian bread is served with a double cruet of peppery, green, fruity Tuscan olive oil. Balsamic vinegar the consistency of light syrup accompanies. The opening is superb.

My experience with this restaurant is limited, having dined here but once. That one experience, however, included the *lombatina alla boscaiola*. At $38 this is the most expensive entrée. Think rib steak from a really, really young animal. The menu describes it thus (grammatical and spelling errors included): "the finest, and freshest veal chop available prepared with out special porcini and champigon mushroom sauce, an amazing feast of a meal once in a Lifetime!" I always wonder when someone uses the adjective "fresh" to modify meat, especially beef. Fresh fish is highly desirable, but beef at its most ideal is dry aged at the finest steakhouses for up to six weeks. Six weeks is hardly fresh. Veal and lamb, served very young, are generally not held in dry aging coolers for more than a week. A week is certainly not fresh, and week-old fish is good only for fertilizer. Regardless of whatever is meant by this menu writer, this is superb white milk-fed veal. It is a light gray tinged with pink and green. The meat is unbelievably tender and gently perfumed. It gives a whole different meaning to "rib steak."

The veal is smothered (literally) in a mushroom wine sauce. Unlike its older brother, the steer, the baby rib steak does not have the pronounced steak flavor beef lovers crave. I would be the first to agree that one should not smother a fine rib steak with a wine mushroom sauce, but this is different. Here the subtleties of the meat become one with the subtleties of the porcini mushroom to form a united whole greater than the sum of its parts.

The menu says "porcini and champigon mushrooms." I don't know what this means. I am sure the menu writer meant to write "champignon"; however, that word means mushroom in French. It is not a type of mushroom, but it is sometimes, incorrectly, used to refer to the basic cultivated white button mushroom. It is deceptive but certainly does not detract from the dish. Of course, if the veal were smothered with porcinis it would be better, but the cost would be $48 instead of $38.

An exquisite pappardelle pasta (a flat, wide noodle) accompanies the veal. I had to negotiate this. It was exchanged for asparagus. The $38 includes nothing else. The noodle was perfectly al dente. The sauce was probably *zingara* (Gypsy style). *Zingara* is a pretty loose recipe, but there is agreement on several fronts. It is white wine based and should have bits of meat (tongue, sausage, chicken, or ham in any order or quantity), tomatoes, shallots, veal stock, and truffles. Tarragon is a frequent herb. This potent sauce is most certainly in that family. I did not taste either tarragon or truffles although I would like to have. A generous sprinkling of Parmigiano-Reggiano, the real thing—potent, earthy, salty—is added to the pasta.

While extrapolating the overall quality of La Bella Vita from this limited sampling may be somewhat arrogant, the general quality is sufficiently high that certain assumptions can be accurately made. Any chef who is capable of doing these things this well is certainly not going to throw together everything else in a haphazard manner. This would mean that I hit upon the only two menu items worth eating. Not likely. On the other hand maybe La Bella Vita is worth more than three stars.

This is possible, but the prices for everything on the menu except the pastas is so high, it probably deserves the yellow light.

Here's the bottom line, especially if you are staying at the Marriott, and even more especially if you do not have a car. You have nine restaurants available to you within one block. La Bella Vita would be my first choice unless I had a major craving for a big American steak. If I were short of cash, I'd still pick Bella Vita and order a pasta: linguine rustica ($18), puttanesca ($16), or fettuccine *zingara* ($18).

La Donna Cucina Italiano

$-$$

Location: 72-624 El Paseo Dr., C-7, Palm Desert, 773-9441. Food type: trattoria. Ambiance: charming indoor and outdoor spaces, with mountain views and murals. Bar: beer and wine. Reservations: suggested. Hours: dinner Monday through Saturday.

La Donna Cucina is a delightful little trattoria with decent food and excellent prices. A few corners are cut. The *tortellini alla panna* is certainly not made with prosciutto di Parma and freshly shucked peas, but then if it were it would not cost $11.50. The pregrated Parmesan cheese, liberally available on every table, is not Parmigiano-Reggiano, but it's free.

Located in the Palms to Pines shopping center, as are Back Street Bistro (earlier in this chapter), Musashi (see Chapter 10), and Trattoria Tiramisu (later in this chapter), it may be a little difficult to find, but for diners on a tight budget in need of a healthy dose of no-frills Italian food, this is just about perfect. The patio, perched on a little hill and ringed by ever-blooming bougainvillea, has views of the Santa Rosa Mountains silhouetted against the setting sun.

An *amuse-bouche* consisting of two little toasts with chopped tomato, basil, and olive oil arrives tableside. These are delightful, crunchy, and redolent of fresh garlic and olive oil.

There are 26 pastas. The description of one will give you a good idea as to how things work at La Donna Cucina. *Tortellini alla panna* translates as "tortellini with cream." Tortellini is stuffed pasta. In a ristorante serving high Italian cuisine, the pasta would be made from scratch on the premises and stuffed with a processed mixture of pork loin, turkey breast, prosciutto, mortadella, egg yolk, grated nutmeg, butter, and Parmigiano-Reggiano. After the pasta is boiled, a sauce of butter, cream, more cheese, and grated white truffle would dress it. It would cost about $45. How is it done here? The tortellini is undoubtedly purchased commercially prestuffed. The stuffing has little flavor. The sauce is a simple *besciamella* with pieces of American ham and peas added. Pregrated Parmesan cheese is sprinkled liberally. It costs $11.50, not $45. It is also tasty and satisfying. What is there to complain about? For light eaters, a half order is plenty for just $5 and change.

Salsiccia con polenta (grilled sausage, polenta, and spinach) at $12.95 is one of the best entrées in this price range in the valley. The polenta, especially, is intriguing. It is quite firm, and I prefer polenta on the firm side although many aficionados of this Italian staple prefer it soft. This one is grilled after it is made, but there is a smoky aftertaste, the source of which I cannot identify. Several fresh, grilled sage leaves garnish the dish. Perhaps the smokiness can be traced to this. Dense sausage nicely flavored with anise, a thick full-bodied tomato sauce, and sautéed spinach complete the plate. It is large, balanced, full flavored, and very inexpensive. Is it great food? No, but so what? It is good food at a great price.

My personal choice for a restaurant of this kind would be Amici, about two miles west. The food at Amici (reviewed earlier in this chapter) is prepared with greater sensitivity and concern for the true Italian flavors and ingredients, but the environment there is less appealing.

Mama Gina

$$$-$$$$
*Location: 73-705 El Paseo Dr., Palm Desert, 568-9898. **Food type:** northern Italian, not quite alta cucina. **Ambiance:** big, open, comfortable, and attractive. **Bar:** full; extensive wine list, often with* Wine Spectator *ratings included. **Reservations:** suggested. **Hours:** lunch Monday through Saturday; dinner nightly.*

Mama Gina is a ristorante, bigger and more elegant than a trattoria, but not as grand as a palace. There are three Mama Ginas. The others are in Florence, Italy, and Newport Beach, California. The environment is attractive and comfortable, though not particularly elegant. There is no stuffiness as might be expected given its reputation and location on chic El Paseo. The décor includes dark reds, beige walls, cream and gold linens, and spotlights affixed to suspended wires. Aggressive abstract expressionist paintings adorn the walls.

Mama Gina's local reputation is strong and its patrons faithful. It has won awards and is featured in several travel guides. Unfortunately, it is simply not quite as good as the hype. Many things that come from this kitchen are superb while others are surprisingly inferior—and for easily correctable reasons. Take, for example, the *tegamino di cozze e vongole fresche* (mussels and clams). The mollusks swim in a delightful bath of white wine (Napa Ridge Chardonnay), olive oil, garlic, and a snappy pinch of red chili flakes. But the mussels themselves are small and tough. Why? This is just an issue of buying better mussels and not overcooking them. They do not have much taste at all, yet the difficult part, the sauce, is excellent.

Pastas range from the magnificent to the ill conceived. *Ravioli neri all'aragosta* (squid-ink ravioli stuffed with ricotta cheese and lobster meat) is in the magnificent column. Everything about it, from the tenderness of the pasta itself to the tomato-cream-lobster sauce to the potent ricotta-lobster filling, works together to deliver a trio of contrasting tastes and textures. On the flip side, the pasta alla puttanesca is a mess. It does not taste bad, it just does not taste like puttanesca. It tastes like spaghetti with marinara sauce—a good one to be sure, but still a marinara sauce. Puttanesca originated in the brothels of Naples (*puttana* means "whore" in Italian). The dish should be spicy, garlicky, and bursting with big, robust flavors. Capers, anchovies, black olives, oregano, basil, fresh tomatoes, and olive oil mingle with a generous portion of chili peppers, both fresh and dried, to produce one of the world's most aggressive pastas. Puttanesca is not for the faint of heart or palate. As most of the lore relates, the hot and spicy nature of the dish served at the sidewalk cafés outside the brothels served as a metaphor for the hot and spicy action within. The puttanesca at Mama Gina is not a call to hot and spicy action, metaphorical or otherwise. This one is bland, bland, bland. The chilies are missing entirely, the anchovies are merely hinted at, the capers are difficult to locate, and the olives are kalamata.

The *gnocchi al Gorgonzola* (potato dumplings with Gorgonzola-cheese sauce) are, on the contrary, quite punchy indeed. The Gorgonzola cheese is a mass of intensity, a result of the interaction of at least three different bacteria. The gnocchi itself is too bland to deal with the force of the sauce. Many gnocchi recipes call for the dumplings to be sautéed in both butter and olive oil after blanching. This would certainly help, but the problem here is the fact that this is an entrée. With this dish comprising the substance of your meal its single flavor will rapidly become tiresome. A half-portion is available as an appetizer. This is the way to go.

Pregrated Parmesan cheese is offered. It is the second-tier Grana Padano variety, not Parmigiano-Reggiano. Very good, but do not put it on the lobster ravioli; it masks the lobster taste.

Brodetto di pesce fresco is actually cioppino. As with the mussel/clam dish, the sauce is magnificent and the fish is problematic. With saffron, red wine, anchovies, garlic, Italian herbs including fennel, and potent fish stock in a traditional tomato base, the liquid alone is one of the best soups ever created. With the addition of seafood it becomes one of the world's great peasant stews (along with bouillabaisse and cassoulet). The liquid here is wonderful, but all the seafood is overcooked. There is no excuse for this. The stock can be made with the leftover shells of every clam, mussel, lobster, and crab that makes its way through the kitchen. That plus bottled clam juice and basic fish fumet is all that is needed to create the sauce. The seafood—whatever that might be—should go in briefly at the last minute. The shellfish used here are the same mussels and clams found in the appetizer, plus Lake Superior whitefish, calamari, and shrimp.

Anitra ai fichi neri e Rémy-Martin (half a roasted duck served with Mission figs and Rémy-Martin demi-glace sauce) is French, not Italian. There is certainly nothing wrong with serving a French dish in an Italian restaurant; French restaurants serve all manner of pasta dishes. I just find it rather amusing that it is listed so meticulously in Italian but the "Rémy-Martin" has to stay in French and "demi-glace" appears in the English translation. Whatever its cultural origins, the sauce is astonishing. It is original, absolutely compatible, enhances the duck's flavor, and introduces contrasting sugars and acids. Figs are cooked into the demi-glace base of veal- and duck-stock reductions. The intense meat flavors already present in the demi-glace are sweetened and heightened with the sensuous qualities of this ancient and exotic fruit. The addition of cognac is inspired. The sauce at this point is in desperate need of something very acidic to balance the sweetness. Vinegar could do the job, but why not try something daring? French sauces have been using reductions of brandy and Madeira for hundreds of years, but those require the alcohol to be burned off. This one retains small amounts of raw alcohol, thus providing a potent acid as well as the flavor of one of the world's finest cognacs. But why does something have to go wrong? The duck itself, skin crisped beautifully, is dried out. Perhaps it is cooked at too high a temperature. The duck is served with spinach—blanched, squeezed, and heavy with garlic—and mashed potatoes. While both garnishes are excellent in themselves, neither is particularly compatible with the duck. The bird has just too much taste. Something like bok choy, which is extremely bitter, and wild rice with its density and nuttiness would complement this duck much more satisfactorily.

The menu has filet mignon Rossini, a wonderful dish I have not seen on any other valley restaurant. It is a filet with foie gras and black truffles with Madeira reduction. A *bistecca alla Fiorentina* is also listed. This cannot be so, as that dish requires a Chianina steer, available only in Italy. It is quite possible they have it in the Florence restaurant, but not here. Osso buco, several veal dishes, and Tuscan-style baby lamb chops are also interesting options.

The Nest
★★
$$
Location: 75-188 Highway 111, Indian Wells, 346-2314. Food type: mostly Italian-American. Ambiance: French country inn; cozy, intimate, and friendly, but can get noisy. Bar: full; adequate wine list; piano bar and dancing. Reservations: taken only for parties of eight or more or for tourists through their concierges. Hours: lunch and dinner daily; early-bird specials.

The Nest is arguably the most successful piano bar in the valley. The unofficial dance floor is always crowded. It's rumored to be a pickup place for those of a certain age, but I cannot speak to the veracity of this. The Nest bills itself as a desert bistro. It isn't really a bistro in the sense that it serves bistro fare such as cassoulet and coquilles St. Jacques. For those dishes, visit Chez Pierre (see Chapter 5). The Nest, on the other hand, looks and feels like a French country inn, with its umbrellas, awnings, trellises, brick, and dark red lighting.

A crab cake appetizer comes with a side of tarter sauce. Tarter sauce, a relic of the 1950s, tastes exactly as it did in 1958. Mayonnaise and sweet pickle relish is hardly competitive in the current culinary world. Lamb loin is not commonly served. The loin chop is the lamb equivalent of the porterhouse steak. The boneless lamb loin is the equivalent of a New York steak cut away from the bone of a sirloin roast. It is not quite as tender as a rack, but it has more flavor and no waste. It should be cooked to no more than medium rare. It has less marbling (internal fat) than a New York steak and becomes tough with overcooking. Here it is served with mint jelly, another throwback to the 1950s.

This sirloin is served with one of the best potato dishes around, the potato soufflé, actually a cross between a soufflé and potatoes *à la dauphinoise*. The potatoes are sliced thinly and mixed with beaten egg yolks, garlic, and nutmeg. Egg whites whipped to stiff peaks are folded into the mixture, Parmesan cheese is liberally added, and the whole thing is baked to a golden brown. The meat is rich and tender; the potatoes, cheesy, sweet, and light. Something bitter is needed for contrast. It comes in the form of sautéed Swiss chard.

Soup and salad are served with every entrée. Again, an anachronism kicks in. A traditional but bland minestrone typical of Italian-American restaurants in 1975—beans, assorted vegetables, herbs—is served automatically. A salad based on iceberg lettuce, another anachronism, with chickpeas, shredded carrots, red cabbage, and black olives in a nice homemade Italian dressing is next.

Veal sweetbreads of excellent quality fail to find their identity. They are neither crispy nor do they arrive braised in a deeply layered Madeira sauce (or some other equally sympathetic accompaniment). They are generally uninteresting, but certainly not bad.

If you are looking for an active bar scene, a good dance floor, and a decent meal at a reasonable cost, the Nest will fill the bill.

The Red Tomato & House of Lamb
★½
$-$$
#
Location: 68-784 E. Palm Canyon Dr., Cathedral City, 328-7518. Food type: Italian and Albanian. Ambiance: fussy, very gay, and crowded but cute; misted patio right on the sidewalk with a view of the traffic. Bar: full. Reservations: suggested. Hours: dinner nightly; early-bird specials.

You can have your choice of lamb shank, spaghetti and meatballs, chicken Parmesan, eggplant Parmesan, or chicken and dumplings for $9.95 between 4 P.M. and 5:30 P.M. Sunday through Thursday. Or, you can take $2 off any of 25 reasonably priced entrées before 5:30 P.M. These early-bird specials include soup or salad, house-baked bread, panzanella, herb butter, and spumoni. Such a deal! Panzanella here is a condiment, a bread and tomato salad with onion, cucumber, and basil.

The restaurant is actually a trattoria and an Albanian restaurant specializing in lamb. The pasta dishes are robust and inexpensive. The lamb dishes are more unusual. There is a spicy lamb stew, *Shkodra* (roasted lamb), *Elbasan* (spicy lamb), and a plain rack. Nothing is excellent, but everything is quite edible. The place is very popular with the locals, so reservations should be made.

Trilussa Ristorante
★★
$$-$$$
Location: 68-718 E. Palm Canyon Dr., Cathedral City, 328-2300. Food type: trattoria with pizza. Ambiance: almost a palace, pleasant patio. Bar: full. Reservations: suggested. Hours: lunch and dinner daily, happy hour 4 P.M. to 6:30 P.M. Monday through Thursday.

Marble floors, granite tabletops, white linens, hanging copper pans, open pizza oven, high ceilings, Italian landscape murals, lovely patio, terrific location in the new Civic Center, mountain views, Mediterranean architecture—what's not to like? The food. Either the chefs or the owners are terrified of flavor. It is the polar opposite of Omri Go Med (see Chapter 5). Omri ramps up the flavor and tells you to go elsewhere if you want bland. Here you get bland and are forced to go elsewhere if you want flavor. There is certainly a place for bland; some people must like it or Trilussa would have faded away.

Take, for example, the *pasta e fagioli alla Toscana,* an Italian classic. The full-flavored Italian version consists of a tomato/meat-stock base heavily impregnated with caramelized garlic, pancetta, herbs (rosemary, thyme, bay leaf), and aromatic vegetables. Pasta, usually ditalini, and cannellini beans (the big ones) are added, and the whole thing is brought together with shavings of Parmigiano-Reggiano. Add a glass of Frascati and some crusty Italian bread, and lunch is ready. This is the dish that reflects the culinary traditions of the culture that created it. What does one get at Trilussa? A thin tomato-flavored liquid more reminiscent of water than the soup base described above. To this liquid are added elbow pasta and Great Northern white beans (the little ones). There is something else that looks like either cabbage or leeks, but since it has no taste, it is impossible to tell. There is some grated (not shaved) cheese (certainly not Parmigiano-Reggiano).

How about the pescatora? Turn to the review of Omri Go Med in Chapter 5 and read the review of Chef Siklai's pescatore. (Note the spelling difference.) On his menu it is listed as follows: "pescatore [mussels+shrimp+clams+ calamari+fish over linguine+spicy pomodoro]." On Trilussa's menu the dish shows up as "mixed seafood, tomato sauce, olive oil and garlic." If you have tasted Omri's dish this one will frustrate you beyond belief. If you have not had that astonishing culinary pleasure, this one will simply bore you. Not only does it have little flavor, but the seafood is overcooked. Mussels and shrimp are tough. Calamari is rubbery.

The entire menu is tried and true Italian-American fare. All the usual antipasti, pasta dishes, chicken, and veal dishes make a dutiful appearance here. Three American-style steaks are offered with Italian names, of course. The one true Italian steak—*bistecca alla Fiorentino*—is not.

Anecdotal information indicates that many Americans prefer their Italian food on the bland side. Trilussa's pizzas are described as subtle. These people do not complain about the "spiciness" or how "garlicky" everything is. For these people add a half star; for others take off a star.

Trattoria Tiramisu
Not rated
$$
Location: 72-655 Highway 111, Suite B-6, in the Palms to Pines Shopping Center, Palm Desert, 773-9100. Food type: more of a ristorante than trattoria. Ambiance: formal and a little sterile. Bar: beer and wine. Reservations: suggested. Hours: dinner nightly.

I have not eaten here, but I have seen the restaurant and studied the menu. It calls itself a trattoria but the menu is more in line with a ristorante, such as Bellini and Castelli's (both reviewed earlier in this chapter) or even La Spiga (Chapter 4), than it is with Amici (this chapter). At first glance—perhaps unfair—it appears formal and a little sterile with its marble floors and pristine white linens.

Several menu items seem to venture away from the safe. A mixed green salad with beets, blue cheese, and walnuts is one of them, as is Mediterranean clam soup. Pappardelle with duck ragù is another. A New York steak sliced and served with Parmesan and arugula is the most expensive thing on the menu at $26.

CHAPTER 7

California Fusion

In addition to *haute cuisine* (French for high cooking) and *alta cucina* (Italian for high cooking), California Fusion has joined cooking's top tier, at least in California. California cooking is closely related to both French nouvelle and Tuscan styles. That is to say, there is an emphasis on quality ingredients, freshness, and simplicity. Ingredients should be allowed to speak for themselves. This goes back about a generation to the 1980s. California Fusion is the latest remake, wherein ingredients, especially herbs and spices, are borrowed from other cultures and merged with California cuisine. French and/or Italian techniques are the standard for California Fusion. Here in the desert, the most popular cuisine to rip off is Japanese. This, of course, has its roots in that short-lived French-Japanese fusion from a generation ago known as "Japonaise." Another popular cuisine routinely fused with California cooking is Southwest, which mixes Mexican and Tex-Mex ingredients with the California style. If a certain culture dominates the fusion menu, I have listed it as part of the food type designation. Many of the finest restaurants in the Coachella Valley are preparing California Fusion.

Augusta
★★½
$$$-$$$$
Location: at Plaza Robergé, 73-951 El Paseo Dr., Palm Desert, 779-9200. Food type: California Fusion. Ambiance: spectacular but nonsensical; noisy nightclub on weekends. Bar: full. Reservations: suggested. Hours: lunch and dinner Monday through Saturday.

Picture this: a slick Polynesian tiki room with a roof of palm fronds and leopard patterns throughout, a large, elegant, multilevel art gallery with a staircase straight out of *Gone With the Wind,* and a harpist playing everything from Vivaldi to "Jailhouse Rock." Plus, it is a ladies-who-lunch venue. Odd but inviting; absurd but attractive.

On weekends, Augusta is transformed into a nightclub. It is loud, crowded, and expensive. The Internet scuttlebutt is if you want to dine, avoid this place at all costs. But let us consider Augusta as a restaurant irrespective of Friday and Saturday nights. Augusta shows a lot of ambition, but it fails on almost all counts. First, it is overpriced. Most entrées are in the low $30s, which, according to my legend, earns it three dollar signs, but this is only part of the story. Appetizers, soups, salads, drinks, and wine are all higher than the average cost for a comparable product, running the total dinner tab easily into the bring-your-banker category.

Mushroom soup with veal sweetbreads is puréed. This is odd in itself, as it deprives the diner of contrasting textures as well as flavor concentrations. It tastes good, however, and with a splash of truffle oil it is very good. The sweetbreads are peculiar. Three little pieces sautéed until crispy, they are virtually tasteless.

A penne pasta Alfredo with shrimp is not good. A great Alfredo is nothing more than Parmigiano-Reggiano, cream, and butter. Additions of parsley, garlic, ricotta, olive oil, basil, thyme, or scallions have at one time or another found their way into the mix, but the essential nature of Alfredo is dairy: cream, butter, and cheese. This one is thin (skim milk?) and not very cheesy. There is some Parmesan cheese, but it is certainly not Parmigiano-Reggiano and there is not much of it. The shrimp are large and full flavored, but they are overcooked. The menu says spicy Alfredo sauce. Spicy? Not on my plate.

Medallions of beef with portobello mushrooms in a peppercorn sauce earn mixed reviews. The meat tastes almost assuredly of a papain-based tenderizer. Papain is a proteolytic enzyme obtained from tropical fruits, especially papaya. When it is used to tenderize meat, the cellular structure is broken down and the meat becomes unpleasantly mushy, as this meat is. The vegetables and peppercorn sauce are both good, solidly traditional in the French manner.

The menu is strictly safe. Nothing at all risk-taking or even the least bit out of the ordinary. Pastas, the ever present ahi with ginger and wasabi, salmon, bass, chicken, rack of lamb, a couple of steaks, and duck. It is a mirror of 50 other restaurants, but here you are paying a lot for location and environment.

Bellatrix
Not rated
$$-$$$
Location: *75-200 Classic Club Blvd., Palm Desert, 601-3690.* **Food type:**

California Fusion (Japanese, Thai, Mediterranean, and Southwest). **Ambiance:** *beautiful room overlooking the golf course.* **Bar:** *full.* **Reservations:** *suggested.* **Hours:** *lunch Monday through Sunday, dinner Tuesday through Saturday.* **Chef:** *Greg Monette.*

Bellatrix, named for a star in the Orion constellation, opened in December 2009 during the final edit of this book. There is, consequently, no comprehensive review, but local respected food writer, Henry Fenwick, described the menu for the local newspaper as follows:

"The different Asian influences are most present on his [Monette's] list of starters, which include Ahi poki, with a pickled ginger cucumber salad, a flash-seared Hamachi carpaccio, and barbecue Korean short ribs with a fresh cucumber salad. The Mediterranean influences are strongest on the entrée menu, in a Parmesan-crusted lamb shank with gnocchi and Tuscan tomato Kalamata olive ragout, and a flavorful grilled hanger steak with spiced lemon hummus, three-olive tapenade, a Vidalia onion marmalade and marinated feta, served with grilled pita.

"Steaks are definitely a big seller. He offers a selection of sauces with the steaks and he'd find it hard to say which is the most popular—the roasted red pepper chimichurri, the gorgonzola butter, the cabernet wine jus or the crab Oscar."

This is a very conservative corporate environment, well off the beaten path of the desert resorts. These elements worked against the culinary genius of Jimmy Schmidt, who closed his four-star restaurant Rattlesnake at this venue and moved to the more sophisticated environs of the La Quinta Resort and Club (see Morgan's in the Desert, Chapter 1). Monette's menu and résumé would seem to argue for something special here, but time will tell.

Cork Tree

$$$

Location: *74-950 Country Club Dr., Palm Desert, 779-0123.* **Food type:** *California.* **Ambiance:** *almost a palace; dark, dark wood, private, walled patio.* **Bar:** *full; good wine list, almost all California varietals.* **Reservations:** *suggested.* **Hours:** *dinner nightly.* **Chef:** *Herve Glin.*

First impressions here are ones of surprise. The first surprise is that this restaurant is part of a shopping center, Desert Springs Marketplace, which is divided in two parts with parking in between. The southern portion features four restaurants: the stand-alone Morton's steakhouse (Chapter 9) and the almost-stand-alone Cork Tree, La Bella Vita (Chapter 6), and City Wok (Chapter 10). Upon entering one is caught by the size and luxurious appointments. This too is unexpected, especially in a shopping center restaurant. It is much larger than it appears from the outside. With its high-gloss hardwood floors and bar, dark wood planks set on their side to form the ceiling, many banquettes along the sides, and soft imbedded lighting, one is startled once again. Capacity is probably about a 100 with another 50 on the patio.

The heated and misted patio is walled off from the street and isolated still again with large terra-cotta pots filled with citrus trees and bougainvillea. Everything is very Barcelona, even the street noise. The proprietors, unfortunately, could not eliminate that. The patio actually sits right on the northwest corner of Country Club and Cook, a busy intersection.

A casual diner once described the food at Cork Tree as "gimmicky," an appellation I have to go along with, at least in part. The chef is Herve Glin, a French transplant trained as a baker in Brittany. His résumé includes stints in Napa, Houston, and Prime 10 steakhouse in Rancho Mirage. (Note: Prime 10 was the name of the steakhouse restaurant at the Agua Caliente Casino [Chapter 3] before it was changed simply to "The Steakhouse.") Our casual diner cited such things as little containers with various sides and sauces and oddly shaped plates, but I find the problem deeper than that. Take, for example, the salad/appetizer "Duck Leg Confit with Boston Wedge, Candied Walnuts, Fuji Apple, Raspberry-Sherry Dressing." Taken as a whole the "salad" is not bad. It has the soft, earthy proteins of duck meat, the crunchy, acidic tang of apple, the sweetness of candied walnuts, and the refreshing body and slight bitterness of butter lettuce all brought together with a lovely vinaigrette redolent of raspberries. What's not to like? There is an arbitrary quality, almost a cavalier "novelty for novelty's sake" character at work. There are also problems with definition and presentation.

The dish is advertised as duck leg confit, but it is listed on the menu under soups and salads. Obviously not a soup, it has to be classified as a salad, but duck confit is not a salad. A duck leg confit is a duck leg that has been cooked and finally preserved in its own rendered fat. When served it is removed from the fat and broiled until crisp. Duck legs done in this manner are terrific, especially when accompanied with something like caramelized onions or bitter greens. (The late and lamented Hedi's Hide-A-Way did a confit in this manner that I can still taste eight years after the fact!) This is not really a duck leg confit. In fact, it is not a duck leg at all, but a few pieces of duck meat of indeterminate provenance. Is it a confit? I don't know. The body of the dish is a wedge of Boston, or butter, lettuce. This is a good lettuce with soft leaves and a fine, subtle flavor. Restaurants tend to avoid it in favor of romaine or even iceberg because the leaves bruise so easily. The duck is only a minor component but the dish is advertised as a duck leg confit primarily. The apple and candied walnuts complement everything nicely and together form the basis of a fine salad. Fresh raspberries, which do not show up on the menu description, offer a second fruit flavor too intense for the whole. Everything dies in their wake except the walnuts, but now we are looking at a dessert rather than a salad.

Finally, we come to the dressing, billed as a raspberry-sherry dressing. The stuff does not look appetizing. In fact, that presentation is so poor it does considerable damage to the dish. The dressing is thick and opaque, resembling something like creamed-beet baby food applied in sporadic clumps about the lettuce. It is the texture, the color (a lavender on the red side), and the opaque quality that conspire to turn off the diner. Were it thinner and transparent the whole dish would improve. Gimmicky? Perhaps.

Pork shank fares better although here, too, arbitrariness seems to be in play. Few restaurants prepare pork shank. It is larger, obviously, than the more popular lamb shank, with a thick layer of fat between skin and meat. BluEmber (Chapter 1) does a nice one with a puttanesca sauce, which is a little jarring at first but is finally successful. This one is less radical. Presentation is beautiful, with the shank placed vertically in a deep red/orange bath. This rust color is echoed nicely with a handful of baby carrots. Asparagus and watercress present the complementary color, and a tureen of mashed potatoes with a pale yellow tint complete the ensemble. The braising liquid/sauce is merlot based, sweetish, and caramelized. It is nicely degreased and offers a perfect complement to the sweet/fatty meat. The shank itself is beautiful to look at, having been tinted a deep burnt sienna by the sauce. However, the thick layer of fat remains. This should have been seared prior to the braising. The meat, nevertheless, is excellent. Both carrots and asparagus, while contributing visually, do little for the final flavor profile. Neither vegetable is finished in any way, the simple steamed asparagus especially presenting awkwardly with the pork.

Whipped potatoes are delightful. This is the kind of texture one always hopes for in a mashed potato. They are light as though cut with meringue. The pale yellow tint is not identifiable, perhaps a pinch of turmeric, its contribution being primarily visual.

Some of the more interesting menu options from the small plate side include mini duck confit tacos; a salmon tower with avocado, apple, mango, tomato, and tarragon-citron vinaigrette; and porcini ravioli with truffle oil. With the exception of the pork shank, entrées are less interesting, featuring the usual fish (salmon, sea bass), steaks (filet, flat iron), chops (veal, pork), and chicken breast.

Cork Tree is a good restaurant. It is a shame that it is not just a bit better. It is moderate to expensive with the veal chop coming in at $43 as the most expensive thing on the menu. There is a major plus for this restaurant that will be of great interest to a certain category of visitor to the area: it is convenient for tourists staying across the street at the Marriott Desert Springs. A delightful walk through the grounds of that resort, across the street (Country Club Drive), and down to the end of the block (going east) is Cork Tree. The food is vastly superior to anything available at the resort and considerably less expensive than Ristorante Tuscany (Chapter 1), the premier restaurant of Desert Springs. On the other hand, La Bella Vita (Chapter 6) is about 100 feet away.

Copley's
★★★½
$$$

Location: 621 N. Palm Canyon Dr., Palm Springs, 327-9555. Food type: California Fusion. Ambiance: postmodern; fun and comfortable. Bar: full; extensive and comprehensive wine list. Reservations: mandatory during season. Hours: dinner nightly; Sunday brunch, bar menu, happy hour (blue plate special—$15). Chef-owner: Andrew Copley.

Cary Grant once owned this property. It was not his house—that was in the much more upscale "movie colony" a few blocks west—it was his guest compound, a series of small bungalows built around a large courtyard with a pool. Built in 1947 and sharing the look and feel of that era with its low ceilings and small scale, the restaurant today presents a somewhat schizophrenic face. A few years ago the property was a Persian restaurant. When that failed, British chef Andrew Manion Copley bought the somewhat run-down complex and converted it into a hugely successful, high-quality restaurant. The property itself is very large, with a parking lot in the front then a couple of odd metal sheds followed by the courtyard. The pool is gone, replaced by an imposing fountain. An attractive climate-controlled outdoor patio is on the right; a vegetable and herb garden is on the left. The restaurant sits at the back of the property: four bungalows all in a row, their partitions removed and divided by a series of archways. Copley has made the most of this peculiar arrangement, not by fighting it but by accentuating its intrinsic quirkiness. The interior has been given the full postmodern treatment. The bar, in the central area is "pebble tech." For those not familiar with current desert swimming-pool design, pebble tech is little rocks, thousands of them. The walls are alternately done with a deep gray grass cloth, maroon paint, and dark gray-green paint. The entire east wall is comprised of windows and glass doors so the restaurant is bright and airy in spite of the dark paint. Floors are the original hardwood. Ceilings are low. Artwork is photorealistic desert flora. All in all, the impression is lively, fun, and somewhat joyous. It is not romantic or intimate.

Copley was educated at Westminster Culinary College in London and has 20 years of credits under his belt at such auspicious venues as the Ritz-Carlton in San Francisco and Maui, the *Queen Elizabeth II,* the Savoy in London, and the Grand Hyatt in Australia.

In culinary terms, Copley's does battle directly with Johannes (reviewed later in this chapter). The food styles are the same, the quality is extremely high, prices are comparable, and even the quirky environments have something in common. Both serve highly creative recipes drawing extensively on Asian, especially Japanese, cuisine. Copley is influenced more by Southwestern and Mexican traditions than is Johannes Bacher, but you can never second guess Bacher. Neither restaurant is perfect, but both deliver very high quality.

Virtually every upscale restaurant in the entire Coachella Valley has some version of a tuna tartare and basic desert salad (nuts, cheese, fruit), and Copley's is no exception. His versions are tweaked a little harder and emerge at the top of the pyramid, but they still follow the set rules. Hawaiian ahi tacos are what he calls his tuna tartare. Copley makes a sweet "taco" shell using sesame seeds (white and black), corn syrup, flour, and miso, a salty fermented bean curd that is a common ingredient in Japanese cooking. Into this taco, he puts chunks of ahi tuna tossed with scallions in a ginger-soy dressing. The shell is crispy and sweet; the ginger and onions, acidic and tangy; the tuna, soft and rich. Everything is different, and everything is complementary. Mainly for presentation purposes the tacos are set upright in a little bed of avocado. Tobiko caviar reinforces the intensity of the fish, and wasabi-treated Tobiko caviar here provides another biting tangent. I find this somewhat problematic. The tacos do not need another flavor strand, as the ginger provides all the bite necessary, and the wasabi treatment eliminates the fish burst of the Tobiko. It looks pretty all in green, but why not double the quantity of the straight Tobiko or, better still, use half the quantity of salmon caviar?

Roasted beet salad is Copley's play on the basic desert salad. It has no lettuce; cold roasted beets replace that venerable salad foundation. The cheese is goat cheese, but this goat cheese is formed into a small cake that is deep-fried. The cheese is served hot in an otherwise room temperature salad, providing still another contrast for the palate. The fruit is a poached pear. It is the nature of the poaching liquid that transforms the pear into the object lying beside these roasted beets. These are poached in wine, ginger, fennel, allspice, and cinnamon. But for the diner, it tastes for all the world like some kind of wassail, that strange, hot Christmas punch from England or Scandinavia made with apple cider, cinnamon, nutmeg, cardamom, cloves, and citrus juice. The pear itself slides into oblivion, but the resulting object is quite interesting and thoroughly compatible with the beets, and while the fruit is no longer fresh, the same acidity is present. Drizzled with honey-mustard and basic balsamic vinaigrette, this salad is unique, surprising, and quite delicious.

Copley's version of the Mexican dish ceviche is at once a huge improvement on the Mexican recipe and a disappointment. This ceviche is tender and is not overwhelmed with lime juice, the problems with Mexican ceviche. First, Copley "cooks" his fish in a combination of citrus juices, predominantly orange juice, which is not so acidic as the traditional lemon or lime. He uses rock shrimp and four different kinds of fish: bass, halibut, salmon, and tuna. Cilantro, onion, and cucumber are introduced to the marinade at the end of the cycle. So far so good, but with the addition of a tomato sauce the fish flavors are lost. All five of them are absorbed into the tomato. There is no point in using five different fish flavors if they do not speak independently.

Entrées at Copley's cover all the trendy bases, but each with a creative twist. Lamb chops, for example, come with sweet potatoes treated with coconut and a mango relish. Salmon is garnished with saffron-truffle butter. A huge char-grilled pork chop is accompanied by a three-cheese polenta cake, spaghetti squash, and meat juices impregnated with cloves, honey, and sage. I would certainly not hesitate to sample the lobster pot pie and 10-ounce Prime New York steak with wild mushrooms, blue cheese, and shallot-Cabernet reduction.

Copley does not have a tandoor, an Indian clay oven, but he does serve a tandoori breast of chicken. This dish is a disappointment. Copley succeeds in taking a piece of meat, which is inherently dry, and cooking it so well that it is less dry than anyone else's, but the traditional tandoori flavors are muted. Meats to be cooked tandoori style must be marinated in plain yogurt, which tenderizes them. Ground annatto seeds, saffron, or turmeric turn the surfaces a bright red. Tandoori-style meats are also traditionally flavored with ginger, garlic, coriander powder, cayenne pepper, and garam masala, a combination of roasted and ground cardamom, cumin, cinnamon, cloves, nutmeg, and black pepper. Of course, there is no rule that states that Copley's tandoori breast of chicken must be the traditional Indian recipe, but if you are going to call a dish "tandoori," you should adhere at least to a certain extent to the tandoori concept. Since he does not cook in a tandoor, at least the complexity of the original Indian recipe should be maintained. While this dish certainly looks like a tandoori chicken, the only spice that emanates strongly from the plate is cumin. Copley stuffs the breast with mango and shrimp. The mango, with its fresh fruit flavors, clashes rather than complements the curry flavors. A pineapple salsa adds the same sort of disconcerting dissonance.

On the flip side, the halibut is superb. This is Alaskan halibut pan-roasted until just cooked. Halibut dries out easily with little margin for error; this one is perfect. Garnished with potatoes mashed with fresh corn kernels and sour cream, this fish quickly sets the tone for something special. The sauce is genuinely interesting and absolutely suited to the mild fish. Once again reaching toward the Orient, Chef Copley combines Chinese chili paste, that fiery mixture of garlic, red chilies, sugar, soy, and ginger. The interesting thing here is the heat. Even local Indian, Chinese, and Mexican restaurants are afraid to put any substantial heat into their dishes, but Copley does what is necessary. It is not blisteringly hot, but it is not timid either. With the addition of a couple "firecracker" shrimp and organic green and yellow string beans (finished in butter) the dish is complete. The shrimp are bursting with flavor; the potatoes are rich and full flavored; and the pungent, spicy sauce brings it all together.

Desserts are not particularly original, but the wine selections include just about everything your heart could desire, from an inexpensive South African Pinot Noir clone for $29 to a magnificent 2002 Merryvale Profile Cabernet at $210. As a nice touch, wine and entrée parings are suggested on the wine list itself, and you are not directed to the more expensive bottles. The $29 bottle mentioned above is suggested with the pork chop.

Firecliff
★★★½
$$$
Location: 73-725 El Paseo Dr., Palm Desert, 773-6565. Food type: California Fusion (American Southwest, Chinese, and Japanese). Ambiance: formal, high tech, and elegant. Bar: full; moderately priced comprehensive wine list. Reservations: suggested. Dress code: yes, but only sporadically enforced. Hours: dinner nightly. Chef-owner: Patricia Hook.

Patricia Hook has been in the valley for years. Her history verges on the ironic: French cooking school, retail gourmet shop, Cuisinart sales representative, national training coordinator for Cuisinart. In this last position, she always managed to wind up in Palm Springs on a Friday. Now why do you suppose that might be? Her past includes a stint as chef in the early 1990s at Biga in the Atrium in Rancho Mirage. She left to become general manager of the La Quinta Grill in 1997. The chef at La Quinta Grill was replaced by the general manager (I wonder how that happened?), and she became one of three partners in the complex. By a two-thirds vote, Patricia Hook dissenting, the Grill was converted into an office complex. In 2006, she opened Firecliff, the most important new restaurant of the year and a significant addition to the desert's dining scene.

Firecliff is quite beautiful, if a little too formal for my taste. Done mostly in a muted gray-green with many unframed abstract expressionist paintings on the walls, New York supper-club music (think Bobby Short without the vocals), and open beamed ceilings with exposed air ducts, Firecliff exudes an upper-class elegance. Officially there is a dress code— no shorts, tank tops, or flip-flops—but, as with most attempts at dress codes in the desert, things tend to dissolve as the temperature rises. The no-shorts policy engendered a firestorm of protest on the Internet.

But forget about all that stuff. What of the food? Superb! The menu is small, but small is good. It means more control and consistency from the kitchen. If a menu has 75 different entrées, walk out. The food is California Fusion in its full and accurate meaning. California cuisine is refined, simple, clean, and relatively small portioned. It is related to Tuscan cuisine and French nouvelle. California cuisine, of its nature, amalgamates ingredients and cooking techniques from the American Southwest and east Asia. Hook does this very well, as do a number of local chefs.

Carrot soup, a purée with layer upon layer of deeply rich carrot flavor, is structured with a carrot stock that includes the stems. Subtle hints of curry power seem to dance just above the surface. The Indian spices, cumin and turmeric, don't really seem to be in the soup, but rather in the air above it. A small crouton impregnated with cinnamon garnishes the dish. The cinnamon works, but the absence of any acidic component seems slightly odd although certainly not destructive.

A unique salad of roasted beets—red and gold—with goat cheese marries the meaty sweetness of beets and the creamy, earthy tanginess of cheese with the bitterness of greens and the astringency of orange vinaigrette. Hook uses a dried and hardened goat cheese. This not only intensifies the flavor but also eliminates most of the moisture that would taint the vinaigrette. When only the beets and the cheese are combined, the beet flavor dominates. When the salad is tasted without the beets there is a certain level of perfection, but on a simplistic level. Put another way, the salad without the beets is perfect, but considerably less interesting than with the beets. This is one of the more fascinating taste combinations around.

Shrimp and scallop chinoise is an example of the chef's remarkable abilities, fusing Chinese flavors with California cuisine. It goes without saying that the jumbo shrimp and sea scallops are cooked perfectly, in other words, until just barely done. In a marinade of ginger, soy, lime, and sesame oil, they retain hints of these potent flavoring agents. They are served on a bed of spinach, snow peas, and bean sprouts, with bits of raw red bell pepper and red cabbage. Conceivably this could be served at an upscale Chinese restaurant, but it is the rice pilaf that defines the dish as Californian. Shunning the usual bland Chinese sticky rice, a condiment used strictly as a foil for the spicy flavors of the stir-fry, Hook opts for basmati rice, creating the light and flavorful pilaf associated with Indian and Middle Eastern fare. This brings an entirely different thrust to the party, a counterpoint of texture and flavor not associated with Chinese food.

Rack of lamb—four large chops cut from Colorado lamb—is spectacular. American lamb is larger, fatter, and more flavorful that that of either Australia or New Zealand. American lamb is also substantially more expensive. At a hefty $38 for four chops, this is one of the more expensive racks in town. This and the New York strip are the only entrées over $29.

As readers of this book are probably aware, virtually every chef in the valley serves rack of lamb, and almost all of them who dress it in any way damage the flavor in one way or another. Chef Hook glazes her rack. Lightly dusted with curry power and a tangerine reduction, this lamb springs to life on the taste buds. The gently acidic tangerine cuts through the rich lamb like a *salsa fresca* on chorizo. As with the carrot soup, the merest hints of curry spices seem to float in the air—like the experience of running past the open door of an Indian restaurant. Mashed potatoes infused with lemon grass are an inspiration. Restaurants all over the valley do mashed potatoes with combinations of garlic, cheese, or rosemary. Often those concoctions are good, but these are a revelation. Lemon grass is not exactly lemony although there is certainly a family resemblance. It is more reminiscent of lemon zest than lemon juice. It is startling how well these potatoes harmonize with the lamb. Hook plays the innate richness of the meat off the opposite flavors of the citrus. With the bitterness of Broccolini as a second side, all the flavors are introduced while the dish remains a simple perfection.

The very popular signature dish, lobster tortilla, is almost as good as the other two entrées but falls victim to the "I gotta add just one more thing to make it perfect" syndrome. Chunks of superb lobster meat are mixed into a buerre blanc with white corn, tomatoes, black beans, and cilantro. This is served with sliced avocado and a simple diced tomato salsa. All of it is served stuffed into a grilled flour tortilla. I think I got lost somewhere in the corn or beans. Lobster is too delicate to handle all of this without damage to its subtle flavors. The tortilla was, at least on one occasion, grilled a little too hot or too long, as a slight burned taste came into play. A little sprig of fresh dill worked surprisingly well with the already overburdened counterpoint. I think what is most interesting with this dish is the buerre blanc. Butter, of course, is the time-tested lobster condiment. The Southwest flavors marry well with the buerre blanc, as does the lobster, but all together it is over the top.

Hoisin-ginger monkfish, seafood linguine, cedar-planked salmon, sea bass, tea-smoked duck breast, and grilled pork tenderloin round out the menu along with a couple interesting steak preparations. The inevitable chicken breast makes a mandatory appearance. This one is done with an Asian pear and Boursin cheese. If you must have chicken breast, this is one of the better ones in town.

The wine list is quite comprehensive except for the lack of late-harvest or ice wines, and most bottles are in the $30 to $50 range. In addition, Hook publishes a $15 corkage fee, which indicates that she is quite willing to accommodate the practice.

Frankie's Fresh Fish
★★-★★★½
$-$$$
Location: 81-944 Highway 111, Suite A, Indio, 342-2228. **Food type:** *Japonaise (French-Japanese fusion).* **Ambiance:** *surely you jest.* **Bar:** *beer and a couple of wines.* **Reservations:** *required for the* omakase *dinner.* **Hours:** *breakfast Monday through Saturday, lunch and dinner daily.* **Chef-owner:** *Frankie Nakasone.*

Tucked away in a nondescript, even run-down Indio strip mall is probably the greatest dining anomaly in the desert. Frankie's runs the gamut from fast food to fine dining. It is sparse even for a coffee shop, with linoleum on the floor and plastic tables. Frankie's does have plates—real ones—but that is the extent of the luxuries. And it does have a wine list. Rothbury (Australian) Chardonnay ($13) is drinkable when cold, but I wouldn't go near the Cab and Merlot. Nakasone has recently added a bottle or two of better whites but his tiny inventory is always changing. That and a few decent beers are the extent of the liquid libations. The wine is poured into water glasses, but the bottle does have a cork, and an ice bucket, albeit a tiny one, is provided. Frankie's corkage charge is only $8; this is the way to go for oenophiles (a.k.a. grape nuts). Purists might want to bring their own glasses too.

You must learn the word *omakase* if you want to experience the true glory of this loopy little place. Learn it and do not forget it. It means "in the hands of the chef." You must make a reservation with Nakasone himself to enjoy this dinner. If he is not there, call back. He is almost always there for dinner but usually only once a week—generally Thursdays—for lunch. If you make a reservation for lunch, Nakasone will probably come just for you. Ask for the $30 *omakase* dinner and your job from that point on is simply to eat. This is a four-star feast of creations worthy of any of the top chefs in the valley.

The juxtaposition of Nakasone's food with this site is so ludicrous as to be funny. His high-end, extremely creative, brilliantly prepared seafood defies all your expectations when served in this funky little storefront. The cuisine is not Japanese food. It is another example of that popular California Fusion cuisine, which usually merges diverse international ingredients with French cooking techniques. Chef Nakasone does it in reverse. He uses Italian and French ingredients in Japanese cooking. The most astonishing case in point is black hijiki seaweed, soft squares of tofu, and pieces of Gorgonzola in sweet rice-wine vinaigrette. It sounds off the wall, but it is fantastic. The pungent Italian blue cheese in the context of these otherwise Japanese tastes is not only astonishing in conception but also amazing in its results.

Have you ever eaten representational food—food designed and presented in such a manner as to represent something else or possibly even that very same food in its original state? This unusual and time-consuming stunt, requiring great skill, seems to characterize a few classical French dishes and some Japanese dishes. Have you ever had oysters on the half shell served on a rock? The rock is made from meringue and salt. When baked it hardens and turns a yellowish brown. It looks like a rock found on the beach. A big oyster shell is placed on the top, and two large, succulent sautéed oysters are nestled therein, swimming in a ponzu sauce.

Well, not exactly a ponzu sauce. The one at Frankie's has garlic, sake, butter, lemon, and soy. Don't eat the rock; it's edible but tastes of nothing but salt. It's just for looks.

What about tuna Poki? Ever have that? It is a Hawaiian tuna appetizer usually served as a "cocktail." Frankie does it in a big "shell" made of something like a wonton skin. Combine chunks of tuna sashimi, ogo (a very expensive type of seaweed that grows like confetti), chives, red onion, chili flakes, sesame oil, and soy and you have a tuna tartare that would sell for $18 all around town. At Frankie's it is $8.50. You have to ask for this last touch, but Nakasone sprinkles the plate with this pink powdery stuff. It looks and tastes for all the world like crushed cotton candy with a fish back taste. It is actually made from roasting cod until it is so dry it can be crushed into a powder. It is then sweetened and artificially colored.

Oddly a pseudo gazpacho cocktail in a thin tomato-based vegetable juice with avocado, cucumber, shrimp, and calamari is rather flavorless. Pass on this one.

Eight pieces of sashimi for $13! Surely you jest? Bluefin, yellowtail, albacore, salmon, and two bay scallops with wasabi, soy, and that peculiar shiso leaf are on this platter. The bluefin and yellowtail are glorious—thick and buttery rich. Taste the leaf; it is most odd, with notes of basil, mint, lemon, and pepper. Pickled ginger and finely shredded jicama provide opposing flavors and palette-cleansing neutrality, respectively.

A salmon filet comes with a sauce of minced tomato, zucchini, onion, shiitake mushrooms, shredded carrot, and dill in a cream base. You might think that all those diverse and powerful flavors would interfere with the salmon, but they do not. The dill is not quite on the mark, but the shiitake cream sauce works well to enhance and complement the salmon flavor.

A small plate with two pieces of sole and a larger chunk of sea bass, seared with a spicy-hot blackened Cajun sauce, arrives. The vicious blast of Cajun heat juxtaposed with the comparative gentleness of the sole is magical. A unique coleslaw and plain sticky rice accompany. You have to admire the sheer guts of anyone who would serve the lowly cabbage with this level of sophistication. Nakasone has no fear. He welcomes danger. This slaw is not sweet. It contains carrots, zucchini, and bean sprouts and no mayonnaise. I suspect the cabbage may be very briefly sautéed.

Lunch at Frankie's is hugely popular. He serves a bento box—eight different ones—for $4.95. In Japan, a bento box is akin to the American brown bag or even picnic basket. Nakasone's box is actually a plate and consists of an entire balanced meal: a fish, shrimp, or chicken entrée, rice, egg roll, and small salad.

Shumai is something a little more unusual. Nakasone processes raw chicken and shrimp with scallions, ginger, garlic, and soy. He adds a few pieces of whole shrimp for texture and undiluted flavor and places a spoonful of this mixture into a wonton skin ravioli style. This little packet is then steamed. A unique sauce of Asian chili sauce (garlic, red chilies, and sugar), sesame oil, and diced tomatoes accompanies.

At present the masterpiece is the baked lobster (currently $15.99, anywhere else $48). The meat is removed from the whole crustacean. The coral and liver are mixed with rice vinegar and flavored Japanese mayonnaise called "Kewpie" (or just "QP"). Nakasone makes a lobster stock by baking, crushing, and boiling the leftover shells. This intense liquid is then strained, further reduced, and added to the lobster-QP filling. The lobster shell is then stuffed with this mixture and baked until golden brown. It is perfect. You will, of course, wish to lick the shell when you are finished. Go ahead. In this place, you can get away with it.

For dessert, Chef Nakasone brings green tea ice cream (Big deal right? Everybody has green tea ice cream) with a red bean paste that tastes like chocolate and a grapefruit-plum wine jelly! The simple ice cream is transformed into a complex dish of powerful contrasting flavors.

Nakasone comes to the table with a devilish twinkle in his eye. "I'm bringing you something else," he says. Better sit down for this. It is lightly breaded, deep-fried jumbo shrimp dipped in chocolate and dusted with bitter cocoa powder. Does it work? You bet it does. The natural sweetness of the shrimp is played up and against the chocolate and against the cocoa. Rather than exploiting its savory implications, Chef Nakasone treats the shrimp as dessert. Shrimp ice cream, anyone?

The uniqueness of this little restaurant cannot be overemphasized. If you are willing to give up elegant surroundings for magnificently creative seafood at very modest prices, Frankie's is the place for you. You can spend $150 a person elsewhere and have all the elegance in the world or $46-$30 for the *omakase* dinner and $8 corkage plus tax and gratuity at Frankie's and get similar quality. May I suggest a Bancrott Sauvignon Blanc available at Trader Joe's for about $8? Bring the wine cold as Frankie's has lousy ice buckets, and I think he only has one.

Fusion One 11

★½

$$$$

Location: 73-850 Highway 111, Palm Desert, 341-5903. *Food type: California Fusion run amuck. Ambiance: black and stainless steel; high-tech space ship. Bar: full; small but well-thought-out wine list.* **Reservations:** *suggested.* **Hours:** *dinner Monday through Saturday.*

In a word, odd. Beginning with the building, the environment is more consistent with that of a Bang & Olufsen stereo outlet than a restaurant. Gunmetal gray, black, and stainless steel are the colors of choice, interrupted by a little violet (seat covers) and blue (ceiling spotlights) here and there. Most striking are the barstools, custom-designed stamped metal of some kind with backs representing martinis. They are fascinating to look at, but as a dining environment, this place is almost as sterile as EAT (see Hotel Zoso in Chapter 2).

Fusion One 11 bills itself as a martini and tapas bar. All dishes are appetizer size. Three of them are the equivalent of a moderately sized meal. Prices range from a low of $9 for a spinach salad to a high of $20 for the king crab ravioli. If you order three of these dishes at the average price and then dessert, the total tab including tax and gratuity without drinks comes to $67. A martini and two glasses of wine bring the total to almost $100 for a rather skimpy dinner.

There are 16 martinis listed on the menu. Three of them are actually martinis; the others are trendy concoctions whose resemblance to a martini is related only to the shape of its container. Southern Bondage, for example, is Southern Comfort, amaretto, peach Schnapps, Triple Sec, and cranberry juice. It tastes like flat peach soda pop. The Downtown would appear to be the abortion of the list: Maker's Mark bourbon, amaretto, and Sprite! Mixing amaretto (not to mention Sprite) with one of the great sipping bourbons in the world is a culinary sin of the most vile kind.

Odd also is the cuisine. This is California Fusion run amuck, California Fusion for its own sake rather than to serve palatability. I have not tasted the following dish—I could not bring myself to try it—but here it is for your consideration: braised lollipop lamb chops over rosemary mashed potatoes and chocolate-mint pesto finished with tobacco onions. A lollipop lamb chop is a single rib trimmed of everything but the head. Now, there is such a thing as mint pesto, but it not really pesto in the Italian sense of the word. It is macadamia nuts, mint, vanilla, and honey instead of pine nuts, mint, garlic, and olive oil. This "pesto" goes well with chocolate, but should you put it on a lamb chop? Tobacco onions are thinly sliced, hot, and spicy deep-fried onion rings. Should you serve them with chocolate and mint?

A salad/bruschetta of roasted julienne of red bell pepper, a large sprig of fresh basil, three little balls of goat cheese, and kalamata olives all served with slices of grilled baguette proves to be an amiable collection of flavors and textures. However, it comes with four sauces. Soy sauce is drizzled on the goat cheese. O.K., I can live with that. Hoisin sauce appears in the lower right corner. This Chinese duck sauce is utterly and completely foreign to the other tastes. Sriracha paste, a red blob on the top of the plate, brings a strange irrelevance to the party. Bites including this paste are not entirely displeasing, but it violently alters the basic Italianate flavors. Sriracha paste is a fiery Thai red chili paste. The final condiment, a curry sauce, is a disaster. It destroys all tastes, including itself. Leave the sauces alone, and this salad/bruschetta is quite satisfying.

A bourbon-marinated pork loin is another quirky success and failure. It is successful when it sticks to the classic recipe and a failure when attempting these bizarre fusions. Slices of pork loin (served nicely pink, thank you very much) are placed over some absolutely wonderful smashed potatoes. Mashed potatoes are starchy potatoes whipped to a smooth texture with some cream or milk. Smashed potatoes are waxy potatoes roughly crushed with maybe some butter. To these potatoes are added red onion, Asiago cheese, and a rémoulade of whole-grain mustard. The combination is perfect. These potatoes are big and bold yet form an astonishingly harmonious relationship with the pork. Rémoulade (repeatedly misspelled as "remolade" on the menu) is essentially a mayonnaise with chopped egg, Worcestershire sauce, mustard, parsley, and horseradish. This unites the meat with the potatoes with uncanny effectiveness. Something is tweaking the chef to do silly things in order to affect some sort of fusion for its own sake. Here it takes the form of a piece of andouille sausage. This is not the true Cajun andouille sausage, which is almost black and is redolent of pecan or hickory smoke. This sausage tastes for all the world like Hillshire Farms Polish kielbasa. In a final nod toward the ridiculous, the word "fusion" is spelled out across the top of the plate in a fancy cursive script with hoisin sauce.

This restaurant seems to be at odds with itself—the juxtaposition of the sublime with the ridiculous. Even the desserts, S'mores Make Your Own and Snicker Bar Pie, leave you scratching your head.

Johannes
★★★½
Lunch: $
Dinner: $-$$$
#

Location: 196 S. Indian Canyon Dr., Palm Springs, 778-0017. *Food type: California Fusion. Ambiance: fun, eccentric décor; bright colors. Bar: full; extensive and reasonably priced wine list. Reservations: mandatory during season; suggested otherwise. Hours: lunch and dinner daily. Chef-owner: Johannes Bacher. Note: If Bacher is not present, quality drops.*

"Old school with a modern twist," says Johannes Bacher, chef-owner of what is one of the finer establishments in Palm Springs. Bacher, born and trained in Austria, toyed with such disparate careers as baker and bodybuilder (he's buddies with Arnold), but it is as a chef that he has made his mark. After years of apprenticeships in Austria and a solid background in classical French technique, Bacher found himself employed on cruise ships. He spent much time in the Far East: Malaysia, Indonesia, and Thailand. Additional time in the Caribbean and around the world with Hilton Hotels has bestowed upon Herr Bacher a knowledge and skill of many cuisines. What better place to marry these diverse cuisines than California?

The physical environment belies its own significance. It is whimsical. Yellow and orange walls and robin's-egg blue asymmetrical door frames set the tone for this *Alice in Wonderland* look. It is very California, very Palm Springs. Even with a small sidewalk patio, bar area, and dining room, Johanne's still cannot boast many tables. Reservations are a must during season.

Expect the unexpected. You never know exactly what Bacher is going to do next. With his vast knowledge of ingredients from just about everywhere in the world, the oddest combinations can show up in any dish on any given day. Take, for example, simple meatballs served as an appetizer. Meatballs, right? Hamburger and breadcrumbs shaped into golf balls, sautéed, and doused with marinara sauce, right? Wrong. Forget the breadcrumbs and use 95 percent fat-free ground beef. Mix in a little coconut milk, make them into ping-pong balls, sauté, and douse with a Thai concoction made with peanuts, almonds, chili paste, coconut milk, fish sauce, and lemon grass. Unexpected? Yes. Irrational? No. All these ingredients have the greatest affinity for one another. How Bacher intuitively knows this is his greatest skill.

How about his take on the basic desert salad of cheese, nuts, and fruit: endive, grapes, pecan praline, Asian pear, buttermilk blue cheese, black current Dijon dressing, and applewood-smoked veal bacon. Sounds like a disaster waiting to happen, but it isn't. The lettuce, grapes, and pear become one element, a fresh, bittersweet, clean, acidic element. The blue cheese marries the mustard and bacon to form an earthy, smoky element. The candied pecans provide sweetness and crunch. Proportionally the endive is about six to one, the six being endive and the one being everything else. Flavors are big but come in small quantities relative to the dominant bitter lettuce. Everything is as one in perfect harmony. It may be a little too sweet, but why quibble?

A magical little summer salad of roasted beets, goat cheese, grapefruit, and pistachios appears. The beets are firm; this is not baby food. With tiny pea shoots and a yellow bell pepper purée another eccentric but completely successful combination is born.

The wild mushroom soup at Johannes ranks way at the top of the list. With mushrooms such as porcini, portobellos, morels, and shiitake puréed with a vegetable stock and thickened with a little potato, one of the most arresting and potent assaults of wild-mushroom aromas fills the air. Bacher uses whatever mushroom is in season. Chanterelles and king trumpets may well appear during another season. This level of intensity is difficult to imagine. Very little in the way of contrasting flavors are employed. Only a little tarragon is introduced and a drizzle of truffle oil, but these are of the same family. They do not add counterpoint but serve to reinforce the already existing wildness. A spoonful of crème fraîche imparts richness.

Bacher also nods to the comfort food of his Austrian roots: schnitzel, spaetzle, and strudel. This Austrian soul food is probably excellent, but unless you are Austrian or German and want to elicit memories of your mother's home cooking, why bother when there is a menu of such daring and originality facing you? The spaetzle, by the way, is made with Gruyère cheese for a terrific mouth feel.

Duck breast served rare has become a California cliché during the last generation, and Bacher serves one as well. However, he does not take the road so many lesser chefs have taken. The sauce is based on Chinese plum sauce, which is a commercial product. Virtually all Chinese restaurants serve it with their duck dishes, and many other restaurants have discovered the peculiar glories of this clear, gingery, almost jellylike sauce. It undergoes some substantial changes in the hands of Bacher, however. He adds honey, Chinese chili paste, mirin, and star anise. Mirin is a low-alcohol rice wine. It is mildly sweet but has a pronounced flavor. This is the sauce for the rare duck breast, pulling it now towards ginger, now towards licorice (star anise). There is a bite of heat from the chili paste and a rush of sweetness from the honey. Bacher's duck sauce is enormously complex but completely coherent. With a garnish of simple blanched spinach and a caramelized Bosc pear, this dish is complete and close to perfect.

Perhaps the most spectacular of the entrées is the trio of lobster, scallops, and Kobe beef. Not only is this unique, but it is hard to believe for its sheer majesty. The meat, from the Greg Norman ranch in Australia, is top sirloin but it is Kobe style, which means it is as tender as filet mignon but with more flavor. Scallops are wrapped in slices of lobster tail. What you have, of course, is a unique take on the venerable American favorite, surf and turf. A vegetable medley sits center stage: strips of roasted bell pepper, zucchini, spinach, carrots, string beans, and shiitake mushrooms. Two sauces alternate across the plate, the first, a tarragon-flavored creation that recalls béarnaise at first. It is not. Danish blue cheese, white wine, shallots, and green peppercorns take both the fish and the meat into one traditional direction, that of béarnaise and steak *poivre.* The second sauce is more radical. It is built on a demi-glace base with a port reduction to which foie gras has been added. Magnificent!

Other entrée options available include Colorado rainbow trout stuffed with spinach and pine nuts, crab and potato hash Riesling sauce, Alaskan halibut on pineapple sauerkraut, and habañero chicken sausage with passion fruit and mango salsa.

Lunch is a relatively new addition. Along with Zin's and Omri Go Med (Chapter 5), this is the best lunch in town for the money. Chef Bacher specializes in a multitude of variously prepared schnitzels for $10.

Kaiser Grille

★ (early-bird special); otherwise not recommended
$ (early-bird special); $$-$$$
Location: 205 S. Palm Canyon Dr., Palm Springs, 323-1003. Food type: Euro-Cali (heavy on Italian). Ambiance: nice if you are on the street side of the outdoor patio, noisy otherwise. Bar: full. Reservations: suggested. Hours: lunch and dinner daily.

The Kaiser Group of restaurants is owned and operated by Kaiser Morcus and his son, Lee. Currently they operate in addition to this, the flagship, the two Chop House locations (Chapter 9), Crazy Bones Barbeque (Chapter 13), and the Hog's Breath Inn (Chapter 8) in La Quinta. If you are surfing the Internet or looking at an older local publication you will note that The Deck (Palm Springs), Big Fish (Palm Desert), and Kaiser Grille (Palm Desert) were all part of the Kaiser family of restaurants. All three are no longer in business.

The early-bird dinner menu is available between 5 and 6. It is a very good buy, reducing many entrées in the $25 range to $14.95. If price and ambiance are at least as important to you as quality food preparation, Kaiser Grille can be a viable option. A word of warning: you will *not* be offered the early-bird menu. You must ask for it.

There is no beating the environment here, especially if you are a people-watcher. Located on a prime corner in the heart of downtown Palm Springs, the lush, misted, and elevated patio offers the perfect cool, tree-shaded spot to observe the action on the street without being seen yourself.

Now for the bad part. The menu is large, too large, offering something for everybody, all in a California vein. Pastas (fettuccine with pine nuts and applewood-smoked bacon), pizzas (Asian pear and Gorgonzola), Mexican (chicken quesadilla), Hawaiian (ahi tuna with mango), Chinese (mu shu napa cabbage wraps), steaks, meatloaf, rack of lamb—it's all here.

The tone of the dinner begins when a strange cakelike bread arrives at the table. An herb, possibly cardamom—sweet, bitter, pungent—suffuses the dough.

"Classic Caesar Salad" is good, fresh romaine with one crouton . . . no, no, there is another one hiding (almost definitely out of a box). What is this cheese? The menu says Parmesan. I guess it is Parmesan, pregrated. Is that an anchovy? There it is, one of them. Ah, the classic Caesar dressing. Would be nice if there were any on here. There is so little in fact that I cannot even tell you if it is out of a bottle.

A big and meaty center-cut pork chop arrives. Requested medium rare, it actually arrives medium rare. This is a surprise, but we get to the heart of Kaiser Grille's cooking problem. Recipes seem to have been created without any concern for proper balance and integrity of the dish as a whole. This chop has a sauce of caramelized red onion. O.K., that works. But apples, probably Golden Delicious cooked to the point of disintegration, have been added. We are now taken toward the traditional American combination of pork with applesauce. This comes in a sweet brown gravy with hints of wine (menu says port) and sage reminiscent of Thanksgiving turkey. The menu says ginger and sundried cranberries. Nothing makes any sense. It is completely unfocused. The final impression is palate confusion with an overriding sweetness.

The menu says au gratin potatoes. In America, "au gratin" generally implies cheese. In France the preferred term is *"dauphinoise"* and there are several variations. Cream, egg, béchamel sauce, and possibly cheese can all be used. Thinly sliced potatoes are layered with these sauces, spiced with a pinch of fresh nutmeg, and baked with breadcrumbs on the top. These "au gratin" potatoes are simply slices of potato drenched with nutmeg and baked until mushy—no cheese, no egg, no breadcrumbs, no béchamel. It is the nutmeg that adds another nail in the culinary coffin. Amidst all the sweetness and confusion wrought by the sauce on the pork chop, the last thing the taste buds need is a blast of nutmeg.

A julienne of carrots is cooked properly but glazed with even more sugar. The sweetness is unrelenting. A bit of plain steamed broccoli offers the only respite. This is hardly cooked at all, but at least it offers some escape from the relentless assault of the sugarplum fairy.

Lavender Bistro
★★★½
$$-$$$
Location: 78-073 Calle Barcelona, La Quinta, 564-5353. **Food type:** California. **Bar:** full, good wine list, half-price wine on Tuesdays, 4:30 P.M. happy hour, free corkage on Sundays. **Reservations:** suggested. **Hours:** 5:30 P.M. daily. **Chef:** Emmanuel Janin.

Lavender Bistro is housed in a sprawling, renovated 1930s ranch-style home. The large and inviting patio is actually the walled backyard of the house. Lavender grows profusely throughout the ample patio. It does not release the kind of fragrance rosemary does, but break off a leaf and crush it between your fingers for a delightful olfactory experience. Majestic palms and small ficus trees wrapped with tiny sparkling lights embrace the diner. Colors are muted gold and beige; linens, white. Heavy Fortessa flatware provides excellent balance in the hand as well as beauty of design. Yet, there is no pretension. It is elegant without being intimidating, beautiful without being stuffy.

Lavender Bistro is also reasonably priced. It offers the kind of quality and value that Zin American Bistro (Chapter 5) and Johannes (this chapter) provide in Palm Springs 22 miles west. To further charge the wallet-batteries, Sunday is free corkage night, and Tuesday sees wine at half price.

I have not had the opportunity to explore this new restaurant as much as I would like. This review represents only one dining experience, but I took steps to extrapolate as much information from that experience as possible. I gave my server a choice of two appetizers and requested that he have the chef select the one he was proudest of. The choices were the wild mushroom soup or beet salad. Chef Janin picked the beet salad. Sliced red and yellow roasted beets with bits of crumbled goat cheese beneath a pillow of greens (mostly frisée) and a drizzle of horseradish-flavored crème fraîche is how the salad is constructed. The beets are perfect: tender, sweet, beautiful to look at. The frisée offers contrasting texture and a touch of bitterness to counteract the intense sweetness of the beet. The goat cheese is not big enough. Beets are an aggressive food. The more complex and intense Humboldt Fog goat cheese with its notes of licorice, allspice, cocoa, and lemon and dry, tangy mouth feel would stand up better to the beets. Another family of cheeses entirely, gorgonzola or Roquefort, would also do the trick. Alas, this cheese did not. The drizzle is only cosmetic. While the salad is lacking in its detail, it is nevertheless flavorful, refreshing, and even rather exciting in its overall effect.

Once again I gave the chef options for my entrée: paella, lamb shank, or pork chop. The pork chop arrives from the kitchen. It is, once again, beautiful to look at. The large and thick (one and a half inches at least) rib chop rests atop a thick mound of tinted and speckled mashed potatoes on a rectangular plate. A bright orange "relish" of some kind is to the right of the meat. On the left side are asparagus spears (green, the complement of red). Janin is a true artist in the presentation department.

I cut into the meat. It is as moist and tender as Kurobuta pork, but it is not. Has it been brined or injected? How matters less for the customer than the fact of its tenderness. It is uniformly cooked throughout with nary a dry spot nor a raw spot, with light caramelization on the surface. The potatoes are a surprise from a French chef. The red tint is adobo sauce; the speckles are chipotle peppers. This condiment is a mainstay of Southwestern cuisine but is as foreign to France as kimchi. And Chef Janin doesn't shy away from the natural heat of the smoked jalapeño. The adobo sauce brings subtle hints of tomato, garlic, and oregano. Not only are the potatoes a perfect side dish for the pork, their complexity of flavors and intense heat complement it exactly. Asparagus brings another aggressive counterpoint to the mix as well as the aforementioned complementary color.

But let us turn to the right side of the plate. What is the orange relish—little dice of bright red-orange stuff resembling candy more than anything else? Some kind of fruit? Tangy. Sweet. In a wine based glaze. Spicy. Not hot spicy, but sweet spicy. Cinnamon, nutmeg? What does the menu say? "Chardonnay-Mango Compote." So it is mango. Its intense red-orange color is probably augmented, as the natural color is more of a yellow to pale orange shade, at least locally. Once again let us forget about the how and focus on the results. Imagine the combinations: tender, moist pork, hot-spicy smoky mashed potatoes, bitter/acidic asparagus, and sweet-spicy mango bits in a fruity white wine. A spectacular dish and a real bargain at $25.

I have not sampled any other dishes at this restaurant. However, if the other offerings are even in the same ball park as these two, Lavender Bistro rates three stars at a minimum. The free corkage on Sundays (for us oenophiles anyway) can result in dinner for two including wine, tax, and tip for about $70. An outstanding buy indeed!

Matchbox

$$

Location: 155 S. Palm Canyon Dr., Palm Springs, 778-6000. *Food type:* *California Fusion and pizza.* *Ambiance:* long, narrow building fronting the *street; balconies and patios reminiscent of New Orleans French Quarter.* **Bar:** *full; adequate wine list.* **Reservations:** *suggested; if you want a balcony table, you will have to beg or bribe.* **Hours:** *dinner nightly; open till 1* A.M.

The environment of Matchbox is fun. It is located in the center of downtown Palm Springs on the second floor of an expansive building. Inside there is wood, stone, and a fireplace. Outside there are balconies, three of them. A single table and two chairs with a view straight down to the street below is the table most in demand. With ornate wrought-iron railings, these balconies elicit impressions of New Orleans.

There are two menus: pizza and California Fusion. The pizza is thin crust, more like a cracker than bread dough. Thin crust is the Italian way, but one of the primary tastes of a good pizza is quality crust. The Italian pizza masters push the dough into a fat ring around the pie. At Matchbox there seems to be an obsession with using as little dough as possible. The signature pizza is called the Matchbox Meat, made with pepperoni, Italian sausage, and bacon. It is unpleasantly greasy. There are ways to prevent this even in a pizza heavily laden with fat meats, but Matchbox seems to conspire to aggravate the problem rather than ameliorate it. The cheese, mozzarella, is put on in chunks with the meat. The layer of cheese, which should form a barrier to the melting fats, allows the grease to soak into the dough. The flavors and intrinsic quality of the meats are good, but after a few slices, the mouth begins to feel icky.

The same problem emerges with stuffed Italian rolls. These are small loaves of Italian bread stuffed with various fillings similar to pizza toppings. The veggie roll is stuffed with crimini mushrooms, onion, red pepper, garlic, and mozzarella cheese and deep-fried. If the roll leaks in any way, the frying fat seeps into the filling. If the oil is not hot enough it soaks the bread also.

The bistro side of the menu is a different story entirely, but the greasiness issue again rears its ugly head. Crab cakes arrive with a stunning presentation, so extreme as to challenge belief. Ribbons of phyllo dough are arranged atop the cakes to resemble some bizarre seaweed or cactus flower. The ensemble is deep-fried, causing the phyllo strips to brown and stick out in a spectacular fashion, but the deep-frying once again renders the ensemble too oily. The cakes themselves are about 80 percent crab, which makes for an excellent balance, but there is too much mayonnaise, which also increases the greasiness.

Yellowfin tuna, seared and dressed with a delightful citrus-based vinaigrette, breaks out of the fried pattern. This is sashimi-grade tuna in a thoroughly enjoyable and subtle sauce of orange, lemon, and lime juices, soy, chicken stock, sugar, and ginger. The acids of the citrus and spice of the ginger cut through the softness of the fish.

A crispy-skinned onaga snapper with a pineapple and basil salsa and a Dijon-crusted pork chop are two entrées worth trying. All things considered, this is a menu that doesn't really have a focus. Quality is wildly inconsistent. Prices, for the most part, are reasonable, and the ambiance is fun. Fish specials are most likely pretty good as the chef seems to specialize in seafood, but there are no guarantees.

There is an ancillary benefit to Matchbox: the Matchbox Vintage Club. Its free corkage is one perk that may be of particular value for wine drinkers.

Pacifica Seafood Restaurant

$$-$$$

Location: *73-505 El Paseo Dr., Suite F2608, Palm Desert, 674-8666.* ***Food type:*** *innovative California twists on a seafood theme.* ***Ambiance:*** *gorgeous second-floor patio with panoramic mountain and valley views; dining room is a little cramped and noisy but well appointed and friendly.* ***Bar:*** *full, including 120 vodkas; good wine list although overpriced; happy hour.* ***Reservations:*** *suggested.* ***Hours:*** *lunch during season; dinner nightly; early-bird specials 4 P.M. to 6 P.M.* ***Chef:*** *Brett Pollock.*

Pacifica is popular. Allow me to rephrase that. Pacifica is *very* popular. The bar is popular, the dining room is popular, and the patio is popular. Popularity is based on a complex combination of factors. Does the quality of the food satisfy the desires of the intended demographic? Is it a fun place? Does it fit within the budget of its target patrons? Occasionally, the reasons for such mass appeal elude food critics. I can speculate, but I cannot provide a definitive answer. Pacifica meets all three of the above criteria, but I still don't get it.

For fans of al fresco dining, there are few venues that can top or even equal this one with its spectacular views of the valley and Indio Hills to the north. The interior is trendy, upscale, contemporary, crowded, noisy, friendly, and active. The ceiling is a distinctive composition of convex and concave "sails," the only apparent reference to the seafood theme. There are 120 different vodkas for fans of that beverage. Tables are close together, and customers engage one another quite freely. Pacifica claims to have the freshest fish in the desert. This may well be true, but it probably is not. All upscale restaurants provide fresh fish. The signature dish is barbecued sugar-spiced salmon. There are serious problems with this dish from a strictly culinary point of view. First, it is not barbecued. In this country, barbecue means smoked. It is definitely not smoked. Is it grilled? Is it broiled? It arrives very hot and seared, which would indicate that it is grilled. The heavily sugared surface caramelizes quickly. When the fish arrives, it is nicely cooked. The first bite is tender and moist, even as the color is beginning to fade. It is so hot that carry-over cooking means that the salmon will be considerably overcooked before it is half-eaten. It begins to dry out and lose its flavor almost immediately.

The fish is paired with garlic mashed potatoes puréed to creaminess. I acknowledge that some people like their mashed potatoes puréed to this extent, but many do not, including me. Most chefs are serving their mashed potatoes in a roughly chopped state. Garlic levels are good. A honey-mustard sauce encircles the plate. The mustard is mild, and the honey provides even more sweetness. Is there nothing to balance the sugar? Blanched green beans neither add nor subtract from the overall taste. Chef Brett Pollock opts for something truly odd, presumably in an attempt to balance the sugar. It may certainly be creative to combine disparate elements but novelty for novelty's sake does not automatically denote success. Pollock tops the potatoes with fermented bean sauce. Fermented black bean sauce is a Chinese condiment. It is a potent mixture of fermented beans, garlic, ginger, rice vinegar, and soy sauce. Its natural home is on a savory steamed whole fish (bass or red snapper) with cilantro and a julienne of various bell peppers. Here it is jarring. None of its flavors even come close to merging with the excessive sweetness of the salmon.

This menu takes delight in the marrying of oddities for their own sakes. I have not tasted any of the menu items I am about to relate, but I ask you to test these combinations in your imagination: scallops with bell pepper polenta and Cambozola cream. Cambozola is a big, smelly cheese, a cross between the French Camembert and the Italian Gorgonzola.

Another is halibut with roasted onion-miso marmalade. Miso is a thick paste made by fermenting rice, barley, or soybeans with the mold culture *k ji-ki.* Imagine swordfish with mushrooms, onion purée, and a red-wine-peppercorn reduction or honey-soy-glazed bass with bok choy and green curry-coconut sauce.

Other combinations would seem to be just fine, such as mahi mahi done with chipotle-corn sauce, *salsa fresca,* and avocado purée (guacamole?). A fine Caesar salad, made according to the rules of Caesar Cardini, is listed on the first-course menu along with several trendy concoctions.

There is something about this menu that attracts a large number of followers. Perhaps I am missing something or perhaps the vodka and the environment are the factors. The prices are reasonable, and the basic quality is there.

Peaks
Not rated
$$-$$$
Location: top of the tram, Mount San Jacinto, Palm Springs, 325-4537. Food type: California Fusion (Japanese). Ambiance: mind-boggling view; Palm Springs Modern architecture. Bar: full; small but adequate wine list. Reservations: recommended for dinner; not necessary for lunch. Dress: temperatures at 8,500 feet can be as much as 50 degrees cooler than at the desert floor. Hours: lunch and dinner daily; last tram leaves for Valley Station at 9:45 P.M. in the winter and 10:30 P.M. in the summer; allow at least two hours to dine. Chef: J. C. Marquez.

There is a maxim that states, "Never eat in a restaurant on top of a building. Never eat in a restaurant that moves. Don't even consider a restaurant that does both." Taken literally, Peaks does not qualify in either category. However, when you have to ascend 8,516 feet in a rotating vehicle, you are at least reminded of the maxim. Peaks transcends these dire warnings, but not entirely. Considering that everything from soap to salt must be brought up from the base station on the tram, it is downright astonishing that Peaks ever got off the ground, so to speak.

Food preparation at 8,500 feet presents another kind of challenge. Boiling point at sea level is 212 degrees F. At 8,500 feet it is 196. This then is the highest temperature that a water-based liquid can reach before it evaporates. Since all cooking liquids are water-based, except for the oil in the deep-fryer, the 16-degree difference in boiling points is significant. Remember Alfred Hitchcock's *North by Northwest?* Can you recall the restaurant in which Eva Marie Saint "shoots" Cary Grant? That's the ambiance: mid-century modern—stone, massive windows, no ornamentation (form follows function), huge wooden beams set into 20-foot ceilings. Peaks is located within the Mountain Station designed by E. Stuart Williams in 1961, its originality and integrity still untarnished. And what a view! Roughly 4,000 square miles of desert floor are visible from your table. We are talking utterly overwhelming, mind-bogglingly spectacular.

This is the third incarnation of this restaurant. The first chef was the very talented Anthony Gusich, and the restaurant was called Elevations. It sold; the name was changed to Peaks. A new chef, David Le Pow, was brought in and quality fell. A year or so ago Le Pow was replaced by Chef J. C. Marquez. Other than the fact that he graduated from the University of Guadalajara in 1985, I cannot find out anything about his training and experience. I have not reviewed the restaurant under Marquez for this edition.

There is obviously a problem here. Peaks cannot attract the local fine-dining customer. That's me. Why? Because it is too bloody much trouble! To get there one has to drive to the north end of Palm Springs then take the tramway road to the Valley Station. This is several miles. If there is any serious traffic one has to hike up the hill from the nearest parking lot. This can be quite strenuous. From the Valley Station, one often has to wait in line to buy a tram ticket, then wait in line again to board. Tickets are a hefty $22.25 per person. Trams leave every half-hour. Last tram down is 9:45 P.M. Twilight tickets are $19.25 even for people going specifically to the restaurant. The tram ride takes 18 minutes, and the whole process has to be reversed on departure. Get the picture? Almost two hours of travel time and $40 (for two) has been added to your dining experience before one morsel has passed between your lips. To attract this customer Peaks would have to offer something that same diner cannot get at sea level (or below sea level as the case may be), namely a unique menu brilliantly executed. When I reviewed this restaurant for the first edition in August 2006, Chef Le Pow assured me he was planning a game-based menu for that fall: venison, antelope, quail, pheasant, boar, and rabbit. It never happened.

Peaks will not appeal to tourists with children. The biggest draw of the aerial tram is the snow in the winter and the technology of the tram itself. Even conservatively estimating that 40 percent of tourists taking the tram ride do not have kids with them, that leaves 60 percent of tourists completely uninterested in Peaks for either lunch or dinner. It is far too expensive and the menu has no interest for children. Of the remainder, childless tourists, some may be interested in a fine-dining experience, but in order to appeal to the broadest range of this diverse clientele, the menu has been dumbed down to the level of cliché. There is nothing on this menu that holds any interest whatsoever for the serious diner, regardless of how well it is prepared. If really hungry, I would rather grab a snack at the cafeteria, return to the desert floor, and drive the few minutes to either Johannes (this chapter) or Zin/Zini (Chapter 5), both in Palm Springs.

The menu consists of carpaccio, calamari, a cheese platter, a chowder, Caesar salad, spinach salad, and a chop salad. Entrées include one chicken, two steaks, a pork chop, a pasta, and a salmon dish. That's it. The lunch menu adds a few sandwiches and deletes the dinner entrées. I don't know what the current wine list is like, but the 2006 list was barely adequate. I cannot address current quality. If you are taking the tram ride anyway and you are happy with a basic fine-dining American menu, that view is utterly gorgeous.

Piero's Acqua Pazza
★★

$$

Location: The River at Rancho Mirage, 71-800 Highway 111, Suite A167, Rancho Mirage, 862-9800. Food type: whatever sells, including American favorites, fish, designer pizzas, and quesadillas. Ambiance: loud, loud, and louder; falling water, mirrors, and a lovely "riverside" patio. Bar: full; happy hour. Reservations: suggested. Hours: lunch and dinner daily.

The River is the trendy, upscale outdoor shopping mall in Rancho Mirage. This impressive feat of engineering has become a hangout for teens and 20-somethings at night. Aqua Pazza fits right into this milieu: flash, noise, and something for everybody, except people who really care about food. It bills itself as a California bistro, but it has none of the qualities that define a bistro, so I can only guess what this means—probably nothing.

The biggest negative at Piero's is the noise. Inside, volume levels are unbearable when it is crowded and irritating when it is not. With huge expanses of glass, hard surfaces throughout, an open kitchen and bar, and no acoustic tile on the ceiling, the din is enough to ruin any meal. Before the patio was opened, a singer/guitarist contributed further to the ruckus. Now, fortunately, he is outside on the beautiful "riverside" shoreline with a delightful view of the Santa Rosa Mountains to the south and west.

The menu is large and safe, as though designed by focus groups and demographers. Quality is wildly inconsistent. The double-cut pork chop with a maple syrup and apple glaze is excellent, more tender than I have come to expect in these days of genetically engineered pigs, nicely charred on the outside and medium rare on the inside. Virtually all entrées, whether meat or fish, come with mashed potatoes and a vegetable medley, appropriate to the entrée's flavors and textures or not. The potatoes are generic, and the veggies are not uniformly cooked. Broccoli, cauliflower, string beans, and carrots all require different cooking times. If they are cooked together and removed from the heat together, either the broccoli is mushy and the carrots are ready or the broccoli is ready and the carrots are raw. My carrots were raw.

Lamb shank is Colorado lamb. The raw material is the best in the world— big, tender, flavorful, and rich with just a hint of wildness. The sauce, the reduced braising liquid, has a superb flavor: white wine, veal stock, essence of aromatic vegetables, and just the right amount of tomato. However, whoever prepares this dish does not bother to degrease the juice. It is swimming in lamb fat. Degreasing is not a difficult operation. Grease can be skimmed quickly, which takes care of about 75 percent of the stuff, but all the chef has to do to get rid of all of it is to place the braising liquid in the refrigerator for a while. The fat cools, hardens, and rises to the top. With a degreased sauce, this could be one of the best lamb shanks in the city. To make matters worse the shank is not seared before placing it in the braising liquid. Caramelizing the surface accomplishes two things. It releases natural sugars that result in another layer of flavor, and it melts the layer of fat just under the skin. The fat problem is thus aggravated. This should have been seared dry and crispy before being placed into the braising liquid. This is truly a shame because this is potentially one terrific lamb shank. Searing and degreasing are simple, basic cooking techniques known to every moderately competent home cook. There is no excuse for ignoring them in a restaurant.

Some of the designer pizzas are not really pizzas at all but toppings on a "cracker." Take for example the lox and caviar pizza. There is no cheese or tomato sauce; in their stead are lox, red onions, salmon caviar, and a squirt of dilled cream cheese. Why put this stuff on a thin slice of baked dough? Here's an original idea: put it on a bagel. Such things as scallops, pears, pineapple, Brie, chorizo, and cilantro all make it onto one of these pizzas.

Shoestring deep-fried onions are greasy little sticks with their flavor burned out of them, and a large piece of bread puffed into the size and shape of a football is not only bad, it is pointless.

The menu is enormous and features everything from porcupine shrimp to a Russian panini (turkey, ham, and Swiss). Prices are generally reasonable. It must be indicative of something although I am not quite sure of what, but Acqua Pazza carries 97 brands of tequila available in two-ounce shots. The wine list is large and reasonably priced.

CHAPTER 8

Traditional American

This is a bit of a catchall chapter. It houses everything from an upscale burger stand, the hugely popular Tyler's, to the ever-so-intensely outré gourmet cabaret Blame it on Midnight. Sports bars (Beer Hunter, Tilted Kilt), "down-home" cooking (Big Mama's, Simba's), quintessential American seafood (Crab Pot), and upscale American dinner houses all find a home in this chapter. If it is comfort food and tradition you are after, from Davey's to Cunard's Sandbar, Shame on the Moon to Cactus Jack's, you need look no further.

The Beer Hunter

$-$$

Locations: 78-483 Highway 111, La Quinta, 564-7442; 34-331 Date Palm Dr., Cathedral City, 770-6337. Food type: fast food and American grill. Ambiance: barn with televisions and games. Reservations: not accepted. Bar: full, but beer is the name of the game. Hours: lunch and dinner daily.

It bills itself as a sports pub and grill. There are 26 television sets simultaneously showing just about every sporting event in the world by way of several satellite dishes. You can watch everything from a paint-ball war to a soccer game, an auto race to curling, plus horses, baseball, golf, and tennis. You have to get used to the sudden and vociferous whoops and hollers of athletic partisans interrupting your repast, but considering the nature of the repasts, that isn't too difficult.

The building is a great big barn covered with sports memorabilia: banners, trophies, plaques, and especially golf bags. Pool, pinball, hoops, and miniature soccer are also found throughout the space. Along with the TVs, this can make for a noisy environment, but nobody seems to mind. No one really comes here to dine anyway. Most of the food belongs in the finger-food category although the menu is extensive.

Children, by the way, are permitted here, and the menu is right up their alley. Most everything on the menu is kid friendly, plus there is a six-item children's menu. Appetizers dominate, with all the usual suspects: Buffalo wings, chicken taquitos, potato skins, chips and salsa, and nachos. Get the Hunter Sampler and forget the rest. Chili, sandwiches, salads, desserts, pizza, pasta, Mexican stuff, and five basic entrées—steak, ribs, fish and chips, shrimp and chips, and a chicken breast—round out the list. Almost everything is well under $15.

Burgers are the staple, and a place like this should be judged by its burgers. There are nine of these concoctions in various permutations. The signature burger is called the Beer Hunter. It arrives on a large plate with coleslaw and steak fries. The fries are excellent, but I am no judge of coleslaw, as I really don't like any coleslaw. This one tasted too sweet to me, but it was not runny with mayonnaise, which I guess is a good thing. The burger is eight ounces, and it is cooked medium rare unless otherwise specified. What this means in practical terms is that the restaurant grinds its own beef or at least knows where it comes from and supervises the grinding. The risk of an *E. coli*-related lawsuit is simply too great a chance to take unless it is sure of its beef. Unfortunately, the beef is the only thing positive that can be said about this signature burger.

A great burger needs contrast as much as a dish at any fine-dining establishment. Street food reacts on the taste buds just like anything else. This burger manages to be bland even with a healthy dose of sautéed mushrooms, cheese, two generous slices of red onion, and shredded lettuce. Why? First of all, mushrooms and meat are too closely related in both flavor and texture. They absorb one another. These are white mushrooms, which do not have a lot of flavor to begin with. The cheese, within the envelope of the meat and mushrooms, also slides into the overall general texture. It is American cheese, that simple slice of mild cheddar-based cheese food. The onion, which should have sparked the combination by providing a pungent acidic contrast, is a mild red onion. It does not have a flavor big enough to do the job of a Spanish onion. Even the lettuce is the most neutral-flavored of all possible lettuces. To compound the felonious burger, no sauce is provided. A big flavorful sauce—say a mixture of mayonnaise, ketchup, pickle relish, chili powder, cumin, pepper, and finely chopped jalapeño— would go a long way toward enhancing this burger. Two strips of salty bacon work well, however, and the bun is big and fresh.

Let's rework this burger in our minds together. What if the

mushrooms were portobellos? Portobello mushrooms are not much more expensive than white mushrooms, and this is a $10 burger. Portobellos might add 15 cents to the cost of the burger, but they would triple the flavor. Substitute sharp cheddar for the American cheese, romaine for the iceberg, and a Spanish onion for the red onion and slather a pungent sauce over the whole thing. Same burger, similar ingredients, but now the ingredients are chosen for the ability to deliver flavor, not dissolve into a tasteless mush. It still needs something. Everyone knows that a big slice of beefsteak tomato is the single most complementary thing you can put on a burger. It is cold, fresh, and acidic, which the other ingredients, except the onion, are not, and has a bit of textural bite to it. Now you have a great burger. But the Beer Hunter is a very popular hangout. Why should it change? No reason at all.

Big Mama's Soul Food
★★
$
Location: 68-510 E. Palm Canyon Dr., Cathedral City, 324-8116. **Food type:** *soul food.* **Ambiance:** *funky.* **Bar:** *beer and wine.* **Reservations:** *not accepted.* **Hours:** *lunch and dinner Tuesday through Sunday.*

This funky little storefront is the only establishment of this type remaining in the entire valley. Big Willie shut down his restaurant in Indio to focus exclusively on catering, and Simba's, a longtime fixture in Palm Springs, is much too compromised to be considered soul food. Big Mama's opened just in time for me to review it here. I wanted to sample its barbecue, as I had hoped for barbecue I could truly recommend, but unfortunately its smoker operates only on weekends and I was there on a Wednesday with no time for a repeat visit. However, considering the quality and authenticity of the rest of the food, I would certainly give its barbecued spare ribs some credibility sight unseen. I did sample the barbecue sauce, and it is worthy—not overly sweet or laden with ketchup and with layers of flavor and a nice kick. This is a gutsy restaurant serving genuine Southern soul food.

The space is peculiar to say the least. An oddly shaped—like a boomerang—storefront is decorated with an ancient brown refrigerator, apartment-sized stove, and a couch and chair covered in plastic. Old pictures of, presumably, family members adorn the walls, as well as a rendition of da Vinci's *The Last Supper* done up in blackface. The first part of the "boomerang" houses tall stool-like tables set for three but at which one is a crowd. After the bend, there is a small dining room with more conventional tables.

Except for a couple salads to provide an alternative to the dedicated Californian who wanders in off the street, the food is strictly Deep South— fried Deep South like battered and heavily breaded and seasoned catfish and okra, for example. A bowl of hush puppies arrives in place of the usual bread. For the uninitiated, hush puppies are little balls of cornbread dough that are deep-fried. Bacon fat is the shortening of choice. They are good: hot, crispy, and not the least bit greasy.

Collard greens are one of the side-dish choices. These greens are a member of the cabbage family and have a flavor somewhat similar to turnip or cauliflower. The texture, however, is like boiled bay leaf. Greens are traditionally boiled or simmered for up to two hours with ham hocks or hog jowls. Most people find the smell of cooking collard greens quite objectionable, but this restaurant does not have that smell. There is no shredded ham in the greens served here.

Candied yams is another side dish. These are shockingly sweet and, with added dessert spices of cinnamon and nutmeg, are essentially inedible. Inedible, that is, when eaten alone, but that is not the way this food is eaten. With a splash of white vinegar on your plate (vinegar is provided at every table) and a shot of Louisiana hot sauce, the bitter greens and candied yams do wonderful things for one another. Most significantly, all the excessive sweetness and turnip-like bitterness are removed, and something new emerges, something interesting and quite palatable indeed.

The deep-fried catfish is breaded so heavily that the fish itself is lost, but everything taken together is balanced and altogether harmonious. The pork chops may be a better choice than the catfish as the flavor of the pig is more assertive. Pulled pork, chicken wings, fried chicken breast, barbecued beef, and the aforementioned pork chops round out the daily entrée list. Cole slaw, mac and cheese, potato salad, and beans are also side-order options. Sweet potato pie is the only dessert. Prices are cheap, cheap, cheap, with lunches averaging about $9 and dinners around $12.

Billy Reed's

★

$

Location: 1800 N. Palm Canyon Dr., Palm Springs, 325-1946. Food type: American. Ambiance: large glorified coffee shop. Bar: full. Reservations: accepted. Hours: breakfast, lunch, and dinner daily.

Billy Reed's is very old fashioned, even anachronistic. It is open all day, every day, the menu is huge, and breakfast is served all day, but it only becomes a viable proposition Monday through Thursdays, when the specials are available. This is high-end coffee-shop food, and unless the special prices are available, better food can be had elsewhere. Monday is prime rib night: eight ounces for $10.95 or 10 ounces for $12.95. Tuesday is either salmon filet or roasted pork loin at $10.95. Wednesday is top sirloin steak for $10.95, and on Thursday filet mignon comes to your table for $12.95. All beef is Black Angus, so these are good deals. Entrées include a choice of two: soup, salad, fresh fruit, vegetables, rice, mashed potatoes, and rolls or cornbread. It is institutional, but it is cheap. Happy hour, with a two-for-one special on well drinks at the bar, is 2 P.M. to 5 P.M. everyday.

Blame It on Midnight

★★½

$$

#

Location: 777 E. Tahquitz Canyon Way, Palm Springs, 323-1299. Food type: American, comfort food. Ambiance: art deco meets Dracula's lair. Bar: full; small but adequate wine list; remarkably inexpensive. Reservations: taken only for parties of six or more. Hours: dinner nightly.

The restaurants Blame It on Midnight and Shame on the Moon (reviewed later in this chapter) both take their names from the lyrics of a song written by Rodney Crowell and made into a hit by the 1982 release of Bob Seger's album *The Distance*. Both restaurants were under the same ownership until 2004, when Blame was bought out. Of all the restaurants in the Coachella Valley, this one is the most hard-core gay oriented.

The elusiveness of the restaurant begins long before you cross the threshold. A sign is just visible from the street, but there is no parking and an entrance is not apparent. To enter you must drive around the block to a rear parking structure and walk down the stairs. Then you meander around through various byways. Eventually you find a doorway that elicits memories, depending on your age and/or knowledge of the art and movies of the 1930s, of art deco design and architecture. An aluminum or stainless-steel curved awning fronts the dark red door. A row of windows revealing a black interior is to the left of the door, and there are tiny ceiling lights. A red glow seeps through the midnight. It is both fascinating and a little eerie. Once inside, blasts of the outré assault the unsuspecting patron. Except for the ceiling stars, lighting is entirely in red. Darkness engulfs you: walls, ceiling, linens, most of the floor, the bar, furniture. Raised banquettes dominate the dining room. A deeply padded couch covering two entire walls encircles the cabaret area. The customers are almost entirely male. The walls are covered with clocks—hundreds of them in all shapes and sizes—and poster art. The legs of chairs and suspended ceiling art are ornate beyond all bounds of the expected. A guest from London once described it thus: "It looks as though a Christmas tree exploded and they never cleaned it up." You have entered the Twilight Zone. Do not bring your Baptist mother from a small town in Nebraska. Bring your metrosexual nephew from Manhattan and his Euro-trash playmate.

This restaurant makes no attempt to emulate the high-end gourmet experience of a four-star restaurant, but on a second-tier level it does remarkably well at half the cost. This is most apparent in the preparation of sauces. That four-star establishment will have a variety of stock bases in either white (poultry) or brown (veal) called "mother" sauces from which a variety of secondary sauces evolve. Here the sauces are greatly simplified; all of them are more or less based on one stock and a white-wine reduction. These sauces do not have the depth or complexity of French sauces, but by deglazing the pan fond with this basic liquid, a successful and quite palatable sauce can be produced for almost any dish.

Comfort seems to be a signature of sorts in many a gay-oriented restaurant. Here it takes the form of a meatloaf, but this one is tweaked by making it with ground turkey and pine nuts. It is not as dense as you are used to with beef-, pork-, lamb-, or veal-based loaves, and the nuts bring an unexpected sweetness as well as crunch. Caramelized onions and a rich, although superficial, gravy ties it all together. Green rice, done with spinach, basil, and parsley, adds an interesting and much needed antiphon for the sweetness. The basil dominates the flavor.

Avocado and shrimp cocktail is refreshing on a hot summer's eve, but nothing special. Composed mostly of cucumber and tomato in a mild tomato-based cocktail sauce, whatever shrimp is in the mix is lost. Hot English mustard contributes a bite, avocado a lusciousness. But still, why bother?

Scallops and risotto are quite fascinating. The scallops are not seared, but sautéed gently. They are not overcooked, but they do take on a not-at-all unpleasant chewy quality with the slower cooking. Traditional risotto with Parmesan cheese accompanies the scallops. Ordinarily I would say that the addition of cheese, especially a dominant cheese like Parmesan, is to be avoided, but strangely, it works here. The menu says Alfredo sauce, as in fettuccine Alfredo. This is not true. Alfredo is simply butter, cream, and cheese. The sauce dressing these scallops is considerably more interesting than butter and cream. White wine, lemon, and a concentrated fish stock are all present. It is a golden brown color. When queried, my server denied these ingredients. I asked for more sauce. I received Alfredo sauce! It was white. A cold, blanched broccoli flower remained uneaten.

Turkey piccata arrives with garlic mashed potatoes. Turkey breast is pounded thin and sautéed briefly so as not to dry out the meat. It is nicely browned, tender, and flavorful. Again, the base sauce arrives. This time it is darker and carries turkey flavor. Yellow beets provide a terrific out-of-left-field counterpoint to the whole package.

Blame It on Midnight is remarkably inexpensive considering the quality delivered. All but two entrées are under $20; the turkey meatloaf is only $15.94. In addition, the wine list, called Grapes of Wrath, while small, has some of the lowest markups around. The Penfolds Rawson label is the house wine. It sells for $17. This is an excellent wine for this price and represents less than a 300 percent markup, remarkable in this age of 400 to 600 percent premiums. Korbel Brut sparkling wine retails for about $10. They sell it here for $18! Drink names are often pregnant with double-entendre: Citroen My Face and Speed Queen, for example. Background music is techno-disco-industrial, thankfully played at a reasonably low volume, although it probably gets louder as the clock approaches midnight. Gay cabaret entertainment is featured Thursday through Saturday.

Cactus Jack's
★★

$$-$$$

Locations: 82-347 Highway 111, Indio, 342-1889; 74450 Highway 111, Palm Desert, 346-1565. Food type: traditional American. Ambiance: Las Vegas steakhouse circa 1974; Palm Desert location is more modern. Bar: full; small, weak wine list; corkage fee of $10. Reservations: dinner only. Hours: breakfast, lunch, and dinner daily.

You are entering a time warp. You firmly believe that you are in the Coachella Valley in 2010, but suddenly it is the Las Vegas of 1974. Not the Las Vegas of the strip with its glitz and glamour, but the outskirts of Vegas: Charleston, Decatur, and Boulder Highway. What happened?

Cactus Jack's has been around a long time. It does good business. Any change would likely threaten its regulars, who undoubtedly like it the way it is. Besides, a little nostalgia never hurt anybody. As you enter through the nondescript double glass doors, there is a small foyer, off of which are the restrooms. A second set of doors points you either to the right to the coffee shop or to the left to the dining room. As a coffee shop, Cactus Jack's is quite ordinary. It is in the "why bother" category. As a dinner house, the restaurant takes on an entirely different character.

It is red and dark. The bar area is full. Two televisions monitor the latest sports events. Tablecloths are red, not pink, not maroon, but red. Vinyl booths line the walls. These are dark red, very dark red. The walls match this color. A wooden half-partition in dark brown separates the bar area from the dining room. Structural wooden beams, in dark brown, are visible throughout. The carpet is another neutral dark color: gray, green, brown, a little of each. Small lamps with red shades are spotted about the room. Hanging light fixtures cast an orange glow.

Even though Cactus Jack's has expanded in the last few years to a considerably more modern building having none of that anachronistic feel of the one in Indio—the proprietors bought out the defunct Chicago Freddy's in Palm Desert—the menu at the two locations still hearkens back to the Vegas of 1974: steaks, chops, seafood, and of course, prime rib. In fact, it is the prime rib for which Cactus Jack's is known. American comfort foods—chicken-fried steak, calf's liver, pasta—fill out the remainder. Prices, however, do not reflect 1974. Steaks come in around

$32, rather than $9.95. Fish dishes are in the mid-$20s. These prices are comparable with the upscale steakhouses a few miles to the west. The difference is that at Cactus Jack's your entrée comes with a side as well as soup or salad.

Food is basic but well prepared. The regular-cut prime rib at $25 is the order of choice here. That the meat is properly cooked is the only requirement defining a good prime rib—that, of course, and high-quality meat to begin with. Here, the meat is Angus Choice, and the preparation is perfect. The regular cut is a slab of meat an inch and a half thick. It must weigh about a pound. Mine was a perfect rare; the couple at the adjacent booth received a perfect medium-rare. The meat is supremely tender, rich, and full flavored, as you would expect from an Angus steer. Horseradish is bottled, shredded horseradish root cut with a little distilled vinegar and oil—potent but not brutal. The meat is served au jus, but the jus tastes slightly of bouillon. For some strange reason, it is increasingly difficult to get a baked potato that is truly baked. When a russet potato has been baked, especially at the recommended temperature of 400 degrees, it becomes dry and fluffy. The inside is pure white with nary a hint of green anywhere. The outer skin is completely dry, and a golden brown inner skin develops. It is nutty and sweet. When a potato is microwaved or baked wrapped in foil, none of these desirable things happens. The flesh is damp and green tinged, the caramelized inner skin does not develop, and the surface remains wet. Unfortunately, this baked potato is of the latter type.

The soup, a spicy corn-bean-chicken chowder, is a surprise. With aromas of cumin and chili powder emanating from the small cup, the olfactory sense is certainly tantalized. It is thickened and flavored by puréeing corn tortilla chips with chicken broth. This not only increases the corn flavor but also supplies a thickener in the form of corn flour. This soup could be served at any number of three-star California Fusion restaurants in Palm Springs as an expensive appetizer. No one would question its humble origins in an Indio coffee shop.

The bottom line here rests on two factors: you find the anachronistic ambiance attractive or at least a worthy novelty, or you have a craving for a fine old fashioned prime rib. Other than that, there are better places to go for everything else on the menu for less money. You can also get a bourbon on the rocks here at six o'clock in the morning, if that idea suits your fancy.

The Crab Pot
★★½
$$-$$$

Location: 78-121 Avenida La Fonda, La Quinta, 564-7333. *Food type:* American seafood. *Ambiance:* big, fun, beautiful outdoor setting. *Bar:* full. *Reservations:* suggested. *Hours:* lunch and dinner daily.

There are currently four Crab Pots nationwide. The original is in Seattle where, presumably, the fish is more or less guaranteed to be fresh. Here that is not always the case. A second valley location is planned for Rancho Mirage and could well be open by the time this edition is in print.

Architecture is Santa Fe/American Indian influenced. It well suits the area. The ambiance is fun. Inside seating is limited, but the patio is large and well placed with fireplace, heaters, misters, shaded areas, and numerous overhead fans. There is an unfortunate wrinkle that needs to be explained, however. The signature dish (four versions) is a fly magnet. Most valley restaurants have al fresco dining options, and flies are generally not a problem. They tend to hit in the late afternoon but disappear by mid-evening. Lunch is generally fly free. There are, on the other hand, some seasons when the flies are unbearable, invading the area like locusts. Well, these signature dishes attract flies from everywhere. Your server will inform you of this problem, asking you if you would prefer an inside table. You will not be able to move inside later should you elect to stay outside, as you will soon find out.

The menu is an enlarged version of Fisherman's Market (reviewed later this chapter); it is also substantially more expensive. In fact this restaurant is deceptively expensive. The signature dishes are called "Seafeasts" for two (or more), which is unfortunate for solo diners. There are four versions, each one expanding on the previous version. The first and smallest, called "The Cove," consists of steamed clams, pacific mussels, shrimp (in their shells), andouille sausage, corn on the cob, and red potatoes (in their jackets). It sells for $15.95. At the other end there is the "Alaskan," $34.95, which adds king crab, dungeness crab, and snow crab. The middle versions have less crab respectively and sell for $23.95 and $29.95. Seafeasts come in a large bowl. The tablecloths (rubberized, waterproof red and white checkerboards) are covered with butcher paper. The feast is poured out on the paper. Guests are presented with mallets and bibs. There is silverware, but it is superfluous. This is a hands-on meal if there ever was one. For those not used to dining like this, it may be somewhat intimidating. A first date, for example, may eternally pair two kindred spirits or ruin an otherwise perfectly good experience.

So how is it? It's good, not great, but good. The corn (very well cooked, soft but with some remaining crunch, flavorful), potatoes (not so well cooked, a little underdone), and an excellent sourdough loaf provide ample stuffing power. These starches serve to mask the fact that this is quite an expensive experience. True, the least expensive Seafeast is $15.95, but this option does not contain any of the more desirable shellfish and consists mostly of the above-mentioned fillers: corn, potatoes, and bread. If a couple elects to go this route they can dine for about $40, including tax and tip. However, to obtain the full Crab Pot experience a couple would need to order at least the $29.95 feast. If a couple of beverages and/or a bottle of wine are included, the final exit for two will easily exceed $125. That said, it is still good. On the occasion of my visit the crab especially was excellent—steamed to the point of fully cooked but tender and moist as well. With a simple drawn butter, it reminded me of a seafood stand in Maine or Nova Scotia. Shrimp, likewise, are excellent. They are probably U20s but have a deep flavor more akin to a larger version. Clams and mussels do not fare as well. Mussels, especially, are small and rather tough. More than a few of the shells are empty. The sausage is a spicy addition pairing nicely with the Cajun spices sprinkled liberally on everything but functioning more as a condiment than anything else. Cajun spices are usually some combination of paprika, cayenne pepper, chili powder, salt, and onion powder. This one tastes primarily of chili powder. It isn't particularly "hot," but the flavor contributes to the overall profile without damaging anything.

The libation of choice should be beer as the Cajun spices will seriously interfere with the balance of any white wine. Unfortunately, the La Quinta restaurant does not have beer by the pitcher. This serves only to drive up the cost. Bud, Bud Lite, and Miller Lite are on tap for $3.75 a glass. They also have Stella Artois on tap for $5.00. A party of two ordering three Stellas each adds $30 to the bill. In Seattle a pitcher of Sam Adams is available for $14, a significantly more reasonable cost for a decent beer.

The bill for me and my dining partner, which included two of the $23.95 Seafeasts and five Stella Artois beers, was $95. This did not include any soups, salads, appetizers, or deserts. While individual prices appear reasonable at first, they are not when anything but a quick lunch is desired. Anecdotal experience suggests that either Fisherman's Market or Oceans would deliver better prepared fish entrees at a more reasonable price; however, no one else has the Seafeasts. The novelty and general fun of the experience is worth a trip at least once, and it really is quite good.

Cunard's Sandbar

$$$

Location: 78-120 *Calle Tampico, La Quinta,* 564-3660. **Food type:** *American.* **Ambiance:** *retro.* **Bar:** *full.* **Reservations:** *suggested.* **Hours:** *dinner Tuesday through Saturday.*

To suggest that the ambiance at Cunard's is retro is to wallow in understatement. This place is a pure anachronism, a throwback to fine dining circa 1955. There are two rooms: the bar room and the dining room. Both are popular although the bar is a little more so. There, a pianist plays jazz-tinged soft-pop standards; think George Shearing playing "The Shadow of Your Smile." The walls are dark red, windows are stained glass, the bar is L-shaped blond wood. The art is pseudo-French Impressionism and Post-Impressionism (Renoir, Degas, Lautrec). The carpet's dark reds, greens, and purples with a busy print scream Las Vegas. Upholstered benches and booths are in red Naugahyde. The customers are loud as befitting a neighborhood bar scene. The parking lot—valet only—is crowded even on a post-season Tuesday. Park across the street.

The menu is as anachronistic as the décor, the bar, the customers, the music, and the overall ambiance. This is a menu one might expect in any upscale American restaurant in the early 1960s. I know, I was busing tables on weekends working my way through college in just such places. Only the prices have changed.

"You want soup or salad with that," asks a black-clad waitress. "That comes with choice of potatoes or rice pilaf, and all of our entrées comes with fresh garden vegetables, and our special today is chicken-fried steak [chicken-fried steak for $29!]. The soup is spinach-cheese." One has to smile. The time warp runs deep.

The menu includes such things as ground sirloin stuffed with blue cheese and topped with sautéed mushrooms, green peppers, and onions. Fried chicken makes an appearance as do a bunch of Americanized Italian standards: various piccatas, Marsalas, and Milaneses, parmagianas, and Bologneses. There is even a big scramble for $24 (hamburger, sausage, spinach, mushrooms, onions, herbs, and Parmesan cheese). Sole, salmon, crab legs, and shrimp scampi are the seafood options. Roast duck and rack of lamb round out the possibilities. There are no appetizers, just the usual side orders of steamed broccoli, iceberg, tomatoes with blue cheese, and sautéed mushrooms.

I had the spinach-cheese soup and the roast duck. In 1964 when I was busing tables, this soup would have been pretty good. Forty-five years later it is ridiculous. Chicken broth (bouillon cubes?), shredded cheddar cheese, milk, and frozen spinach is a recipe for a nostalgic moment but not much else. The spinach supplies nothing but a variation in the texture. Cheddar cheese and chicken broth don't taste bad together; it's more of a "why bother." It also cries out on deaf ears for a little nutmeg.

We served an orange duck on our menu in 1964. It was the Saturday night special of the non-lethal kind. In retrospect, it was an unbelievable buy: house cocktail, soup, salad, entrée, and dessert all for $3.85! This one costs more than seven times that one, comes only with the aforementioned soup, and is half as good. That one came with wild rice and carrots. This one comes with "baked or mashed" and "fresh garden vegetables." That one had a rich, deeply flavored orange sauce made by a genuine French chef; this one has an "apricot brandy" sauce. The duck is actually cooked perfectly. The meat is tender and moist, the skin is caramelized and crispy, but the sauce is peculiar. There is no depth here and there is an excessively bitter aftertaste. Burnt sugar is a flavor that often works well in dishes like this one, but here it is overdone, the bitterness masking the duck itself. The lack of depth is probably caused by not basing the sauce on a duck stock. It tastes only of burnt sugar and thinned and melted apricot jam flamed with brandy.

Mashed potatoes, overly whipped but of a good flavor with cheese and chives, retain the retro theme. "Fresh garden vegetables" are actually carrots and zucchini. These are probably steamed together as the carrots are undercooked and the zucchini is overcooked. Vegetables are unfinished. Bread is sweet and cakey, not at all appropriate with a savory dish.

Dessert anyone? Sandbar's Famous Toll House Pie à la mode, $8.99.

A glass of Sterling Pinot Noir is replaced by Rodney Strong ("Sorry, we're out of the Sterling"), a reduction in quality for the same price. The Strong is old and picking up both bitterness and a metallic edge. I ask the waitress when the bottle was opened. She says it was brand new, just opened three days ago, "But the cork was in it!" She doesn't have a clue. It is replaced without a problem with a newly opened Mondavi Coastal Cab for the same price, a further reduction in quality.

This restaurant is attracting a faithful following. One has to ask why. The La Quinta Cove is no desert when it comes to restaurants. The superb Lavender Bistro (Chapter 7) is two blocks away, and Morgan's in the Desert at the La Quinta Resort and Club (Chapter 1) is around the corner to the north. It is obvious, therefore, that people are coming here for its old-fashioned menu and ambiance. If hard retro is your taste, Cunard's may be just the place for you, but if it is fine dining you are seeking, go to Lavender Bistro. You'll save a little money too, especially on Sundays when corkage is free.

Davey's Hideaway
★★½
$$
#

Location: 292 E. Palm Canyon Dr., 320-4480. Food type: American. Ambiance: dark, intimate, and comfortable; New York-style. Bar: full; adequate wine list. Reservations: recommended. Hours: dinner Monday through Saturday.

Davey's Hideaway is a bastion of good, old-fashioned American cooking. Not quite comfort food, if that is defined as meatloaf and pot roast, but first-rate preparations of such things as calf's liver, prime rib, pork chops, fish, some adapted Italian dishes, and a steak or three. The lamb rack is a customer favorite. Davey's is a very comfortable place with a warm, inviting, buzzy, big family atmosphere.

The menu taken at face value is nothing special. The preparations are not complex, but they are well executed. Split-pea soup is included with the entrées. I know split-pea soup is really easy to prepare at home, but that doesn't make it any less rich, flavorful, and satisfying. Here the carrots are not puréed with the rest of the vegetables, a nice touch. In fact as I write this, a split-pea soup is simmering on my stove, and I have no intention of puréeing the carrots.

The rack of pork isn't really a rack in the "rack of lamb" sense. It is two rib chops cut from the rack. A whole rack of pork would feed a small marching band. Since 1964, food scientists have been systematically breeding the fat out of hogs. They have succeeded. They have created the other white meat, but they have also removed both tenderness and flavor. This is especially true with the naturally lean cuts like the loin and ribs. The good news is that Davey's chops have most of the tenderness and flavor associated with a big, fat, old-fashioned pig. How do they do it? I don't know, but there are a couple of techniques. First is the overnight brine soak. The whole rack is placed in a bath of water, vinegar, herbs, kosher salt, and something like honey or molasses. This saturates the tissues with a flavorful and fat-free liquid. The second method is injection. By the use of a large hypodermic needle, the tissues can be injected with either fat or flavored salt brine to restore the tenderness. Whatever the chef has done, this meat is not dried out or tough.

The pork is served with applesauce and a Merlot-peppercorn sauce. Applesauce comes way too close to comfort food for me, but the Merlot-peppercorn has a nice tanginess and piquancy that is both unusual and highly complementary. You usually encounter sweet and/or fruity sauces with pork so this one provides an interesting bit of variety. With a choice of rice, roasted red potatoes, or pasta and served with simple but beautifully prepared red peppers and string beans, this is excellent basic American fare *and* a complete meal for $20.

But wait! Before 6 P.M., there are five menu items for $14.95: prime rib, salmon, pasta, chicken, and the pork.

Fisherman's Market & Grill
★½
$-$$
Locations: 235 S. Indian Canyon Dr., Palm Springs, 327-1766; 44-250 Town Center Way, C2, Palm Desert, 776-6533; 78-575 Highway 111, La Quinta, 777-1601. Food type: grilled seafood. Ambiance: Palm Springs location is older and a little funky; Palm Desert has pleasant misted patios; La Quinta is the newest, but the patio is almost in the parking lot. Bar: beer and wine; happy hour. Reservations: not accepted. Hours: lunch and dinner daily.

This is simple grilled fish, fresh and of good quality. The happy-hour price is $8.95, which will get you sole, mahi mahi, salmon, fish and chips, or catfish. This is not fancy, and they have a tendency to overcook, but for fans of fish grilled simply, this restaurant cannot be beat at these prices.

Grill-a-Burger

$

Locations: 166 N. Palm Canyon Dr., Palm Springs, 327-8175; 73-091 Country Club Dr., Suite A-2, Palm Desert, 346-8170. *Food type:* diner; soda fountain. *Ambiance:* beachy and fun; tiki room. *Bar:* full; 60-ounce margarita for $25. *Reservations:* not accepted. *Hours:* lunch Tuesday through Sunday; dinner Tuesday through Saturday.

Ever feel like just having a burger and fries? How about a strawberry malt with that order? This is not a Children's Corner restaurant, as featured in Chapter 16. The portions are too large, the prices too high, and the booze flows too freely. Take the little ones to a chain like Ruby's Diner or Islands for their burger fix. Grill-a-Burger does fill the bill nicely for occasional adult cravings, however. Dogs and burgers are what they do, and they do them very well.

The room and patio minimally reference a Hawaiian burger joint, with palm fronds, bamboo, wicker, and wallpaper covered with banana leaves. The patio is crowded, noisy, and great for people-watching. Here, crowded and noisy is actually a plus, quite compatible with your Frank-n-Stein, your dog of choice and a draft beer, for $7.95.

There are 24 different burgers, all well thought out and made to order. Meat is USDA Choice chuck (probably), buns are freshly baked, and all garnishes are freshly sliced to order. A whole range of cheeses accompany the various burgers depending on the particular recipe. Boursin, for example, comes on the Oooh La La, with onions caramelized in red wine, bacon, and garlic mayo. Mozzarella accompanies the Mama Mia, with fire-roasted red bell peppers, grilled onions, and sautéed mushrooms on a toasted focaccia bun with basil mayo, and Pepper Jack garnishes the Babaloo, with jalapeño peppers, grilled onions, and bacon on a toasted jalapeño-cheese bun with chipotle mayo. As so it goes 24 times over. The intrinsic quality is high, and the prices are in the $6 to $15 range. Fifteen dollars gets you a triple-decker called the Kong.

In addition, there are 14 dogs and 12 burgers made with something other than beef, mostly chicken. Fountain treats and salads occupy a substantive part of the menu, and liquid libations of an alcoholic nature play a major role, including an almost two-quart margarita for $25 and beer by the pitcher.

Shakes and malts come with a spray of canned whipped cream on the top. If you are like me and prefer your malts pure, ask them to leave it off. Fries arrive in the strangest of shapes, indicating that they were cut in house. They are crispy, hot, spicy, and cooked through.

Hog's Breath Inn
★★½
$-$$
*Location: 78-065 Main St., La Quinta, 564-5556. **Food type:** American. **Ambiance:** new building faked to resemble an old Mexican village. **Bar:** full; large wine list. **Reservations:** suggested for dinner. **Hours:** lunch and dinner Tuesday through Sunday; bar open all day.*

When you first enter this building, there is a sense of confusion. The restaurant is upstairs, highly unusual in this area. In Italy, yes; in Palm Springs, no. At the top of the stairs—there is an elevator, too—you are confronted by huge murals of Clint Eastwood snarling and mugging for the camera, his six-shooter or .44 Magnum pointing right into your eyes. The floor is Saltillo tile designed to look 200 years old. The walls are hand textured to appear as adobe, when in reality they are plaster and dry wall. You are in Old Town, La Quinta's own movie set. A couple years ago, most of the old town of La Quinta was ripped out to make way for the new Old Town, two square blocks of kitsch. The Clint Eastwood posters are not intended as an ironic reference to the movie-set quality of the entire place but as homage to Eastwood's own ego. He built the first Hog's Breath Inn, arguably the worst name for a restaurant ever conceived, in Carmel many years ago. In 2005, he built the one in La Quinta. In 2006 a local restaurant corporation, the Kaiser Group, bought both restaurants.

Trappings aside, this place has consistently good first-quality American food that is clean, simple, and well prepared. This generalization is occasionally transcended, as it is with the artichoke soup. At first glance this seems an unlikely marriage. I must confess to never having experienced artichoke soup, and I approached it with not a little trepidation. It jumps right out of its league; it could grace the table of any three-star restaurant in town. Artichoke hearts puréed with cream is nothing unusual, but there are other layers happening here. Garlic, both in its fresh form and as garlic salt, is one of them. A subtle vinegar, rice wine perhaps, adds acidity. The addition of fresh bread croutons serves to provide textural contrast, but the croutons are whole grain or multigrain and add nuttiness more akin to breakfast cereal than does, for example, the sourdough crouton found in onion soup.

A hanger steak sandwich on ciabatta bread slides right into the trendy niche this restaurant is designed to fill. Hanger steak, like its close relatives from the belly area (brisket, flank, and skirt), is flavorful but tends to be tough if not treated with lots of skill and TLC. At Hog's Breath Inn, skill and TLC are in ample supply. A generous portion of steak, a marinade supplying the tenderness and flash grilling to keep it rare, results in an excellent primary component. Grilled onions and red bell pepper strips provide contrasting acids and textures. A slice of provolone—a good choice—brings a rich earthiness to the party. But there is not enough cheese; it is gone before the sandwich is half eaten. The ciabatta is problematic, too. This Italian bread, currently experiencing its 15 minutes of fame in this country, shows up in everything from fast food to *alta cucina*. The word "ciabatta" doesn't really mean anything except to refer to its slipper shape. It is not a recipe, per se. However, a ciabatta, as commonly understood in the United States, is flavored with an intense Tuscan olive oil and an herb such as marjoram or rosemary or even sun-dried tomatoes. It has a crispy surface and an airy, spongy interior that is based on a bread starter called "poolish." This intense, herb-flavored ciabatta does not allow for the flavors of the meat, vegetables, and cheese to speak clearly. Also the open spongelike texture of the bread quickly absorbs the juices of the fillings and renders it soggy—a poor choice of bread for an otherwise excellent sandwich

The menu at Hog's Breath Inn is uninspired. But for the diner without an adventurous spirit, this restaurant could fill dining needs at a relatively low cost, and lunch is an excellent buy. A few steaks, a couple chickens, a bit of barbecue (braised spare ribs and brisket—not recommended), and a smattering of fish round out the entrée options.

John Henry's Café
★
$-$$
#

Location: 1785 E. *Tahquitz Canyon Way, Palm Springs, 327-7667.* **Food type:** *American.* **Ambiance:** *a cute place in a strange place.* **Bar:** *full; poor, even frightening, wine list.* **Reservations:** *required.* **Hours:** *dinner Tuesday through Sunday.*

This immensely popular restaurant is in the oddest of spots, an alley. That's right, in an alley behind the Jensen's shopping center at Sunrise and Tahquitz in Palm Springs. Drive past the center heading east and turn into the first alley you come to. It will still not be clear where it is exactly, but that unmarked building on your right is the place. There are two entrances into the patio, none into the restaurant except by way of the kitchen.

Its cuisine is best described as pseudo fine dining. The draw here is cost. John Henry's is cheap. There is a direct competitor with a similar menu but much better food about two miles away called Café Scandia (Chapter 5). It is popular, too, but the crowds at John Henry's are uncanny.

The owners have managed to turn a seemingly disastrous location into something quite charming, made all the more so by its oasis quality. A circular patio completely enclosed by a seven-foot concrete-block fence is ringed within by flowers and trees decorated with Christmas-tree lights. Ample heating keeps the al fresco environment warm and cozy on even the coldest nights. The only view is that of the stars and a brick wall of an adjacent building. Inside are a few tables and some outré paintings—faux Lautrec done in a primitive semi-pornographic style. Black, white, and glass constitute the color scheme.

An appetizer consisting of a large wedge of Brie baked on a piece of French bread is served with candied walnuts and sliced apple. This is a variation of the popular desert salad: cheese (usually Gorgonzola), nuts (usually pecans), and fruit (usually pear) on a bed of lettuces (usually romaine and arugula) with a honey-mustard vinaigrette. Here the bread substitutes for the lettuce. This dish would have worked were it not for the choice of apple. A Red Delicious simply does not have the sufficient crunch and acidity to function as a foil for the cheese and bread. A Granny Smith or Pippin would add the necessary sparkle to bring the blandness to life. Walnuts are glazed and plated still hot, resulting in their sticking to the plate. All entrées are served with soup or salad. The mushroom soup tastes like Campbell's with extra mushrooms added. These would be the white cultivated variety. The base is thick with a decidedly commercial aftertaste. Osso buco is served with polenta and the vegetable du jour, carrots. The carrots are canned! Remember the cafeteria at your high school? Those are the carrots. A dubious polenta more reminiscent of cornmeal mush than polenta rests ominously on the plate. The recipes for grits and polenta are essentially the same—cornmeal and water—but polenta has evolved into complex delights in recent years. Made with stocks, cream, wild mushrooms, and sun-dried tomatoes, Italian polentas have added a whole new layer of fine dining to the local scene. The osso buco itself is not bad, though small. The sauce is on the greasy side but not objectionably so. Its flavors are traditional; the sauce, puréed.

Anecdotal evidence clearly states that the fish should be avoided. The rack of lamb, a small but full New Zealand rack roasted and served with the safe and ever-so-old-fashioned mint jelly ($17.95), is the most popular entrée. The house wine is Hacienda; avoid it like the plague.

This is the perfect venue for those who desire an elegant restaurant, have a limited budget, and whose palate is not particularly discriminating. Avoid the fish and the pasta, and bring your own wine—the corkage fee is $12—or stick with the either the Clos du Bois Chardonnay ($23) or Cabernet Sauvignon ($22).

Oceans

$-$$

Location: 67-555 E. Palm Canyon Dr., Suite C-101, Cathedral City, 324-1554. Food type: American, seafood. Ambiance: faux oceanfront eatery. Bar: full; small but thoughtfully chosen wine list with excellent prices. Reservations: accepted but not required. Hours: lunch and dinner Monday through Saturday. Chef: Jose Puentes.

Oceans, although located in an open mall, is designed and decorated in such a manner as to evoke the ambiance of a pier or beachfront restaurant. In fact, it would be right at home on a pier on a California beach. A patio with trellises, flowers, talkative parrots, and an overhanging wooden roof render it quite apart from its otherwise mundane Cathedral City environs. Inside, sand colors and ocean blue dominate the environment. Walls are adorned with paintings that at first glance resemble those of Sam Francis. At second glance, you notice they are actually abstract representations of swimming fish. It's all very clever and peaceful.

Oceans has three items on its menu that are excellent. The first is Mussels Oceans, briny and fresh and served in a thick Pernod-infused cream sauce. Pernod, with its notes of anise, is a common flavoring for mussels, but it is easy for a chef to pour too much or too little. Here the balance is perfect. Manufacturer's cream (cream with at least 36 percent butterfat) with bits of onion and tomato create the perfect nest for these little gems. The norm at most establishments is a watery, garlicky wine broth, but here the heavy cream offers a much more interesting medium with an excellent contrasting texture. Green-lipped mussels, or even larger black ones, would be an improvement, but the serving is large, 14 of them. Elsewhere the usual appetizer portion is eight.

Another outstanding menu offering is—surprise—escargot. I would expect the valley's best escargot to come from some upscale French establishment like Cuistot (see Chapter 4) or a classic bistro like Chez Pierre (see Chapter 5). To begin with, this is a textbook traditional recipe. I have had escargot with hazelnuts and lemon and in various concoctions with mushrooms and puff pastry. Most simply do not work. The snail inherently does not have much flavors so it is easily overwhelmed. A snail needs to be big, soft, and fresh. Small, rubbery, and stale just does not make it in the escargot world. Ever since ancient Roman chef Flavius Lupinus first fattened this gastropod for culinary purposes, butter, garlic, and a bit of herbs have proved to be the most successful interpretation. Served blistering hot in a sea of garlic and butter, Oceans' escargots are big fat and flavorful, relatively speaking.

Paella is the major surprise, if inconsistent. I have enjoyed paella from Madrid to Palm Desert. My favorite chefs have done it: Siklai, Pelech, Hamrouni. All of them are good, but this one is better, and from such an unexpected source. The chef is one Jose Puentes, and he has been with Oceans almost since its inception in 1997. This one at $21 is also the least expensive. It is served only as a special most weekends, so call ahead or request it in advance.

The biggest problem with paella is that it all begins to taste the same after a few bites. There is certainly enough flavor and textural contrast in this memorable dish that this should not happen, but it does. Whether it is prepared in the classical Valencia tradition with snails, rabbit, and chicken or under Cuban influence with shellfish, paella always seems to homogenize. This paella not only does not become homogenized, but it actually improves as you eat it. Puentes uses basmati rice, which is not only unusual but in fact acts in the opposite manner of the specified Bomba or even Arborio. Basmati is a dry, fluffy rice; the rices called for are starchy and creamy. Against all tradition, the basmati works and works well. Clams, mussels, a smoky, spicy sausage, an enormous shrimp—six inches long with shell on to retain maximum flavor—and a chicken thigh are added to the mix. Using the thigh whole prevents it from drying out and disseminating its flavor. The traditional peas provide a vegetal kick and another contrasting flavor to the dominant meat and rice. Saffron balance, a problem Puentes has with his bouillabaisse, is perfect here, but unfortunately, a recent tasting revealed a complete lack of that defining ingredient. (Paella without saffron is not paella.) Pierre Pelech at Chez Pierre (see Chapter 5) buys Bomba rice from Spain especially for this dish, but as superb a chef as Pelech is, his paella does not have the variety and depth of flavor as this one when it is prepared correctly. Chef Nyerick at the Miramonte Resort (Chapter 1) uses a rice similar to Bomba, Arborio, with more traditional results. I think the interest created by Chef Puentes derives from the combination of sausage, chicken, and shellfish. It is inauthentic but highly successful. With a rabbit leg in place of the chicken, a more authentic and wild taste could make this paella even more interesting. Or perhaps a turkey tail.

On the other hand, Oceans has shown itself inconsistent, especially with its specials. The chef has an instinctive touch with fish. He buys high quality, and he knows exactly when it is cooked, but he does not seem to know quite what to do with his perfectly cooked fish. That problem is called *capellini alla checca,* which accompanies virtually everything. Capellini is angel-hair pasta. *Alla checca* does not work with everything, and worse, it is not always *alla checca. Checca* is a raw tomato diced with the usual Italian ingredients: olive oil, garlic, basil, and chunks of mozzarella. There is no mozzarella here (fortunately), but sometimes a marinara sauce is substituted. This is a disaster. The fish, whether a salmon filet or a piece of sashimi-grade bluefin tuna, is squashed by a full-bodied tomato sauce. This experience has happened to me twice without a word from the staff. If it happens to you, send it back. You may also order these fish blackened, that is, Cajun style. The spicy surface is especially good with the salmon. The fish entrées served at Oceans are not complex recipes with weaving independent lines of contrasting flavors. These are simple grilled fish whose innate flavors are allowed to speak for themselves. Pasta Oceans—shrimp, scallops, clams, and mussels with capellini—also works well.

Even though there has been some minor deterioration in quality here since the first edition—I experienced a lobster tail that was thoroughly dried out, rubbery, and flavorless, and a paella was delivered without saffron—Oceans is still a satisfying, inexpensive restaurant with simply prepared fresh fish. I would prefer it to both Fisherman's Market and Grill (this chapter) and Pacifica Seafood Restaurant (Chapter 7). Prices at Oceans are reasonable, and if you order with its limitations in mind, you will have some wonderful seafood and save a bundle. As a rule, avoid the meat dishes.

Riccio's Steak and Seafood Restaurant
★★
$$-$$$
Locations: 495 N. Palm Canyon Dr., Palm Springs, 325-3111. Food type: steak, seafood, and Americanized Euro-American. Ambiance: cute, no frills. Bar: full. Reservations: suggested. Hours: lunch and dinner daily.

Let's all sing along now: "M-I-C-K-E-Y M-O-U-S-E. Mickey Mouse, ya da ya. Mickey Mouse, ya da ya."

If you are into faux, this the place for you. Born of desperation, Riccio's attempts to offer you everything their focus groups and PR advisors think you might want. Perhaps you do; perhaps this is right up your alley. Who am I to question focus groups? It is not bad, mind you, and it is also not particularly expensive. Lunch actually is cheap. Nevertheless, one has to ask, "Why bother?" There are so many other venues out there with so much more to offer.

The old Riccio's, some two miles north of this one and well off the beaten path, was a failed Italian restaurant with a long and notable history dating back to the Golden Age of Palm Springs. The new Riccio's has moved downtown where the bulk of the tourists wander. The menu tries to straddle trendy and easy American dishes and Italian favorites. Both suffer. All the while, Frank Sinatra croons favorites.

I order the New England clam chowder. Riccio's calls itself a "steak and seafood" restaurant, right? Clams are definitely seafood, so this should be indicative of the kind of work the kitchen does well. We'll see. When it arrives, it is very white, too white. It has a pleasant aroma but one more of bell pepper than of clams. There is no green, but little specks of red and yellow. I taste the red and yellow. Hmmmm. Too small to taste but probably tiny pieces of red and yellow bell pepper whose reality has dissolved into the cream base. The bell pepper flavor and aroma is pervasive but nice. I taste the clams independently. They are big and tender but lack flavor. I try another, then another. Virtually flavorless. I look for potatoes. This soup is not loaded down with potatoes; there are only a few pieces. The overall sensation is one of palatability, but the more thoughtful analysis consists of "Why can't I taste any clams?" I finish it. A greenish herb-infused olive oil with a peppery Tuscan finish and some fresh Italian bread go well with the soup.

The menu clearly denies its Italianate history; therefore, I pass up the cioppino in favor of the paella. Seafood, right? My plate arrives. Service is paced well: nothing is rushed. The dish looks odd. It is not yellow, but red. Paella absolutely *must* be yellow. The defining ingredient is saffron, which dyes yellow everything in its wake. I take a deep breath, expecting the distinctive blast of the world's most expensive food, the saffron thread (up to $2,000 per pound). Nothing. Paella without saffron is not paella; maybe it's cioppino over rice. I take a close look at the rice. Long grain! Paella is supposed to be built on the distinctive short-grain rices of Valencia, Spain. This looks and tastes like generic American long-grain rice.

I ask my waitress what fish are used in the cioppino. She is quite happy to tell me: shrimp, scallops, salmon, mussels, and clams. I look carefully at my paella: shrimp, scallops, salmon, mussels, and clams. There are also pieces of chicken and sausage here though. Hmmmm. Something is beginning to smell fishy, and it is not the clam chowder.

I try a clam. It is excellent, terrific flavor, cooked just long enough. I try a mussel. Poor. Tiny. Rubbery. I try a piece of chicken breast. Worse. Completely dried out and stringy. A piece of salmon is next. Good. Fat and tender. Not overcooked. Portuguese sausage, a.k.a. *linguica*? Fine.

Scallop? A little over cooked, but OK. Shrimp? Terrible! These have a most peculiar aftertaste. A chemical smell and taste, a preservative? This is a *"melosa,"* or juicy, paella. Tradition calls for a *"seco"* dish, but I like the wet ones too. This juice, however, is tomato based. This is a fish stew of the cioppino variety, not a paella. I try to think of the dish as a seafood stew over rice, setting aside all preconceptions of paella. Taken out of context the dish, except for the shrimp, is fair. The broth is Italianate. I imagine a chicken thigh and bigger mussels. It is difficult to imagine away the chemical aftertaste of the shrimp, but I do my best. As paella it is ridiculous, as a fish stew with rice it is better. The *linguica* would appear to be an exception to the paella/cioppino theory. Cioppino should certainly not have *linguica* in it as this cinnamon/cumin-flavored sausage has no place in a fish stew from Genoa.

There are five steaks on the menu ranging from $22 for a "petite" filet (presumably eight ounces) to $45 for a porterhouse. Sizes are not listed on the menu . . . curious. Rack of lamb, veal chop, pork chop, salmon steak, ahi steak, chicken breast, shrimp scampi, catch of the day, scallops—this is a masterpiece of originality.

The immediate neighbor to the south of Riccio's is another Riccio restaurant called "Al Dente," owned and operated by Kendra Riccio. It has been at the same location for at least 15 years. That restaurant has not been reviewed for this book. (One of the ones that fell through the cracks.)

The Right Bank

$ (with two-for-one coupon only)
Location: 70-065 Highway 111, Rancho Mirage, 202-9380. Food type: American (faux French). Ambiance: ancient Rome meets Las Vegas. Bar: full. Reservations: suggested. Hours: dinner nightly.

There is a standard two-for-one coupon for the Right Bank. The coupon is usually available in Wednesday's food section of the local newspaper, *The Desert Sun.* Unless you have the coupon, do not even consider dining here; it is ridiculously overpriced. However, with the coupon, the average price of an entrée including soup or salad is $13. This is so much of a bargain it makes eating the food worth it, at least for some.

The best way to describe the Right Bank is with the word "silly." It is silly in every respect. First, it looks silly: ancient Rome meets Las Vegas, with black carpet; black linens; a high, dark "cottage cheese" ceiling with track lighting; faux marble walls in beige; statues; busts; and plants. The menu is silly too. It is big and impressive looking at first glance, but after some careful analysis it doesn't make sense. It appears to parrot almost every other restaurant in town, but not quite. It is as though a serious-minded chef with big ideas and no talent decided to build it in his image.

Deep-fried wontons arrive with a liver paté and a shrimp paté. The liver version is not bad but looks most unappetizing. It is probably chicken liver processed with so much cream that it turns a gray color. The shrimp version tastes remarkably like Thousand Island dressing with pickles. Any hint of shrimp is found only in the imagination. Could it be the sauce from a shrimp cocktail? Battered and deep-fried carrots are at least funny. They taste a bit like doughnuts, but interesting, flavorful doughnuts.

Take the raspberry-beet soup, please! The color is an intense magenta. At first I think it is food coloring, but it can't be. No one would deliberately color food like this. It looks, feels, and tastes like a yogurt Push Pop. As soup, it is dreadful; as a little kid's frozen dessert, it might be pretty good. Or take the mushroom soup—condensed and canned but not thinned out. Opt for the salad. It is not good, but at least it is not outré. The blue-cheese dressing tastes like Ranch to which a few tiny bits of cheese have been added.

There is a whitefish Sanebel. As far as I can tell, "Sanebel" is meaningless. Sanibel, with an *i,* is an island off southwestern Florida near Fort Myers. With an *e,* it draws a blank from all sources. The menu advertises it as served with a rémoulade. Granted they are related, but this rémoulade is tarter sauce. Both are mayonnaise based, but a real rémoulade has parsley, tarragon, anchovy paste, chervil, capers, onions, and gherkins. This rémoulade has sweet pickles. The fish is quite good, fresh and not overcooked. It comes with a corn soufflé. The corn is crunchy as though scraped from the cob, or at least flash-frozen. The corn doesn't exactly match the wonderfully light soufflé, but all things considered it is good. Side vegetables are a different story. Carrots are blanched but almost raw and glazed with far too much sugar; string beans taste as though they are finished in rice wine and creosote—medicinal.

The rack of lamb Cabernet is actually half a rack, four of the tiniest chops ever seen, but—and this is a major but—it is excellent. The Cabernet reduction is actually wine-flavored brown gravy, but it does not entirely mask the lamb. This dish comes with mashed potatoes heavy on the garlic and the same vegetables as the fish.

So why bother? Price is why. Two entrées with accompanying salads can be had for under $30, and there are many choices. Just stay away from the soup.

Shame on the Moon
★★★
$$
#

Location: 69-950 Frank Sinatra Dr., Rancho Mirage, 324-5515. *Ambiance: misty moonlight; seductive.* **Food type:** *California and comfort food.* **Bar:** *full; remarkably inexpensive wine list.* **Reservations:** *recommended.* **Hours:** *dinner nightly.*

Almost invisible from the street, Shame on the Moon projects a dark, almost kinky moodiness—once you manage to find it. The ever-so-courtly Ann Drogeny, maven to the stars, escorts you to a private table, a rendezvous bathed in seductive darkness, a retreat of shadows and eerie moonlight. Lighting is by tightly focused spots embedded in the ceiling. Outside the main dining room is a long row of semiprivate nooks and crannies.

Shame on the Moon's food is best described as California-gourmet comfort food. The recipes are sophisticated, imaginative, and consistent. These days when $30-plus entrées are the norm and $40 entrées are becoming all too frequent, such prices are a welcome relief. And soup or salad is included. At $23, a Burgess Zinfandel, with hints of berries, pepper, and leather, is downright cheap for this wine in a restaurant.

Gazpacho is the antithesis of those watery concoctions reminiscent of V8 juice. This one projects notions of green pepper, onion, cucumber, and garlic, all subsumed within a thick tomato purée. This one is served very cold and slightly spicy with hints of cumin and chili pepper.

Flank steak—often a tough cut, but not here—is served with a peanut-teriyaki glaze, barbecued Mexican onions, corn flan, and roasted-eggplant compote. The result is layers of flavor coming from deep within the meat.

Imagine a teriyaki sauce—soy, vinegar, sugar, and garlic—blended with peanut butter. Sounds Indonesian, but the astonishing corn flan anchors it to the Southwest. Flan is a custard usually served as dessert. This one is packed with corn and served as a savory garnish.

Calf's liver, that lowly American diner staple, is transformed with deeply caramelized onions, applewood-smoked bacon, and garlic mashed potatoes. The main reason so many people dislike liver is that it is often cooked into shoe leather. Very fresh calf's liver, at least a half-inch thick, sautéed to medium or medium rare, is a delight. It has none of that unpleasant livery taste most people recall from their childhoods.

A 10-ounce pork chop is split and stuffed with green Swiss chard, ricotta, and mozzarella and served with dried-cherry chutney. The pork is dry, but the flavors are big and interesting. The bitterness of the chard is balanced by the richness of the cheese, while the cherry chutney offers a big dose of both acid and natural sugars.

Duckling with fig sauce is tender and moist, and the unique fig sauce is earthy, dense, succulent, and sweet. Actually, it is too sweet, probably a Bellona fig. The sweetness does wonderful things to the extremely tender duck meat, but it needs some kind of bite for balance, perhaps ginger. The port wine reduction and wild rice are superb.

"Dessert anyone?" A misty phantasm, Ann Drogeny, emerges from the moonlight.

"Not a chance. Just bring us the bill."

Dinner for four including tax, tip, and two bottles of Zin averages less then $45 a person. Slip out of the Moonlight into the moonlight.

Simba's

$-$$

Location: 190 N. Sunrise Way, Palm Springs, 778-7630. **Food type:** *down-home cooking.* **Ambiance:** *large cafeteria-style dining room.* **Bar:** *beer and wine.* **Reservations:** *suggested.* **Hours:** *dinner Tuesday through Sunday.*

From the street, Simba's appears almost like a palace, but inside the environment is more school cafeteria than fine dining, with large wooden tables and chairs filling the huge space. A large buffet offers diners the most variety, as well as the most value. Most of the menu is on the buffet,

242 THE PALM SPRINGS DINER'S BIBLE

excluding, unfortunately, the pork ribs and Louisiana hot links. Beef ribs are on the buffet, which gives some idea as to the quality of the barbecue in general.

The bottom line here is that most of the tastes are homogenized, overly sweet, and occasionally greasy. Cornbread, in particular, errs not only on the sweet side, but the ration of cornmeal to flour is so low the final product is more like cake than cornbread. It is nothing like Southern cornbread, which is three-to-one cornmeal to flour and has no sugar at all. Barbecue beans with pineapple are routine. Corn kernels come in a thin cream sauce. Turnips are interesting, not because of any turnip flavor, but because of the seasoning, which references east Indian cuisine. Collard greens are significantly more tender than those at Big Mama's (reviewed earlier in this chapter), but they are also sweeter. Yams are done with marshmallows that are even sweeter than the candied yams at Big Mama's. However, at Big Mama's vinegar is available on the table to temper the sugar rush. Because the collard greens here are also relatively sweet, they do nothing for the yams either. A "split-pea" soup is made with lima beans and ham hocks. It is not puréed, which makes the texture interesting. Whether you prefer this to actual split-pea soup depends on whether you like lima beans.

The barbecue is a disappointment. The meats, for the most part, are smoked, but it is hard to say what exactly is wrong. The beef ribs clear the bone nicely and have good flavor—both meaty and smoky—but the texture is stringy and tough. A nondescript barbecue sauce does not help. Smoked whole turkey results in nice dark meat, and an uninteresting but serviceable country gravy accompanies. It is, however, on the greasy side.

For my taste buds, the seafood gumbo is the winner all around. There are as many recipes for gumbo as there are cooks making it, but except for a layer of floating grease, this one is excellent. It is served as a soup, not as an entrée over rice. The seafood is catfish, battered and probably deep-fried, before going into the gumbo. Tiny cocktail shrimp are here also, but they do not matter much. What is particularly interesting are the multitude of flavors, both fish and vegetable, and the heat. Okra, jalapeños, and whole Roma tomatoes are simmered in a fish stock since forever, giving their all to a dense liquid boasting layers of complex flavor. Onion, bell pepper, celery, thyme, garlic, and bay leaf—they are all there weaving their magic. I have no idea why this gumbo is greasy, but it most definitely is.

As a buffet at $15.99, it is one dimensional. The buffets at any of the casinos do a significantly larger spread for only a few dollars more. If you are partial to the Southern style of cooking, this will satisfy for a reasonable financial outlay. Kids up to 10 years old eat for $10, which seems steep. Very small children are charged $7.

Tilted Kilt

Not reviewed

$-$$$

Location: 72-191 Highway 111, Palm Desert, 776-5554. **Food type:** *American.* **Ambiance:** *sports bar with Scottish theme in a Hooter's-style environment.* **Bar:** *full.* **Reservations:** *not accepted.* **Hours:** *Sunday through Thursday 11 A.M. to midnight; Friday and Saturday 11 A.M. till 2 A.M.*

This is a chain of some 40 restaurants. It is promoted as a Scottish (or Irish) sports bar with sexy waitresses. It appeals primarily to (just barely) postadolescent males. The menu is strictly American, or perhaps I should I be accurate: it is Italian, but nobody mentions the fact that pizza and pasta are Italian not Scottish (or Irish). They attach Scottish (or Irish) names to some American sandwiches (the Scottish cheese steak) or English dishes (fish and chips or a shepherd's pie), but that doesn't change anything. If anything, both the shepherd's pie and the cheese steak have been Italianized with Parmesan and provolone cheese, respectively.

The aforementioned waitresses are done up in "tilted kilts" more evocative of Las Vegas than Scotland: plaid miniskirt, push-up matching plaid bra, and little white tie top dipping rakishly beneath the plaid bra.

They offer lots of beer on tap (mostly American, but they do have Guinness and Dos Equis), a tiny selection of generic wine (mostly Sutter Home), and overpriced cocktails, bombers, and "bevis." So what is a bevi? It comes from the Italian *"mangia e bevi,"* which literally means, "drink your fruit" and idiomatically means an ice-cream sundae. Here it refers to a Polynesian-style fruit cocktail like the Caribbean Kilt (rum, pineapple, orange, and cranberry juices).

If you do not have anything to drink, the food is inexpensive: burgers, chicken wings, pizza, pastrami, French dip. Therefore, if you are a 22-year-old straight male who wants a pizza while he watches a basketball game and a waitress in a "tilted kilt" this is the place for you.

Rumor has it that the food is passable. I really wouldn't know; I haven't been 22 for quite some time.

Tyler's
★★
$$

Location: 149 S. Indian Canyon Dr., Palm Springs, 325-2990. Food type: burgers and dogs. Ambiance: stand, small counter, cute "tent" outside. Bar: beer. Reservations: no. Hours: 11 A.M. to 4 P.M. Tuesday through Saturday. Note: cash only.

The wait here can be horrendous. It is rumored that Bill Gates waited half an hour for a burger. Lines down the block are common. What is all the fuss about? These burgers are not cheap. In fact, they are expensive. A regular burger—no chili, no cheese, no bacon—is $6.75. That is $7.25 with California's exorbitant sales tax. You want fries with that? Four dollars more, please. You want to sit down, maybe have a beer or a Coke? Add another $4. Three dollars more for the tip. Your total is now in the neighborhood of $20 for a burger, fries, and a Coke. Tell you what. You want a burger for lunch? Walk across the parking lot to Palm Canyon and about half a block to the left. Stop at Zin American Bistro (Chapter 5) and order the Zin Burger: a half-pound of Kobe beef sirloin, caramelized sweet onions, Fiscalli cheddar, and fries. That's set you back $11. Add smoked bacon or avocado for another buck. Sit at a table next to the open window. Mindy herself may wait on you. No standing in line! Have a beer ($3.50). Tax, tip, beer, burger, fries $19. Hello!

For those who actually like standing in line, Tyler's burgers are good. Are they great? No, but you do get a substantial piece of meat, at least twice as thick as any fast-food chain's quarter-pounder. But here is the downside: if you order a burger at a real restaurant like Zin, described above, you can have it cooked medium or medium rare. It will retain its juices, be more tender, and deliver twice the flavor. Tyler's is a fast-food stand. Legally they *have* to cook their meet well-done or risk bacterial infection. *E coli* is life threatening. Yes, you get a nice fresh bun, Thousand Island dressing, onion, pickles, lettuce, and tomato, and you can pay an extra $2 for cheese or bacon. It is a good burger. O.K.? Get over it. Stand in line; what do I care?

Alternately, you could move to L.A. and get a Tommy's burger. Two dollars gets you the world's best fast-food chili burger: tomato, cheese, chili, pickle, onion, and a bunch of pickled jalapeños on the side. Bring your own six pack. No service, no tip.

Uptown Grill
★ (with early-bird coupon only)
$-$$$
Location: 150 E. Vista Chino, Palm Springs, 320-6116. **Food type:** *American.* **Ambiance:** *cute French country home.* **Bar:** *full.* **Reservations:** *suggested.* **Hours:** *lunch Monday through Friday; dinner nightly.*

Like its estranged sister across town, the Right Bank (reviewed earlier in this chapter), Uptown Grill is only recommended if you have the two-for-one coupon. Here the coupon is only good between 5 P.M. and 6 P.M. and applies only to six of the least expensive entrées. The coupon is available regularly in the Wednesday food section of the local newspaper, *The Desert Sun.* Without the two-for-one coupon, this restaurant is not recommended. There is much better dining available elsewhere, even in this discounted price range.

CHAPTER 9

Steakhouses

Steakhouses are perhaps *the* major dining attraction in the valley. At last count, there were 24 of them and the count is still growing. Of those 24, 17 serve USDA Prime steaks. In addition, most of the fine dinner houses of whatever culinary persuasion carry either a Choice or Prime steak on the menu, usually with the appropriate appellation. Thus in a French bistro an *entrecôte* can be enjoyed, and in a ristorante a *bistecca* is much admired. This fact brings the number of establishments where you can order an excellent steak up to about 200. What are we to make of this phenomenon? Perhaps a social anthropologist could attempt an answer, but I just eat the stuff and write about it. "Why" is well beyond my expertise.

Cuts

It is a confusing list to be sure: chuck, rib, Spencer, Delmonico, cowboy, New York, Kansas City strip, stripper, round, porterhouse, flank, hanger, cube, top sirloin, sirloin tip, filet mignon, T-bone, rib-eye, bone-in this, and bone-in that. My goodness! What is a body to do?

The first thing is to forget about that list. There are really only three steak cuts worthy of the broiler: rib, New York, and filet. Let us look at the three cuts and attempt to slide out from beneath the baggage.

T-bone is the classic cut of USDA Prime beef from the midsection of the short loin. It is really two steaks in one—the New York strip and a small filet—joined by the famous *T*. When the filet is full size, the steak is a porterhouse, the "king of steaks." A 24-ounce porterhouse is the best of both worlds: 14 ounces of New York steak and six ounces of filet mignon, with four ounces of bone.

The rib steak is one rib cut from the rack or rib cage and broiled or grilled. When served as a rack it is a standing rib roast. It is a roast, not a steak, and it is baked. Rib roasts can be as small as two ribs serving three or four people to entire racks serving upwards of 20 people, such as one finds in a Vegas buffet. Some steers are larger than others, but generally speaking a rib steak will range from about 12 ounces to perhaps as much as 30, bone-in. The bone weighs four to six ounces. The rib steak contains a lot of connective tissue and fat (exclusive of its marbling), most of which melts away during the cooking process. Excluding the bone and fat, a 12-ounce rib steak will deliver about eight ounces of excellent meat or one adequate serving for a normal adult.

The rib is not a hard-working muscle, so the meat is extremely tender. It is second only to the filet for tenderness. Because it is not hard working, it also delivers only moderate flavor. The most intense flavor of any meat cut lies next to the bone. Removing the bone may make for a more elegant presentation, or compensate for poor knife skills, but the meat that was around the bone will lose its flavor and tend to dry out more quickly. A Spencer steak, an almost obsolete term, is rib-eye in current terminology. It is supposed to be the center of a rib steak completely trimmed of its waste. A cowboy steak generally refers to a thick bone-in rib. It began life as a marketing ploy but is now becoming generally accepted.

The New York steak is cut from the sirloin at the base of the spine. The New York steak is the most flavorful of all the three major steaks. It is a semiworking muscle and has the defining flavor of steak. Unlike the rib, which is tender by its very nature, the New York steak is unpredictable. Logic then tells us that a super tender New York is the best of both worlds—both tender and flavorful. New York steaks can be cut to any size, but servings generally range from about eight to 16 ounces. This cut is usually not served bone-in and has little waste. So eight ounces means eight ounces.

Nowhere is terminology more confusing than with the New York. The Delmonico, another term moving toward obsolescence, is a bone-in New York. The Kansas City, Kansas City stripper, and strip steak are all boneless New York steaks.

The filet mignon, or great filet, has no waste and is the tenderest of all steaks. This muscle, cut from the short loin, does no work. It is not as flavorful as the rich and nutty New York, but its buttery softness is irresistible. The entire filet—approximately 16 inches long and five inches in diameter—can be cut to any desired thickness. When used for steaks, this means one to two inches thick. When used as a roast, the entire filet can be baked unadorned or done as one of the greatest accomplishments of culinary history, a beef Wellington. The filet is rarely served on the bone. It is rather pointless as the bone area is not very large, and the filet's flavor, subtle as it is, suffers little from being boneless. Four-, eight-, and 12-ounce servings are readily available.

Other steak cuts are of a different nature. The top sirloin is cut further up the back and is less tender and less consistent than the New York and filet. It is the middle-class substitute and can work very well in skillful hands. The chuck eye is the poor man's substitute and can also work well but requires even more skill. The flank, hanger, or skirt steak is from the belly area and is a working muscle. These are highly flavorful but tend to be tough. Again, in skillful hands—interesting marinades, braising, smoking, or sensitive grilling—the flank can become a fine meal. A few local chefs prefer flank and hanger steak to the more tender options because of their greater depth of flavor, but these cuts are not generally served in the steakhouses. Interestingly in these steaks, the method of carving is crucial to a tender steak. The meat must be cut across the grain or it is almost inedible it is so tough.

Other "steaks" are not worth your time or energy. For hamburger or stewing meat, the chuck or seven-bone steak or roast is the best. The fat-to-meat ratio is approximately one to three, resulting in a burger that is both juicy and flavorful. Braised in a stew or simmered in a chili, chuck is tender and flavorful but the fat must be skimmed. Sirloin tip makes a fine roast beef. Chuck roasts are the basis of pot roasts, and brisket becomes corned beef or the object of 24 hours of smoking for a Texas barbecue.

USDA Grading

The United States Department of Agriculture grades meat as Prime, Choice, Select, or Standard. Within each grade there are three levels: plus, neutral, and minus. The grades are a composite evaluation of factors that affect palatability of meat: tenderness, juiciness, and flavor. These factors include carcass maturity, texture, firmness, color of lean, and the amount and distribution of marbling within the lean. Marbling is intramuscular fat. It refers to the intermingling or dispersion of fat within the lean meat itself. Prime steak has the most marbling. Select is what you usually get at the supermarket unless you seek out and are willing to pay double for the Choice product. Locally, Jensen's carries Prime and Choice. Pavilions and Costco carry Choice. Ralphs, Vons, Albertsons, Stater Bros., and Wal-Mart deal fundamentally in Select, but Choice may be available at some locations.

What does marbling mean for taste? As a rule, the more fat in the tissues, the more tender and juicy the meat. However, this does not mean that increased fat is always a good thing. Aside from the obvious health disadvantage, there is the cost factor, and some cuts do not benefit from increased marbling.

The big winner here is the New York/T-bone steak. Already the most flavorful of the line-up, the New York is the chewiest of the major steaks. A Choice New York steak is excellent, but a Prime New York steak is marvelous. A Select New York is inconsistent. On the other hand, the rib steak and the filet are already so tender that the Choice cuts melt in your mouth anyway. Why bother paying the extra money? A Prime filet mignon is a waste of money—and we are talking a lot of money. Choice filet mignon is like soft butter. A Select filet mignon is as tender as a Prime New York. Unless you left your false teeth at home, there is no point to the Prime filet. The rib steak is not quite as tender as the filet, so some may opt to spend the extra money on Prime, but not this foodie. A Choice rib steak compares favorably with a Prime New York in the tenderness department. A Select rib steak, however, is not as good, but it is what I buy for home use. Black Angus, which is the preferred steak of many a fine chef and gourmet, is sold in higher-end supermarkets as Choice. The Black Angus, however, is a type of cow, and therefore can be any grade. Certified Black Angus Prime All-Natural is arguably the finest beef in the world—or at least the United States.

But what of the porterhouse? I have been known to spend the money on a Prime porterhouse. The combination of Prime New York and Prime filet is irresistible, even if Prime filet is overkill.

Kobe is a Japanese-style beef. It is fed beer and sake, and gin is rubbed into the skin. The animal must get no exercise because the result is a super-fat Prime. At $50 a pound for the New York (available at Jensen's), is the added level of tenderness worth the money? That is your call, but for the other cuts, it is simply not worth it by any standard. In recent years many restaurants have begun serving a Kobe burger. This is a marketing ploy, and it is ridiculous. Chuck steak makes for the best burger. When the meat is ground, the tenderness issue vis-à-vis fat is entirely irrelevant. Chuck steak is about 30 percent fat, which is the ideal ratio for a tender hamburger. Ground Kobe is so fat it tends to fall apart when ground.

Cost

Costs for Choice vs. Prime in a restaurant are remarkably similar. While the supermarket price of Choice New York steak is roughly half that of Prime, in a steakhouse the Choice product is only a few dollars less. A Choice rib steak served at Capri (reviewed later in this chapter), for example, is the best of both worlds, combining value and taste in one package.

Cookery

Cooking a great steak requires tremendous heat—between 900 hundred degrees to a blast furnace at 1,800! Steak lovers want a charred surface and a rare, even cold, center. A high-tech overfired broiler is the secret. This kind of broiler delivers tremendous heat that is both predictable and consistent. Some establishments use the underfired version, which has the advantage of searing the bits of dripping fat, which gives the meat a barbecued taste. As Daniel Garvin, director of marketing and sales at cooking-equipment manufacturer Montague, explains, "These fats drip down onto hot surfaces, where they are vaporized and drift back up around the meat as a flavor-infusing smoke." The disadvantage of the underfired grill is the potential for flareups, which can cause a burned spot or carbonization. Not only do these taste bad, but they are also carcinogenic. Home grills are underfired; they must be watched carefully.

At upscale restaurants that serve the better cuts of meat, the trend is away from the underfired grill to the overfired broiler, which employs a combination radiant-infrared ceramic burner that radiates cooking heat down onto the meat below. The upscale professional steakhouses in the Coachella Valley prefer this type of broiler. The Montague Radiglo C45 generates heat in the neighborhood of 1,800 degrees. Overfired broilers also are excellent for cooking thick lamb chops. "The higher-temperature radiant heat produced by overfired broilers quickly sears the meat, sealing in the juices, while the infrared heat penetrates the meat to cook the inside," Garvin says. "It is a method that produces an especially succulent cooked piece of meat, and this is what customers expect."

"How would you like that cooked?" That is the third question asked by every waiter in every steakhouse in the world. The first is, "Can I start you off with something from the bar?" followed by, "Are you ready to order?" The options according to current terminology are black and blue, rare, medium rare, medium, medium well, and well. For the steak lover, only the first three count. For the true steak aficionado, only black and blue counts. Black and blue is derived from the French term *bleu,* or blue, which, in food jargon, means raw. So a black and blue steak is one that has been "blackened," or seared on the surface to a dark crust, but raw in the center. What this does is provide for the maximum contrast of tastes and textures: hard-soft, seasoned-unseasoned, hot-cool, cooked-raw. Rare behaves in the same way, but without the extremes of hot and cold. The center is red but warm. Medium rare lessens the effect even more. Any more cooking than that and the point of a great steak is lost.

Capri Steakhouse
(See Capri Italian Restaurant, Chapter 6.)
★★★
$$
Location: 12-260 Palm Dr., Desert Hot Springs, 329-6833. **Food type:** *Italian and steaks.* **Ambiance:** *throwback to 1960; nice bar area; oppressive and claustrophobic dining room.* **Bar:** *full; adequate wine list.* **Reservations:** *suggested; required for bar room.* **Hours:** *dinner Tuesday through Sunday.*

Desert Hot Springs is a vastly different world from the resort cities on the other side of the valley. Its claim to fame as a resort city is based on water: natural, hot mineral water bubbling up from fissures resulting from the convergence of two faults. Other than this feature, which has resulted in a number of spa-oriented resorts, Desert Hot Springs is a rather sleazy small town with nowhere to go and little to do. With the exception of Casino, the restaurant at Two Bunch Palms Resort (see Chapter 1), Capri is the only restaurant in town worth considering unless you want Korean food.

Capri was built in 1962 by the Santucci family. The whole family still works the place, but the two sons, John Jr. and Joe, bought it from their parents in 1976. The bar room is very pleasant in a retro sort of way: low ceilings, a circular wall of windows, and an oak bar. Faithful regulars occupy the tables and bar stools. The dining room, however, is oppressive and claustrophobic. This means that reservations *must* be made for the bar room.

Capri is essentially two restaurants in one. The Italian food at Capri is mediocre at best, but Capri shines with its steaks. A USDA Choice 12-ounce rib-eye for $15.95 (16 ounces for $19.95) is a regular special.

252   THE PALM SPRINGS DINER'S BIBLE

Try that on the other side of the valley! This is an excellent piece of meat aged on premises for another 10 days before grilling. The regular prices for all the steaks, except the 16-ounce filet mignon, are in the mid-$20s. Steaks are grilled over an open gas flame. This low-tech cooking method cannot deliver a true black and blue, but an excellent rare is routinely delivered. Joe Santucci has developed something unique, within my experience, with his steak presentation. A small bowl, perhaps three ounces, of hot Marsala and melted butter is poured over the sizzling platter just as the steak is delivered. The liquid evaporates within seconds, but the most delightful residual flavor remains. There is nothing in this somewhat sweet fortified wine that diminishes the steak in any way. The sugars and acids of the famed apéritif from Sicily in fact enhance it. With a side of the simple oil-garlic-anchovy pasta, this steak compares favorably with any number of crosstown steakhouses at half the cost.

Other steaks are a New York strip, porterhouse, T-bone, and top sirloin. Because these steaks are Choice and not Prime, I would recommend the rib cuts or possibly the porterhouse. The porterhouse, at 25 ounces, is easily enough for two, but there is a $7.50 split charge, bringing the total to $37.45. It is not worth it.

Mama Julia makes a rum cake that is apparently well loved by the locals. I don't understand that. It is just a slice of ordinary pound cake with some rum poured over it served with a spray of canned whipped cream.

Chop House
Not recommended
$$$$
Locations: 74-040 Highway 111, Palm Desert, 779-9888; 262 S. Palm Canyon Dr., Palm Springs, 320-4500. **Food type:** *Prime steakhouse.* **Ambiance:** *Palm Desert location is an upscale coffee shop; Palm Springs is high tech but view impaired.* **Bar:** *full; adequate wine list.* **Reservations:** *suggested.* **Hours:** *dinner nightly.*

There are two Chop Houses in the valley, one in Palm Springs and one in Palm Desert. They are Prime steakhouses and are part of the Kaiser group of restaurants (see Kaiser Grille, Chapter 7).

Chop House is an oddity. For some reason, the steaks are cooked slowly. Lee Morcus, co-founder of the Kaiser group, has this to say about the peculiar slow-cooking aberration: "We broil meats at lower temperatures to retain the juice. Searing at too high a temperature destroys the fibers. When meat is cooked, the juice goes to the center of the meat. As meat cools, the juice should flow back into the extremities of the fiber. But if the fibers are destroyed, the juice just pools out onto the plate."

Of course, high-temperature searing destroys the fibers. That is the idea. This forms a sort of crust, which prevents the juices from pouring out. The purpose of standing time is to allow the juices to recede back into the meat. But the main reason for high temperatures is to caramelize the surface, releasing huge, sweet flavors and creating a contrast between the hot, seared, salty crust and the soft, cool, meaty center. At lower temperatures, the cooking is more even and this contrast is lost. With everyone else in town investing in high-tech broilers in order to sear their Prime steaks at 1,800 degrees, you have to wonder what is going on in the minds of Kaiser and Lee Morcus.

I sampled four different steak entrées at Chop House. All four were uninteresting and uniformly overcooked, even when ordered blood rare. This slow cooking cannot deliver properly cooked rare steak. Fortunately our party had a $50 promotional discount coupon or the dinner would have been vastly overpriced.

Dillon Roadhouse
★★
$-$$

Location: 64-647 Dillon Rd., North Palm Springs (Desert Hot Springs), 251-1991. Food type: steakhouse and miscellaneous American. Ambiance: roadhouse. Bar: full; do not even think about ordering wine; mixed drinks are iffy. Reservations: not accepted. Hours: lunch and dinner daily.

By definition, a roadhouse is an inn, usually outside city limits on a main road, providing meals and liquor, dancing, and sometimes gambling. It can also be known as a barrelhouse, a honky-tonk, or a juke joint.

Dillon's is not an inn, and it does not have gambling, but it is definitely outside the city limits—way outside. Officially, the address says North Palm Springs, an unincorporated area north and west of Palm Springs. However, the reality is that this roadhouse is closer to Desert Hot Springs than anything else. I venture to guess that not one person in the place would say that it is not in Desert Hot Springs, including the employees. The percentage of people who live in the resort cities other than Desert Hot Springs who have ever heard of this place is close to zero. Why do I know about it? Because I enjoy exploring, especially on a bicycle. I encountered it several years ago when it was called Ray and Joe's Office. Is it worth it? Yes and no. Dillon Roadhouse is absolutely not for everyone, but if you are comfortable with this profile, it may be just the place for you.

To get there (as no one knows about it, you cannot inquire) drive north on Palm Drive from Interstate 10 towards Desert Hot Springs. Turn left on Dillon Road and drive west about two miles. It will be on your left in the middle of nowhere.

The building is old, dark, and rather gritty. There are no tourists. The menu is mostly fast food with a few notable exceptions: a good rib steak, steak sandwich, and beer-can chicken, a first in my experience in any restaurant. Beer-can chicken was invented by barbecue guru Steve Raichlen, and it is a terrific recipe. The bird is heavily seasoned with paprika, brown sugar, mustard, garlic, onion, and chili powder. An open 12-ounce can of beer is inserted into the cavity, and the chicken is roasted standing up and covered on a grill over indirect heat. The beer steams the bird from the inside, keeping it moist throughout the cooking process. The dry heat on the outside crisps and caramelizes the skin. I cannot speak to how well it is done at Dillon Roadhouse, but anybody who advertises beer-can chicken had better do it right because anyone who knows this recipe will torture the chef who does it wrong. A full bird is $15. That is easily enough for two, or three in a pinch. The biggest inducements are the monthly specials. Smoked whole hog, for example, is offered at $9 a person, all you can eat. This is a terrific buy, but call to find out when it is happening.

Everything comes with French fries, undoubtedly precut and frozen, but perfectly adequate. A salad of iceberg, tomato wedges, cucumber, and shredded carrot is also included. A bottled blue cheese or Italian dresses it. A pitcher of Budweiser will set you back about $12. Not a particularly good buy, but certainly better than across the valley.

Live country music, naturally, and sometimes karaoke set the tone for the evenings, and you can dance the night away with no cover charge and plenty of raucous company. This is what a roadhouse is all about.

The Falls

Steak: ★★
Everything else: ★
$$$$

Locations: 78-430 Highway 111, La Quinta, 777-9999; 155 S. Palm Canyon Dr., Palm Springs, 416-8664. Food type: Prime steakhouse. Ambiance: Vegas glitz; aggressively commercial and noisy. Bar: home of the smoking martini; adequate wine list. Reservations: suggested. Hours: dinner nightly; "halfy-hour" with half-priced menu items.

There are two of these Falls, one in Palm Springs and one in La Quinta. They are so named because their décor includes sheets of glass functioning as shields for cascading water. These steakhouses target a younger, hipper crowd more interested in showing off than eating well. Fire pits, twinkling periwinkle lights, and Vegas glitz begin even before entering. The bar area, which is the center of the action at the Falls, is studded with retro lava lamps. Behind the bar, jets of water are fired through the air. The atmosphere in the bar area is loud, high energy, and very trendy, with aggressive fusion-jazz music filling in the blanks. There are as many diners in the bar area as there are drinkers.

This is the home of the smoking martini. I opted for one of these things in the interest of dispassionate journalism, despite my better aesthetic judgment. From the nine offerings I selected a Diane Grod-tini, a blend of rum, Midori (melon liqueur), banana liqueur, pineapple juice, and dry ice. The dry ice evaporates as a gas not as a liquid, which makes the drink appear to be smoking. It's actually rather pretty if a bit embarrassing. (Imagine yourself ordering one of these things in a waterfront bar in, say, Liverpool!) The martini tastes predominantly of banana and pineapple; any resemblance to an actual martini is derived solely from the shape of the glass.

The menu at first glance is impressive. It is large and offers what appear to be interesting variations on many traditional dishes: blue-crab cakes with sugar-coated sliced mangos finished with roasted red pepper sauce and flash-fried leeks and Colorado rack of lamb with roasted red pepper crème brûlée. I did not taste either of these so I will not comment except to ask the reader to run those ingredients around in your imagination and see where they lead.

Portions are not large; they are gigantic. The 30-ounce porterhouse

($51) will satiate two of the most voracious appetites. For price comparison purposes, look at LG's untrimmed 30-ounce Prime porterhouse at $54.49. This is a *trimmed* 30-ounce Prime porterhouse.

I asked for my steak black and blue. It came rare, but not black and blue. The meat was Prime tender but sorely lacking in flavor. Decidedly underwhelming when compared to LG's or Morton's of Chicago (both reviewed later in this chapter).

All steaks come with barbwire onions and a half-head of roasted garlic. The onions are tough, greasy, and flavorless. I love a roasted garlic head, but this one had something else on it, perhaps balsamic vinegar and/or sugar, significantly interfering with the essence of garlic. The Falls' chef even manages to produce a subpar baked potato, not an easy task since all that is required is a hot oven and an hour or so. It is underdone and retains a dampness characteristic of cooking in foil or a microwave.

New for 2009, the Falls has added a "halfy-hour." This is an excellent discount good between 5 P.M. and 7 P.M. Monday through Saturday and all evening on Sunday. Bar service is minimally discounted, but there is a bar menu that is downright cheap. I have not sampled this bar menu, but the offerings appear to be both interesting and a certainly a terrific value: roasted oysters with crab, shrimp, corn, topped with Parmesan cream ($7) or a steak sandwich with caramelized mushrooms and onions with melted Gruyère ($7). How about a smoked poblano chili stuffed with shrimp, cheese, and corn. Four dollars! Are you kidding me? Even if these specials aren't any good, with a $3 Stella Artois how bad can they be?

Fleming's
★★★
$$$-$$$$
Location: at The River at Rancho Mirage, 71-800 Highway 111, Rancho Mirage, 776-6685. Food type: Prime steakhouse. Ambiance: the usual dark wood, plus an "ocean" view. Bar: full; 100 wines available by the glass. Reservations: suggested. Hours: dinner nightly; bar menu; happy hour.

There are 32 Fleming's restaurants in North America. Fleming's is part of the multinational OSI restaurant group, which also owns Outback Steakhouse. Its claim to fame rests partly on the fact that it has 100 wines available by the glass. This represents a huge and dangerous investment as resealing methods are notoriously unreliable. Fleming's is either selling a whole lot of wine by the glass or the prices are inflated in order to cover the cost of spoiled wine.

Fleming's is located on the southeastern shore of The River, a spectacular outdoor mall constructed around and within a huge circulating artificial river rather like a moat. It is located in Rancho Mirage at Bob Hope Drive and Highway 111. Fleming's lays claim to an "ocean" view, albeit slightly man-made.

Is there a steakhouse in town that does not use vast quantities of dark polished wood? The interior space of Fleming's appears not as coherent as Morton's of Chicago, with whom it bares a family resemblance, but it is certainly comfortable, and the bar area is striking.

Fleming's is a notable exception to the rather dreary rule that states that steakhouses are notoriously lax in the side-dish department. Breaded Brie and a warm spinach salad are worthy creations. Five sticks of Brie approximately four inches long are thickly coated with breadcrumbs and either pan- or deep-fried. The cheese is unctuous, rich, buttery, and meltingly sensuous; the coating, crunchy. The combination is terrific. That is just the beginning. The Brie needs something tart, cold, and acidic. The solution is slices of pippin apple, but the chef is not finished. Thin slices of ginger contribute a unique heat and bite, and finally, a jalapeño jelly finishes it. This is a bit too sweet and doesn't have enough pepper kick, but the idea is right on. The dish in its entirety is well thought out and perfectly prepared.

The spinach salad is a different take on the usual, and this one is a high point in steakhouse side dishes. Sautéed mushrooms tasting mostly of portobello, red onions, bits of red bell pepper, tangy goat cheese, and spinach are served with balsamic vinaigrette. The chef is working the same contrasting set of tastes he used so effectively in the previous dish. The mushrooms are soft and full flavored; the red onion is hard, crunchy, and acidic. All elements work together and at the same time provide diverse tastes.

Baked potatoes are not fluffy. Have they really been baked? Perhaps they have been wrapped in foil or microwaved? The string bean special is garden-fresh baby beans blanched to an al dente state and finished in butter with almonds and bits of tomato. There is a reason why the French

"french" their *haricots vert*. "Frenching" means that the bean is cut into halves or quarters lengthwise. When the bean is thus cooked, its natural starchiness dissipates without damaging the bean's delicate flavor. These are not frenched. Creamed spinach is ordinary but thoroughly enjoyable. Because of the outstanding quality of these sides, I am tempted to suggest a few others although I have not tasted them. The tenderloin carpaccio with a caper-Creole mustard sauce and red onion could be excellent, but do not order it if you are having a steak, as it would be redundant. Sweet chili calamari served with crispy rice noodles is another potential winner. If you are unfamiliar with sweet chili sauce, expect a huge blast of sugar, garlic, and hot peppers. It is very popular in East Asian cooking. Rather than the usual baked potato, Fleming's potatoes with cream, jalapeños, and cheddar cheese could be an excellent alternative.

Undoubtedly, you have noticed that I have not yet mentioned the raison d'être of the steakhouse, the steak. A 20-ounce Delmonico, named for the famed *fin de siècle* New York restaurant where this steak was served, is a bone-in New York. Nowadays the name "Delmonico" is sliding into oblivion. Indeed Fleming's advertises it as a bone-in New York. The advantage of the bone is, of course, that the meat retains more of its juices. It arrives black and blue, as ordered, but considering that the Delmonico is the most flavorful of all beef cuts, this one is curiously bland. In a blind tasting, I might well have called this a filet mignon, as its tenderness is uncanny. Is the subdued flavor a characteristic of this particular steer? In every other respect the steak was superb, and Fleming's cannot possibly know if a particular steer has more or less flavor than any other.

I tasted both its béarnaise and peppercorn sauces. The béarnaise has a fine texture but is remarkably underpowered in the tarragon department. The peppercorn sauce is curiously bland as well.

Fleming's is well balanced when it comes to the pairing of steaks with sides. The steaks may not be as spectacular as they are elsewhere, but the side dishes are generally better, and the prices are not off the charts.

Hibachi Steakhouse

(See Hibachi Sushi Bar, Chapter 10.)
Not recommended
$-$$$
*Location: 71-680 Highway 111, Rancho Mirage, 674-0078. **Food type:***

Japanese teppanyaki-style steakhouse. **Bar:** *full.* **Reservations:** *required; timed seating.* **Hours:** *call for regular hours; early-bird and two-for-one specials frequently available.*

The Japanese-style steakhouse is more about entertainment than food. Going once can be fun, especially if you have children along, but do not go expecting to dine or even eat particularly well. Seating is timed. Audience members sit around a horseshoe-shaped bar that encloses the grill master/juggler. Dishes are surf and turf in various combinations: steak and lobster, steak and shrimp, steak and scallops. The meat—New York steak—is diced, which automatically diminishes the flavor. It also causes the meat to either be overcooked or stewed, damaging the texture that Americans especially love about steak. The temperature of the teppanyaki grill is much too low to cook a whole steak American style, but raising the temperature for these little cubes would burn them. The actual quality of the steak does not matter here, as any steak is reduced to its lowest common denominator when subjected to this type of cooking.

Unless you are truly interested in the show to the extent that the food becomes secondary, the Japanese steakhouse should be avoided. All three Japanese steakhouses listed here have good early-bird specials. Hibachi does have a terrific sushi bar. See the review in Chapter 10.

Ichiban
Not recommended
$-$$$
Location: 1201 E. Palm Canyon Dr., Palm Springs, 318-1622. **Food type:** *Japanese teppanyaki-style steakhouse.* **Bar:** *full.* **Reservations:** *required; timed seating.* **Hours:** *dinner nightly; early-bird and two-for-one specials frequently available.*

See review of Hibachi Steakhouse.

Kobe
Not recommended
$-$$$
Location: 69-838 Highway 111, Rancho Mirage, 324-1717. **Food type:** *Japanese*

teppanyaki-style steakhouse. **Bar:** *full.* **Reservations:** *required; timed seating.* **Hours:** *dinner nightly; early-bird and two-for-one specials frequently available.*

See review of Hibachi Steakhouse.

LG's
Steaks: ★★★★
Everything else: ★★½
$$$$
Locations: 74-225 Highway 111, Palm Desert, 779-9799; 255 S. Palm Canyon Dr., Palm Springs, 416-1779; 78-525 Highway 111, La Quinta, 771-9911. **Food type:** *Prime steakhouse.* **Ambiance:** *Palm Desert is a very old but comfortable building with Santa Fe-style architecture; Palm Springs location is intimate and comfortable with an interesting layout and beautiful patio; La Quinta is high-tech contemporary in pseudo Santa Fe style with a receding roof that opens to the sky.* **Bar:** *full; extensive award-winning wine list; $25 corkage fee.* **Reservations:** *suggested.* **Hours:** *dinner nightly.*

LG's was born in 1991, founded by retired steak lover Leon Greenberg, who was frustrated that he couldn't get a good steak in the Coachella Valley. Just east of Deep Canyon on Highway 111 stands the oldest and still premier steakhouse in the desert. According to Tom Horan's America's Top Ten Club, LG's is one of the country's top 10 steakhouses, the only one from California so designated. Horan is a former restaurateur, author of several dining guides, and founder of the Independent American Restaurant Association. LG's is also the recipient of the DiRoNA (Distinguished Restaurants of North America) Award of Excellence. Only 800 restaurants have achieved this list.

There are three LG's in the desert resort areas: Palm Desert (the original), Palm Springs, and La Quinta. The ambiance is different at each of them. The original is the homiest. It has a definite lived-in feel that comes with the patina of age. The building itself dates from the late 1940s and has the high ceilings and rough wooden beams characteristic of the Sante Fe style. A central wood bar beckons as guests arrive. Colors are light. It is comfortable but not intimate.

The success of the Palm Desert venue prompted the opening of a second restaurant in Palm Springs a few years later. It is in an existing building in a Spanish/Mexican style of architecture common in downtown Palm Springs. The smallest of the three, it has a charming heated and misted outdoor patio with a firepit. The interior space meanders around, resulting in spaces that are more isolated. There is privacy to be had here that is not available at the other two locations.

The La Quinta restaurant, built expressly as an LG's, is the newest. An attempt was made to retain at least a pseudo Sante Fe look—high ceilings and wooden beams—but the feel is high-tech contemporary. A central ceiling panel can be opened to the stars, weather permitting. There is a large outdoor patio and fireplace similar to the Palm Springs location, but the ambiance is somewhat sterile.

Exactly how good is LG's? Is it really the best in the valley? Service is impeccable from the moment you call for a reservation till the moment the valet closes the car door. As to the steaks themselves, they cannot be faulted. The jewel in the crown, a 20-ounce porterhouse, is tied for the best steak I have ever tasted. The same quality is present throughout the menu. Only USDA Prime is served—the top 2 percent of corn-fed Kansas beef dry aged for approximately 35 days. The meat has already been hung for three weeks before it arrives at LG's, where it is hung for another two. This aging process reduces the water content of the meat, concentrating the flavor and imparting a unique nuttiness. The steaks at LG's are magnificent, but the 24-ounce porterhouse at Morton's of Chicago is just as good and the 20-ounce T-bone at Ruth's Chris is clearly competitive.

LG's is very expensive, the most expensive in the desert outside of the casinos. The Gold Striker, a 30-ounce untrimmed porterhouse is $54.49 as of this writing. By the time you actually read this, it may well be $60. Everything is à la carte. A tomato and onion salad is $9. A portobello mushroom cap is $13. Escargots are $14, and a Caesar salad for two is $20. Seasonal berries for dessert are $9. Sharing is a viable proposition, however. The restaurant is happy to provide extra plates at no charge, but remarkably few people elect to go this route. The award-winning wine list is enormous and offers bottles within a wide range of prices from $28 to $500, with most bottles in the $40 range. Should a couple elect to order full meals—predinner drinks, appetizers, median-priced bottle of wine, steaks, potatoes, vegetables, desserts, and after-dinner drinks—they would be looking at a total cost in the neighborhood of

$400. On the other hand, a couple could order the Caesar salad for two, split the 20-ounce porterhouse, potato, and vegetable, forgo the dessert and drinks, and bring their own wine and pay the $25 corkage fee. Their final bill would be about $130, including tax and tip. They would leave not the least bit hungry and would probably enjoy the experience more because it did not cost them $400. They also wouldn't have a bunch of doggy bags to take home. Nevertheless, LG's regular clientele generally opt for the former not the latter. This fact should in no way deter a more budget-conscious diner. Greenberg is perfectly amenable to the choices of his more frugal patrons.

The issue of side dishes in a steakhouse is a touchy one. As a general rule, they tend not to be of the same caliber as the steak. At LG's, I can recommend with complete confidence the Caesar salad. This is the only truly authentic and genuine full-flavored Caesar in the entire desert. Caesar Cardini's memorable recipe is followed almost to the letter. Romaine hearts, crispy and fresh, are chopped into uniform one-inch squares. A dressing of anchovies, Dijon mustard, Worcestershire sauce, coddled egg, olive oil, lemon juice, and red-wine vinegar is prepared tableside. House-made croutons and freshly grated Parmigiano-Reggiano are added. Cardini specifies that the cheese is to be shaved tableside; here it is grated back stage, but it still packs the wonderful punch that only Parmigiano-Reggiano can. With freshly ground pepper and served on chilled plates, this Caesar is virtually perfect.

The creamed spinach, likewise, is superb, with its heavy cream and garlic flavors supporting and complementing the spinach. Parmesan-garlic mashed potatoes are good but curiously lacking in flavor considering the potency of their ingredients.

I would not order ethnic-specific cuisine such as escargots. Nor would I order an entrée that is not a steak. Steak is the raison d'être of LG's. If you want something else, go somewhere else.

LG's does not offer sauces on its steaks. Sauce béarnaise and *poivre* are the options most often available at other locations, but in my opinion these concoctions, which have a solid place in French cuisine, do not belong here. Not only are they generally not prepared well by steakhouse chefs, these huge American-style platters of meat are at their best adorned with nothing but salt and pepper. LG's does well by understanding the true aesthetic of the American steak.

Morton's of Chicago
Steaks: ★★★★
Sides: ★
$$$$

Location: 74-880 *Country Club Dr., Palm Desert,* 340-6865. *Food type: Prime steakhouse. Ambiance: dark, wood-paneled men's club; high energy but not noisy. Bar: full; extensive wine list. Reservations: suggested. Dress: In their words, "Jeans, T-shirts, shorts, and sandals are not appropriate for dining at Morton's." This is one of only three explicitly stated dress codes of which I am aware. I do not know if it is enforced, but my guess is that a woman wearing designer jeans or a man in dress shorts will not be turned away. Hours: dinner nightly.*

Morton's is a formidable steakhouse chain in direct competition with Ruth's Chris. This international corporation with 65 restaurants arrived in the desert in 1993. Morton's defines "the look": dark, wood-paneled men's club, subdued lighting, Sinatra singing in the background. Martinis, scotch and soda, and bourbon on the rocks are the libations of choice. Morton's exemplifies the Platonic idea of the great steakhouse better than anyone.

A sample tray displaying the menu choices is presented tableside. This is an excellent idea, especially for those not quite sure how much 14 ounces really is or those with uncertain knowledge of the various cuts of meat. Offered are a New York strip at 20 ounces, a 14-ounce rib-eye, and a 14-ounce double filet. The 24-ounce USDA Prime porterhouse, ordered and delivered black and blue, is genuinely magnificent, and it is the only bone-in steak on the menu.

With a black and blue steak, this is what happens in the mouth. The first experiences are heat, crunch, and salt. A few moments later exactly the opposite happens: cool, soft, and the intense flavor of the meat without seasoning. If you are squeamish about ordering your steak like this, I urge you to try it at least twice. Remember you can always return it for more cooking. Also, keep in mind that your steak will continue to cook after it has been removed from the heat. This is called carry-over and is true of all cooked food. Treat yourself to one of the most wonderful taste experiences in the world.

As for the side dishes, the lyonnaise potatoes are cut too coarsely with too much onion to lay claim to the label "lyonnaise." They are overcaramelized—burned—and rather rustic. Beefsteak tomatoes with blue cheese is a dependable side dish. The tomatoes are large, meaty, and full of fresh tomato flavor, but perhaps the vinaigrette and red onion version would better serve the meat.

Morton's offers two classic sauces for their steaks: béarnaise and a five-peppercorn cognac-cream sauce. The use of different kinds of cracked peppercorns introduces a heat quite unlike that of a chili pepper. Steak *poivre* is a classic steak recipe, but I find cream to be problematic. Cream on steak? Not for my taste buds! The béarnaise, though a little thin, is a true béarnaise. Steak with béarnaise, especially filet mignon, adheres to the standards and principles of haute cuisine. The primary flavoring of a béarnaise is tarragon, a potent herb with notes of licorice. I ordered a taste of both of these sauces, but did not use either of them. Best advice with a steak like this: Leave well enough alone.

Outback Steakhouse
★½
$$-$$$
Location: 72-229 Highway 111, Palm Desert, 779-9068. Food type: Choice steakhouse. Ambiance: barn with Australian tchotchkes. Bar: full. Reservations: not accepted, but you may call ahead for "preferred seating," which reduces your wait. Hours: dinner nightly.

OSI is the parent company of the Outback Steakhouse chain. It is a gigantic multinational linked either directly or indirectly with Fleming's (reviewed earlier in this chapter) and Roy's (see Chapter 4).

The barnlike room in mostly wood is ornamented with Australian trappings like neon crocodiles, stuffed kangaroos, and boomerangs. Booths are the norm, with tables available only for large parties.

Outback serves Choice steak with the addition of chicken, ribs, and fish in different locations, depending on demand. Food is moderately priced and adequately prepared. The most expensive item on the menu is the Melbourne, a 20-ounce porterhouse at $25.99. This includes a choice of two sides from an extensive list. That is 40 percent of what the same would cost at LG's (reviewed earlier in this chapter). Outback is enormously popular. Why? The simple answer is that it is the restaurant of default—the same reason some Americans might go to McDonald's in Tokyo but not in Chicago. The menu is familiar and undemanding. Food is prepared simply, and the quality is high. You don't have to worry that you may have to unravel a complicated French menu or be confronted by some weird sauce. Outback is also child friendly—although the "littlies" (Australian slang for kids) are considered adults here at age 10—with steaks, chicken, ribs, and burgers available for around $6. Perhaps in many parts of this country or some parts of the world, an Outback is a much-needed addition to the local dining scene. But here in the desert, more and better can be had with intelligent ordering at any number of establishments for the same money.

Even my brother, a foodie of some stature, will occasionally pay a visit to Outback. These are his exact words: "I actually like Outback. When I'm not in the mood for cooking or paying big bucks for a nice meal, I go there. The price has gone up a bit lately, but it is still one of the best buys around for a rack of lamb, a bottle of wine, an appetizer, tip, and tax for under $50. Colleen and I did just that a few weeks ago. We split the meal, and that is exactly what we paid, all-inclusive." He lives in the Boston area and is a fine cook himself, so there is not exactly a dearth of options available to him.

Players Steakhouse
Steak: see text
Everything else: see text
$$$$

See full review in Chapter 3 under Fantasy Springs Resort and Casino.

Ruth's Chris
Steaks: ★★★
Sides: ★★
$$$$
Location: 74-740 Highway 111, Indian Wells, 779-1998. *Food type: Prime steakhouse. Ambiance: Southern aristocratic estate; formal. Bar: full; extensive wine list. Reservations: suggested. Hours: dinner nightly.*

Ruth's Chris founder Ruth Fertel pioneered the sale of Prime steak in the United States, in New Orleans to be exact. She was also the first to bring Prime steak to the Coachella Valley.

The story of Ruth Fertel is well known but an interesting one nevertheless. A chemistry major in college, she taught school briefly and later become a medical technician. She took a plunge in 1965 and bought the defunct Chris Steakhouse with a $22,000 mortgage on her house. The rest is history. With 130 restaurants worldwide, Ruth's Chris became the original Prime American steakhouse.

When you enter Ruth's Chris you enter a world apart, an ambiance that evokes the Southern aristocracy. It is formal, elegant, and quiet. Cell phones must be turned off. Everything from linens to carpeting is of the highest quality but without ostentation; old Southern money has no need to show off. Discipline and reserve, quality and manners, these are the organizing forces behind this venerable dining establishment. Service is faultless (as though it could be otherwise). Even the decanting of the wine is performed with efficiency, élan, and without having to ask.

Side dishes are inconsistent. With the recommendation of my waiter, I ordered lyonnaise potatoes and a small Ruth's chop salad. A lyonnaise is thin slices of potato sautéed until three-quarters cooked. Chopped onion is added, and the sauté is complete when the potatoes are golden. These potatoes are dark brown, a bit greasy, and overcooked. The salad consists of julienne of iceberg, spinach, radicchio, red onions, mushrooms, green olives, bacon, eggs, hearts of palm, croutons, blue cheese, and lemon basil dressing with cherry tomatoes and crispy fried onions. The result of this concoction is surprisingly rather bland. The vast numbers of competing flavors tend simply to nullify all of them.

Steak here is just about as good as it gets: thick, juicy, tender, flavorful, USDA Prime, Midwestern corn-fed, custom-aged, and perfectly cooked (rare) T-bone. Cost? $35 for about 16 ounces, excluding the bone. Like LG, Fertel believed that a great steak is best served au naturel. Salt and pepper is about it. A porterhouse for two, rib-eye, New York, and filet in various sizes round out the list.

Spa Steakhouse
Not recommended
$$$$

See full review in Chapter 3 under Spa Resort Casino.

The Steakhouse
Not recommended
$$$$

See full review in Chapter 3 under Agua Caliente Casino.

Sullivan's
Steaks: ★★★
Everything else: ★★
$$$-$$$$; $5 bar menu
Location: El Paseo Gardens, 73-505 El Paseo Dr., Palm Desert, 341-3560.
Food type: Choice steakhouse. **Ambiance:** Chicago men's club circa 1928;
terrific outdoor patio; live jazz. **Reservations:** suggested but not accepted for
patio. **Bar:** full; good wine selection. **Hours:** dinner nightly.

Sullivan's is another international chain to enter the desert in the last
few years. A stroll into Sullivan's . . . Oh, wait. You can't stroll into
Sullivan's. With the doors open—as they usually are—Sullivan's seems
to be everywhere. Some of the best live jazz in the valley (especially on
Thursdays) emanates from the huge bar. Many of the patrons are actually
listening to the music. All along the patio, which is part of the second
floor of El Paseo Gardens, there are diners, drinkers, schmoozers, and
jazz aficionados. The dining room is packed. Stylized boxing murals
reminiscent of the paintings of George Bellows are painted on the walls.
Sullivan's refers to John L. Sullivan, the 19th-century bare-knuckle
heavyweight. With its lavish use of dark wood paneling, this place
emerges as a Roaring Twenties-style speakeasy or Chicago men's club. It's
fun, loud, aggressive, and busy. It is absolutely nothing like Ruth's Chris.

Service here is friendly—crushingly friendly—but it is neither
knowledgeable nor accurate.

The steaks here are not Prime; they are Choice. This matters little
except in the New York and the porterhouse. For comparison purposes,
I usually order the porterhouse at all steakhouses. Here it is thick, juicy,
and flavorful. How does it compare with its exact Prime parallel, the
24-ounce porterhouse at Morton's or LG's? The Prime is better, and the
cost difference is marginal at Morton's but substantial at LG's.

I ordered the baked potato with all the stuff on it, a Caesar salad, and creamed spinach. I substituted split-pea soup for the iceberg wedge that comes with the steak. The potato is as you would expect. The Caesar is dull: no anchovies, ordinary Parmesan. The creamed spinach is good with lots of garlic and cheese. The soup is undistinguished.

The issue at Sullivan's is reduced to two factors: cost and ambiance. The cost of dining at Sullivan's is marginally lower than at Morton's or Ruth's Chris and substantially lower than LG's. In the ambiance department, Sullivan's has everyone beaten if high-quality live jazz is something you desire while eating. The outdoor patio is both delightful and far enough away from the musicians so that the music does not intrude yet close enough to listen should you so desire. The dining room is crowded, noisy, and separated from the music. The bar area, which is where the jazz trio performs, is also crowded and noisy, but here the noise is the music. An inexpensive bar menu allows diners who are also jazz aficionados a first-rate place in which to hang out.

CHAPTER 10

Chinese and Japanese

Chinese

Chinese food is not done particularly well in the Coachella Valley. In contrast with Japanese restaurants this seems particularly odd, as Japanese cuisine is less well known but more demanding, at least in its popular American form. There are Chinese restaurants scattered about all over the valley. Most are all-you-can-eat neighborhood buffets guaranteed to make you feel just a little bit ill, but several notable exceptions exist.

Canton Bistro
★½
$

*Location: 79-405 Highway 111, La Quinta, 771-9129. **Food type:** Chinese. **Ambiance:** well-done storefront. **Bar:** full. **Reservations:** taken only for parties of six or more. **Hours:** lunch and dinner daily.*

What can I say? There is nothing really wrong with Canton Bistro. It's just that I cannot think of any reason to recommend it except perhaps the duck. The menu is ordinary Chinese-American cuisine. The preparations are routine stir-fry; nothing special happens here. The duck is nothing special either, except that is it $9.95. A half-duck for $9.95 with rice and veggies—even boring ones—is a really good buy, especially considering the fact that a half duck probably cost them $5. Duck is a daily special, which means that it is not on the menu but they have it all the time.

Citi Wok
★
$-$$

*Location: 74-970 Country Club Dr., #450, Palm Desert, 341-1511. **Food type:** Chinese. **Ambiance:** austere, with takeout counter, small patio close to the noise of a major intersection. **Bar:** beer and wine. **Reservations:** not accepted.*

Hours: from 11 A.M. weekdays and 11:30 A.M. weekends. Special note: delivery.

This is your usual neighborhood Chinese restaurant. Along with Morton's Steakhouse (Chapter 9), La Bella Vita (Chapter 6), and Cork Tree (Chapter 7), it is also part of the big four restaurants of the Desert Springs Market. The dining room is an austere L-shaped room with lots of plastic and plywood. The patio consists of a few tables set up along the south wall. There is plenty of street noise.

If there is one thing Chinese food is generally not, it is boring. Citi Wok manages to earn high grades in the dubious task of producing truly bland food.

Hot and sour soup is neither hot nor sour, but it does have cornstarch in copious quantities. And tofu—don't forget the tofu. In the world of bland, tofu ranks near the top. Woodear mushrooms, perhaps my least favorite of all mushrooms, are the only noticeable flavor ingredient. This soup is marked with two red chili peppers on the menu indicating that it is hot and spicy. It isn't. But it does have a lot of cornstarch.

I opt for the catfish with black bean sauce. (*Catfish in Black Bean Sauce* is also the name of a movie made by Vietnamese writer-director Chi Muoi Lo in 1999.) This is the most original thing on the menu; I have great hopes. I used to patronize a little Chinese restaurant in L.A.'s Chinatown. They served a whole fish in black bean sauce with scallions, garlic, and cilantro that knocked my socks off with its potent flavors. I was hoping for something along those lines. What I got was just another stir-fry with chunks of catfish dredged in cornstarch (maybe somebody here owns stock in some cornstarch factory) and fried. Yellow squash and bean sauce are added. This is not the recipe for catfish that I know. The one I know calls for a whole fish with slivers of fresh ginger inserted under the skin. The fish is then deep-fried, bathed in black bean/soy sauce, and served with fresh tomatoes, scallions, and lime wedges. That is not even close to what I got. This has no taste at all, not even a bad taste, just nothing.

Citi Wok's *gyoza bao* does not fare as well. These are not just bland but also unpleasant. *Gyoza bao,* or dumplings, are actually Japanese not Chinese and unlike Chinese dumblings, *gyoza bao* are first fried then steamed. They are *supposed* to be made of bao dough (which is just flour and water) stuffed with ground pork, shredded cabbage, soy sauce, ginger, mirin, sugar, and scallions. They are *supposed* to come with a dipping sauce of soy, rice vinegar, mirin, sugar, and garlic. (Mirin is a very sweet rice wine.) These are not bland ingredients. What does one have to do to remove all the flavor from these things?

The best thing I taste is the shrimp with lobster sauce. This is nothing special, but it, at least, has some flavor, traditional Chinese-American-corner-restaurant flavor though it may be. Bamboo shoots, water chestnuts, peas, carrots, mushrooms in a pleasant lobster-flavored sauce complement the shrimp nicely. One out of four? One star.

P. F. Chang's China Bistro
★★½
$-$$
Location: *at The River at Rancho Mirage, 71-800 Highway 111, Rancho Mirage, 776-4912.* **Food type:** *Chinese (Mandarin and Szechuan).* **Ambiance:** *big, beautiful palace; riverside patio.* **Bar:** *full; extensive wine list for a Chinese restaurant.* **Reservations:** *suggested.* **Hours:** *lunch and dinner daily.*

There are 27 P. F. Chang's restaurants in California alone. In addition, P. F. Chang's operates the Pei Wei Asian Diner and the Taneko Japanese Tavern chains. What is surprising is that a chain of this magnitude can be so successful and relatively uncompromising at the same time.

The building is spectacular, with slate walls and alcoves for the banquettes. Statues of Chinese warriors and delicate vases are recessed into the walls. A huge horse appears at the entrance. A lovely patio sits "riverside," heated or misted for temperature control. An enormous semicircular bar adorns the rear wall. A mural depicting rural Chinese tradition mirrors the bar shape. Huge orange lights evocative of flying saucers or stylized mushrooms are suspended from the ceiling. Red lanterns hang over the banquettes. Overall, it is much more suggestive of postmodern America than traditional China, but this does not really detract from its beauty. The fact that there is no aroma, however, does detract.

The mandarin side of the menu is comprised mostly of the usual stir-fries: the ever-popular kung pao chicken, moo goo gai pan, and beef with broccoli. There are, even here, a number of more interesting offerings such as oolong-marinated sea bass and wild Alaskan sockeye salmon, which are broiled and steamed, respectively. The Szechuan menu proves to be the more unusual. These Szechuan dishes do not compromise on the signature

Szechuan heat. On a one to 10 scale, they come in at around a nine, which is virtually unheard of in these parts. Locally, even Thai and Indian restaurants, traditionally hotter than Szechuan, hold back the chili peppers. Flaming red wontons is a case in point. These are poached pork dumplings in a spicy garlic-sesame-soy broth. Nothing prepares the casual diner for the major league punch of scallions and pickled red chili peppers. Be forewarned: when a dish is labeled "spicy" on the Szechuan menu, it is true. It is not true on the Mandarin menu.

Szechuan green beans are fabulous. The beans themselves are cooked until just a hint of crunchiness remains. They are stir-fried, garnished with pickled vegetables, and dressed with chili peppers and garlic. The heat and chili flavors complement the intrinsic flavor of the beans, which retain their integrity in spite of the onslaught of heat.

The menu claims the sea bass is broiled. This does not appear to be the case as there is no seared crust. While the fish is glazed with sweet ginger soy, it is tender and uniformly cooked through as though it were steamed or poached. It is supposed to be garnished with corn and spinach, but at the time I sampled this dish, all spinach had been removed from the market due to an *E. Coli* outbreak. The bass was prepared as per the salmon recipe, which I did not sample. This consists of Chinese black mushrooms, bok choy, tomatoes, and asparagus. Anything I say about this accompaniment is possibly irrelevant, but I will say that the chunks of tomato are weird with the bass. I imagine them to be equally strange with the salmon, but I cannot be sure.

Hot Fish, as it is known on the menu, is thin slices of catfish dredged in cornstarch and deep-fried before going into a stir-fry with various vegetables. The fish itself is so light and crunchy it almost seems to be coated with meringue. However, once past the delightful texture, the dish became quite ordinary.

There is an extensive wine list. Considering the fact that Chinese food is not particularly compatible with wine, this is odd. But they must be selling it or they would not carry it.

Sunrise Chinese Food
★½
$

Location: 1751 F-5 N. Sunrise Way, Palm Springs, 323-9881. Food type: Chinese. Ambiance: austere storefront. Bar: beer and wine. Reservations: not accepted. Hours: lunch and dinner daily.

Generic menus and Americanized Chinese fare is the name of the game at Sunrise, as it is at most Chinese restaurants in the desert. This is a tiny Chinese restaurant in the Albertsons shopping center at Vista Chino and Sunrise that straddles the Chinese-American line more successfully than most. The sign simply says, "Chinese Food," but the menu says, "Sunrise." Yes, it has a buffet, but do not eat the buffet. Yes, it serves all the expected dishes. There is, however, another side to this humble diner. Sometimes it takes some influence or knowledge or pressure or whatever. But by and large, the owners and chefs do not eat deep-fried battered orange chicken nuggets. What they make for themselves is quite different; however, they will make anything they are able per customer request.

Bok choy comes in a presentation with Chinese black mushrooms in what is probably a ketjap manis sauce. Ketjap manis is a sweet Chinese soy product. It can be effectively faked in a Western kitchen with equal parts soy sauce and molasses. These mushrooms are unique. Hard and chewy, they look a bit like shiitake but taste more like oyster mushrooms.

A shrimp curry features large shrimp coated with an aggressive sweet garlic-curry sauce. String beans with garlic are done with a sauce based on black beans. They are crunchy, full flavored, and a surprise from this essentially generic menu.

Wor wonton soup is shrimp, chicken broth, snow peas, scallions, and wonton skins stuffed with a flavorful pork filling. The Mongolian beef is tender enough but bland. Peking duck is not on the menu, but they make it. Call ahead for availability or to place a special order. All they can say is no.

Chinese hot mustard and Chinese chili sauce come in yellow and red squeeze bottles. They'll blow your socks off, so do not make the mistake of thinking these are American mustard and ketchup.

The libation of choice here is Tsingtao beer. Unless you are a tea drinker, order this. Do not even think about wine.

Shanghai Inn
★★½
$$

Location: in the Albertsons shopping center, 40-101 Monterey Ave., A-3, Rancho Mirage, 568-5812. **Food type:** *Chinese.* **Ambiance:** *well-designed storefront.* **Bar:** *full; inexpensive; small but adequate wine list.* **Hours:** *lunch and dinner daily.*

With a floor of textured and painted concrete, accents in red, a faux driftwood and copper fountain, Chinese screens, and tables and chairs in mahogany, Shanghai Inn manages to create a pleasant enough environment although it can hardly be called elegant.

There is an active full bar, unusual in most Chinese restaurants, but not in the desert. A full page of wines offered at reasonable markups comes with the menu. It has been my experience, however, that wine with Chinese food is usually not a happy marriage. The tannins of a full-bodied red obliterate the subtle, often spicy-sweet flavors of many stir-fries, and the whites, while certainly preferable, do not hold up as well as beer. My recommendation in most instances for a liquid libation with Chinese food is Tsingtao beer. It arrives at Shanghai Inn in a frozen mug—nice touch.

One half a roasted duck is crisp of surface and tender of meat. The fat has all but melted away. This is one of the better entrées. Request both the Chinese plum sauce and hoisin sauce. The plum sauce is redolent of ginger and is quite sweet. The hoisin is made from soybean paste, sugar, garlic, and vinegar and is also sweet. Most importantly, order the bok choy as a side. The meat is sweet, the sauces are sweet, and the rice with which it comes is sweet. Bok choy is just about the only thing on the menu that is not sweet. With its bitter bite, it is the perfect accompaniment. It comes with Chinese black mushrooms that do nothing for the duck. In fact, they taste very strange with the duck. Request the bok choy without the mushrooms. The duck, fried rice, and an order of bok choy actually makes for a dish resembling a European presentation. If the traditional Chinese rice were a potato dish or wild rice, it actually would be. This is the only item on the menu with which I would pour a red wine, a Pinot Noir.

Lobster with black-bean sauce is an impressive dish. One tends to think of all Chinese stir-fries as looking more or less the same. This one comes with the tail shell as garnish. The lobster is cut into chopstick-sized pieces and is dipped in an egg wash and dusted with cornstarch before hitting the wok. With a black-bean sauce, onions, and red and green bell peppers, this dish is a winner on all counts. The sweetness of lobster meat is complemented well by the sweetness of the bean sauce, while the aromatic vegetables provide the necessary contrast.

Bao San Ding is comprised of shrimp and scallops with macadamia nuts in an intense fish broth. The nuts provide textural contrast for the softness of the shellfish, but in spite of the garlic and the same aromatic vegetables as with the lobster, the prevailing taste is one of sweetness.

Honey-walnut shrimp is a customer favorite. The shrimp are dipped in a mixture of thin mayonnaise and orange-blossom honey before hitting the wok. The mayonnaise adds an interesting, unidentifiable creamy tang to an otherwise very sweet dish. The walnuts are so seriously fried that a dark crisp "skin" forms around them while the inside is softer than when raw. These shrimp are excellent if pricey.

Shanghai Sao-Mai are steamed shrimp and chicken dumplings. The addition of scallions and ginger is a welcome relief from the relentless sweetness. A dipping sauce of Chinese rice vinegar, soy sauce, and ginger is provided with these dumplings, but I find that the dumplings are more flavorful without it.

Snow peas, wood ear mushrooms, and chicken in a *Ju-chow* rice mixture is a most interesting dish. This particular type of rice cooks into almost a mush. It more or less disappears into the overall texture but imparts a sweetness that is quite surprising. With the exotic wildness of the mushrooms and the snap of the peas, this dish functions as a fine side dish but lacks enough identity to serve as an entrée.

Hot and spicy dishes are marked with a chili pepper icon. This is a farce. I asked John Liu, the manager of Shanghai Inn, for an order of the hottest, spiciest dish on the menu. The sesame beef was delivered to me. No only was it not hot, there was nary a hint of spice anywhere in the background. This is ridiculous. Liu explained to me that most of his customers do not like spicy foods. I can understand the need to serve the customer, but why label it hot and spicy on the menu? Obviously if you want a hot dish this must be explained to the server when ordering.

The general tone of overall sweetness is a problem here. Unless you are knowledgeable and careful when ordering, this sweetness could easily become cloying. It also makes for an overall lack of taste variety.

Tsing Tao
Not recommended
$-$$
Location: 74-040 Highway 111, Palm Desert, 779-9593. *Food type: Chinese. Ambiance: coffee shop. Bar: full, but no physical bar. Reservations: suggested. Hours: lunch Monday through Friday, dinner nightly.*

Pale blue and white set the tone for this austere Chinese restaurant. With a menu change, it could pass for an American coffee shop. Tsing Tao is a rather ordinary Chinese restaurant. Its single claim to fame is the fact that Peking duck is prepared daily. This is northern China's signature dish. In Chinatowns all over the world, the spectacle of hanging duck, its skin tinted a dark red, can be observed. The ducks must be hung for up to 12 hours, but the use of an electric fan can reduce this time by as much as 50 percent. They are then blanched in the famous marinade of water, dry sherry, honey, ginger, vinegar, and cornstarch. In more scrupulous restaurants, an air pump is used to create a balloon between the skin and the meat. This results in a sublimely crispy skin. The ducks are then hung again for up to 11 hours. (Chinese restaurants in America have run into problems with government health agencies over this practice, but in recent years, they seem to have worked out their differences.) Finally, the ducks are roasted. The skin is separated from the meat to retain its crispiness, and the duck is cut into exactly 120 uniform chunks. This is the Chinese way. In Britain the meat is shredded, which, in my opinion greatly reduces its flavor as well as bringing it down to room temperature. It does, however, make it much easier for the diner. Slices of scallion and cucumber garnish the meat, and little Mandarin pancakes are smeared with hoisin sauce and filled with portions of meat and/or skin at the diner's option.

So how is it done at Tsing Tao? Sadly many corners are cut. The duck lacks the intensity of the genuine article. It is served shredded with the skin on. This is the most distressing fact, but shredding also removes all the fat and bone, which are responsible for so much of the flavor. The shredded duck is evenly divided among four large Mandarin pancakes and dressed tableside by the server. Personal options are thus removed unless the diner wishes to unravel the whole thing. Traditionally up to 24 small pancakes are brought to the table. The bottom line on Tsing Tao's Peking duck is, don't bother. Go to Shanghai Inn (reviewed earlier in this chapter) and order the roasted half-duck.

A couple of the house specials—hot braised fish, lobster Szechwan— appear to be interesting, but other than that, Tsing Tao is quite ordinary. All the usual Chinese-American dishes are represented; any menu item with a chili pepper attached is a heat warning, but nothing is the least bit spicy. Kung pao chicken, for example, is bland and flavorless.

Japanese

In contrast with the Chinese restaurant, local purveyors of Japanese cuisine are often exciting, original, and even occasionally spectacular. Okura and No Da Te in particular rank very high on the Japanese quality list.

Hibachi Sushi Bar
(See Hibachi Steakhouse, Chapter 9.)
★★★
$$$
Location: 71-680 Highway 111, Rancho Mirage, 674-0078. **Food type:** sushi. **Ambiance:** one big room; attractive bar; red wall. **Bar:** full. **Reservations:** suggested. **Hours:** dinner nightly.

This place is filled with anomalies. Hibachi was opened primarily as a teppanyaki steakhouse. These dining-as-theater shows are especially popular with children. That one of the three finest sushi bars in the valley is located within this circus is bizarre. Second, the sushi chef is not Japanese; he is Vietnamese, and he got into this profession quite by accident. His name is Chuong Vo, and he makes some of the most daring and unusual sushi around. Filet mignon with asparagus, crab, avocado, mayo, sake, and special sauce is an example. Or try this one: cucumber and miso flakes with kimchi, pickled cabbage—pickled cabbage with huge amounts of garlic and chili power! Kimchi is Korean. Or try these: an Anaheim chili stuffed with spicy tuna and deep-fried or the famed Hibachi roll.

For interesting, even fascinating sushi Hibachi is a must-go, but it frequently veers away from the traditionally Japanese.

Kiyosaku
Not rated
$$$
Location: 1555 S. Palm Canyon Dr., Palm Springs, 327-6601. **Food type:** Japanese. **Ambiance:** traditional sushi bar; few tables; blond wood dominates. **Bar:** beer and wine. **Reservations:** not accepted. **Hours:** dinner Thursday through Tuesday.

Kiyosaku was the first sushi restaurant in the Coachella Valley, and it still boasts of a fine reputation, especially among the cognoscenti. It is also the only establishment in the west valley—Palm Springs, Cathedral City, Desert Hot Springs—where quality sushi is available. Reportedly, the astonishing skill of chef-owner Kiyoshi Ishikawa and his fanatical concern about the freshness of the fish has led him to select fish flown into the area from such diverse ports of call as Tokyo, Brazil, Ecuador, Canada, and Alaska.

I have not yet had a chance to visit this restaurant, but for those staying in the Palm Springs area this restaurant has a reliable and credible reputation.

Matsuri
★★
$-$$

Location: 73-759 Highway 111, Palm Desert, 776-6655. **Food type:** Japanese. **Ambiance:** cute, small "Hawaiian" coffee shop. **Bar:** beer and wine. **Reservations:** not needed for small parties. **Hours:** lunch and dinner Monday through Saturday.

With its pale yellow colors, translucent panels, blond-wood sushi bar, and hanging red lanterns, Matsuri's ambiance emerges as more Hawaiian than Japanese. The background music is mostly traditional Japanese, but it is interspersed with thinned-out surfer rock, which reinforces the Polynesian impression.

The menu is similar to that of Musashi (reviewed later in this chapter). The major differences between the two venues are environmental, with Musashi presenting a quiet, peaceful ambiance and Matsuri, the hustle and bustle of a Polynesian diner. For comparison purposes, I ordered the tonkatsu in both places. This is a pork cutlet, or pork steak, egg washed, lightly breaded, and deep-fried. The dredging delivers a tender and juicy piece of meat. The high heat of the fryer cooks it quickly, and the coating protects it from becoming dried out. The meat is good at both places, but certainly nothing spectacular. The differences emerge with the sauces. Here I ordered the curry sauce. Japanese curry is popular in Japan although most Americans do not think of curry as being particularly Japanese. Japanese curry tends to be mild and contains diced vegetables. This one has carrots, peas, onion, corn kernels, string beans, and soybeans.

Its "curryness" comes from curry powder (basically coriander, cumin, turmeric, and whatever else the individual curry maker wishes to add, including ginger, mustard, saffron, or garlic) and garam marsala (toasted cardamom seeds, cinnamon, cumin seeds, cloves, black peppercorns, and nutmeg). This curry sauce resembles American-style country gravy more than an Indian or Thai curry. It is thick—starchy thick as with flour or cornstarch—mild, and opaque. With a large mound of sticky rice, the totality of the dish is satisfying and flavorful, but it is remarkably unsophisticated.

Pickled radish called *fukujinzuke* provides a very nice crunchy and tangy condiment for the otherwise thick, rich entrée. It performs the same function as pickled ginger, that marvelous little "I wonder what the heck this sparkling taste could be" tidbit that so often accompanies Japanese food. By the way, any transliterated Japanese word with "zuke" in it means "pickled."

By contrast, the sushi-sashimi side of the restaurant is unusually sophisticated and offers 17 different kinds of sushi, including chirashi (assorted fish over rice), Tekka Don (tuna over rice), and tuna, yellowtail, halibut, salmon, and mackerel sashimi.

Musashi

$-$$

Location: 72-785 Highway 111, B-4, Palm Desert, 340-9780. **Food type:** *Japanese.* **Ambiance:** *an oasis of tranquility in a Palm Desert storefront.* **Bar:** *beer and wine.* **Reservations:** *suggested for dinner; not necessary for lunch.* **Hours:** *lunch and dinner daily.*

Musashi is a quiet little place, unassuming and easily overlooked. Open the door to a world of minimal design and repose, of wood and pale pink, of sushi bars, strange ideograms, and exotic aromas.

Enoki mushrooms are served as an appetizer in a ponzu sauce. Soy, lemon, rice vinegar, and sake provide sweetness. The sashimi plate is yellowtail, yellowfin tuna, Alaskan farmed salmon, and mackerel with wasabi, pickled ginger, julienne of radish, and a shiso leaf. The fish is soft, mild, gentle, and glorious. The tuna and salmon pale in comparison with the yellowtail. It is exquisite and expensive. The mackerel establishes itself in marked contrast. Mackerel is fat and fishy tasting. That's why it works so well. As counterpoint to the yellowtail, it is the perfect foil. Then there is that funny-looking leaf shiso. Mint, lemon, basil, and possibly tarragon tease the palate.

A deep-fried pork cutlet, tonkatsu, is out of context but not a big deal. Good as it is, this simple pork steak, egg washed, breaded, deep-fried, cut into thin slices, is not in the same league as the sashimi. The sauce is thick. I taste carrots, but the look and texture is that of molasses. The waiter says it is a vegetable reduction with a sweet and sour base: carrots, tomatoes, garlic, and onions. The cutlet comes with a side of sticky rice and iceberg lettuce with a ginger-mustard mayonnaise. Nothing special.

Zoru soba are cold buckwheat noodles. I personally find them most uninteresting, but they appear on almost every Japanese menu. Somebody must like them.

No Da Te
★★★
$$-$$$$
Location: 73-655 *El Paseo Dr., Suite L, Palm Desert,* 340-3797. **Food type:** *Japanese.* **Ambiance:** *a little austere but still inviting.* **Bar:** *beer and wine.* **Reservations:** *required during season, not taken at sushi bar.* **Hours:** *dinner nightly, lunch Tuesday through Saturday.*

It is a summer special, but it is the best sushi deal in town, possibly the world: all you can eat for $25. I am eating $100 worth of some of the best sushi available. Almost everyone at the bar is ordering the special, and they are all here several times a week. They are requesting this and that from the sushi chef, altering recipes at will, and in general having a terrific time. The chef is having a good time too. He passes out tastes, increases spiciness, puts more caviar on this, and drops a quail egg into an oyster/sake shooter. Customers and chef alike are schmoozing about everything: sushi, tennis, sushi, golf, sushi, the economy, but mostly about sushi. These people are experts. Two teenage boys are the masters. They are here three times a week and tweak almost every order. They also do not eat the rice. Since sashimi is not part of the special, if one just eats the fish, one can order twice as much and effectively get sashimi for the price of sushi. No one seems to mind, and the chef-owner is visiting with everyone.

During the high season No Da Te is packed. Reservations are mandatory, but the sushi bar is standing-room only. No reservations permitted. The location is the heart of El Paseo, the ritziest street in the area, just a door or two west of Mama Gina's (Chapter 6). The front is seriously smoked glass giving the restaurant the austerity that a large black window provides, yet the interior belies that elegant but somewhat intimidating appearance. The interior is simple, almost plain, with beige walls and dark wood. Simple bamboo wall hangings are the only ornament.

The menu is large, running the gamut of Japanese dishes: teriyaki (chicken or beef), sukiyaki (chicken or beef), pork cutlets, grilled steak, salmon, white fish, chicken, tempura, hibachi-grilled toro (the well-marbled belly of a bluefin tuna: highly prized and very expensive), crab, scallop, clam, abalone, vegetables, mushrooms (shiitake and matsutake), various noodles, and combos, salads, soups, 10 cold appetizers, and 12 hot appetizers, even a few desserts (tempura-fried ice cream with raspberry sauce). However, this review will cover only the sushi bar. Why? Because that's where I am eating. Most of the reviews of Japanese restaurants in this book cover only the dining room; it is time for a change. One can obviously extrapolate from one to the other. It is unlikely that a restaurant would have an excellent dining room and a poor sushi bar and vise versa. Also, many of the dishes available at the sushi bar are rolls provided by the kitchen. I am therefore willing to go out on a limb (albeit only a short one) and award No Da Te three stars based on the outstanding performance and value of the sushi bar.

Once again the menu is huge. Rolls and No Da Te signature rolls take up a page and a half of the bar menu. The "Justin" is spicy tuna and avocado roll. It is about 8 pieces. Three of these and a normal person is quite sated. The rice roll is "deep-fried." That's what the menu says. I don't know how it is possible as the finished product is not greasy at all. Perhaps it is pan-fried, but still it is not greasy. Regardless of how it is done the rice has a marvelously sweet, crunchy surface. It is bathed in a sweet eel sauce and liberally sprinkled with tobiko caviar. The effect of the sweet eel sauce is surprising, much like molasses. The ratio of rice to tuna, on the other hand, is probably about eight to one, which doesn't make for great tuna flavor, but the overall effect of the dish is excellent.

The No Da Te rolls are the house signatures. There are four of these numbered two through five. (I have no idea what happened to number one.) These are the most popular rolls. I had the number two, which I found rather bland. The number two is shrimp, crab, and egg (like an omelet). With both shrimp and crab it should have had more flavor than the Justin, but the rice to seafood ratio is simply too large and this rice is not fried. The number three is lobster based and is not permitted on the all-you-can-eat menu for obvious reasons.

The spider roll is very interesting. "Spider" is soft-shell crab, which is deep-fried and rolled with bits of carrot (raw), avocado, pea shoots, and cucumber. The crab in this case has plenty of flavor, thanks, in large part, to the fact that the soft shell is eaten, crushed by the molars in a defiantly primitive manifestation of dining technique. Once again tobiko caviar is the condiment.

Were I to eat all the rice from these three rolls I'd have been finished. That would have been extremely foolish. It is on to the sushi.

Most sushi is not a recipe per se. Its worth is judged not by the skill of the chef in the kitchen but by the basic quality of the fish. This is top of the line: yellowtail—soft, buttery, creamy, mild, my personal favorite; salmon—beautifully marbled, melt-in-your-mouth tender, subtle; squid—chewy, bigger flavor; octopus—tough (I didn't like it); white fish—big flavor, sinewy; mackerel—always a good contrast, naturally oily, serious fish flavor.

Salmon roe is wrapped in nori (seaweed). I love this. About the size of a small pea, each egg when crushed against the roof of the mouth explodes in a rush of concentrated brine and fish essence. (This is part of the $25 deal! How can that be?) Be careful not to crush the eggs before putting them in your mouth, as the "pop" of the big caviar egg is magical. Never, ever spread caviar on a cracker (or whatever) and crush the eggs in the process. This is a culinary sin worthy of at least 30 lashes with a cane switch.

A large raw oyster comes in the little nori cup just like the salmon roe. This I do not like at all. It is not the fault of the chef or the oyster. I have only myself to blame, but the room temperature and size of the raw oyster is just too much for me.

The scallops come in a preparation. Here bits of scallop are mixed with kewpie (a.k.a. QP, Japanese mayonnaise) and a secret ingredient the chef would not reveal. This I love, but this late in my ordering I really don't want mayonnaise.

Also coming in a kitchen preparation is the eel. Slices of the definitely ugly snakelike fish are deep-fried, sliced on a bias, and smothered in sweet eel sauce. This is a bar favorite. The chef is passing pieces of it around. In a blind taste test, most people would probably identify it as some kind of barbecued pork product.

The fish is the freshest of fresh. The ambiance is terrific, the price is certainly right (at least for this summer special). How bad can the dining room be? *Bon Appétit!*

Okura Robata Grill and Sushi Bar
★★★
$$-$$$

Locations: Point Happy Plaza, 78-370 Highway 111, #150, La Quinta, 564-5820; 105 S. Palm Canyon Dr., Palm Springs, 327-1333. **Food type:** *contemporary Japanese.* **Ambiance:** *dark, high tech, Zen-like; meager patio; annoying music.* **Bar:** *full.* **Reservations:** *suggested.* **Hours:** *dinner daily, bar menu, happy hour.*

Okura in La Quinta opened sometime around 2005. The chef was a man named Yoshi Kojima. He was a genius. Within hours, it seemed, Okura was the favorite haunt of all the top chefs in the Coachella Valley. From far and wide they came on their days off: Pierre, Bernard, Eric, Keith. These and other brilliant chefs would all hang out at Okura marveling at the wonders conjured up by Yoshi. The Yoshi magic opened new vistas of aesthetic and culinary delights. Yoshi was a genius.

Then suddenly, not much more than a year later, on the cusp of Okura's expansion to Palm Springs, tragedy! Yoshi was gone, fired. How? Why? I do not know, but Yoshi was no more. Yoshi was by close to unanimous opinion of foodies and chefs alike the greatest chef in the valley; he was my favorite. Okura then closed for lunch and adopted a happy hour with bar menu. Their prices dropped marginally. And the magic went away.

The new Okura is not the magnificent four-star glory that once was, but Okura is still a very good restaurant. Food is best described as contemporary Japanese and Japanese fusion. Fusion with what? you ask. The answer: French technique, French conception, and some French ingredients. While most of the menu is solidly Japanese, the entrées reflect the fusion side of the menu. *Robata* in Okura Robata Grill literally means "by the fireside" in Japanese. It means to cook over an open flame in the style of Japanese fishermen. A *robata* grill, then, is a hot charcoal grill. The charcoal is imported from Japan. There is also an extensive sushi/sashimi bar and oven-prepared dishes.

Black linens set the tone. The inside is dark, elegant, refined, and aggressively contemporary. Black slate, stone, and wood establish a neutral color palette. Subtle track lighting and red translucent canvas screens provide contrast. The outside patio is formed by separating it from a parking lot by a row of large, tall, black pots. The use of misters and umbrellas creates a pleasant enough ambiance, but it certainly does not rank with the many beautiful patios around town. Background music strikes an odd note. It is, I think, Japanese technopop, electronic and relentlessly thumping. Fortunately, it is not played at a disturbingly high volume though it can become quite irritating, especially inside.

Gyoza dumplings are not dumplings or dim sum in the Chinese style, boiled buns stuffed with something like sweet and sour pork. These are more like pot stickers, pan-fried until crispy. The filling of pork, ginger, scallions, sesame, and garlic is spicy and full flavored. The gyoza skins are thin enough to turn into a paper-like "ravioli" when fried. These are dressed in chili oil and served with a few bitter greens. They are an excellent appetizer, and as a happy hour bar dish they are only $4.95.

Dynamite Mussels are a genuine challenge. I do not know what to make of these. I do know that I do not like them. Why is a question more difficult to address. I cannot honestly tell you whether it is the recipe that is at fault or my sense of taste or experience. These are New Zealand mussels: big, soft, flavorful. My cherished experiences with mussels are along the Ligurian coast of Italy. Steamed in white wine, basil, tomatoes, and a fistful of mashed garlic and served with a loaf of freshly baked Italian bread and a liter of house Frascati wine, this is a rustic lunch fit for king and peasant alike. That is my benchmark experience, my basis for comparison, prejudiced though it undoubtedly is. Here we have the famed green mussel. It is bigger than the more commonly served black one. It has more of the "organ meat" character than does the black one. Crabmeat is cooked with a cream and kewpie (QP, a Japanese mayonnaise) sauce and placed on top of the mussel. The menu says, "topped with tobiko caviar" but this is not evident. The concoction is then broiled for a minute to crisp and brown the surface. It sounds wonderful. I do not think it is. The crab mixture has the distinct flavor and texture of a soft crab cake. There is certainly nothing wrong with this except that it forms a stark and uncomfortable alliance with the mussel. Not only do I find that neither aspect of this dish complements the other, but they seem to be in opposition. As I say, this may well be my fault and not the fault of the dish, but this is my experience.

Okura has the reputation of being one of the finest sushi bars in the valley, and the sushi/sashimi side of the menu is extensive. I wanted to experience the menu from all sides, so I am limited to one sampling. I had the *shiro* (albacore). This is white tuna: soft, buttery, mild. Served on short-grain sticky rice with the delicate sweetness of rice vinegar shining through and accompanied with pickled ginger and wasabi, it is superb in every respect.

From the *robata* grill come the grilled spareribs. For those of us whose experience of barbecue is limited to the Texas smoker, you are in for a treat. Six ribs arranged into a tower stacked "Lincoln logs" fashion make for a unique presentation. These ribs are cut from a St. Louis slab, that is, with the chine bone removed. These ribs are not smoked. The telltale signature of American (North or South) barbecue is not here. These ribs are probably first braised in sake/soy sauce/rice vinegar and honey before grilling over Japanese charcoal. They are as tender and moist as the smoked Texas version, but their flavor is entirely different. The sauce in which they are served is different also. Instead of the usual taste of Texas (corn syrup, chili pepper, and catsup), this one delivers the more sophisticated combination of sake, rice vinegar, soy sauce, miso, marin, ground sesame seeds, and some mysterious fruit. Apple, mandarin orange, and peach cross my mind, but all are rejected. It is beyond my experience. An Internet search of Japanese barbecue sauces led me to the umeboshi, a salty Japanese plum. It might be this, I don't know. These ribs come with deep-fried scallion shoestrings, not much flavor, but they look pretty.

In a definite nod to the West, scalloped potatoes are advertised as the side dish. This is not to be as the potatoes are not available at my early dining hour. This is a shame, as it would allow me my chance to explore the "fusion" side of the menu. Instead, a large round of fried rice accompanies. This side dish works well with the ribs. I cannot imagine the potatoes doing as well, but I don't know for sure.

Okura is a solid, high-quality Japanese restaurant with an extensive menu and reasonable prices. The happy hour offers a good selection of appetizers at an even greater discount. One cannot help but think of the genius Yoshi Kojima even as one crosses the threshold.

CHAPTER 11

Vietnamese, Korean, Thai, and Indian

There is one Korean restaurant; a number of Thai restaurants, including one fine-dining establishment, Bangkok Five; and several Thai fast-food chains in the valley. The chains are not reviewed. Thai food fares rather well here considering that it is more demanding on the American palate than Chinese food, which does not do as well. Indian restaurants come and go. One excellent establishment, Monsoon, has passed into the hands of longtime Palm Springs fixture Delhi Palace, which is currently the only Indian restaurant in town. Le Basil opened, adding Vietnamese cuisine to the area.

Vietnamese

Le Basil
★★★
$-$$
Location: 72-695 Highway 111, #A10, Palm Desert, 773-1112. Food type: Vietnamese and miscellaneous Southeast Asian. Ambiance: upscale shopping center location but attractive and peaceful. Bar: full; good beer selection, adequate wine list. Reservations: accepted; recommended for weekend evenings. Hours: from 11 A.M. Monday through Saturday, from noon Sundays; closed Tuesdays.

This is a terrific little spot. Located on a corner a few doors east of the Von's market that anchors the Palms to Pines shopping center, its patio boasts of two views: south and west to the Santa Rosa Mountains. Since the restaurant itself rests more or less at the top of a sloping parking lot, the parking itself is lost amidst a sea of palm trees. Inside is all blond wood radiating the usual East Asian calm. The first impression is a wonderful smell: a mixture of charred meat (duck skin?), garlic, basil, fresh fish, and soy sauce. Hunger pangs begin after roughly the first whiff.

Many preparations of fresh fish are the focus of the menu. Filets of orange roughy, salmon, or halibut are the featured trio. Sadly, whole fish does not seem to be an option. Various preparations of shellfish, chicken, and pork comprise another portion of the menu; curries, noodle dishes, and a honey duck, the final third. Phở, the amazing concoction of beef, beef stock, and vermicelli is a mainstay at both lunch and dinner. The secrets lie in the stock. The details remain hush-hush, but the primary flavoring agents are licorice bark and star anise. Simmered for 24 hours, these ingredients, along with onions, carrots, celery, and the aforementioned secrets, impart a depth to the beef broth reminiscent of molasses. Thai stocks come to mind but these are less sweet. This signature dish is under $8.

Highly recommended is the appetizer *bánh xèo,* literally translated as "sizzling cake." This is a fascinating dish and one difficult to come by except in places with large Vietnamese populations like Orange County, California. Its unique quality is that the diner has the option of changing both its flavor profile and texture with each bite. The star of the show is a stuffed crepe. It is a yellow color, but the yellow does not come from egg as one might expect from a crepe, but turmeric. The batter is essentially a mixture of rice flour and coconut milk. A thin pancake about 10 inches in diameter is made from this batter and pan-fried in hot oil with bits of pork, shrimp, and scallions. When the meat-filled crepe is half-cooked, bean sprouts are stuffed into it. The crepe is crispy/brittle, hot, and slightly oily. The meats are hot, soft, full-flavored, and earthy; the bean sprouts are cool and crunchy. But this is only the beginning of the dish. On the same plate a salad of iceberg lettuce (functioning as wraps), pieces of baby carrot, cucumber, and jicama (*bengkuang*), mint, and cilantro are to be mixed and matched with the crepe. Thus, one bite may be tweaked with mint and another with cilantro. The heavy crunch of carrot may influence another while the subtle and refreshing apple/pear flavors of the jicama influence yet another. A sweet and garlicky fish sauce used for dipping called *nuoc cham* accompanies everything. But this is not all. Four additional condiments are served on the side: a hot-spicy-sweet tamarind, a jalapeño, a hot-sweet-garlic chili paste, and the traditional soy. With the possible exception of the tamarind sauce the latter three are all out of a bottle. The jalapeño sauce is probably green Tabasco. For around $8 this remarkable dish can serve alone as a light lunch or as a most satisfying and unusual appetizer.

The fresh fish entrées are arguably the featured house specialties and the halibut, at $19, is the most expensive thing on the menu. The triumvirate of orange roughy, salmon, and halibut may be had a number of different ways from char broiled to steamed with various sauces. The ginger sauce particularly seems interesting, but I opted for the red chili sauce. This is a combination of sugar, garlic, and sun-ripened hot red chilies. It is popular all over Southeast Asia and comes in a bottle. I don't know whether or not this sauce is house made for the fish, but I suspect it is not. Regardless of its source, it did work with the fish, complementing and not interfering with it.

My fish is a little overcooked, in spite of a specific request that care be taken, but I suspect this was a serving error not a kitchen error. Many customers have reported somewhat frantic service during the crowded dinner hour.

Beer mates particularly well with this kind of spicy cuisine and Le Basil has an ample selection at a reasonable price. Red wines are generally a disaster; even a peppery Syrah or Zinfandel tends not to work with this kind of food. The only exception might be with the honey duck, but I have yet to try that. Big, fruity, dry, metallic white wines, New Zealand Sauvignon Blancs, for example, can pair well. The wine list is rather sparse, but corkage is a reasonable $12.

Le Basil remains one of the more interesting Oriental alternatives in the valley.

Korean

Palm Korea B.B.Q. Restaurant

$$

*Location: 13-440 Palm Dr., Desert Hot Springs, 329-2277. **Food type:** Korean. **Ambiance:** plain square room; bare wood tables and chairs. **Bar:** Korean beer, rice wine, soju, ginseng, and herb wine. **Reservations:** not accepted. **Hours:** lunch Monday through Friday; dinner Monday through Saturday.*

This is the only venue for Korean food in the Coachella Valley. It is a small, spare building, almost a shack, with a single dining room done in a pale yellow. There is almost no ornamentation or decoration, and the tables and chairs are plane bare wood.

As there is no basis for comparison, it is difficult to measure the quality of this restaurant. The staple of Korean food is kimchi, or pickled cabbage. To the inexperienced palate, kimchi is bizarre and not in a good way. Salted cabbage (salted to purge the liquid) is fermented with a potent mixture of garlic, scallions, sugar, ginger, and a large dose of hot chili powder. The fermenting process takes a few weeks. Kimchi ranges from hot to very hot, and the garlic is pronounced. It garnishes everything on the Korean menu.

Another peculiarly Korean accompaniment is bean jelly. The bean is the soybean, and although it has almost no flavor, it is used to flavor this gelatin. The jelly comes with soy sauce, cilantro, and finely chopped scallions, which have plenty of flavor. Seaweed soup, with an undefined type of seaweed, improves as you eat it. At first, it is ridiculously bland, but the subtleties of the seaweed begin to emerge about halfway through the bowl. The seaweed itself is like a briny, rubbery collard green.

Chili paste is a ubiquitous condiment. This one is not blisteringly hot, but it is hot enough, and the diner controls the quantity. Chili paste is made from dried chilies soaked in water and puréed. It is thick, almost like creamy peanut butter.

Palm Korea is a barbecue joint. Korean barbecue is actually grilled. The meats are generally thinly sliced and placed in a marinade of soy sauce, rice vinegar, garlic, sugar, scallions, and cilantro. Purists insist on the addition of kiwi (apple or pear will do as well) as it aids in tenderizing and provides a delightful fresh flavor. The grilling is fast, more like a flash sear than anything even remotely similar to an American barbecue pit. Because they are cut so thin, all meats are tender regardless of the cut, even brisket. Palm Korea barbecues brisket, pork belly (*samgyupsal*), rib-eye, pork, and chicken. It has soups and stews—no, it does not serve *boshintang,* the infamous dog-meat stew—a number of vegetarian/tofu dishes, squid, octopus, whole baby chicken, eel, and broiled mackerel. First-timers might consider the *bibimbap*, a combo plate of barbecued beef strips, shiitake mushrooms, vegetables, and a sunny-side-up egg.

All the above-mentioned condiments, as well as rice, come with every dish. The interesting thing is that very little of this food has much taste independently—bean sprouts, sticky rice, bean jelly, seaweed, and lettuce are not hallmarks of flavor—but together some startling things begin to happen. Each element contributes to the whole in unexpected ways, and the whole is bursting with flavor. Add the chili paste as liberally as you like; it does not mask the other foods.

Beef, pork, or chicken *bulgogi* are the most popular items. *Bulgogi* is a plate of barbecued meat served with rice, kimchi, and vegetables. In a unique touch, a pair of scissors is provided for cutting the strips of meat. In the liquid libations department, Palm Korea serves OB (or Oriental Brewery) beer. At $6 for a 12-ounce bottle, this is not cheap for an undistinguished Pilsner. More interesting, but certainly not for everyone, is the *Bek Se Ju,* or ginseng rice wine. It has a taste rather like the combination of raisins, ginger, green tea, bay leaf, and Pinot Grigio. It is also expensive, at $13 for 12 ounces. Soju, a fortified wine made from rice, barley, sweet potato, and tapioca, is also on the menu. It is 20 percent alcohol, so something other than straight fermentation is happening here. I have not tried this.

Thai

Bangkok 5
★★★
$$
Location: 70-026 Highway 111, Rancho Mirage, 770-9508. *Food type: Thai. Ambiance: big, dark, dramatic cube. Bar: full; exotic specialty drinks. Reservations: suggested. Hours: dinner nightly.*

Copper roof, volcanic rock, teak slatted shutters, beamed ceilings 20 feet above the floor—Bangkok 5 is a palace. With a dining and bar area surrounding a stone-paved atrium accessed by 16-foot glass doors, the effect is imposing and dramatic but user friendly at the same time. The walls are clay colored and softly illuminated within the dictates of the aesthetic concept known as *wabi-sabi,* or "imperfect beauty." Weathered rice paper and wooden lanterns adorn the environment. White-linen-clad tables are pin-spot lit and centered with a single flower.

Despite its placement in this chapter, Bangkok 5 *is* a palace. There are a number of Thai restaurants in this valley; however, like the chain Thai Smile, which is not reviewed, most are in the fast-food category. Bangkok 5 is the premier venue. Food is excellent.

All cultures produce their own unique tastes. Some develop a complex cuisine combining these tastes in a variety of aesthetically pleasing manners. Few achieve artistry. Thailand ranks with the big boys, not exactly France or Italy, but certainly with Spain and Greece. Appetizers are a marvel of variety and interesting tastes. Thai satay, for example, is chicken, pork, or beef strips marinated in brown sugar, curry powder, peanut butter, soy sauce, lime juice, garlic, and chili flakes, skewered and grilled. A spicy-sweet peanut sauce with coconut milk, chili paste, molasses, and cilantro is provided for dipping.

Star of Bangkok is comprised of little cups of pastry filled with minced chicken, corn, and onion. These are mild, and the corn is quite surprising, having none of the associations connected with grits, polenta, tamales, succotash, cornbread, or Fritos. These tastes are homogenized with Oriental mystery.

Poh Piah Todd are spring rolls with shrimp, pork, and glass noodles. The shrimp and pork are merely flavorings; it is the glass noodles that are featured. Dipped into Thai plum sauce (similar to Chinese plum-duck sauce but without the ginger) with pieces of fresh cucumber, these can be fascinating, but don't go looking for the pork and shrimp.

Thai pot stickers are dumplings of wonton skins stuffed with ground shrimp, chicken, and vegetables. There is no evidence that they ever actually were pot stickers, that is to say they never did actually stick to the pot. These appear to be dumplings from beginning to end.

Fresh New Zealand mussels are dusted with crushed peanuts and broiled. New Zealand mussels are the favorite of every mussel fan because of their large size and intense briny flavor, but the cooking process here renders them dried out and rubbery.

Thai soups are a marvel. Tom Yum Talay is mixed seafood in a clear lemon grass-infused stock. It is spicy-hot and sweet. The seafood consists of shrimp (overcooked), scallops (perfect), calamari (full flavored and chewy), a crab claw (mushy), and mussels (slightly overcooked). Mushrooms, lemon grass, shiso, and tomato provide a vegetable contrast. There is a strip of what appears to be a jalapeño pepper. I ate the entire strip all at once. It was not a jalapeño. It was a serrano! This is a serious warning. A jalapeño chili has as few as 2,500 Scoville units (the measurement of chili heat); a serrano chili can have as much as 25,000 units. In other words, eating one serrano chili can be like eating 10 jalapeño chilies. I hit the extreme end and seriously burned my mouth. I was in pain for about 15 minutes, coughing, sneezing, swollen sinuses, and tongue on fire. In spite of some of the seafood being a little overcooked, this soup is magnificent.

Entrées range from the common pad thai (traditional Thai noodles with chicken and shrimp) to the esoteric Pla Duk, a brutally hot whole catfish served swimming in chili sauce. Panang Moor is a pork dish. Slices of pork about a quarter-inch thick are quickly sautéed and served with a panang curry sauce. Panang is a red curry sauce (the red ones are sweet). Dried chilies, shallots, garlic, galanga (ginger), lemon grass, lime zest, coriander, shrimp paste, cumin, cloves, cinnamon, coconut milk, sugar, peanuts, and star anise are ingredients for this complex sauce. The depth of flavor is enormous. You will find yourself eating it with a spoon or soaking it up with the plain white rice. Order more of the sauce on the side as the chef makes it up special order. I ordered extra about halfway through my meal. I was finished by the time it arrived.

Bangkok 5 is set up for the American/European dining tradition. Tables are set with knives and forks; entrées come as self-contained units with meat, rice, and veggies all served on the same plate. But this Americanization is not reflected in the food.

There is an amusing aside. A lamb chop appears on the menu served with portobello mushrooms and a Merlot reduction. If you don't like Thai food, don't go to Bangkok 5. If you do like Thai food, do not order the lamb chop. Would you order Pla Duk in an Italian restaurant?

Indian

Delhi Palace
★½
$-$$
Location: 1422 N. Palm Canyon Dr., Palm Springs, 325-3411. Food type: Indian. Ambiance: sultry east Indian den with exotic sounds and aromas. Bar: none. Reservations: dinner only. Hours: lunch buffet and dinner daily.

Indian restaurants come and go in this area every two years. Delhi Palace is the only veteran. It is basically a glorified storefront, but when infused with the aromas of cumin, turmeric, coriander, and saffron and the exotic sounds of the tabla and sitar, a suitable atmosphere is created.

All the usual suspects appear on this inclusive menu, but in spite of the huge variety of foods represented within Indian cuisine, they seem remarkably homogenized. Chicken curry fails to impress. It isn't bad; it is just rather dull. Lamb curry also lacks interest. The sauce is bland, and not just in the spicy/heat department, and the chicken is, well, chicken. The lamb is considerably more interesting. Mint chutney—effervescent, sparkling, and refreshing—accompanies especially well. The mint chutney is particularly good with the tikka dishes.

Baigan bhurtha, a.k.a. *baingan bartha,* is an eggplant stew consisting of eggplant roasted until it is mush with onions, tomatoes, and a whole battery of Indian herbs and spices. It is excellent with plain basmati rice.

Matar paneer seems like a fascinating concoction according to the ingredient list, but it fails to deliver. Paneer, a soft white farmer cheese, is mixed with peas. These are the defining elements. The remainder of the recipe is more or less the same as for *baigan bhurtha* without the eggplant. I do not know what paneer tastes like, but I didn't taste anything like a farmer cheese here. Various recipes state that tofu or yogurt may be substituted, but the menu clearly states "cheese." Because of this fact, the dish slipped into the same taste profile as the eggplant.

Chicken tikka is always good if the kitchen has a tandoor, which Delhi Palace does. Boneless chicken (supposed to be legs, but here it is breast, which is dryer and less flavorful) is marinated in yogurt and Indian herbs and spices, including chili powder and turmeric, which turn it a deep orange red. It is slapped against the side of a tandoor, where it is cooked lightning fast. A tandoor is a clay oven that can reach temperatures approaching 900 degrees.

Aloo is the Hindi word for potato; look for it on the menu. *Aloo baigan* is potato and eggplant. The treatment for these vegetables is mostly the same, which creates the homogenous quality.

Tamarind chutney and mango chutney are also available. The mango is thick with large chunks of fruit and enough chili fire to make it interesting. My favorite chutney is the tamarind, but it doesn't seem to go with anything. It is tangy and sweet and the spiciest of the three. I wound up eating it straight with a spoon. The cold fresh mint offers the greatest contrast with the dominant flavors of the food.

Vege pakora, a.k.a. *veg pakora,* provides a fun shift. This is basically onion rings made with any of the following cut into thin slices or florets: onions, carrots, celery, bell pepper, parsnips, cauliflower, or broccoli. They are battered, fried, and heavily salted. The result is dry and crispy. The various vegetables are lost in the mix, but this is mostly about salt and crunch. Considering the fact that most of the dishes are in a stew, this is almost a required side dish.

Indian desserts can be fascinating. The most curious is *gulab jamin,* a.k.a. *gulab jamun,* cream balls in a sweet syrup. How do you make a ball out of cream? The ingredients are actually powered milk, flour, cream, and baking soda. From this mixture, balls are formed and deep-fried. A saffron—and cardamom—flavored simple syrup is poured over them. They have the texture of ricotta cheese, but the flavor is more subtle.

Delhi Palace is not great, but it is the only game in town. For more punch, ask your server for a side of chili paste and add it yourself. The lunch buffet is an excellent way to sample many dishes and keep the tab to a wallet-friendly $9.

CHAPTER 12

Brazilian, Mexican, and Southwestern

In the first edition this chapter was called "Latin American." That chapter included a Cuban restaurant as well as the three cuisines named above. The Cuban restaurant has since closed and Southwestern really isn't Latin American anyway, so I thought it best to rename the chapter entirely. One Brazilian restaurant and one Southwestern restaurant operate in the Palm Springs area, but Mexican restaurants abound. There is Mexican fine dining, trendy Americanized Mexican restaurants, and even a few genuinely authentic Mexican restaurants. Countless little Mexican diners and taco stands spot the landscape, most of which are not in this book. Disregarding the fast-food outlets like Taco Bell, a number of quite decent chains can be found locally. El Ranchito (Chapter 16) comes readily to mind.

Brazilian

Brazil is a huge country (Brazil, Australia, and the USA, excluding Alaska, are all about three million square miles). Its cuisine is as diverse as one would expect of such a large landmass. Portugal exerts the dominant influence, but it is liberally mixed with Amerindian and African culinary forces. Cattle were brought to Brazil from the Portuguese-controlled Cape Verde Islands in the early 16th century, and the rest is barbecue history. The gauchos of southern Brazil developed a style of barbecue called *churrasco,* and Brazil's most popular cooking style can be found in the Cathedral City of the 21st century.

Picanha
Picanha Pronto

$$$

Location: 68-510 E. Palm Canyon Dr., Cathedral City, 328-1818; Picanha Pronto telephone is 324-7778. **Food type:** *Brazilian barbecue.* **Ambiance:** *big hacienda-style dining room.* **Reservations:** *suggested.* **Bar:** *full; Brazilian* *cocktails (Caipirinha); adequate wine list.* **Hours:** *lunch and dinner Monday through Saturday.*

Picanha has moved since the first edition from a prime location in Palm Desert to a rather mundane location in Cathedral City. Service and quality are down, prices are higher.

Picanha is unique in the desert, being more like a buffet than your usual conception of a full-service restaurant. It is officially a *churrascaria,* which in Portuguese literally means (Brazilian) steakhouse. *Churrasco* is a cooking style referring to barbecue, but not American barbecue. The latter at its most accurate means "to cook for a long time with warm smoke." In America a *churrasco* would be a grill. In the rest of South America, the barbecue method of cooking is known as *asado.* Picanha is also not really a steakhouse although certain cuts of steak are served. Meat at Picanha is not smoked, so don't expect an American-style barbecue. What we have here is an open grill over which many different kinds of meat, from garlic chicken to leg of lamb, are placed on a rotisserie. Sound confusing? Read on.

The building is fairly dark, with a reception area in front and bar to the left. Dark wood and faux adobe tan walls define the environment. Brazilian pop music is piped in. A large open dining room is to the right. This room is much brighter, with the north wall mostly of glass. Paintings of rural Brazilian life decorate the walls. Artifacts reminiscent of Pampas gauchos appear as ornaments. Waiters adopt a gaucho look as well. The dining room is reminiscent of a large communal dining room presumably found in a hacienda on a large Brazilian ranch. Resting on each table is a wooden block, a cylinder about four inches long and one and a half inches in diameter. The top is green, the bottom is red, or vise versa.

A waitress brings me a wine list. A card featuring a list of exotic Brazilian cocktails, called Caipirinha, is on the table. There does not seem to be a menu. Other customers are descending on a buffet line or salad bar; I cannot tell. I do the same. It is an odd mixture: grilled vegetables—eggplant, zucchini, strips of red bell pepper, Parmesan-covered tomatoes—tabbouleh, chickpeas, some interesting looking corn kernels, string beans with something or other, bow-tie pasta with Parmesan cheese and sun-dried tomatoes, green beans with wedges of tangerine and candied walnuts, and the usual salad fixings. I ignore the salad stuff and try each of the grilled vegetables. The corn is the most interesting, quite spicy, a hot paprika rather than a chili powder. One of the dressings is red. It tastes a bit like Chinese chili sauce with a tomato base. "Try the soup," says the waitress, "and you will find rice and beans up there also. Oh, and turn your block so that the green is on the top." I turn my block green up and shrug.

The eggplant is not sufficiently purged of its liquid. It is mushy. The zucchini and red bell pepper have a good flavor, but their cold temperature makes them less than desirable. The soup is cream of zucchini. It is surprisingly interesting. There's something in there other than zucchini and cream, something I cannot identify.

Suddenly I am accosted by a gaucho, a swarthy young man in boots, a big military-looking belt, and blue blouse carrying a "sword" and a 12-inch chef's knife. Small Brazilian sausages fill one of the "swords," actually skewers, and Polish kielbasa, the other. With his huge chef's knife, he slides one of each onto my plate. I sample the small Brazilian sausage: mildly spicy, smoky, good pork. I expect something more like *linguiça,* the hot-spicy sausage from Portugal redolent of coriander, paprika, cloves, chilies, allspice, and cinnamon. But no such luck; these are much more bland. I don't want the kielbasa. Why sate myself on a large piece of commercial meat available at the local supermarket?

The gauchos arrive promptly at my table whenever the block is turned green-side up. All manner of *churrasco* are delivered to my plate: chicken wrapped in bacon, top sirloin roast, spare ribs, garlic chicken, tri-tip, leg of lamb, garlic steak, lemon steak, barbecued chicken drumstick, Parmesan-crusted pork loin. Everything is done on a rotisserie over an open grill. For serious carnivores, those addicted to meat to the exclusion of all other food groups, this is a marriage made in heaven. They can stuff themselves silly at no extra cost. Be forewarned, however. You may not take anything home with you.

For omnivores, those of us who prefer a balanced plate of meats and vegetables, something is seriously lacking. Only some of these meats can be successfully paired with the buffet items. As it is only human nature to want to sample all of the *churrasco,* most people will wind up sated but not satisfied. If that seems like a paradox, consider this. The tri-tip (wonderfully rare, by the way) pairs beautifully with the rice and Cuban-style black beans. The beans are particularly good, prepared with garlic, bay leaf, and sausage. With some corn and a small simple salad or cup of soup, this is one terrific meal. It is also overpriced and does not take advantage of the uniqueness of this restaurant.

Try it Middle Eastern style. Request several slices of the leg of lamb and make a buffet run for rice, tabbouleh, eggplant, and zucchini. Try the green beans. They are quite interesting, but they don't seem to be compatible with anything. Try making an Italian-style dinner. Request the garlic steak, Parmesan tomatoes, sautéed red peppers, and pasta. While the leg of lamb and the tri-tip are superbly cooked, the steak is medium well, overdone for most tastes. The meats with barbecue sauce on them—American style—do not pair well with anything from the buffet. The garlic chicken will work with the Italian-style presentation as will the pork loin. The lemon steak is not worth the effort. It is overcooked and tough.

There is a conspiracy to sate your appetite before the introduction of the more expensive meats. In fact, filet mignon is advertised but did not come my way during the early-bird special. Bread and butter are rushed to your table—refills are prompt and happen without request—and the salad bar is your first stop. The nature of human desire is such that a salad bar is perceived as free; ergo, by the time the meat begins to make its rounds you are already half-full. The cheaper cuts—sausages and chicken—are first to arrive. That big piece of Polish kielbasa will dampen anyone's appetite. You have to eat smart to make a place like this work for you. This is a carnivore's delight; all others should go elsewhere.

Picanha Pronto is a fast-food outlet right next to the main dining room. There is a separate entrance, but the address is the same. I have not eaten at Picanha Pronto, but their basic repertoire consists of a hamburger-style sandwich made with the various meets served next door. The same salad bar is also available. Prices are between $6 for most of the "burgers" and $14 for the salad bar, a meat selection, choice of any two sides, and the Brazilian cheese bread.

Mexican

Californians like Mexican food. The Mexican population is large, and Mexican restaurants flourish. Although most are owned and operated by Mexicans, they generally do not serve authentic Mexican food but an Americanized version that has been dumbed down for gringos. It is easy to determine to which group a restaurant belongs; just look at the customers. The most Americanized—Don Diego's and Las Casuelas—have no Mexican customers. The least Americanized—El Campanario and Taco Salsas—have all Mexican customers.

There are scores of small Mexican restaurants in the Coachella Valley. Only the most well known and most distinctive in terms of quality and/or authenticity are included in this book. The vast majority of these restaurants serve the cliché fast-food trio, tacos, enchiladas, and burritos, with the ubiquitous splat of Spanish rice and refried beans. Getting past the clichés and searching for authenticity is my goal here.

Adobe Grill
★★★

$$$

See full review in Chapter 1 under La Quinta Resort

Don Diego's
★

$$

Location: 74-969 Cook St. (behind Le St. Germain), Indian Wells, 340-5588. Food type: Americanized Mexican. Ambiance: rather sterile in spite of efforts to the contrary. Bar: full; no wine list. Hours: lunch and dinner daily.

Don Diego's is the quintessence of bland: Mexican food Americanized to the point of denaturing it. This is on par with the Las Casuelas chain (reviewed later in this chapter) and possibly even one step more extreme. The environment is not as nice, as Las Casuelas Terraza in Palm Springs has a terrific outdoor patio, live music, and a dance floor.

The first thing you notice at Don Diego's is the total lack of aromas, not just Mexican aromas—fire-roasted peppers, deep-fried snapper or tilapia, fresh salsas—but any aromas. There is nothing, just the pure, fresh, cool recirculated air of a highly efficient air-conditioning system. Never trust a restaurant that does not smell of anything. There is a kitchen on the premises preparing dishes for a hundred people or so. How can there not be a smell?

The décor is primarily green: dark green acoustic ceiling tile; dark green carpets; green vinyl upholstery on all the booths; green-, red-, orange-, and yellow-patterned vinyl tablecloths; and green awnings. With faux Tiffany lamps, wooden paneling, and paintings of cowboys and bullfighters, it all comes together as a kind of nebulous pseudo ethnic kitsch. These very nebulous qualities are mirrored in the food.

The food isn't exactly bad, it is just completely neutral: afraid to be Mexican and afraid not to be. It emerges as nothing. From reading the menu I would expect the *pescado* Veracruz to be one of the more interesting offerings. The menu describes it as "grilled fresh fish selection (ask your server) served in a savory Vera Cruz style sauce of tomatoes, onions, green olives, capers and white wine. Very flavorful!" What is served is *possibly* fresh halibut moderately overcooked so the flesh is hard and dry. The sauce is a tomato base with onions and green peppers. *Veracruzana* actually means onions, yellow peppers, tomatoes, olives, capers, garlic, white wine, and herbs (usually Mexican oregano, thyme, and marjoram) simmered until a deeply flavorful broth emerges. The Veracruz sauce at Don Diego's is the sort of American institutional cooking you might expect to find on meatloaf. Rice with little corn kernels and a vegetable medley of carrots, broccoli, and cauliflower are served with this fish. The veggies are blanched or steamed to an al dente state and finished in butter. They are bland, but at least they are not mushy.

Sizzling fajitas are "world famous, legendary . . . a must!" says the menu. Actually, they are grilled pieces of filet and chicken with a nice marinade, but overcooked. The chicken, which is breast naturally, is tough and stringy. This is served with a Spanish rice, refried beans, guacamole, *salsa fresca,* and sour cream. It seems that it would be extremely difficult to make this combination bland, but Don Diego's has mastered bland. Except for the filet, nothing has any taste.

Cochinita pibil emerges as the best entrée. This is shredded pork tenderloin in a mildly spiced achiote sauce. Why anyone would shred pork tenderloin is beyond reason. The tenderloin is the filet mignon of the hog. Shredding is traditionally done on a pork shoulder that has been smoked for 20 hours. Pork shoulder is fat and tough with a lot of waste, but it has huge flavors. The 20 hours of smoking leaves it butter tender, and the fat melts. The tenderloin is lean and tender automatically. It needs a fast, hot sauté. All that happens here is that the tenderloin becomes dried out and tougher than is was before shredding. Makes no sense.

Achiote sauce is supposed to be made with a battery of potent spices and peppers, including the bitter achiote (annatto) seed, cumin, black peppercorns, allspice, cloves, habañero peppers, orange juice, vinegar, lots of garlic, lemon juice, and tequila. The habañero is the most brutal chili pepper ever created. That little orange devil can knock you out by sharing the same room with you. This shredded pork tenderloin is served in a "mild" achiote sauce! What does that mean? Cuban-style black beans and the same rice served with the fish comes with this dish. Why bother? Three truly delicious slices of fried plantains, tender and sweet, act as catalyst for the disparate flavors, bringing the whole thing together. Without preconceived notions, this dish really is pretty good. But in the context of Mexican expectations it is bland.

The remainder of this menu is a compendium of the usual Mexican stuff served in fast-food joints all over the country: tacos, enchiladas, burritos, tamales, quesadillas, and a carne asada or two. Don Diego's is popular—although not with Mexicans—and it is obvious that many people like their food bland. You know who you are. Try Don Diego's.

El Campanario
★★★
$-$$
Location: 44-185 Monroe St., Indio, 342-3681. **Food type:** *authentic Mexican.* **Ambiance:** *coffee shop with postmodern colors and a full bar.* **Bar:** *full; excellent selection of Mexican beers; terrible wine list.* **Reservations:** *suggested, but only necessary for dinner.* **Hours:** *breakfast, lunch, and dinner daily.* **Chef:** *Samuel Vasquez.*

With scores of restaurants dishing up Mexican-American fast food, this one is an unexpected delight. It is off the beaten path just beneath and west of the bridge that passes over the railroad tracks in north Indio. Its address is on Monroe, but it is much more accessible from Indio Boulevard. Physically it resembles a large coffee shop done in the postmodern colors mauve and avocado. Seating is mostly banquettes, even in the dining room. There is a full bar, but it is not a hangout.

Molcajetes are the name of the game here. *Molcajetes* are hand-carved lava stones. Once carved, they function as a mortar and pestle, but that is only the beginning of the story. *Molcajete* is also the name of six dinner entrées. They are as spectacular as they are unique. These entrées are not, repeat, *not* something found in any other local Mexican restaurant. For under $15, they are not only superb but also cheap by local standards. All are variations on a theme. I sampled the *molcajete mar y tierra,* a combination of asada meat, shrimp, ranchero cheese, *nopal asado* (cactus), and scallions in a *molcajete* sauce. More about this in a minute. All permutations of the *molcajete* share the sauce, cheese, cactus, and scallions. The meats are different. There is an asada-quail combination, a rib-eye, a shrimp, a chicken, a pork, and a crab, scallop, and shrimp combination. The *molcajete* sauce is really a misnomer. The chef, the very talented Samuel Vasquez, creates the sauce from ancient Mexican traditions and named it for the container in which it is served. Disregard the linguistic quirks and savor the magnificence of the sauce itself: roasted tomatoes, various chilies, chicken stock, cilantro, and pumpkin and sesame seeds. The ingredients are processed into a thick salsa. It is genuinely hot with billows of flavor encircling everything, but it is truly marvelous when unifying the diverse meats and vegetables. Asada is thin, flash-fried steak. Medium-sized shrimp with tremendous flavor are immersed in the sauce. Fried strips of prickly pear cactus (the flavor is closest to bell pepper) and Mexican scallions are added. Slices of ranchero cheese complete the dish. The richness of the cheese and the pungency of the sauce marry the surf (shrimp) and turf (beef) to create a harmonious whole the likes of which you have probably not experienced in a Mexican restaurant.

The *molcajetes* may be the most interesting things on the menu, but the remainder is not to be ignored. The *Sabana de pollo campanario* is a pounded chicken breast, flattened to no more than an eighth of an inch thick, topped with a thin layer of refried beans, sautéed onions, strips of poblano chili, over which a liberal serving of Monterey Jack cheese has been melted. I would expect the base of this dish to be a tortilla, but the "tortilla" is actually a thin layer of chicken. O.K., so we have a tostada, but the "tostada" is chicken breast. Now, on top of the "tostada" we put some poblano chili. Poblanos are mild chilies, four steps up from green bells on the Scoville scale. (Bell peppers have zero Scoville units; poblanos have 2,000 units; jalapeños have up to 8,000; habeñeros have 350,000; police-grade pepper spray has 5.3 million; pure capsaicin has 16 million.) Sautéed onions and sour cream are put on the top, and finally the whole thing is covered with Monterey Jack cheese and placed under the broiler. What is particularly interesting is the simultaneous use of heat (capsaicin) and cooling (sour cream).

The shrimp-octopus cocktail is another variant worth investigating. Most sauces for shrimp cocktail are nothing more than glorified ketchup. This one is thin and sweet—rather like V8 juice mixed with cilantro, lime juice, sugar, and Mexican hot sauce—unusual, and quite delicious. Several dishes appear on the menu that, at first glance, appear to be American alternatives. Interestingly, management assures me it is just the opposite, saying they are for Mexicans who want to try something different. Since almost 100 percent of the clientele of El Campanario is Mexican, the statement does have a certain degree of credibility. Whatever the actual take, rib steak and salmon with baked potato and chef's choice of vegetables are also on the menu. But forget this stuff and go for the *molcajetes*. When in Rome.

Breakfast is also a viable option with a more interesting menu than is usually found in Mexican restaurants. I can recommend the signature omelet made with shrimp. Diced red potatoes, onion, and green and red bell peppers make a terrific alternative to the usual Spanish rice. Creamy refried beans covered with melted cheese garnish as well. Considering the care and creativity lavished on the dinner menu, you can probably conclude that such things as *huevos divorciados* could well be worth the $7.50 being charged. That is two eggs, one with ham and the other with tortilla, one in red salsa and the other in green salsa, served with refried beans and house-made potatoes. Twenty offerings are available for breakfast. Some seem a bit silly, like eggs Florentine and eggs Benedict, but most of the remainder would seem to be interesting and culinary-stimulating options.

The kitchen can be slow. Give yourself plenty of time. Special note: This restaurant is the only restaurant within close proximity to either Fantasy Springs Casino or Spotlight 29 Casino. It is not within walking distance, but only a few miles by car if you are staying at Fantasy Springs Resort. There is also a $5 children's menu. Casino dining usually has age restrictions; this restaurant does not.

El Gallito
★★

Location: 68-820 Grove St., Cathedral City, 328-7794. *Food type:* Americanized Mexican. *Ambiance:* small old house; cute in a cheesy way. *Bar:*

beer and wine. **Reservations:** *not accepted.* **Hours:** *lunch and dinner daily.*
Note: cash only; ATM on premises.

El Gallito is a Cathedral City landmark that was struggling for its life
in 2007. This had nothing to do with its financial health; El Gallito was
as popular then as it is now. It was because of *Kelo v. City of New London.*
The city wanted to demolish the building and sell the land to a private
developer. El Gallito's customers were furious. As of this writing El
Gallito has been spared, even as all the land to its immediate east has been
cleared for development. Even if the city eventually forces it to relocate,
the restaurant will remain a viable and popular Mexican restaurant.

Gallito is the Spanish word for braggart or showoff. You could assume
that the restaurant is showing off its food of which it is proud. This
converted house of indeterminate age with room for maybe 40 customers
if they are trying to pass for sardines is a funny-looking little place, funky
and rather endearing rather than off putting. Red vinyl booths, cream-
colored plaster walls covered with Mexican tchotchkes, and faux brick
arches just about define this space.

The patrons of El Gallito are largely not Mexican. The food at El
Gallito is much like that of the Las Casuelas chain—Americanized—
but here it is less bland. The use of ample quantities of sour cream and
cheddar cheese and the concurrent diminishment of chili-based heat
makes the food particularly palatable for the American customer.

The menu is conservative, serving the usual amalgam of tacos, egg
dishes, enchiladas, burritos, a handful of specials, and combination
plates. There is no fish. Two blocks away is Taco Salsas (reviewed later
in this chapter) whose food is not only more authentic, but also more
interesting. El Gallito does, however, deliver high quality. The burrito,
for example, is not particularly Mexican, but in terms of both food
quality and preparation, it is outstanding. The meat, beef chuck braised
in chile verde (green chili sauce, mostly ortega chilies), is full flavored and
tender. Lengthy braising of this cut of beef often results in an unpleasant
stringiness characteristic of American pot roast. This is not the case here.
It is also not the least bit greasy. On the other hand, what should be a
punchy chile verde sauce is not. An advertised ranchera sauce also lacks
flavor. These are supposed to be thick vegetable-based sauces pregnant
with variety of chilies. They are bland. In a strange decision, this burrito

plate is covered with melted cheddar cheese and sour cream. Cheddar cheese is an American cheese delivering strictly American tastes, and sour cream is an American addition as well. Taken as a whole without the baggage of a label—in this case Mexican—this is a good dish although perhaps with too much dairy product. However, when your taste buds are expecting Mexican, it is a disappointment.

Refried beans are also bland, but they carry the authentic creaminess that comes from making them with lard rather than canola oil. Guacamole, too, has the consistency of a good ripe and fresh avocado purée but without the tastes that make guacamole something other than puréed avocado. Where are the tomatillos, jalapeños, onion, and lime juice?

A *salsa fresca* served with seriously deep-fried corn chips packs a lot of heat, but in a curiously simple tomato sauce. Cilantro, onion, various kinds of chilies, both hot and mild, are all missing.

The usual fine Mexican beers are sold, but wine is generic—Chablis, rose, Burgundy—all chilled. Prices are higher than you might expect in so modest an establishment. There are also surcharges for rice and beans on many dishes, and $2 extra for requesting eggs prepared separately in egg and chorizo dishes.

El Mirasol

$$

Location: 140 E. Palm Canyon Dr., Palm Springs, 323-0721. **Food type:** *Americanized Mexican.* **Ambiance:** *comfortable Mexican-style interior with good view and sidewalk patio.* **Bar:** *full; excellent beer selection; house wine by the glass only.* **Reservations:** *not accepted.* **Hours:** *lunch and dinner daily.*

With the last vestiges of brilliant sunlight reflecting off a lone cloud, an 8,000-foot rock escarpment looms almost violently to the west of El Marisol's street-front patio in Palm Springs. This is the view from one of the more popular Mexican restaurants in the area.

Mole is arguably the most significant contribution of indigenous Mexican cuisine to the larger world of cooking. Of course, the Mexican grandmother, like the proverbial Italian grandmother, alters, adjusts, and adapts her recipe according to her own taste and family traditions. No two are exactly alike. The use of nuts, raisins, coriander, pumpkin seeds, and dessert spices are unusual enough in savory cooking, but it is bitter chocolate in a brutally hot sauce that makes mole unique. Pasilla chilies, mulato chilies, and ancho chilies are the basis for that heat. Onions, garlic, and a stock made from whatever meat is being served with the mole, whether turkey, chicken, or pork, form the base. Mole is as wonderful as it is startling. Authentic mole is also demanding, extremely hot, and bitter. It is a shock to those not familiar with its peculiar virtues. The mole at El Mirasol is mildly spiced, and the chocolate is semisweet. The flavors are deep and complex, but the use of semisweet chocolate detracts from its basic nature. It is frustrating.

At El Mirasol the mole is served with a chicken breast, *pollo en mole poblano*. Boneless, skinless chicken breast is popular in California; it conforms to all the politically correct dietary rules. It is also vastly overrated from a culinary standpoint. Whole chicken, turkey thigh, or pork shoulder would make for a more interesting and significantly more complex, not to mention richer, taste.

Shrimp *doña diablo* lives up to its billing. Five shrimp are briefly sautéed in hot garlic oil. They then go into a chipotle and arbol chili sauce with lime juice and vinegar. This is a potent mixture. Chipotle is a smoked jalapeño; the arbol chili is that very thin red one you see occasionally at the supermarket. They create a genuine blast of chili heat. On a scale of one to 10 it would be an eight. The shrimp are a good size jumbo, about four inches long uncurled, and they are fully capable of retaining their flavor even against the chipotle fire. In fact they are complemented rather than smothered by it.

Scallops in Pipian sauce are a frequent special. New England deep-sea scallops (seven to nine of them, depending on size) are flash-fried in garlic oil and served in a nest of medium spicy Pipian. Pipian is like mole, a totally unique, indigenous Mexican concoction. It is a purée of pumpkin seeds and ancho chilies simmered in chicken stock. Pipian is a very friendly complement for fish, but it can also be found with turkey, duck, chicken, or pork. Curiously, I taste a base of fish stock, not chicken. The scallops themselves are large, succulent, and cooked not a moment too long.

A vegetarian burrito of spinach, broccoli, tomatoes, bell peppers, scallions, garlic, and Monterey Jack cheese arrives in a luscious, mild tomatillo sauce. Sounds a bit weird, but it is quite good. With vegetables lightly sautéed and a fresh—probably homemade—flour tortilla redolent of melted cheese, this entrée provides a delightful and offbeat alternative to the usual fast-food meat-and-beans-style burrito found everywhere. A sauce of processed tomatillos, green chilies, scallions, and cilantro, simmered until flavors are intermingled, brings the whole thing together. The ubiquitous rice and beans accompany. Neither is particularly interesting, but truly wonderful homemade corn tortillas thick and pregnant with powerful corn flavor contribute their natural gifts. The crab enchilada is an excellent option, and ceviche is served on weekends.

Las Casuelas
★½
$$

Locations: Las Casuelas Nuevas, 70-050 Highway 111, Rancho Mirage, 328-8844; Las Casuelas La Quinta, 78-080 Highway 111, La Quinta, 777-7715; Las Casuelas Terraza, 222 S. Palm Canyon Dr., Palm Springs, 325-2794; The Original Las Casuelas, 368 N. Palm Canyon Dr., Palm Springs, 325-3213; Casuelas Café, 73-703 Highway 111, Palm Desert, 568-0011. **Food type:** *Americanized Mexican.* **Ambiance:** *Las Casuelas La Quinta and Las Casuelas Nuevas are the newest and tend to exchange quirkiness for the big, safe palace. They are comfortable enough but lack soul. The patio at La Quinta is the premier spot on the east side of the valley. The most interesting is Las Casuelas Terraza, in Palm Springs. This is a kind of indoor/outdoor affair with tables right next to the sidewalk separated only by a half-wall and open windows. The building is old and meanders about in an irrational manner. Entertainment here tends toward rock 'n' roll and there is a dance floor.* **Bar:** *full.* **Reservations:** *recommended.* **Hours:** *vary by location but most are open lunch and dinner.*

There is a formula for these restaurants, and the owners have it down pat: build a big, safe, friendly Mexican hacienda. Serve lots of big, safe, friendly American food with Mexican names. Throw in big, safe, friendly margaritas with some big, safe, friendly Mexican-flavored guitar music played by big, safe, friendly Mexicans and, voila, success! The food is bland, bland, bland. Regardless of what it is, it all tastes the same. Rice, refried beans, and whatever the entrée might happen to be called. It arrives on a big platter with a flourish and melted cheese. American tourists with no stomach for Mexican food scarf it down by the truckload. The original, founded in 1958 by the Delgado family (all of the locations are owned by various members of this family) is in Palm Springs. Las Casuelas Terrazo, just up the street, has a live band and a dance floor. Terrazo has ample sidewalk seating and a terrific old-fashioned character.

If this is to your taste, by all means, go for it. The food does not taste bad; in fact, it doesn't taste much of anything. Just be forewarned.

RosAmarillo
★★½
$$

Location: in Ralph's Shopping Center, 49-990 Jefferson St., Suite 120, Indio, 777-1175. Food type: Mexican. Ambiance: elegant storefront with uniquely Mexican contemporary décor. Bar: full; small wine list; excellent beer list; excellent but expensive margaritas. Reservations: recommended for prime time. Hours: lunch and dinner daily. Chef: Rosario Enriquez.

Yes, it's a storefront, but it's a new one created from scratch by owner Christina Tristan with intelligence and an uncommon aesthetic sense. Maroon and gold dominate the room. Walls, linens, dishes, and even the menu sport the signature colors. The high culture of Spanish and Mexican painters—Picasso, Dalí, Rivera, Kahlo—is represented with gallery-like precision. Does the food measure up? Indeed it does, with a single exception.

This menu is multilayered. Tacos, tamales, enchiladas, and burritos are all available. Chimichangas and combination plates are too. Rice and beans accompany everything. But RosAmarillo has another side, a deeper, richer side.

But why are rice and beans the universal accompaniments of every Mexican entrée? Is it so in Mexico City, Acapulco, Veracruz? I ask the waitress. She laughs. "No," she says, "they have all kinds of side dishes there, but Americans sort of expect rice and beans. I don't really know why." By the way, this is not true of Adobe Grill (see Chapter 1) at the La Quinta Resort and Club.

A beautiful *salsa fresca* is presented with the addition of green bell pepper. It is mild but nicely flavorful and bursting with that "I chopped these vegetables three minutes ago just for you" taste.

Thick black-bean soup is the first order of business. Complex to say the least: bay leaf, garlic certainly, but bacon, and jalapeño? No, says Chef Rosario Enriquez without offering the correct ingredients. Enriquez speaks little English, but it matters not. With a dollop of sour cream—the menu says crème fraîche but it was too sour for that French delicacy—this is a superb soup.

Huachinango frito is a whole deep-fried red snapper with *mojo de ajo.* There is something wonderful about this dish, but you must rethink all your biases. It is cooked like a potato chip: crispy and brittle. The bones, too, become brittle and contribute to the overall crunch. Most of the bones are edible, as are the skin, fins, tail, and much of the head. It is unique. RosAmarillo serves a large fish whose fillet has been deeply scored. This improves contact with the hot oil. Served on a huge platter of romaine, lemons, avocado, cucumber, and scallions, along with the ubiquitous rice and beans, this is a genuine feast. Chunks of fish wrapped in a corn tortilla, doused with *salsa fresca,* and washed down with Dos Equis beer—Mexican food does not get much better than this. Be careful though, not all the bones are brittle enough to eat. And don't even think about pealing the skin off the meat. It will not come off, as it has been permanently bonded with 385 degrees of hot oil. Besides, the skin is the best part.

Camarónes ala Veracruzana is shrimp with *Veracruzana* sauce, one of the glories of Veracruz-style regional cooking. Onions, yellow peppers, tomatoes, olives, capers, garlic, white wine, and herbs (usually Mexican oregano, thyme, and marjoram) are simmered until a deeply flavorful broth emerges. The sauce is perfect, but the shrimp are badly overcooked. This could be an anomaly, but they should not be served this way.

The mole here is better than the one at El Mirasol (reviewed earlier in this chapter) but not as good as the one at Adobe Grill. Now if someone would only serve mole on a turkey thigh or slice of pork shoulder instead of a chicken breast.

Serenata

★★

$-$$

*Location: 73-325 Highway 111, Palm Desert, 836-9028. **Food type:** Americanized Mexican. **Ambiance:** intimate, brightly colored, and friendly; mariachi band on Thursdays. **Bar:** full; all the great Mexican beers; almost no wine. **Reservations:** suggested. **Hours:** lunch and dinner daily.*

Of the Americanized Mexican restaurants, this is perhaps my personal favorite. The food is not completely denatured as it is at Don Diego's, nor is it as commercial as it is at the Las Casuelas chain. The restaurant itself is utterly charming. It is small with an aggressive paint job; gold and red, actually a rust color, burst forth as you enter. A small but fully stocked bar is on the left; the dining room, on the right. A bamboo ceiling and Mexican tchotchkes are sprinkled about. A mariachi band entertains on Thursdays, when reservations are a must.

The menu is decidedly ordinary, but the quality of the food and preparation is high. A terrific *salsa fresca* arrives immediately. This medium-hot salsa is best described as sprightly, extremely refreshing, and bursting with garden-fresh flavor: fresh tomatoes, cilantro, onion, and a hint of cucumber. A hotter salsa that is made with tomatillos is also available. The waitstaff describe it as habañero salsa. This is a blatant lie. They probably carry a single habañero chili through the room as they make it. At something like 350,000 Scoville units, the habañero is roughly 45 times hotter than a jalapeño pepper. We are talking liquid hell! The sauce is, however, nicely warm. For those inclined to a little heat, ask for it.

They do a nice chiles rellenos spiked liberally and effectively with cumin. Fans of this dish are frustrated by so many rellenos, soggy with grease, produced by countless incompetent Mexican kitchens. They are labor intensive and tricky to make, and the bad ones are hideous. For those readers unfamiliar with this dish, chiles rellenos consist of large mild peppers, usually poblanos. These are baked and peeled then stuffed with some kind of filling: egg and cheese, spicy pork, ground meat, vegetables. Usually Monterey Jack cheese is included. A batter is made from egg whites and flour. The chilies are dipped in the meringue batter. This is the difficult part as the batter must form a tight seal. The sealed peppers are then deep-fried. If the seal is not tight, the oil leaks into the peppers and the resultant chiles rellenos are revolting. The principle is not unlike that which defines baked Alaska: ice cream sealed with meringue and baked. Good chiles rellenos are terrific. Serenata does good chiles rellenos.

Carnitas Morelia is also a fine dish although for more authentic Mexican tastes I would probably go for the similar chile verde or chile Colorado. Chunks of seasoned pork are steamed until tender then sautéed. The steaming results in a tender and flavorful piece of meat; the sauté adds a caramelization. A choice of beans—refried, black Cuban style, or *frijoles de la olla* (whole pinto beans in a juice)—and Spanish rice come with virtually everything. The black beans are the best by a substantial margin. *Frijoles de la olla* are the same as refried beans but they are not mashed up. Guacamole and sour cream also garnish everything.

Serenata does a chocolate mole sauce, but this one is the sweetest of all those sampled. The Aztec recipe calls for bitter chocolate and huge selections of spices, chilies, and roasted seeds. It should be bitter and blisteringly hot. The current practice by Mexican restaurants in the United States of using semisweet or, worse, sweet chocolate results in something totally unrelated to the Aztec mole sauce. Ice cream anyone?

Taco Salsas
★★
$

Location: 69-020 E. Palm Canyon Dr., Cathedral City, 321-6612. **Food type:** *Mexican.* **Ambiance:** *cheesy storefront.* **Bar:** *beer, wine, and fresh fruit juice.* **Reservations:** *not accepted.* **Hours:** *lunch and dinner daily; breakfast Sunday only.* **Chef-owner:** *Miguel Hernandez.*

Yes, it is cheesy with its yellow and orange vinyl tablecloths, gold walls, and blue indoor/outdoor carpet, but you do not come here to admire the scenery. You come for some of the more authentic Mexican food around.

Begin with the salsa bar. It looks at first like a salad bar. Five homemade salsas and assorted condiments—various chilies and cilantro—grace this bar. Help yourself. The salsas are a fascinating study in the art of Mexican salsa making. The first is a *salsa fresca,* the kind everyone knows (at least those of us who live in border states): finely chopped tomatoes, various chilies, cilantro, onion, vinegar, a bit of sugar, all fresh. But then there are the less-well-known versions: ancho, California, and arbol chilies roasted, dried, and crushed with garlic and vinegar; arbol chilies with garlic, pepper, allspice, Mexican oregano, and cloves (this one is surprising); tomatillos with serrano and jalapeño chilies; tomatillos, roasted arbol and California chilies, and garlic. Take a sample of each to your table. Regulars go to the bar first and bring six or seven little cups of their favorites to their table before ordering. All are spicy-hot, but none is brutal.

Mexican beer is always a good choice of libation here, but do not overlook the fresh Mexican fruit juices. Papaya, mango, and guava juice with their mild sweetness and thick melon flavors seem to temper the heat of the chilies almost as well as milk. (Milk would be horrible with this food. Do not even consider it.) Soda drinkers should try the Jarritos Tamarindo (tamarind soda).

Ceviche cocktail or tostada offers a profound contrast to the ceviche at the much more upscale Adobe Grill (see Chapter 1) at the La Quinta Resort and Club. The fish here is ground Alaskan whitefish and it is "cooked" in the lime juice for two hours. At Adobe Grill, is it diced halibut "cooked" for eight hours. The difference? The halibut is tough and stringy; this one is as tender as prime filet and much more flavorful. The halibut is also five times more expensive.

Mole con puerco (pork in mole) is not the chocolate mole common in the southern states of Mexico. This one is made from all the chilies and seeds but has no chocolate or cinnamon. The pork is shredded shoulder meat—rich, tender, and full flavor

Pulpo a la diabla (octopus in red-hot sauce) is an excellent dish. Chef Hernandez seems to have solved the problem of cooking octopus. Cooked too little and it is tough as shoe leather; cooked too long and it turns to baby food. Hernandez boils it furiously in plain water for five minutes, turns off the heat, and covers it and allows it to steam for 15 minutes. He then boils it again for five minutes. This method, he explains, breaks down the muscle but is not enough time to destroy the texture of the meat. The final texture is something like an avocado or banana that is not quite ripe. The diabla sauce is definitely spicy-hot although certainly not unbearable. The heat is forward in the mouth and tempers well with mango juice. Both dishes arrive on a platter with shredded lettuce, tomatoes, and cucumber, offering a strong contrast to the spicy meats. Spanish rice and creamy refried beans accompany.

There are some interesting *sopas* offered at Taco Salsas. Beef soup with beans, bacon, and onion is one of them. Thin slices of roast beef in a hearty broth with deep layers of bacon and onion flavors would be perfect were it not a bit on the greasy side.

The most expensive thing on the menu is $11.95, and there is a seafood platter for two at $21.95, which puts Taco Salsas definitively in the cheap-eats category.

Southwestern

This is a flexible category. It can mean a lot of different things depending on where you are standing. Put as simply as possible Southwestern cuisine hinges on the chili pepper and the general spiciness that results from its use. It is influenced to be sure by Mexican cooking, but it is not the same. Big cuts of smoked or grilled beef and pork rubbed with chili powder, cumin, sugar, and garlic are not Mexican, but Texan. Chili cookoffs are indigenous to the American Southwest not Mexico. Menudo and mole are Mexican and not American Southwest. That being said, restaurants billing themselves as "Southwest" usually feature a lot of Mexican dishes.

Blue Coyote Bar and Grill

$$

Locations: 445 N. Palm Canyon Dr., Palm Springs, 327-119; 44-100 Jefferson St., Indio, 772-2600. *Food type:* Tex-Mex/Southwestern. *Ambiance: Palm Springs location has stunning misted patio with fountains and umbrellas; Indio location is a dull storefront.* *Bar: full; the margaritas have a terrific reputation.* *Reservations: suggested.* *Hours: lunch and dinner daily.*

A second Blue Coyote has opened in a strip mall in Indio. The food is the same as the one in Palm Springs, but the most interesting thing about the Palm Springs restaurant is its location and ambiance. Here there is only the food. If you have a choice, go to Palm Springs or go elsewhere. El Campanario (this chapter) in Indio has excellent Mexican food.

Blue Coyote in Palm Springs is a popular restaurant and hangout, especially with 20-somethings. Its location on the main drag downtown and its delightful misted patio with fountains and blue and yellow umbrellas make it the ideal spot for people-watching and consuming the enormously popular Wild Coyote margarita. The extra half-star on the quality rating is for the ambiance; the food earns one and a half stars.

There are a number of dishes that are strictly Southwest and would not be found on a typical Mexican menu: chipotle baby-back ribs, Yucatan lamb, Yucatan mahi mahi, paella, jalapeño filet medallions, a Southwestern-style porterhouse steak, and Southwestern-style rack of lamb. Several dinner specials do not follow the Mexican formula, including Cajun salmon, Argentinean-style rib steak, and Southwestern meatloaf.

Service at this restaurant earns decidedly mixed reviews. This is a common complaint here, but for me it exhibited itself when the waiter brought my entrée within two minutes of my appetizer. I really hate this. *Posole,* or *pozole,* is a traditional Mexican soup made with hominy and pork. Hominy is corn kernels that have been nixtamalized then simmered until they pop. Nixtamalization is the process by which dried corn has been heated and soaked in an alkaline solution to loosen the skin. Chunks of pork are sautéed with onions, garlic, and chilies. The hominy goes into a broth, which could be water or chicken broth and Mexican spices (cumin, chili powder, Mexican oregano) and possibly tomatoes. The pork joins the corn, and everything is simmered until the pork is tender. This is a good recipe, but the soup at Blue Coyote is not good. To begin with, the hominy vastly outnumbers the pork chunks. They are supposed to be of equal quantity. Cumin dominates the balance to the extent that everything else is lost, and the pork is tough and stringy.

Southwestern carnitas should be easy as this pulled or shredded pork steamed in a banana leaf and served with rice, beans, guacamole, pico de gallo, and sour cream is standard Mexican fare. The beans are Cuban black beans, which is a good sign, but they are undercooked. Undercooked beans are unpleasant. The rice, too, uninteresting to begin with, is undercooked. The guacamole is excellent with tomatoes and jalapeños. Pico de gallo is just *salsa fresca*— tomatoes, onion, cilantro, and chilies—without the liquid or the chilies and is consequently quite bland. But the real story is with the pork. Pulled pork is a standard of Texas barbecue. A pork shoulder is smoked forever then pulled apart. This pork is not smoked, so it is possibly braised. Whatever the case, the meat is much drier than it should be. The pieces touching the banana leaf are hard and almost burned, as though the leaf were stuffed the day before then baked to reheat it.

The salsa fresca is excellent, with a nice moderate burn and the full flavor of several different kinds of chilies. Ask for extra and use it liberally on most dishes. Flour tortillas are delivered automatically.

CHAPTER 13

Barbecue

Barbecue, like country music, is in short supply in the Coachella Valley. For the most part, what barbecue there is tends to be housed in much more upscale environments than you would expect to see in Texas, Missouri, or Kansas. The two flashiest establishments are Babe's B-B-Que Grill & Brewhouse in Rancho Mirage and Jakalope Ranch in Indio. There are also the usual chains like Tony Roma's, but since these are well-known chains whose food is consistent nationwide, there is no point in including them here. We also have the shacks and joints. Palm Springs sports Cowboy Way BBQ, Cathedral City has Big Mama's and Tootie's, and Harry's Oklahoma BBQ is in La Quinta. For my taste the best barbecue locally does not come from these western-style smokehouses, but from Japanese grills. Okura (Chapter 10) especially does wonderful grilled ribs. Japanese-style barbecue is not listed in this chapter, but in Chapter 10 under Japanese restaurants.

Babe's B-B-Que Grill and Brewhouse
★★½
$$
Location: at The River at Rancho Mirage, 71-800 Highway 111, Rancho Mirage, 346-8738. Food type: American barbecue. Ambiance: pseudo barbecue barn; more like plush Chicago steakhouse heavy on the kitsch. Bar: full; heavy on the microbrews. Reservations: not accepted. Hours: lunch and dinner daily.

The ambiance at Babe's is rather odd. It is not what you tend to expect at a barbecue joint: the down-home atmosphere of plastic plates, sawdust on the floor, picnic benches, beer served in huge pitchers, and a bathtub in which to wash up. There is a place in Santa Barbara with a bathtub, not for bathing, but serving as a gigantic sink for patrons to wash their hands. Rockabilly or country should be blaring from speakers too large for comfort. Babe's isn't even remotely like this. It actually tries to emulate some of the atmosphere of a traditional barbecue joint but it comes off as kitsch. Three huge bronze hogs stand guard at the entrance. A mural of galloping horses does not make a barbecue joint. Babe's is more like a Chicago steakhouse trying too hard. The patio could actually be lifted from a four-star restaurant with its firepit and misters. Even the location is wrong; The River at Rancho Mirage is just about as upscale as you can get around these here parts.

Many of the customers at Babe's are not here for the barbecue but for the brews. Ale, stout, porter, lager, and Pilsner fanatics are right up there with wine fanatics when it comes to the intensity of their analysis. Because this is a book fundamentally about food, let me just say that I am not a beer fanatic. I like the stuff, but it fulfills a much less important niche in my life than does either food or wine. I did, however, thoroughly enjoy a large (25-ounce) Blackfin brew. It is a big, dark lager in the German style and winner in 2003 of the bronze medal at the Australian International Beer Awards. Babe's brews five beers on the premises, ranging from the monster Bighorn IPA (6.2 percent alcohol) to a Pilsner in the Czech style. Twenty other beers are also available either on tap or by the bottle.

St. Louis ribs are a misnomer. They are definitely ribs, and they are definitely the St. Louis-style cut, but this is not St. Louis-style barbecue. The St. Louis cut is the preferred cut of some rib aficionados. They are not baby backs, and they are also not country style, which are really chops. The classic barbecued ribs are the spareribs, the lower section of rib cage remaining after the chop has been removed. When the chine bone and the brisket bones are removed from the bottom of the rib rack, the rib section is called a St. Louis cut. St. Louis ribs are prepared similar to Memphis barbecue, which specifies a spicy dry rub and a savory vinegar-based mop sauce. Cider vinegar, apple cider, bay leaf, garlic, Tabasco, salt, and a spicy dry rub are the basis for the St. Louis-style barbecue. Southern barbecue sauce is thin and vinegar based; it is not very sweet. The sauce at Babe's is western style—ketchup and corn syrup based—very sweet and not spicy at all, just like the stuff available in a bottle. Worse, Babe's does not use a dry rub either. The ribs themselves are wonderful, smoked in hickory wood for 18 hours at something like 250 degrees, but they are too sweet and remarkably lacking the kind of spiciness you generally associate with great barbecue.

Meat prepared by smoking has a pink smoke ring just under the surface, even when fully cooked. This is caused by myoglobin in the meat reacting with carbon monoxide in the smoke to form a heat-stable pigment. These ribs have that ring.

Sides include choice of two: fries, sweet potato fries, beans, or coleslaw. May I suggest the sweet potato fries and the beans? Sweet potato fries are tricky to make. The density of the sweet potato makes it difficult to get them crisp, and the high sugar levels mean that they burn easily. Babe's manages to do sweet potato fries perfectly (I wish I knew the secret; mine are lousy). The beans are too sweet, quite ordinary, and without much depth of flavor, but are the next best option unless you are a diehard coleslaw fan. I cannot speak to the quality of coleslaw, as I do not like the stuff; however, a friend speaks highly of it. I thought it too sweet and with too much mayonnaise.

Babe's cornbread is a marvel. The finest cornbread in the world comes from Virgil's Deli in New York City. Its uniqueness comes from the addition of grated sharp cheddar cheese, corn kernels, cilantro, Tabasco, and scallions. It is also prepared with buttermilk, which provides an acid base allowing the use of soda as a leavening. Virgil's cornbread has multiple levels of flavor; it is moderately sweet, light but moist, and extremely complex. The use of more flour than cornmeal eliminates the grittiness associated with Southern cornbread. Babe's cornbread comes close to the Virgil ideal. The texture is the same and the flavors almost as complex. There is no cilantro, no scallions, probably no Tabasco, but there are bits of red peppers, corn kernels and probably cheese. It boasts of more depth than any cornbread in my experience other than Virgil's.

Chili is thinner than most but is not laden with beans. Beef, tomato, onion, peppers, and a heavy dose of cumin define its taste profile. Babe's does a lot of chicken, a Texas tri-tip, pork tenderloin, short ribs, and three steaks. Oddly there is a pulled-pork sandwich but no pulled pork as an entrée.

The Cowboy Way BBQ

$$-$$$

Location: 317 N. Indian Canyon Dr., Palm Springs, 322-0265. Food type: barbecue. Ambiance: lunch counter at converted bus stop. Bar: beer and wine. Reservations: not accepted. Hours: 11 A.M. to 8 P.M. Note: cash and ATM only.

Cowboy Way is a converted Greyhound bus terminal. It consists of a countertop in a sterile room. There is a view: the heavy traffic of Indian Canyon Drive. It is one-way if that is any consolation. The place even

318 THE PALM SPRINGS DINER'S BIBLE

faces east so there are no mountains in the distance. But there is smoke! Lots and lots of delicious smoke generated by hours of "low and slow" cooking. You do not want to dine here even if the smell of smoking pork is enticing, but you might want to do takeout. They have beer and wine, but the thought of ordering dinner with wine and sitting down for a meal is ludicrous. Besides, finding a wine that will pair well with this food is next to impossible.

Somebody at Cowboy Way made the choice not to serve spareribs. Spareribs *with* the top flap are the most flavorful of barbecued meats. Increasingly, California barbecue establishments are electing to serve the St. Louis cut, which eliminates the top flap. Yes, it does make them easier to eat for those with poor manual dexterity. (Hey, eating ribs is messy business! You don't like getting grease and barbecue sauce on your hands? Go elsewhere. Ribs cannot be negotiated efficiently with a knife and fork.) Other places, such as Cowboy Way, are electing to eliminate even the St. Louis cut, which is already a compromise, and serve only baby backs. The baby back is not even a rib, but it is even less messy than the St. Louis cut.

Spareribs are cut from the pig's belly. They are true ribs. They are tough and contain lots of fat and connective tissue. The meat is hard to get at, and they take forever to cook. If the top flap is removed, they become easier to eat and cook more evenly, but the most succulent meat is cut away. When the whole sparerib is cooked properly, that is to say, smoked for upwards of 18 hours, all the connective tissue breaks down to a form of gelatin and most of the fat melts away. The result is a supremely tender, massively flavored rib. All that fat and connective tissue are part of the rib experience. It is the same kind of thing that makes a braised lamb shank different from a lean slice of lamb leg. The baby back is cut from the back, the loin area. They are naturally more tender, have little fat, and no connective tissue. The result is a meat that cooks much faster, is all meat, and is nowhere near as messy. Baby backs also have half the flavor. The "Grayhound bus station" serves only baby backs. (They do carry beef ribs.)

How are they? They are well prepared baby backs if you like baby backs. They are as you would expect: meaty, falling off the bone, no fat, no gelatinous connective tissue, little flavor. They are also expensive, the most expensive in town. In fact, the cost for a whole rack is more even than Jackalope Ranch (this chapter). Jackalope is a $36 million food Disneyland; Cowboy Way is a bus station with a lunch counter! A whole rack of baby backs at Jackalope is $26; at Cowboy Way, $26.95. Explain that.

The only available sauce is a mild tomato/corn syrup Western sauce. It is nicely balanced, but there should at least be a second spicier option. Jackalope has three interesting sauces; Tootie's (this chapter) has their "Kick Ass" version. This one is similar to the one at Babe's (this chapter).

Kansas City Slaw is the least sweet of its competition. Kansas City-style coleslaw is vinegar based, rather than mayonnaise based. Cowboy BBQ makes theirs with very little sugar, which is a nice change, but it is still dull. No local barbecue joint has an interesting slaw. Considering what is currently being created out there in food land, this fact is not only a shame but also embarrassing. Consider this one by Tyler Florence of the Food Network: green cabbage, carrots, red onion, green onions, red chili pepper, mayonnaise, Dijon mustard, cider vinegar, lemon juice, sugar (pinch), celery seed, hot sauce. This is not difficult, and it is a whole lot more interesting than shredded cabbage, sugar, and mayonnaise or white vinegar. I even might become a slaw fan.

Barbecue sandwiches are a fast-food option. Pulled pork, brisket, and tritip for $8, $9, and $11, respectively, are available. These are anything but cheap. On the other hand, Tyler's (Chapter 14) gets $11 for a burger and fries.

Harry's Oklahoma Style Smokehouse BBQ
½
$-$$

Location: 47-150 *Washington Blvd., La Quinta, 564-4929.* **Food type:** *barbecue.* **Ambiance:** *sterile barn.* **Reservations:** *accepted.* **Bar:** *beer and wine.* **Hours:** *11:00 A.M. to 8:00 P.M. Sunday through Thursday, 11 A.M. till 9:00 P.M. Friday and Saturday; free delivery.*

Well, it smells really smoky. Ceilings are really high, even ridiculously so. It is located next to Louis's Pantry (Chapter 15), but entrance is around the back.

There are two one reasons to dine here, hence the half-star: poverty and hunger. Sundays feature the "All You Can Eat Pig OUT Buffet" for $16.95 (adults) and $8.95 (under 12). There are all kinds of specials: two-for-one Monday night madness, etc. Happy hour features full dinners for $10.95. Of course, the poverty and hunger must be accompanied with indiscriminate eating habits. Harry's is just plain bad, even aggressively so.

Harry's features a whole range of barbecued meats excluding only brisket: baby backs, St. Louis-style spareribs, beef ribs, chicken, hot links, tri-tip, and pulled pork. All the usual sides are also on the menu: dirty rice, baked beans, potato salad, coleslaw, and cornbread. Desserts are peach cobbler, pecan pie, and Key lime cheesecake.

To begin with, the pork ribs are undersmoked. They need another three hours at least before all the connective tissue is broken down and they are falling-off-the-bone tender. Tri-tip is oversmoked. It is dried out and verging on stringiness. Chicken breast is smoked just right. Served on the bone, it has kept its moisture and is perfectly cooked. There is something wrong with a barbecue joint when the chicken is better than the ribs.

Cornbread is inedible. Perhaps a new batch is in the oven and so I received the last of yesterday's version. But why serve it at all? At least dried-out cornbread can be somewhat rescued by sprinkling a little water on it, wrapping it in plastic, and giving it a few seconds in the microwave. This is cold and dry. It is also boring and too sweet. There are many fine new recipes for more interesting cornbread with various additions: cheddar cheese, cilantro, scallions, chili peppers, etc. This is the ancient recipe found on the box of cornmeal.

"Molasses baked beans" tastes for all the world of a can, perhaps with the addition of a little molasses.

Coleslaw is drowning in a mayonnaise-based "cream" sauce, cloying and sweet. Fortunately the fresh cabbage does provide a respite from the other tastes, which all seem to fall under the same umbrella.

Sauce is generic. There is a mild and a "spicy." Tomato sauce, vinegar, and corn syrup are the basic ingredients. The "spicy" is only marginally spicy, but a genuine Louisiana hot sauce is thankfully provided at every table.

Peach cobbler is actually pie. There is a layer of soggy dough underneath the "peaches" as well as on the top. Cobblers, crisps, betties, crumbles, and pandowdies are all basically deep-dish fruit pies with a pastry (often a biscuit of some kind) or crumble on the top. The ratio of fruit to pastry in a good cobbler should be three to one. Here it is the other way around. To add insult to injury the peaches have absolutely no flavor and arrive in a thick syrup.

At least it's cheap.

Jackalope Ranch
★★½
$$-$$$$

*Location: 80-400 Highway 111, Indio, 342-1999. **Food Type:** barbecue plus. **Ambiance:** grand Texas lodge. **Bar:** full. **Reservations:** suggested. **Hours:** lunch and dinner daily, happy hour, bar menu 3:30 P.M. to 6 P.M., Sunday brunch.*

This is another in the seemingly endless chain of Kaiser Group restaurants. No sooner does one close than another pops up. Readers of the first edition will note my review of Crazy Bones, a Kaiser Group barbecue establishment in Palm Springs. Crazy Bones was built on The Deck, the prior Kaiser Group generation. Both restaurants failed. They have now tried the barbecue format again with the more elaborate (6.4 acres of elaborate, actually) Jackalope Ranch. The total cost of this massive Texas-style lodge is estimated at $36 million. It originated as the last and greatest project of Don Calendar, founder of the Marie Calendar chain and the successful Babes B-B-Que (this chapter) in Rancho Mirage. Unfortunately the 80-year-old Mr. Calendar died before the project was completed, and the property was bought by the Kaiser group.

So what is a jackalope? Lee Morcus of the Kaiser Group can be seen discussing the presence of the horned "killer" rabbits on his property. Black-helicopter conspiracy theories abound on the Internet. Wikipedia says, "mythical animal . . . a cross between an antelope and a jackrabbit." Apparently, there is an actual species of jackrabbit called the "antelope jackrabbit" because it can run really, really fast. Lee Morcus says it is good for smoking and tastes like chicken. I find that hard to believe, especially since neither antelope nor rabbit tastes anything like chicken. PR hype or whatever, when they start serving the mythical killer rabbit with horns, I will be the first in line.

The food at Jackalope is termed "Progressive Southwest BBQ and Steaks." The hype reads, "The Coachella Valley's newest dining sensation is getting rave reviews from the media and our guests." Progressive Southwest? Well, Southwest generally means Texas, New Mexico, Arizona, and Southern California with some serious Mexican influence, but the barbecue tradition is Texas. "Progressive"—one has to wonder if it means anything at all. I can't figure it out even after having dined here. If pressured to come up with something I would compare it to Firecliff (Chapter 7).

The facts not in dispute are these. The 21,000-square-foot building is absolutely stunning both inside and out. No expense has been spared. The use of the most expensive building materials and construction techniques are in evidence: copper, leather, wood, slate, stone. Open beam ceilings are in the 20-foot-plus range. Various dining rooms, bar areas, banquet rooms, and private dining rooms abound. The huge heated and misted outdoor two-tiered dining area has an enormous bar traversing its entire length. Fountains, huge grassy areas, pig sculptures, and a foyer larger than many restaurants showcase the exorbitance of the ranch. One dining room has five enormous flat-screen television sets. The wine cellar can be examined up close and personal as it is set up on both sides of an open aisle. Kitchen and state-of-the-art smoker are also visible. Bar stools and booths are covered in raw cowhide. (I guess it's cowhide. I am completely ignorant about these things.)

The saloon is serviced by cocktail waitresses dressed awkwardly in denim miniskirts and corsets. It is only somewhat embarrassing. The Tilted Kilt (Chapter 14) manages it a little better, but only Las Vegas seems to do this sort of thing well. I remember back in the 1970s at Caesar's Palace . . . Oh well, never mind that now.

Internet reviews, local word of mouth, and my own experience is that service ranges from mediocre to truly hideous. Our party requested that our dishes be brought out one at a time with an interval in between. This did not happen. Our party asked for bread service. Our waitress said, "Certainly." It took four requests.

The food is surprisingly good. I say "surprisingly" because everything about this mega-hacienda seems to be more about entertainment than about food, and the menu is enormous. The other Kaiser restaurants also generally serve mediocre food. (See Chop House in Chapter 9 and Kaiser Grill in Chapter 7). Here it is certainly overpriced but creative and well prepared.

First course is the "smoked shrimp and local sweet corn chowder with fried red chili biscuits and red onion salad." The red onion salad never materializes but we do not notice. The "chowder" is actually more of a bisque. What is the difference? A bisque is a smooth, thick shellfish (usually) soup. It is pureed and cream based. Lobster, crab, and shrimp are the most popular versions. A chowder is a chunky ·stewlike soup often made with come kind of seafood. This is a shrimp bisque with corn kernels in it. The bisque is excellent. Flavor like this cannot be achieved except by the traditional French techniques of crushing the shells with butter, straining, and adding pureed shrimp and cream. It is potent and luscious with butterfat. It arguably becomes more of a chowder by the addition of the corn kernels, but its thickness and fundamental nature argue against it. The corn itself neither adds to nor subtracts from the otherwise lusciousness of the bisque although it is flavorful and well cooked to a pleasingly crunchy al dente. The "red chili biscuits" bring nothing to the party. They are little bread garnishes floating on the top.

Second course is the "three pepper crusted Ahi with cucumber-red onion salad, cilantro-chili pequin [*sic*] dressing, tamarind glaze, and spicy peanuts." The described salad is not what arrives. Instead, I am served a salad of primarily spinach with shoestring deep-fried onion on top. There were a few spicy peanuts sprinkled about but they did not contribute anything to the overall effect. A "pequin" is a type of chili. It is red and about six times hotter than the relatively mild jalapeño, which puts it solidly in the medium-hot range along with the serrano. I cannot detect any cilantro-chili pequin (that should be cilantro-pequin chili) in this salad. Tamarind is a tart and acidic fruit. When sweetened it makes for a terrific soda popular in Mexico. This glaze actually is squeezed about the plate upon which the ahi rests. Considering the potency of the tamarind this glaze has little or no taste. On the other hand, the ahi is superb. The natural quality of the meat is easily sashimi grade, and the quick sear is perfect, leaving the center completely raw. The "three pepper" crust is weak and listless, but if the tamarind glaze had more punch, it would be fine.

No barbecue restaurant review can possibly be relevant without a serious look at the restaurant's raison d'être, spareribs. Jackalope has several barbecue plates and various combinations: baby backs, St. Louis-style spareribs, tri-tip, pork shoulder, and chicken. (No jackalope!) All of these entrées are in the $20 range, and portions are small. I got only four ribs for my $24. However, the barbecue process is right on. The distinctive pink myoglobin ring indicates a perfect smoking time. They are rich, meaty, tender, full flavored, and falling off the bone. The St. Louis cut is the only way to get spareribs. See the review of Babe's (this chapter) for an explanation of the St. Louis cut.

Three different sauces are delivered with the meat. Essentially, though minor flavorings occur, they are mild, medium, and hot. All of them are catsup and corn syrup based with vinegar and assorted flavorings. The mild is the same as any bottled barbecue, better than some, worse than others. The medium is actually the most interesting with a distinct back note of guava. The ever-interesting chipotle pepper supplies the heat here. The hot version is flavored with the prickly pear cactus and the blistering habañero chili. The cactus flavor is lost in the heat, but for those of us who like a bit of the capsicum burn, this one does fill the bill nicely.

Coleslaw is silly. Coleslaw is already too sweet for my taste, but this one comes with a big helping of raisins, including sultanas. With a better balance and perhaps some onion and shredded carrot, the slaw could offer a much needed contrast to the sweetness and texture of the barbecue.

Sweet potato fries are excellent (they are underseasoned, but I eat too much salt anyway). Sweet potato fries are harder to make than the russet version as the sweet potato needs more time to cook. More time in hot oil means either a lower temperature or a burned surface. Lower temperature means a greasy fry. Sensitive compromise is needed. We have that here.

Also on the menu are a filet mignon, buffalo rib, and veal rib, all with apparently interesting Southwest preparations; a duck breast in adobo sauce; and a couple of fish. Various hamburgers and ceviches round out the menu.

What is the bottom line? The building, grounds, and cocktail waitresses (depending on your hormones) are worth a visit. Service is poor. Food is inconsistent but for the most part quite good and prices are marginally too high.

Tootie's Texas Barbecue
Barbecue: ★★½
Sides: not recommended
$
*Location: 68-703 Perez Rd., Suite A1, Cathedral City, 202-6963. **Food type:** Texas barbecue. **Ambiance:** bus station chic. **Bar:** beer only. **Hours:** lunch and dinner Tuesday through Saturday.*

Tootie's looks and feels like a bus station in San Antonio: galvanized steel sheeting, matching trash cans, green paint, linoleum, and Texas-style "ort" on the walls.

But let's talk pork ribs. Each slab of hog is rubbed with sugar, garlic powder, salt, and cayenne pepper then goes into the smoker. Tootie's smokes with green oak for seven hours at 200 degrees. The result is a thick, meaty slab of full-flavored ribs. The meat is never placed on a grill, which means no surface char. This is a perfectly legitimate style of barbecue. It is not a criticism. These ribs are not falling off the bone as many a place brags, but then I really don't see the advantage of having the meat fall off the bone.

Combos of ribs, hot links, and pork shoulder—smoked for 12 hours—are spicy enough, but certainly not aggressively so. The pork shoulder is succulent and flavorful. Shredded and stuffed into a jalapeño cheese bun this makes for a terrific and inexpensive lunch at $5.95.

All this barbecue comes with either the regular or Kick Ass sauce. The regular is thin and tomato-y; the Kick Ass is much better. That appellation may be a bit enthusiastic, but it is not out of the ballpark.

Tootie's offers eight side dishes: potato salad, coleslaw, cowboy beans, baked beans, macaroni, creamed corn, dirty rice, and Texas caviar. The winner is the Texas caviar. This is a salad based on the black-eyed pea (really a bean), combining it with some or most of the following: celery, green and/or red bell pepper, garlic, jalapeño, tomato, onion, cilantro, cumin, sugar, vinegar, and oil. This one had no tomato, and I didn't taste any cumin or cilantro. Texas caviar in Texas is generally mushy. This is much better, as these black-eyed peas have a little crunch left in them. None of the other side dishes is any good. They are bland and unworthy of pairing with this barbecue. The meat cried out for a Jamaican baked-bean recipe with rum, molasses, and dry mustard. The cornbread and jalapeño bread are pathetic.

Another plus for this restaurant is the price. All barbecue is in the $7-$11 range and includes two sides. Shiner Bock, a Texas dark beer and excellent complement to the barbecue, is available on tap for $2.25. Disposable plates and counter ordering help keep costs down. Tootie's also caters any event from family picnics to corporate parties.

CHAPTER 14

Potpourri

Restaurants difficult to categorize for one reason or another—delis, pubs, clubs, and novelties—can be found here. Just because a restaurant is in this chapter does not automatically make it suspect as to quality. The last three years have seen the demise of two terrific and fun little places, the quirky Mad French Lady gourmet market and sandwich counter and the Market on El Paseo, a little wine and cheese shop. On the other hand, Bouchee has expanded to a second location, and the Camelot Theatres have added a happy hour and bar menu with ridiculously low prices ($4 appetizers) in the upstairs lounge.

Bouchee Fine Foods

$

Locations: Rancho Las Palmas Shopping Center, 42-410 Bob Hope Dr., Rancho Mirage, 340-5311; 46-600 Washington St., Suite 1, La Quinta, 771-0293. Food type: gourmet store, deli, and sandwich bar. Ambiance: big square room; muted colors; relaxed and comfortable. Bar: wine only; limited to five different labels. Hours: lunch and dinner (till 6 P.M.) Monday though Saturday.

Bouchee has a larger selection of deli items and sandwiches than its competitor, Jennifer's Kitchen (reviewed later in this chapter). The choices here, however, do not always work as intended. The problem here is that many of the deli dishes are better hot, and they either cannot be reheated or don't do well in the microwave. Take, for example, the grilled rack of lamb. This is an eight-bone trimmed Australian rack grilled medium rare. These little lovelies sell for $13 each—a very good price as they cost about $9—but they are cold. Lamb does not share with its bovine counterpart that quality which renders its cold version palatable. Cold lamb simply does not taste good. The quality of the fat—lanolin— is so dense it makes for a wonderful ingredient in soap, but not in the mouth. So what can be done? Heat it up, right? Microwave it? I think not. It will be cooked to destruction before it is hot. A rack this size takes only 20 minutes to roast. Reheating it in any manner simply overcooks it. The solution is to call ahead. Tell them what time you will be there, and they will have the rack hot off the grill upon your arrival. As for other dishes, the meatloaf, which comes with a rather fascinating chutney made with tomatoes, raisins, onions, and curry spices, is good cold but could probably take a reheat. The chicken breast would be destroyed reheated, but it, too, is edible cold. A very nice spinach-feta-stuffed ravioli dish is garnished with fresh red peppers, scallions, and feta. Cold, the pasta is doughy. Reheating it requires that the garnish be removed, defeating the purpose of ordering out.

There is a way to make Bouchee work well for lunch or even an early dinner, but it requires some serious planning. Order the rack of lamb as described above and ask them to microwave some fingerling potatoes and grilled vegetables when you arrive. Alternately, have the orzo salad (this is excellent cold) or ask them to warm up one of the Gorgonzola-stuffed twice-baked potatoes. One of the larger racks will easily serve two, reducing the total cost for two to about $18 total.

Bouchee does not charge extra for drinking a bottle of their wine with your food as is the practice at Jennifer's Kitchen. There is a very nice Napa Cabernet—Cartlidge and Browne—available for under $10. This is one way to go.

Another option is to use Bouchee more as it was intended, by ordering soup and/or a sandwich. How about a chicken, artichoke, and Gruyère cheese panini? Alternatively, you could try a panini of roast beef, roasted onion, and Gorgonzola. Order a side from the deli case. The kidney bean salad and orzo salad are excellent cold pairings with the hot sandwiches. Wine (both a red and a white selection of the day) is available by the glass.

You may have to ask, but there is an *amuse-bouche* (amusement for the mouth) here that is terrific: Peppadew peppers stuffed with goat cheese. The Peppadew is a new discovery from South Africa; it is a wonderful little thing about the size of a Ping-Pong ball. Hot, spicy, and sweet, it lends just the right degree of zing to everything it touches.

Bouchee is also a gourmet shop with specialty salts, including fleur de sel ($13 for 4.4 ounces), various mustards, jams, and oils. Beautiful dishes and the usual trendy coffee bar round out the establishment.

Camelot Café
Camelot Cinebar

★
$

Location: Camelot Theatres, 2300 E. Baristo Rd., Palm Springs, 325-6588. Food type: California trendy and/or healthful-appearing snack bar. Ambiance: theater lobby and sidewalk café. Bar: beer and wine; Cinebar Lounge upstairs has a full bar. Reservations: not accepted. Hours: Cinebar lounge happy hour is 3 P.M. until 6 P.M. Wednesday through Sunday. Note: Admission to the theater is not required to eat at the café.

Unfortunately, the Camelot Café is a better idea than it is a reality. Movie theaters have relied for decades on snack foods for a large portion of their income. At Camelot Café, you can eat real food and have a glass of wine at the same time. I do not know if you can take your Thai curry chicken wrap and white wine into the theater, but nobody seems to want to anyway. It is just not that kind of a place.

The Camelot Theatres is what was once known, somewhat derisively, as an art theater. This became an absurd anachronism when someone in Hollywood actually figured out that *All About Eve* and *Apocalypse Now* were more art than a typical French bedroom farce. Yes, the Camelot Theatres plays foreign movies, film-festival prize winners, low-budget flicks, and films that have no stars and sad endings. It also draws patrons who might actually be attracted to the tempura sole burrito or turkey Brie on a focaccia onion roll. The tempura sole is panko crusted and wrapped in a flour tortilla with napa cabbage, wasabi mayo, roasted peppers, and avocado. Ironically, prices are about the same as you would pay elsewhere for a large popcorn and Pepsi—about $7.

The chili with onions and cheddar is adequate. The pizzas are acceptable. The grilled portobello ciabatta is pretentious nonsense, rather like a steak sandwich with a grilled portobello mushroom standing in for the steak. With mozzarella, grilled onions, tomato, and a pesto vinaigrette, it tastes just about as it sounds. As you might expect, you can get chai tea, smoothies, a Mocha Glacier, and a caramel macchiato with any of your entrées. Not being a fan of fancy coffee drinks, I had to look up "caramel macchiato." It is espresso, milk, vanilla syrup, and caramel sauce. I do not know what a Mocha Glacier is—iced coffee, I guess—but I figure anybody who wants one knows what it is.

The Cinebar Lounge upstairs has an excellent happy hour with various appetizers from the café for $3 or $4, beer for $3, well drinks for $4, and martinis for $5. Appetizers include individual pizzas and crab cakes for $4.

Casey's
★
$$

Location: 42-455 Washington St., Palm Desert, 345-6503. Food type: American favorites. Ambiance: anachronistic American neighborhood cocktail lounge. Bar: full. Reservations: suggested. Hours: bar opens at 10 A.M.; lunch and dinner daily.

Casey's is not so much a restaurant with an active lounge scene as it is a cocktail lounge that serves food. This should not be a destination for those looking for good food if food is the only motivation. Casey's is fundamentally a neighborhood bar with entertainment such as karaoke and a sing-along piano bar. People do dance, but only when they've had a few too many. A big-screen TV presents major sporting events. Casey's is very much the anachronism, eliciting recollections of 1977. It is off the tourist path and neither looks nor feels like anything else in town, with the possible exception of Cactus Jack's (see Chapter 8). It is dark, with the lounge on one side of the bar and the dining room on the other. From late afternoon until closing, the lounge is packed with locals.

The food is basic American with a few borrowed items and a smattering of comfort food. Prices are low to moderate. Chicken-fried steak or pot roast can be had for around $13. Steaks, prime rib, surf and turf, and halibut are in the $20-$30 range.

Tomato blue cheese soup can only be described as weird. It is neither good nor bad, but strange, the result of a generally mild blue cheese pureed with generic tomato soup. The tomato flavor is preserved, but the cheese is absorbed into this thick goop.

The prime rib sandwich fares even worse. The meat only comes well done, but that is only a part of the problem. It is served open face on a generic piece of white bread with a completely flavorless au jus of water, beef bouillon, and grease. A dill pickle, slice of raw carrot, wilted French fries, and catsup complete the presentation. Upon request, however, 100 percent fresh grated horseradish can be had. It has been a long time since

I have experienced a horseradish with the ability to rip into my sinuses with this much vehemence.

Undoubtedly there are many items on this substantial menu that fare considerably better than these two, but any kitchen that delivers these has to be viewed with not a little skepticism.

Hair of the Dog English Pub
Not rated
Location: 238 N. Palm Canyon Dr., Palm Springs, 323-9890. **Food type:** *none.* **Ambiance:** *London's Carnaby Street.* **Bar:** *full.* **Hours:** *8 A.M. to 2 A.M. daily.*

This is not an English pub at all but a saloon with English memorabilia on the walls and excellent rock 'n' roll on the jukebox. There is no food, but patrons are invited to bring their own. Decent NYPD Pizza is just down the street. Regulars love to hang out the "pub." They love the jukebox and wish there were a dance floor. They also speak highly of the cold beer and happy-hour prices.

Jennifer's Kitchen
★★½
$-$$
Location: 70-225 Highway 111, Rancho Mirage, 324-3904. **Food type:** *California Fusion deli.* **Ambiance:** *primarily a store; postmodern décor.* **Bar:** *interesting selection of beer and wine.* **Reservations:** *not accepted.* **Hours:** *10 A.M. to 7 P.M. Monday through Saturday.* **Chef-owner:** *Jennifer Johnson.*

Once upon a time there was Tastebud Tango. No, allow me to begin again. Once upon a time there was Omri & Boni. They set up shop in a wonderful little bistro in Palm Desert. Omri & Boni got rich and built a $4 million palace in La Quinta, which was later sold and renamed Amore (Chapter 4). Jennifer Johnson and a partner bought the bistro, named it Tastebud Tango, and began serving California-Southwest fusion. Then Tastebud Tango vanished, and Indian restaurant Monsoon emerged in its stead. Monsoon morphed into Delhi Palace (see Chapter 11). Foodies valleywide held a wake as Johnson resumed her catering career.

But wait! Jennifer Johnson is back. She has opened a gourmet shop. It is quite large for a little store. With granite counters, tile floors, wooden tables, and an open ceiling, the interior ambiance is a comfortable postmodern set piece. A wine/coffee/dessert bar is to your left as you enter. To your immediate right, but partitioned off, is the dining area. All along the back wall and filling most of the interior space are all manner of gourmet goodies and libations from Dr. Bob's specialty ice creams to Johnson's own frozen dinner entrées. Whether it is boeuf bourguignon or enchiladas, Johnson makes something for everyone's taste. Have lunch in her "kitchen" and buy your dinner to take home. Pick up a nice bottle of wine to have with that entrée while you are at it. Johnson does not mark up her wine. Wine and beer selections are idiosyncratic, even quirky. A dry and fruity Spanish white for under $7 sits next to a Stag's Leap Cab for $50. This store reflects Johnson's taste, not that of some marketing boffin.

The left side of the building is the deli where Johnson's talents are on display day in and day out. Everything in the deli case is prepared that morning. Johnson moves in whatever direction the muse takes her. Customers can't be sure of the availability of their favorites from one day to the next, but you should regard this as an opportunity to experiment with new and different creations. Failure is rare in Jennifer's Kitchen.

Chicken breast stuffed with ricotta and pesto manages one of the great culinary rarities of our time, a moist chicken breast. The oil in the pesto and the milk of the ricotta serve as lubricants for the naturally dry meat. A salad of huge cannellini beans dressed in an Italian style provides an excellent side dish for one of Johnson's hot sandwiches. She does a paella with chicken and Italian-style turkey sausage. Other times she opts for the Cuban version and puts in all manner of shellfish. Saffron flavor is weak, and I found it a little disconcerting to have it cold, but nothing prevented me from buying a pound of it, taking it home, and warming it up. The pasta primavera is superb. She uses orecchiette pasta—so named because they resemble ears—with peas, black olives, red onions, and parsley in a terrific thin mayonnaise made with white balsamic vinegar, egg yolks, and olive oil.

Then there is the couscous, something I generally find irritatingly bland. Johnson's is not bland. She does it with the typical north African sweet-savory use of fruit, in this case currants and dried apricots. Kalamata olives prevent it from becoming too sweet. A beautiful squash salad made from zucchini, Italian yellow squash, and onion can substitute for the cannellini bean salad for a little more pungency. Johnson uses flank steak for her beef Thai salad because of its pronounced flavor. The downside of flank steak is that it is naturally tough. The distinctive Thai flavors of ginger, lime, chili paste, and Thai basil suffuse the salad throughout.

Hot sandwiches are the most popular: Black Forest ham, Swiss, and Brie with grilled apples, onions, and aïoli on country French bread that is based on a sourdough starter called levain and an albacore melt with sharp cheddar, tomatoes, balsamic vinegar, and onions on sourdough.

Try Jennifer's Kitchen for a interesting lunch alternative for under $10. Pick any wine in the store, pay an additional $8 corkage fee, and turn lunch into a gourmet feast.

Native Foods

½

$

Locations: 73-890 El Paseo Dr., Palm Desert, 836-9396; 1775 E. Palm Canyon Dr., #F, Palm Springs, 416-0070. Food type: international vegan. Ambiance: spiffy little shop with counter service. Bar: beer and wine. Reservations: not accepted. Hours: Monday through Saturday 11 A.M. to 9 P.M. Chef-owner: Tanya Petrovna.

Aside from the conceit by implication, that milk, eggs, and hamburger are somehow not "native," Native Foods fulfills a popular dining niche in the Coachella Valley. Lunch here is popular, as retail employees flood the place for their huge and interesting salads. But every restaurant does a number of salads, many of which are vegan by definition. "Vegan" means absolutely no meat, fish, eggs, or dairy products (yeast spores excepted). It is in their "meat" menu that the defining elements of Native Foods' type of cuisine emerge. The Bali surf burger contains tempeh, lettuce, and tomato but no meat. The BBQ Love burger is made with seitan and the MadCowboy's Delight with soy chicken, chipotle barbecue sauce, corn, and avocado.

Seitan is primarily wheat gluten with the following added: yeast flakes, vegetable broth, soy sauce, tomato paste, garlic, and lemon zest. Tempeh is a cultured (think cheese) cake of beans or grain. The bean cake is injected with the bacteria *rhizopus oligosporus* and fermented. A thick white mat of mycelia (the vegetative part of a fungus) develops on the cake. It is then steamed and is ready to use as fake meat.

Thai sticks claim to be satay made with tempeh. Traditional satay is strips of pork or chicken in a spicy marinade of brown sugar, curry powder, peanut butter, soy sauce, lime juice, garlic, and chili peppers. They are served with peanut sauce punched up with molasses, chicken stock, heavy cream, garlic, cilantro, and cayenne pepper. Traditional satay is a brutally hot and spicy strip of grilled pork. The Native version is a strip of tempeh both sautéed and grilled (?) and served with their own peanut butter sauce. There is no flavor here at all. Tempeh tastes like a piece of hard, undefined porridge, like oatmeal or cream of wheat. There is no marinade, spicy or otherwise, and the peanut sauce tastes only of a thinned peanut butter.

A jerk burger made with seitan "steak" does not fare much better. The best way to describe the taste of seitan is to think of meatloaf made with unseasoned, finely ground chicken and veal. To this mixture is added at least 50 percent grits. Again, the porridge similarity arises, but here there is some semblance of a generic meat. The reference to Jamaican jerk marinade found on the menu is disingenuous. You would think that vegan cooking would attempt to compensate for the inherent blandness of fake meat by ratcheting up the spices. This is the reason I ordered the Jamaican jerk burger, but it didn't happen. I didn't expect anything like the actual Jamaican pork recipe where the meat is "jerked," that is, punched full of holes and stuffed with potent herbs and spices (the defining ingredient of which is the habañero chili) and buried in the ground to cook over hot rocks. Nevertheless, I did expect something resembling a jerk sauce or marinade. What I got was a thick slab of steamed seitan, lettuce, shredded carrot, red onion, and vegan mayo on a bun. Jerk marinades are spicy and brutally hot. What is the point of advertising something as jerk and delivering a product bearing no resemblance to jerk at all?

The soy taco meat is kicked up with the traditional Mexican condiments *salsa fresca* and guacamole on corn tortillas. With cumin, coriander, garlic, onion, and chili powder, this taco meat at least covered up the fact that it is tofu. The "meat" here has some resistance in the mouth, like shredded pork.

The Native iced tea is a hibiscus tea lightly sweetened with apple juice. It is remarkably refreshing, but then you would expect that of ice water flavored with apple juice.

Native Foods is the brainchild of author, chef, and entrepreneur Tanya Petrovna. I do not know what the limits are for a cuisine founded upon faking meat and/or dairy products. Petrovna has a good reputation in her field, and perhaps this is as good as it gets, at least compared to whatever else is out there. I looked through her cookbook and was frequently appalled. Her recipe for hollandaise sauce is a particularly egregious example. The nature of hollandaise is founded on the protein-rich emulsification properties of the egg yolk and its ability to absorb enormous quantities of butter without breaking down. Can something like hollandaise possibly be made without either eggs or butter? Petrovna's hollandaise is soy milk thickened with corn starch, which makes it more akin to a simple béchamel than hollandaise. She then calls for a flavoring of tarragon and shallot. These are the flavorings of béarnaise, not hollandaise. I don't get it.

PALM SPRINGS AERIAL TRAMWAY
1 Tramway Rd.
Palm Springs

There are two restaurants at the top of the Tram: Peaks and Pines. Peaks is a legitimate fine-dining establish. A review of this restaurant can be found in Chapter 7 as well as a description of the Tramway itself. Fees for the tram ride are rather expensive, but discount coupons, group rates, senior discounts, and season passes are available. Adults are $22.95; children, $15.95. Ride and dine options are also available. Cars depart at least every half-hour with the first car up Monday through Friday at 10 A.M.; the first car goes up weekends and holidays at 8 A.M. Last car up is 8 P.M. and the last car down 9:45 P.M.

Pines
★
$
Location: top of the tram, Mount San Jacinto, Palm Springs, 325-4537. Food type: American buffet/cafeteria and snacks. Ambiance: barn with spectacular views. Bar: none, but there is a bar just around the corner. Reservations: not accepted. Hours: daily 10 A.M. to 9:30 P.M. during summer; daily 10 A.M. to 8:30 P.M. during winter.

Do not confuse Pines with Peaks (see Chapter 7). Peaks is a fine-dining restaurant; Pines is a cafeteria. For the last several years, Pines was known as Top of the Tram, and it had the reputation of being one of the worst dining experiences possible in the Coachella Valley. Word of mouth was, "Avoid it at all costs." Its gourmet sister restaurant was known as Elevations. Several years ago, Elevations was a fine restaurant but it deteriorated in quality and has since been sold and renamed Peaks. Though both restaurants are at the top of the tram, once you get up there you will notice that they are two separate entities. The cafeteria survives because it is a tourist trap. Once a family of tourists is up the mountain, they are trapped. The only way down, unless this particular tourist family is capable of, and prepared for, a brutal eight-hour hike, is back the way they came. Valley residents usually bring a sack lunch. A tuna sandwich and banana taste pretty good following a two-hour romp through the snow at 9,000 feet.

Under new ownership, Pines has improved dramatically. The best deal is the Ride-n-Dine ticket. For $35.50, an adult gets a tram ticket ($22.95) and dinner ($12.55). A child's Ride-n-Dine is $23. If the same lunch or dinner is purchased separate from the tram ticket, it is $5 more. Dinner includes salad, entrée, veggie, potato or rice, and roll. Entrées change biweekly but generally include prime rib, a couple of pasta dishes, barbecue chicken, and a fish. Salads might include a Palms salad (green beans, tomato, cucumber, iceberg, and blue cheese vinaigrette) or Caesar. I kid you not, they advertise shaved Parmigiano-Reggiano. I find this hard to believe considering that the Caesar salad costs $6.75, but management claims it is true. I have not independently verified this claim. Freshly made sandwiches, pizzas, and salads are served all day.

PALM SPRINGS AIR MUSEUM
745 N. Gene Autry Trail
Palm Springs

The museum consists of two large hangars devoted primarily to the military planes of World War II. Cravens Hangar, on the north side features planes of the European theater, and Pond Hangar on the south, planes of the Pacific theater. Outside on the grounds in front of the museum are several jet fighters of the Vietnam era.

The most spectacular exhibit is a B-17G heavy bomber. Also known as the Flying Fortress, this early monster was the state-of-the-art killing machine of the European theater. Many Hollywood notables, including James Stewart (pilot), Robert Altman (co-pilot), and Walter Matthau (gunner), were with the B-17. Docents abound to answer questions and conduct tours, and you can climb through this huge plane and explore the conditions (cramped and undoubtedly freezing cold) and technology of the 1940s. One generation later the extreme and radical change in technology is in evidence by such planes as the F-14 Tomcat jet fighter outside on the grounds.

Entrance fees are $12 for adults, $10 for seniors, military, and teens, and $5 for children. There is a little café called Freedom Fighters. To dine at the café it is not necessary to purchase a ticket to the museum, but I can't imagine why anyone not visiting the museum would want to do so.

Freedom Fighters' Café
Not recommended
$
Location: inside the Palm Springs Air Museum, 745 N. Gene Autry Trail, Palm Springs, 778-6262. **Food type:** *American with Americanized Italian and Mexican "sandwiches."* **Ambiance:** *roped-off section of airplane hangar.* **Bar:** *no.* **Reservations:** *not accepted.* **Hours:** *10 A.M. to 4 P.M. Monday through Saturday; 11 A.M. until 4 P.M. Sundays.*

This glorified snack bar is enclosed in a fenced-off area of Cravens Hangar. The overhead glare of the florescent lighting makes for an unpleasant dining experience. The menu and prices here are identical to that of the Palm Springs Art Museum (this chapter), but several factors work to weaken the experience at this venue. Here there are daily specials of burgers and dogs. I had the misfortune of ordering the pepperoni pizza.

A pizza with a diameter of four inches arrives with a small package of Lays potato chips and a soda of my choice. The bill is $5. The pizza is doughy. I don't know how one can manage to produce a crust like this on a pizza—certainly not in a pizza oven, or really, any oven. I make pizza at home and bake it on a clay tile heated to 500 degrees in an oven. I can only guess that this one comes frozen, is thawed in a microwave, and placed in a toaster oven to melt the cheese. The doughy/cakey texture of the crust is unpleasant to say the least. The pepperoni is of a cheap American salty/chemical variety.

The menu proper consists primarily of several sandwiches with pedantic names, all in the $9 range, including a Capresse Panini (mozzarella cheese, basil leaves, tomato, and pesto spread on a baguette), a Tuscan (turkey, Swiss cheese, pesto on a baguette), and a pita pocket (chicken, lettuce, tomato, roasted pepper, and hummus). Three quesadillas (chicken, salmon, cheese) round out the more interesting side of the menu. There are also a few salads and a soup of the day. The pita pocket or Tuscan Panini can not help but be better than the pizza, but the fact that they would even serve something this poor does not speak well for the general quality.

PALM SPRINGS MUSEUM OF ART
101 Museum Dr.
Palm Springs

The experience begins on the street. The building is stunning, designed by architect E. Stuart Williams in 1976. This style is known locally as Palm Springs Modern, but it is best understood as High Modern, embracing truth to materials and unity with the environment. Stone, textured concrete, glass, and wood dominate. Williams himself said this about his achievement: "The rocks on the mountain have a beautiful patina they acquired over the millennia. Inside, the galleries are incredibly friendly to people." Palm Springs was evolving from a retreat into a full-fledged city in 1976 and building codes prohibited structures more than 35 feet in height. Williams' creative solution was to place the museum's outdoor sculpture gardens and theater below grade. Twenty years later, Williams came out of retirement to draw plans for a third-story addition to the museum. He was 86. It is absolutely seamless.

For a medium-sized art museum in a small city, this museum is quite astonishing not just for its building but also for the quality of both its permanent collection and its special exhibits.

A small auditorium (400 seats) is beautifully laid out even as it is somewhat lacking in the acoustics department. A concert series is presented every season.

The café is cleverly named Muse Café and is adjacent to the auditorium on one side and sculpture gardens on the other.

Muse Café

Location: inside the Palm Springs Museum of Art, 101 Museum Dr., Palm Springs, 322-4800. Food type: American and Americanized Italian and Mexican

"sandwiches." **Ambiance:** *charming, informal space architecturally consistent with rest of the building, large photographs of Palm Springs' celebrities from the 1950s and '60s adorn the walls.* **Bar:** *beer and wine.* **Reservations:** *not accepted.* **Hours:** *Tuesday, Wednesday, and Friday through Sunday 10 A.M. to 5 P.M. Thursdays 12 P.M. to 8 P.M. Closed Mondays.*

The menu and prices at Muse Café are identical to those of the Freedom Fighters' Café at the Palm Springs Air Museum (this chapter), but this one manages to do a little better. Part of this is a significantly improved environment. Another part is the presence of beer and wine, and Muse Café does not appear to have fast-food-style snacks like burgers and dogs (and frozen pizza!).

I sample the soup of the day, lentil, and it is surprisingly good. It is certainly not a great lentil soup like that which was to be found at the late/lamented Café Paris of Hedi Hamrouni, redolent of harissa (North African hot chili paste) and complex vegetation. But it is certainly better than the pureed baby food of Kabobz (Chapter 17) or the bland concoction of Lord Fletcher's (Chapter 4). The lentils are cooked until they are tender but not falling apart. The mixture is not pureed and vestiges of a *mirepoix* (carrots, onion, and celery) are still evident. Flavor is full, even if lacking the sparkle of harissa. Still, for a café of this type . . .

Reilly's Irish Pub & Restaurant
Not recommended
$
Location: *36-200 Date Palm Dr., Cathedral City, 324-9600.* **Food type:** *American.* **Ambiance:** *coffee shop.* **Bar:** *full; heavy on the Irish beer.* **Reservations:** *accepted but not necessary.* **Hours:** *10 A.M. to 11 P.M. Monday through Thursday, 10 A.M. through 1 A.M. Friday and Saturday, closed Sunday.*

A check on the Internet will reveal the presence of two Reilly's Irish Pubs, both with addresses on Date Palm. This information is out of date. The new Reilly's is *not* on Date Palm, despite what its address claims. If you look for it at this address you will not find it. The number 36-200 is the address of the Date Palm Country Club. To find the pub you must turn into the country club and follow the signs to the 19th hole, which means you must turn left at the first opportunity and meander around the entire golf course. You will eventually come to the clubhouse, but, trust me, you will wish you hadn't.

Reportedly, Friday and Saturday evenings there is live music and dancing. There is lots of Irish-style drinking, and people supposedly have a good time. I cannot speak to that. I can, however, address the food. It is dreadful. Airline food is a gourmet feast by comparison; even the school cafeteria fares well; hospital food may be in the same ballpark but my vote goes to the medical profession.

This is a coffee shop, not an Irish pub. There is no Irish food on the menu. The closest thing is corned beef and cabbage, which is New York Irish American. Everything else on the menu is straightforward American coffee shop fare. There is one anomaly, Shepherd's pie. Shepherd's pie is English, but let us overlook that for the moment. I made the mistake of ordering the only thing on the menu that is not served in every American coffee shop from Bar Harbor to Chula Vista. Shepherd's pie is savory pie made with ground lamb with mashed potatoes servings as the "crust." Even a bad traditional English Shepherd's pie contains carrots, mushrooms, garlic, and onions. Grated cheddar cheese on top of the potatoes gives the final presentation a nice color. What I got at Reilly's Irish Pub is something else entirely. The meat is a mystery. It is probably very old hamburger: dried out, gray, stringy, and with a rancid flavor. Could it have been lamb? Yes, it could have been anything, even let's-tour-the-Soviet Union mystery meat. Powdered potatoes in great quantity appear above and below the mystery meat along with canned corn. I give it two bites. One to taste it; and the second to make sure it is really true. The accompanying salad is, you guessed it, chopped iceberg with French, Thousand Island, or blue cheese.

They don't even have Guinness on tap! Eat here at your own risk.

Village Pub

$-$$

Location: 266 S. Palm Canyon Dr., Palm Springs, 323-3265. **Food type:** *multiethnic fast food.* **Ambiance:** *big, sprawling, two-story, multiple bar hangout; live and canned rock 'n' roll.* **Bars:** *three of them; good happy hour.* **Reservations:** *not accepted.*

There is no cover charge and food is served until 2 A.M., but by and large no one really goes to the Village Pub to dine. There is a huge menu, but it is mostly fast food of one type or another. Its raison d'être, however, is the environment: a huge patio, three bars, a dance floor, and indoor dining on the main level. The second floor is devoted to games and televisions. Drinks are cheap by valley standards.

Burgers, pizza, nachos, stir-fries, wings, tacos, chips and salsa, salads, and pastas define the bulk of the dining options. Chicken pot pie and fish and chips are the extent of its pub grub. It is inexpensive, and if this kind of environment appeals to you, it is worth a visit.

CHAPTER 15

Breakfast

I like breakfast. I mean, a real American breakfast, what the tour companies call "American plan" as opposed to "European plan," which is a piece of bread and a cup of coffee. The interesting thing about coffee shops, roadside diners, resort restaurants, and other purveyors of such staples as biscuits and gravy, center-cut ham steak, and poached eggs is how similar they are in terms of both menu and price.

Nevertheless, let us begin with what to avoid. First and foremost, use your olfactory sense. If the restaurant does not smell fresh and clean, go elsewhere. Second, avoid too-good-to-be-true prices. No one can serve you decent pigs in blankets for $0.99 unless subsidized by a casino, and even then it probably is not any good. A roadside diner may well sell a plate of ham and eggs for $5.99. It is surprising but absolutely true that most upscale restaurants in such places as Miracle Springs Spa and Resort sell the identical item for about the same price. Actually, in this example, a dollar cheaper! The roadside diner has to survive on its own. It has no captive audience, nor does it have a hotel, casino, or bar to subsidize it.

Bit o' Country
★½
$
Location: 418 S. Indian Canyon Dr., Palm Springs, 325-5154. Food type: American coffee shop. Ambiance: sidewalk café; view is primarily of traffic. Bar: none. Reservations: not accepted. Hours: breakfast and lunch daily.

Bit o' Country is a quintessential country diner. Outdoor seating is provided just off Indian Avenue on high-tech-looking aluminum chairs. It serves up big, hearty American breakfasts in the traditional mode. Everything is fresh and well prepared, and prices are marginally reasonable if not downright cheap. If you want dill and thyme in your biscuits and gravy, try Rock Garden or Michael's (both reviewed later in this chapter). Here biscuits are plain baking powder—flavorful and fluffy—and the gravy is a plain cream sauce. You can also opt for grits rather than hash browns, but forget about Yukon Golds sautéed with paprika. However, Bit o' Country's hash browns are crisp and with nary a hint of the latent greasiness characteristic of lesser establishments. Fresh salsa is a processed concoction of tomatoes, onions, bell peppers, and jalapeños. Oddly, there is no cilantro, but this one packs quite a bit of burn. Taste it before slathering your ham steak with it.

Bit o' Country also lives up to its moniker in the proportions category. Check out the house omelet: three eggs, sautéed mushrooms, onions, peppers, tomatoes, olives, chili peppers, sausage, bacon, ham and cheese topped with Spanish sauce, sour cream and avocado for $5.95. But wait! For $6.95 you can have it with five eggs! Bring the family.

The one odd note is the Greek omelet made with onion, peppers, feta cheese, and Spanish sauce. I don't know about you, but I find feta cheese in a breakfast omelet most unpleasant.

Grove Artisan Kitchen
(See Chapter 1 for a full review of Grove Artisan Kitchen's lunch and dinner menu.)

★★

$$

Location: Miramonte Resort, 45-500 Highway 111, Indian Wells, 341-2200. Food type: gourmet breakfast. Ambiance: rather ordinary interior; beautiful patio with views of lush grounds and mountains. Bar: champagne, Bloody Marys, and excellent coffee. Reservations: not necessary. Hours: breakfast, lunch, and dinner daily. Chef: Robert Nyerick.

It is a pity that Grove Artisan Kitchen's breakfast is not as good as its lunch and dinner. Chef Robert Nyerick is in charge of the kitchen for all meals, but there are some strange irrationalities here that are not present later in the day.

The only genuine failure is the lobster omelet. This appears to be the most interesting thing on the breakfast menu, as well as the most expensive at $17. The problems are threefold. First, the recipe is so cluttered that none of the ingredients, especially the signature lobster, are allowed to speak. Chunks of lobster, woodland mushrooms, asparagus, and tarragon all conspire effectively to block any flavor. Tarragon—far too much tarragon, with its sweet, lingering licorice aftertaste—is the only lasting impression. Second, where is the egg? An omelet must fundamentally be about the egg not the fillings. Here the egg functions more like pita bread or a tortilla wrap. The egg is seriously overcooked without any of the creamy, light lusciousness you associate with a truly fine omelet. Third, the asparagus isn't even peeled properly. It is stringy. Fortunately, everything is uphill from there. Breakfast potatoes—rounds of hash browns in a ramekin—or roasted fingerlings are quite delicious, crispy, and flavorful. Homemade corned beef hash, thick-cut peppered bacon, sage sausage, and the six-ounce Choice New York steak form the basis of a fine breakfast. Hollandaise is thick and flavorful. But eggs remain a problem.

Eggs Benedict is made with prosciutto di Parma and topped with a roasted red pepper hollandaise, an interesting variant. The prosciutto is not. It is also too salty, but nothing else is salted so overall the salt level is acceptable. As with the omelet eggs, poached eggs also fail. The absolute magic of eggs Benedict is the spilling of the yolks. These eggs should be jumbos, and overpoaching ruins the effect. The eggs are too small, and the yolks (requested soft) are delivered almost hard.

The menu is interesting. It shows genuine care and creativity, but some serious work on the skillful preparation of the egg is needed.

Chalkboard Café Grill
★
$

Location: in the Desert Courtyards shopping center, 46-900 Monroe St., Suite 302, Indio, 347-8100. Food type: coffee shop. Ambiance: new building in new shopping center. Bar: none. Reservations: not accepted. Hours: breakfast and lunch Monday through Saturday.

This café bills itself as "self-serve gourmet." It is definitely self-serve, but the gourmet is less clear. There is certainly an effort here to produce a product of higher quality than the norm. At lunch, for example, there is an onion soup, but the cheese is Parmesan not Gruyère. There is a salmon fillet with dilled mayonnaise, but the mayonnaise is out of a jar with the dill added at the restaurant. A grilled club sandwich is made with chicken breast, bacon, jalapeño Jack, and cheddar cheese on grilled

Parmesan-dusted sourdough bread with lettuce, tomato, and mayo. This is a substantive effort, but is it worth $9?

Tabbouleh, chili, fries (house-made with the skin on), burgers, quesadillas, salads—you have seen it all a million times before. Everything is served on paper and plastic and there are no service personnel, which means you have no gratuity to pay. But it also means you bus your own table and pick up your own food. Want more water? A refill on that coffee? Get it yourself.

Omelets are well made with sensitivity to exactly how an egg cooks. They are fluffy and moist in the center. They are all the same price, $6.95, regardless of the fillings. Chili has an excellent flavor with just the right degree of spicy heat, but the grind is much too fine for a traditional chili. This is ground finer than hamburger, whereas chili grind should be coarser than hamburger. Breakfast burritos, pancakes, cinnamon French toast, and the usual bacon-and-eggs combos round out the breakfast menu. Hash browns are chopped up French fries browned with red onion and peppers. They taste all right but are overseasoned. Toast is a cheap, grilled English muffin.

Considering that you are eating on and with plastic and serving yourself, prices are probably a little too high. The whole thing is an odd marriage, but if you find yourself in need of a quick lunch and considering the dining limitations of the location, the grilled club with the onion soup (included) is probably worth both your time and money.

Chuckwalla

½

$

Location: Miracle Springs Resort and Spa, 10-625 Palm Dr., Desert Hot Springs, 251-6000. Food type: American coffee shop. Ambiance: pool area with magnificent views. Bar: full. Reservations: not necessary. Hours: breakfast, lunch, and dinner daily. Recommended only for breakfast and only as a matter of convenience.

There is a minimal dining scene in Desert Hot Springs. Aside from the Casino room at Two Bunch Palms Resort (see Chapter 1), there is no fine dining. The Capri (see Chapter 8) fills the mid-range slot. Chuckwalla is the restaurant at Miracle Springs Resort and Spa. Miracle Springs is at the top of the hill on the west side of Palm Drive. If you are staying in Desert Hot Springs, Chuckwalla will suffice for breakfast. The interior of Chuckwalla is modern, elegant, and clean, in keeping with the overall tone of the resort. The patio, on the other hand, while pleasant enough, seems a bit of an afterthought.

The Bloody Mary is a major disappointment: spicy enough but watery and without any citrus tang. This one is garnished with not only celery and lime, but also two olives and a pickled onion. What is that about? Those are garnishes for a martini and a Gibson, respectively. At the Rock Garden (reviewed later in this chapter), a thermal pitcher for coffee is provided at the table. Here the waitress is always refilling a small cup, which cools off rapidly on the patio. The hash browns are finely grated and fry up nicely with a good crunch. They are well seasoned, fully cooked, and exhibit no greasiness. Poached eggs are also done properly, a rarity in most coffee shops. The ham is cut from a formed loaf! I cannot imagine why. Prefab ham is not less expensive than the real thing. Is it convenience? Biscuits and gravy fail on all counts. The biscuit is fine, but this gravy is a huge mound of cream sauce thickened to library paste and packed with a spicy sausage. This is down-home, truck-stop country gravy, the kind that holds your fork at attention without any encouragement. A half order is large enough to sate the appetite of the entire Russian army (O.K., just the officers).

Coffee Break Café
★½
$

Location: 78-900 Avenue 47, Suite 100, La Quinta, 564-0226. Food type: American coffee shop with a healthful twist. Ambiance: new, trendy, and comfortable. Bar: a few inexpensive but decent wines. Reservations: not accepted. Hours: breakfast and lunch Monday through Friday.

This is a coffee shop in an out-of-the-way and unexpected spot in what appears, at first glance, to be a residential neighborhood. Sporting the now nearly ubiquitous black ceiling with exposed duct work and pale yellow walls, a relaxing and comfortable mid-morning (or mid-afternoon) getaway has taken root in this odd little location. The food is both surprisingly good and surprisingly inexpensive. There is a health-food bent with nothing on the menu that is fried. "Steaming" is the word of the day. I wonder about steamed scrambled eggs, but the poached eggs cannot be faulted except that the edges have been trimmed off, reducing the quantity of egg whites. Potatoes are not served with breakfast orders unless requested. Hash browns are not served at all. The potatoes that do come are sliced and baked russets with olive oil, herbs, and onions. They are a nice change from the usual hash browns or home fries.

Homemade *salsa fresca* packs a nice little chili pepper punch, but it hits late. Wait for it before piling it on your ham. It has the usual ingredient—tomatoes, onions, cilantro, and chilies—but is processed almost into a purée. I prefer my salsas on the chunkier side, but this is a perfectly valid way of making them.

The owner is a pastry chef. Her repertoire is not huge, but her creations are the main attraction, especially the fruit-filled scones. She makes them with a variety of flavors, including blackberry, raspberry, boysenberry, cranberry orange, blueberry, apple cinnamon, and chocolate chip. They are big and light and have the texture much like that of a baking powder biscuit. Muffins and cinnamon rolls round out her limited offerings.

A portion of the room is allotted for a lounge with a leather couch, chairs, and coffee table. Order a bottle of wine. Believe it or not, drinkable bottles of Chardonnay, Merlot, and Cab are available for $12. Lattes, café mocha, espresso, and fancy fruit drinks are also part of the menu.

Lunches consist of salads and sandwiches with an emphasis on whole-wheat bread and fresh fruits and vegetables.

El Campanario
★★★
$

See full review under "Mexican" in Chapter 12.

French Corner Café and Pastry
★
$-$$
Location: in the Desert Crossing Shopping Center, 72-423 Highway 111, Palm Desert, 568-5362. Ambiance: somewhat austere for a "French" restaurant. Food type: mostly "Frenchified" American. Bar: beer and wine. Reservations: not necessary. Hours: daily 8 A.M. to 8 P.M.

This place is a major disappointment, especially since the menu is interesting, the pastry counter is gorgeous, and prices are reasonable. The little patio is separated from the parking lot with a ring of tall potted bushes and trees, and the restaurant itself is rather antiseptic with its three walls of glass and innocuous ochre linens beneath sheets of glass. The first jarring note is the complete lack of smells wafting from the kitchen. One should not enter a French restaurant and be denied the glorious aromas associated with French cooking: herbs, garlic, cheeses, braising meats. Here there is nothing, not a whiff of anything at all except clean, fresh desert air. Some nondescript French music is piped in; a few small Lautrec poster copies ornament the walls; some larger generic Euro-landscapes are on the only wall that is not all glass.

The menu lists dishes for breakfast, lunch, and dinner. Food seems to be mostly safe American food translated into French for the menu, but this pattern is interrupted by a handful of genuine French bistro staples like frog legs, escargot, and coquille St. Jacques.

Breakfast features all the usual American things with the edition of *crepe maison*. Based on three samples, this is the only successful breakfast. The crepe is large, light, and "springy" with a crispy surface. It is stuffed with a superb and flavorful thinly sliced ham. A nicely cooked poached egg rests on the top, its yoke spilling lusciously into the crepe. Unfortunately, it is all downhill from here on. Potatoes are little chunks of deep-fried russets. They are well cooked with a crispy surface and no greasiness, but a French fry is a French fry regardless of the shape. Toast appears to be the cheapest bread on the market—mostly air and little flavor. This is odd considering that this restaurant advertises itself as a bakery.

Orange juice is wonderful, either fresh squeezed on premises or something equal to that of Florida's Natural (with pulp, thank you). Coffee is French roast. It comes in demitasse cups requiring six or eight refills for the American appetite. It, too, is excellent.

Scrambled eggs should be flawlessly prepared anywhere, but especially in a French restaurant. These are not really overcooked, but they lack that buttery-creamy fluff one associates with French technique. These are just like those at any chain coffee chop. The same is true for bacon. There is nothing wrong with it, but one expects more at a "French" corner café. Applewood smoked, hickory smoked, maple, pancetta, artisan cured, Canadian—the world is full of interesting bacons.

An omelet stuffed with spinach, Brie, and mushrooms should have been a perfect test of the Frenchness of this café. It is almost tasteless. How does one manage to take three aggressive ingredients such as these and neuter them so effectively?

At an adjacent table an eggs Benedict is served. The hollandaise sauce (billed as hollandaise on the menu) is frozen in place as though made of plastic, such as a hollandaise in the display window of a Chinese restaurant. How is that possible? Hollandaise is made from egg yolks, clarified butter, and lemon juice. All three of these ingredients are a liquid. The thickening power of the proteins in an egg yolk are impressive but not this impressive. Either this is not hollandaise or it has been modified with something else. Its color is also too much to the orange side of yellow. I did not ask to taste the stuff as that would have seemed quite gauche, but melted cheese comes to mind.

The pastry display is gorgeous, featuring a large number of fascinating looking creations. My waiter is bragging that they are all made "in house." "The best in California," he insists. Such ingredients as mango, lime, and chocolate seem to cry out for purchase. I asked my waiter for his choice as the best in the case, the most representative of the skill of the pastry chef, and his personal favorite. He selects a lemon meringue tart. The meringue is most peculiar. It is more like marshmallow than meringue. The lemon custard is fine, but nothing out of the ordinary. One has to wonder what exactly the "best in California" actually means.

I have not sampled lunch or dinner here. This is my experience with the kitchen at breakfast. Whether or not this experience transfers to lunch and dinner, I do not know. That will have to be your call. Prices are quite reasonable for dinner with entrées in the $18 (lobster ravioli) to $26 range (eight-ounce filet).

Louise's Pantry
★½
$

Location: *47-150 Washington St., La Quinta, 771-3330.* **Food type:** *American diner, coffee shop, and soda fountain.* **Ambiance:** *new coffee shop but not sterile; customer friendly.* **Bar:** *none.* **Reservations:** *not accepted.* **Hours:** *breakfast, lunch, and dinner daily.*

In 1943, a young Jewish woman named Louise Lavelle or Levelle, probably some Americanized form of Levine, opened a tiny lunch counter in a long since defunct drug store in Palm Springs. People liked Louise's cooking. She was successful, and in 1945 she opened up shop in a small restaurant right on Palm Canyon Drive. In time, Louise's Pantry became the most successful business in Palm Springs. People lined up down the block. So what was Louise's secret? No one knows. This little shack lasted until 1986, an astonishing feat for any restaurant. Louise sold it, and a second Louise's Pantry opened in Palm Desert. Astronomical price increases in downtown Palm Springs forced the closure of the original, but the Palm Desert version thrived. By and by the new owner died, and the name was bought in 1999. Six years later Louise's Pantry arose in the sands of La Quinta. The name is the same, and there is a certain provenance. But I guess it is like those 1950s rock groups such as the Coasters who continue to perform when all the original members are dead. The menu remains the same, but Louise is no more.

The new Louise's is in a new building. That alone decreases the intended ambiance, but the menu is reminiscent of a 1950s diner in its soda jerk glory.

Primarily a breakfast venue, Louise's offers the usual battery of eggs and pancakes. The signature Original Joe's eggs is probably not the way to go. It is one of those scrambles packed with so many ingredients its identity is all but lost: spinach, mushrooms, onions, and ground beef. Nothing can be recognized for what it is. It also looks unappetizing.

The Spanish omelet fares much better. I've never encountered anyone who makes a true *Spanish,* Spanish omelet, which is made like a frittata containing potatoes and with no sauce. American Spanish omelets are usually onions, green bell peppers, and a mildly spiced tomato sauce. This one is no exception. The eggs themselves are well prepared, with a low heat and an interior that remains soft. The sauce could have considerably more bite, but with the addition of Mediterranean oregano some nice flavors emerge.

Country potatoes are excellent—thinly sliced rounds of russet potatoes fried in just enough hot oil to render the surfaces crunchy and golden, but not so much as to load them down with grease. Homemade jams—strawberry, raspberry, and grape—are terrific. The raspberry and strawberry would make wonderful sauces for an ice-cream sundae. These are thinner than the usual sugar- and pectin-laden commercial products. They are mostly fruit and carry a lot more flavor.

A compilation of sandwich classics—Monte Cristo, Reuben, Philly cheese steak, French dip, BLT, burgers, and dogs—set the standard for lunch. Dinner is comfort food straight from the '50s: meatloaf, fried chicken, Texas chili, fish and chips, pork chops, and liver with onions and bacon. From the fountain come root-beer floats, milk shakes, and various ice cream and sherbet combos. Cakes, cream pies, fruit pies, custards, and Danish are all baked on premises.

Manhattan in the Desert

$$

Location: 2665 E. Palm Canyon Dr., Palm Springs, 322-3354. Food type: Jewish-style New York deli on a large scale. Ambiance: upscale postmodern coffee shop; busy, buzzy, and noisy. Bar: beer and Glen Ellen wine. Reservations: not accepted. Hours: breakfast, lunch, and dinner Monday through Saturday.

They charged me a buck and a quarter for the salsa. Is that New York or what? At first, Manhattan in the Desert is a bit overwhelming. If there is a palace of a coffee shop, this is it. Everything is big, even excessive, from the parking lot to the brownies. We are talking cubes six inches on a side. This goes for the cheesecakes, the pastries, and everything else. Bakery prices range from $2.50 for a simple muffin to $8.95 for one pound of the seven-layer rum cake.

More than a hundred different sandwiches, albeit mostly variations on a theme, are dished up, massively confusing the unwary diner who happens to wander in off the street. You want a glass of wine with that roast beef, pastrami, tongue, turkey, avocado, knockwurst, tomato, onion, sauerkraut, and bean sprout "megawich"? Better make that Glen Ellen because that is all they have. Or go for a beer. Dinner entrées follow the American comfort food catalogue: meatloaf, liver and onions, cabbage rolls, short ribs, chicken in a pot, pot roast.

Manhattan in the Desert is a bakery, deli, and restaurant. It is a Jewish-style New York deli, but it does not promote itself with the misleading kosher label, as does Sherman's (reviewed later in this chapter), with whom it most directly competes.

The building is postmodern from its moderne appropriation on the outside to its use of color and materials on the inside. Gray-green defines the space, with huge hanging light fixtures in yellow and orange, pop art, faux silver tabletops, and faux copper ceiling panels as ornament. Large curved glass displays for the bakery items and deli items to go are in the foyer. Customers echo the New York ambiance. They are loud, buzzy, and busy, even boisterous. The food, unlike everything else, is unsure of itself. An unusual plate of crudites arrives: sauerkraut, strips of cucumber and dill pickle, and half a pickled tomato. In addition, coffee—Douwe Egbert from Sarah Lee—is a strange match. Douwe Egbert's is a Dutch coffee made primarily from arabica beans, but it has a rather sweet and nutty component almost as though it has been doctored. In itself it is fine coffee, but I found it odd with the food. This could well be a personal quirk, however.

A large platter of pastrami and poached eggs with an onion bagel seems simple enough. Poached and boiled eggs are the tests of an accomplished short-order cook. They cannot be done assembly-line style, which makes them a nuisance. Boiled eggs must be timed; poached eggs must be closely monitored for customer preference. A stale egg will not poach or boil properly. Poached eggs break easily; often the white part is brushed away. Poached eggs should be drained in the kitchen, not served in a bowl of water. The whites should be firm and intact; the yolk, soft, large, warm, and sensuous. A properly poached egg is a work of art.

Manhattan's poached eggs are served in a bowl of water. The whites have all but disappeared. A large mound of first-quality pastrami occupies much of the oversized platter. A little time on a hot grill to caramelize the edges would be nice, but this is fine pastrami nevertheless. A toasted onion bagel, tasting remarkably like Van de Kamp's bagels, surprised me. I like Van de Kamp's onion bagels; I buy them all the time. But I expected a larger, baked-on-premises New York-style bagel from this establishment. They bake 16-ounce bear claws but not bagels! Whipped cream cheese is superb, but that is to be expected here.

The potatoes are the first indication that someone somewhere is making odd decisions. Red potatoes are used. They are cut into bite-sized chunks and sautéed until the surfaces are wonderfully crisp. Strips of fresh green bell pepper and red onion are added at the last minute. The potatoes are excellent—by themselves. They are awkward with the pastrami, bagel, and cream cheese, but good with the eggs. Their pronounced tastes sap flavor from the pastrami rather than complementing it. Traditional hash browns would be a better choice here.

Salsa is odd—mostly tomatoes, scallions, and what looks and tastes like cooked green bell pepper. A good *salsa fresca* is easy—minced onion, diced tomatoes, two or three types of hot chili peppers, and cilantro with a little vinegar and sugar. This one is peculiar and does not complement anything on the platter.

Maxcy's Grill
★½
$

Location: 79-305 Highway 111, La Quinta, 564-0613. *Food type: coffee shop. Ambiance: big room, big windows. Bar: beer and wine. Reservations: not accepted. Hours; breakfast, lunch, and dinner daily.*

"Generic" is the correct term to apply here. Prepare yourself not to be surprised by anything either on the good side or the bad side. Maxcy's is exactly what you expect. It is the quintessential American coffee shop. Everything on the extensive menu is fresh and well prepared according to designated skills of a graduate short-order cook. Everything is also quite ordinary, even boring. Even the prices are ordinary: a really cheap weekday special and around $8 for everything else. Even its location is generic—the parking lot at Walmart.

If you find yourself in La Quinta and hungry for ordinary coffee shop food, it sure does beat Denny's.

Lantana
★½
$$$

See Hyatt Grand Champions in Chapter 1 for review.

La Quinta Baking Company
★★½
$-$$

See review in Chapter 5, French Bistros.

Michael's Café
★★
$-$$

Location: 35-955 Date Palm Dr., Cathedral City, 321-7197. *Food type:*
American coffee shop. *Ambiance:* gay, with Elvis, Judy, and Marilyn décor
carried to a level approaching the absurd. *Bar: full.* *Reservations:* not accepted.
Hours: breakfast and lunch daily.

I have lowered the rating on this coffee shop since the first edition.
After a recent dining experience, I have found an unfortunate drop in
the quality of both the food itself and the care of its preparation. The
more interesting aspects of this restaurant, its herbed hash browns and
sauces, seem to have given way to the more conventional. It is still one
of the better coffee shops around, but all things considered I would favor
Sunshine Café over Michael's.

Despite the questionable quality, Michael's offers an interesting
environment. The owners seem to be obsessed with Marilyn Monroe,
followed closely by Elvis Presley and Judy Garland. Images of these
American icons are everywhere, even to the point of absurdity—kitsch
carried to hitherto undreamed of levels. Covered sidewalk seating is
comfortable and does not really reflect the fact that Michael's is actually
part of an outdoor shopping mall.

Michael's shares much with Sunshine Café (reviewed later in this
chapter). The menu is a bit more sophisticated with such things as a Nova
lox plate and a deli omelet, and the prices are about a buck more but
quality is somewhat less. The perfectly sautéed pork chops and poached
eggs with, for example, hash browns, biscuits, and gravy is one of the
finest traditional breakfasts around. Corned beef hash or country smoked
ham are alternatives.

My favorite coffee-shop test, the Denver omelet, passes, but not with
flying colors. The fresh, crunchy dice of green bell pepper, ham, and
onion are just right, but the omelet is dry when requested easy. Biscuits
are not always big, fresh, and fluffy. They do not ever fall into the rock-
hard microwaved version delivered at inferior establishments, but they
can be less than perfect.

Gravy is excellent. Thinner than most country gravies, this one is most likely a sauce suprême (cream and chicken stock) with bits of sausage. It is subtle and clean, with a velvety texture. I'll bet money that the *salsa fresca* is out of a jar. It is medium hot with a heavy back note of green bell pepper and no discernible cilantro taste.

Pancakes and hash browns are excellent. The home fries are large potato dice that have been deep-fried—think French fries. The cold lox plates are wonderful: bagel, cream cheese, Bermuda onion, cucumber, tomato, kalamata olives, and capers.

The J. D. Original, billed as "a legendary creation piled high, open faced, and smothered in gravy—two scrambled eggs and two sausage patties on an open biscuit," sounds much better than it is. It may well be a legendary creation, and it is certainly piled high, but it is more of a big mess than anything else. It is all mixed together so there is only one taste.

Lunch is salads, burgers, and sandwiches, all of which can be quite interesting: cobb, teriyaki deluxe, and Ruben, respectively. The full bar is also an unusual feature for a coffee shop.

The Nest
★
$
Location: 75-188 Highway 111, Indian Wells, 346-2314. **Food type:** *American breakfast.* **Ambiance:** *French country inn; cozy, intimate, and friendly.* **Bar:** *full.* **Reservations:** *not accepted.* **Hours:** *hours seem to be constantly changing, best to call in advance.*

Something strange happens when a dinner house decides to offer breakfast: the breakfast is either better or worse than the benchmark coffee shop. In this case, it is worse. Using Sunrise Café (this chapter) as our benchmark, the Nest comes in at "why bother." Yes, it is pretty. The Euro countryside look is attractive and enticing. Coffee is good. Service is adequate. Palms Café in Palm Desert is several miles west; Sunrise Café in Cathedral City is a lot more miles. The Miramonte Resort is almost right across the street, however, and the La Quinta Resort and Club is not much farther to the east, as is the funky little Teddy's (all this chapter). Again, why bother?

Take, for example, the corned beef hash with poached eggs and a slice of honeydew melon. Shouldn't be difficult. Let's start with the toast. Why?

Because it comes already cold, unbuttered, and five minutes before the corned beef. Saving money by buying really cheap bread is a spurious savings. The toast is 90 percent air and is reduced to panko as soon as it is buttered. Needless to say air does not have much flavor and even less texture.

Before ordering the corned beef I inquired as to whether it is made on premises or bought elsewhere. I should have specified as to whether I meant the corned beef itself or just the hash. I do not know what this meat is. Corned beef is made by brining a beef brisket for 10 days in a spicy pickling liquid containing such things as sugar, saltpeter, cinnamon, mustard seed, peppercorns, cloves, allspice berries, berries, bay leaves, and ginger. It is then braised in a broth with onion, carrot, and celery for three hours until fork tender and finally cut thinly across the grain. That is corned beef.

Corned beef hash combines, usually in equal measure, corned beef and boiled potatoes with chopped onion and parsley. It is formed into patties and pan-fried in butter. Sometimes the mixture is processed. I prefer it chopped rather than processed, but at the Nest it is not to be. With a proper corned beef hash, the beef is spicy and earthy, the potatoes add starch and body, the onion brings acidity and tang, and the parsley (when cooked), an herby hint of tarragon. It is time consuming but not difficult.

The "hash" at the Nest is mystery meat. It is tough, chewy, and filled with gristle. Some shredded potato is added along with tiny bits of onion. Nothing tastes but the mystery meat. It also arrives cold.

Poached eggs are medium cooked and cold. I ordered them easy.

The honeydew, by the way, is excellent, but still, why bother?

Omri Go Med
★★★

Location: 73-676 Highway 111, Palm Desert, 341-7004. **Food:** *American/ Middle Eastern coffee shop.* **Ambiance:** *big triangular room, one-table patio in rear; good use of greenery and bougainvillea.* **Bar:** *beer and wine.* **Reservations:** *not accepted for breakfast.* **Hours:** *Monday through Saturday, Sunday brunch.*

When I sampled the breakfast menu at Omri's, he had been open exactly three days so it was very much a work in progress. Some offerings were superb; others he was still working on. By the time you read this, knowing Omri's track record, all the bugs will have been worked out. If you want something a little more daring for breakfast, something other than your basic coffee-shop menu of bacon and eggs, hash browns, and pancakes, try Omri's. Yes, he does have rolled oats, but they are Middle Eastern style with chopped dried apricots, dried currants, fresh pomegranate, and honey. Your French toast is made with challah and comes with sautéed Granny Smith apples, roasted walnuts, and maple syrup. Omri's version of eggs Benedict is made with spinach, arugula, a brioche biscuit, and either pancetta *or* lox. He's got an omelet made with goat cheese, kalamata olives, scallions, bell pepper, and tomato.

There are three skillet dishes: the shakshuka, the corned beef, and the roast pork. The shakshuka is a Turkish ratatouille and is the most unusual thing on the menu. Eggs baked with a ratatouille of tomatoes, eggplant, onions, peppers, chilies, cumin, turmeric, and a healthy dose of Omri magic. The whole skillet is covered with mozzarella and baked. Omri's corned beef is not corned beef hash, but slices of his own corned beef. This is absolutely superb corned beef—packed with flavor. I have not tried the roast pork skillet, but that is first on my list for the next time. It comes with a hash brown/onion crisp. Don't know . . . try it yourself.

Prices are lower than at Palms Café (this chapter), for example, and this is a time to expand your breakfast experience. There is a great chef in the kitchen here as opposed to a short-order cook.

Palms Café
★★★
$
Locations: 44-150 Town Center Way, Palm Desert, 779-1617; 69-930 Highway 111, Rancho Mirage, 770-1614. Food: American coffee shop. Ambiance: pretty, upscale, beautiful patio, flowers and greenery. Bar: beer and wine. Reservations: not accepted. Hours: breakfast and lunch daily.

Palms Café is a spinoff of Sunshine Café (this chapter). The menu is largely the same, and the quality is very high. Portions are huge and the kitchen will happily split for you. The Trailblazer Omelet, for example, will easily serve two. The Palm Desert location is the most modern and attractive by contemporary standards. Rancho Mirage is rather ordinary: a large box with a pleasant sidewalk patio.

For a full review of the food, see Sunshine Café. The Palm Desert location is usually crowded, especially on weekends, but the restaurant is large and wait times generally are not more than 10 minutes. The Rancho Mirage location is new (winter of 2009) and I have not yet eaten there.

Peabody's Café
½

$

Location: 134 S. Palm Canyon Dr., Palm Springs, 322-1877. Food type: American coffee shop. Ambiance: fun and funky little sidewalk café. Bar: full. Reservations: not accepted. Hours: breakfast and lunch daily; dinner Thursday to Saturday.

So why, with only half a star, is Peabody's on the recommended list at all? Because it is just so darn cute, that's why. If cuteness is on your short list of desirable qualities, Peabody's must rank accordingly. Don't count on quality food, but for people-watching right in the heart of downtown Palm Springs, this place can be equaled, but can't be beat. With tables covered in vinyl and stapled together, crowded next to the windowed front, and a few more tables right at curbside, Peabody's does have a French/Italian street-scene ambiance about it. California's governor, Arnold Schwarzenegger, has been known to visit Peabody's. Since Arnold is friends with Johannes Bacher, I would expect him to visit Johannes (see Chapter 7) rather than this coffee shop, but who can second guess the wily ways of politicians. The building itself is old and a bit ratty, which only adds an element of authenticity to its Euro trash-wannabe charm. It is just a shame that the food is not better than it is.

A Denver omelet is always a surefire test of a short-order cook's finesse. For a Denver omelet to succeed, the vegetables must be absolutely fresh, diced fine, and raw. Green bell pepper and red or sweet onion have to crunch, crackle, and release springlike flavors into your mouth. The ham, too, should be cut right from the bone. However, a great omelet is about the egg not the filling. The fillings should never overpower the egg in terms of either quality or quantity. Here they do both. There is too much filling, and nothing is fresh or raw. A group sauté succeeds only in turning the whole thing into mush.

O'Brien potatoes are not O'Brien potatoes. Most people do not know what O'Brien potatoes are, so they never complain. Imagine that you ordered a tuna sandwich and you got ham and cheese. You complain, and the cook says, "This is our version of a tuna sandwich, Mr. Know-It-All!" Well, I'm, sorry, but tuna is not ham, hollandaise is not cheese sauce, and O'Brien potatoes have onion, green bell pepper, and pimiento. These potatoes have red and yellow bell peppers and possibly some onion, and everything is so overcooked that nothing tastes like much of anything. They are also swimming in grease.

A Black Forest ham sandwich fairs little better with a ham that is indistinguishable from any packaged sliced ham. Potato salad, on the other hand, is remarkably good, especially in context. This is not a Smart & Final tub of russets, mayonnaise, and pickles, but a homemade concoction of diced red potatoes—skins on—black olives, and onion with a hint of dill. It needs more onion, salt, and dill, but who's complaining? Eggs Albuquerque—two poached eggs on an English muffin, topped with avocado, sour cream, and mango salsa—are worth a look. Mango salsa, in fact, finds its way into several dishes.

With its full bar, you might order a mimosa or Bloody Mary, enjoy the buzz of downtown Palm Springs, and forget all about the mediocre food. Friday and Saturday feature karaoke from 8 P.M. till last call. On Thursday there is karaoke for the under-21 set from 6 P.M. to 8 P.M.; after that the kids are kicked out.

Pinocchio in the Desert
Not recommended
$-$$
*Location: 134 E. Tahquitz Canyon Way, Palm Springs, 322-3776. **Food type:** standard American. **Ambiance:** Parisian-style sidewalk café. **Bar:** full. **Reservations:** not accepted. **Hours:** breakfast, lunch, and dinner Wednesday through Monday.*

It is with a heavy heart that I have to announce the demise of the desert's best and most interesting breakfast establishment, More Than a Mouthful. That restaurant was very successful, but its owners tired of the daily grind and sold in February 2007. The new owners have renamed the downtown Palm Springs café Pinocchio in the Desert.

More Than a Mouthful was a riot of gay camp with its walls copiously adorned with outrageous pop art—Andy Warhol and Roy Lichtenstein on Dexedrine. It is all gone now. While the terrific location and sidewalk ambiance are still intact, everything else, including food quality, is gone. The signature blue-crab cake Benedict from the old restaurant remains on Pinocchio's menu. What was a marvel of hedonistic delight now consists of a cold and runny hollandaise. Hollandaise is a mayonnaise made with clarified butter rather than oil. It should have the consistency of mayonnaise, not diesel fuel. The crab cake here is shredded crab and mayonnaise cut with corn kernels and bits of red and green bell pepper. It is not a cake; it is not even fried. The English muffin is not toasted. Because of this, all the liquid from the crab, remaining poaching water, and hollandaise soaks into the muffin, leaving it soggy. Poached eggs, requested soft, arrive firm, eliminating the glory of Benedict. Potatoes, advertised as O'Brien, are not O'Brien, but they are caramelized nicely.

The dinner menu is inexpensive and contains several dishes that, if prepared well, could be excellent buys—pastas, turkey breast, and meatloaf between $7 and $11; steaks, prime rib, and rack of lamb averaging $18. With reasonable prices for cocktails and wines and an excellent street-side environment, this could be a real winner, but I am not holding my breath

Randy's
★
$

Location: 73-560 Highway 111, Palm Desert, 340-3036. Food type: American. Ambiance: storefront off a parking lot. Bar: none. Reservations: not accepted. Hours: breakfast and lunch daily; closed all summer. Note: cash only.

This is an odd call. Randy's is very popular, but I don't recommend it in large part because I do not like it. This kind of bias does not make for good criticism, but there is an element that is objective. Randy's crams everything into a scramble or an omelet, a practice that renders the eggs irrelevant. It often even renders the stuffing irrelevant. A sample scramble contains tofu, salsa, spinach, potatoes, rice, beans, and the kitchen sink, it seems. With every conceivable sausage, cheese, and vegetable combination offered, these overstuffed wonders draw a big crowd but fail on the aesthetic front.

If you like big piles of overcomplicated breakfast food, this is your place. Salma Hayek may drop by when she is in town. Does that help?

Rock Garden Café
★★½ (only for breakfast)
$

Location: 777 S. Palm Canyon Dr., Palm Springs, 327-8840. *Food type:* American. *Ambiance:* rock house, babbling brook, parklike patio, and a view. *Bar:* full. *Reservations:* not accepted for breakfast. *Hours:* breakfast, lunch, and dinner daily.

Located smack up against the base of Mount San Jacinto, this quirky upscale establishment is utterly charming. Made entirely of rocks, it exudes both the feeling of an old-fashioned country home and a custom-designed getaway. With sparkling waterfalls and babbling ponds, the outdoor patio is an absolute must, especially when showing visiting friends and relatives our winter wonderland.

The Rock Garden, coming as it does with a fully equipped bar, prompts thoughts of an early morning Bloody Mary. A great Bloody Mary is concocted from ice cubes made from fresh-squeezed lemon and/or lime juice spiked with lemon pepper. Water from melting ice is a disaster. Add a rich and potent homemade tomato juice and a gin with enough flavor to cut through the tomato. You do not get any flavor from vodka. Dashes of Tabasco, horseradish, and Worcestershire round out the recipe. The traditional garnish is a celery stick and lime wedge. Bartender, feisty octogenarian Lou Suboter, who has been pouring his own tomato-juice recipe since 1949, puts together a fine Mary. It lacks what I consider to be the ultimate touch—the frozen lemon or lime juice—but his addition of the seldom-used freshly grated horseradish works beautifully with the Tabasco.

The food is a cut above the usual coffee-shop fare. The eggs are large and fresh; the Nova Scotia lox, clean and smoky. The classic—and then some—omelets are packed with fresh and flavorful meats, cheeses, and veggies. Thermal pitchers are provided on every table, insuring a hot refill at your disposal, a nice touch especially when dining outside. House potatoes are Yukon Gold wedges seasoned with salt, sugar, and paprika and sautéed until tender. The skins are left on for additional flavor. The biscuits and gravy, always a tell-tale indicator separating the fine breakfast establishment from the second rate, are light and soft. The gravy is effectively original. Your usual country diner might go so far as to serve commercial cream of chicken soup. This gravy is a velouté rather than a simple béchamel. It is also fused with herbs: thyme, Italian parsley, and dill.

Salsa is another café test. Is it bottled or prepared in the kitchen by a chef who knows and understands what a *salsa fresca* is all about? Freshness is mandatory. The classic salsa contains onion, tomato, a variety of chili peppers fresh or smoked, and cilantro. This one is Italian parsley, scallions, onion, tomato, and either lemon or lime juice. It was not spicy at all, but a successful variant.

The menu features a battery of interesting omelets, from the Butcher Shop through the Baja Breakfast, all at reasonable prices. In addition, Rock Garden Café has a daily special for $3.99 or $4.99. This is more than your basic two eggs, toast, and hash browns. It ranges from a banana waffle to huevos rancheros to a ham and cheese omelet. Rock Garden Café is also a bakery serving up such things as Napoleons and fruit-custard tarts.

Sherman's Deli
★★
$

Locations: 73-161 Country Club Dr., #D, Palm Desert, 568-1581; 401 E. Tahquitz Canyon Way, Palm Springs, 325-1199. Food type: New York deli and coffee shop. Ambiance: upscale coffee shop. Bar: beer and wine. Reservations: not accepted. Hours: breakfast, lunch, and dinner daily.

Sherman's bills itself as a "kosher style" deli, a term I find offensive. It is true that no observant Jew will believe for one second that the restaurant is kosher, but it is at least mildly deceptive for everyone else. Is it kosher style because kippers and onions are sandwiched between the sausage and eggs and the ham steak? The Monday-night special is pork tenderloin. The early-bird specials include barbecued baby back ribs and a rib and chicken combo!

Having said this, Sherman's isn't a bad coffee shop, perhaps a cut below Sunshine Café and on par with Michael's Café (both reviewed in this chapter). The only thing particularly notable are the potatoes. They are little balloons. Let me see if I can remember this story correctly. Some big-wig politician was coming into a train station in a small French town some time in the 19th century. The chef, who was preparing *pommes frites* (French fries), did not realize that the train was going to be late and dropped the potatoes into the oil too soon. They were partially cooked when the chef was informed of the delay. He removed the French fries half-cooked. They had absorbed a considerable amount of oil and were in a generally yucky state. He cranked up the temperature of the oil, and just before arrival of the train, he refried them. They blew up like balloons, forming a super crisp outer surface and a large air pocket inside. They were a huge success. Sherman's serves potato balloons about the size of a fifty-cent piece. They are a bit greasy, but otherwise enjoyable.

Cream cheese is whipped, which is always nice, and in keeping with its kosher-style appellation, multiple varieties of bagels are offered along with pastrami, potato pancakes (latkes), corned beef, tongue, brisket, blintzes, borscht, knockwurst, and brisket. Prices are on a par with Michael's.

Sunshine Café
★★★

$

Location: 36-815 Cathedral Canyon Dr., Cathedral City, 328-1415. Food type: American. Ambiance: coffee shop. Bar: none. Reservations: not accepted. Hours: breakfast and lunch daily.

Sunshine Café is a funky 1950s-style diner. The main room is fun, the counter is friendly and often hilariously informal, and the back room is boring. This is one of those places that grew past its own success as the back room is obviously the adjacent shop bought out and connected by an awkward hallway. Service is aggressive and funny.

This is a well-above-average coffee shop with all the expected breakfast and lunch items. There is nothing unusual here except that the quality of the food itself is better than the norm, and the preparation, more considered. It is improving all the time. In fact since the first edition, I have upgraded Sunshine Café from two to three stars. For example, I like eggs boiled with the whites just solidified and the yolks soft. It takes about five minutes to render a large egg thus. Most coffee shops tell you they cannot do boiled eggs. It is true that a short-order cook hates making them as it breaks up the flow of his assembly line. Every short-order cook in the world prefers fried or scrambled. I have been refused in this request many times. At Sunshine Café, my eggs came in exactly five minutes accompanied with the following request from the waitress,

"Sir, the cook wants you to try these now, and if they are not right he will make them again." No, they did not know I was a food critic. I was most impressed, and the eggs were perfect.

Truly competent short-order cooks are hard to find and omelets are one of those tests. The Trailblazer, Denver, bacon-mushroom-cheese, and Mexican are highly recommended versions. Fresh, crunchy, perfectly sautéed ingredients wrapped into a moist egg pillow defines the American omelet.

Home fried, hash browns, biscuits and gravy, ham steak: almost everything is a cut above the coffee shop norm—even the coffee. Pancakes are particularly good and come in many interesting variations. Prices are above the lowest in town, but certainly lower than the highest.

Sunshine Café is crowded and reservations are not taken. There are two tables outside, but these are basically right over the street. I tried to eat out there once and they forgot about me. If dining alone, the counter is the place to be.

Sunshine Café has inspired a spinoff, named Palms Café (this chapter), with two locations, one in Palm Desert and the other in Rancho Mirage.

Teddy's
★½

$

Location: 77-965 Avenida Montezuma, La Quinta, 771-1000. *Food type: Mexican-American diner. Ambiance: counter service, takeout, snacks, and minimal table service. Bar: beer. Reservations: not accepted. Hours: breakfast and lunch daily.*

This is a funky little Mexican dive located behind the post office in the La Quinta Village (next to the Village Gas Station). It is not much more than a glorified stand with a semi-self-service counter and a few tables. A fuzzy old television set hangs from the ceiling in the corner. Teddy's does, however, make one of the best huevos rancheros in town. With soft, lightly grilled corn tortillas, *queso blanco,* hot salsa, and over-easy eggs, this is an excellent version of the Mexican staple. The one negative is the salsa, which is out of a jar. There is a hot version and a medium version. The hot version is genuinely hot. Order them both and mix them to your taste. If Teddy's would make its own *salsa fresca,* I'd give it another half-star. Order a Negra Modelo with your huevos.

Twenty6

★★★

$-$$

Location: La Quinta Resort and Club, 49-499 Eisenhower Dr., La Quinta, 564-5720. Food type: gourmet American breakfast. Ambiance: Mediterranean villa. Bar: full, but French roast coffee and fresh-squeezed orange juice is what you want. Reservations: not accepted for breakfast. Hours: breakfast, lunch, dinner, and room service daily 6 A.M. to midnight. Chef: Chris Swenson.

French roast coffee and fresh-squeezed orange juice should open the party. The executive chef is Chris Swenson. Swenson worked his way up the ranks the hard way, beginning with washing dishes in Minneapolis at age 14. He trained in all phases of the culinary arts by apprenticing himself with an older master. Now he is responsible for breakfast, lunch, and dinner in an exclusive four-star resort.

The crab Benedict is an interesting dish. Chef Swenson builds his Benedict around lump and Dungeness crab—not a crab cake—and uses a béarnaise rather than a hollandaise. What is the difference? A hollandaise is flavored with lemon, and a béarnaise, with tarragon. Does the béarnaise work as well with the crab as the more traditional lemon-based sauce? Unequivocally, the answer is yes. It results in a more savory twist, but both are superb. At Twenty6, a slice of grilled tomato and leaf of spinach are placed beneath the crab. These actually work better with the béarnaise than they would with hollandaise. In both cases the poached egg spills its golden loveliness over the crab to marvelous effect. Which do I prefer? It is a split decision. I like the complexity of the béarnaise, but I prefer the crab cake.

The Twenty6 signature omelet is composed of a chicken-apple sausage, a particularly inspired pairing. With a few baby red potatoes for texture, teardrop tomatoes for acid, and mushrooms and cheese for earthiness, this omelet fulfills the desire for conservative tastes while pushing ever so slightly into the more exotic.

The Humboldt Fog goat cheese omelet is a different story. This one pushes dramatically. Made with a potent northern California cheese more suggestive of a Camembert than a goat cheese, this omelet takes the unwary diner way out into left field. Chef Swenson is well aware of this and has created the perfect foil: a tomato jam made with corn syrup, shallots, olive oil, and cardamom. This is one of those instances when the whole is decidedly more than the sum of its parts. The omelet without the tomato jam is just too odd, too quirky, to work alone. The jam without the omelet is some kind of fake savory-sweet relish that is too weird to use as jam and too sweet to work as a relish. Together they bring out the best of one another, resulting in a truly inspired omelet. All egg entrées are served with baby red potatoes—parboiled and sautéed—with a strawberry and wedge of kiwi.

For those inclined to the traditional flapjack, the Indio sweet-corn pancake is the way to go. This is a basic buttermilk batter to which fresh, locally grown corn kernels are introduced. When made well, the pancakes are spongy, elastic, and not too thick. The kernels are blanched just slightly, which makes for a surprising textural twist. A honey butter complements the corn.

For a radical departure from the trucker's special of biscuits and gravy—you know the kind where the fork stands erect in the gravy and the sausage is Farmer John bulk—Chef Swenson introduces a gourmet version. These biscuits are the lightest within my experience, and the gravy is not so much gravy as a reduced cream sauce laced with a serious addition of rosemary. There is no thickening agent such as flour or cornstarch, which impart the stiffness commonly associated with gravy. Thickening is strictly by way of reduction. Slices of a high-quality mild pork sausage and pieces of mushrooms round out this dish.

Other offerings include pecan-raisin French toast, Virginia ham, corned beef hash, lox, and an Angus rib-eye steak.

Not Recommended

The following coffee shops are not recommended for one reason or another: Cactus Jack's (Indio), Don and Sweet Sue's (Cathedral City), Elmer's (Indio and Palm Springs), Empire Polo Grill (Indio), Keedy's (Palm Desert), Main Street Bar and Grill (La Quinta), Mimi's (Palm Desert), Niko's Café (Indio), Rick's Restaurant (Palm Springs), and Ruby's Diner (Palm Springs and Palm Desert). They may be overpriced for what they deliver or the quality elsewhere may be better for the same or less money.

John's (Palm Desert and Palm Springs) and Goody's Café (Cathedral City, Indio, Palm Desert, and Rancho Mirage) are aggressively bad; avoid them at all costs.

CHAPTER 16

Children's Corner

As a general rule, do not take the little ones to dinner in a fine-dining restaurant. Most parents do not make this mistake while at home, but on vacation, with limited time and no babysitter, they often do. Or should I say, we often do. I have made this mistake several times myself. It simply is not worth it. Do not take your kids to Cuistot or Wally's (Chapter 4). Even if they are wonderfully behaved and polite as can be, children will not enjoy the food. At best, you, as parents, will simply try to finish quickly to spare your children any more suffering. Rare is the child with a sophisticated palate. Rare is the child who will remain well behaved through a two-hour, $200 repast when he hates the food. At the other extreme, perhaps the best dining spot for families has shut its doors since the first edition. I am speaking of longtime Palm Desert resident Romano's Macaroni Grill. Below is a guide that will keep your wallet under control, please your children, and provide something better than fast food for you.

Ciro's Ristorante and Pizzeria

$-$$

*Location: 81-963 Highway 111, Indio, 347-6503. **Food type:** Italian-American diner. **Ambiance:** austere coffee shop. **Bar:** domestic beer on tap and house wines (Inglenook, Cribari, Estate Cellars). **Reservations:** accepted for parties of six or more only. **Hours:** lunch and dinner daily.*

Ciro's is a New Jersey-style Italian diner. The menu is large: 24 pizzas featuring all the traditional Italian toppings and such West Coast variations as pineapple, jalapeños, cashews, shrimp, and smoked oysters; 13 pastas ranging from spaghetti and meatballs to *mostaccioli ala Siciliano;* 10 sandwiches; four children's entrées; daily soup specials; salads; appetizers; seven desserts; and 12 house specialties. Sea scallops in parsley, white wine, and cream and fettuccine primavera with grilled shrimp are the high-end extremes.

The quality is good enough, the preparation is consistent, and the prices are family friendly, sometimes downright cheap. Lunch, for example, is $6.25 for your choice of the daily soup (or salad) and pasta, sub sandwich, or personal pizza. At dinnertime, $8.95 will get you the three-course early-bird special: soup, salad, and entrée.

Manicotti stuffed with ricotta and its attendant herbs—mostly oregano—and covered with tomato sauce, a slice of provolone, and baked in a hot oven is simple, good, basic, Italian-American fare, a definitive step above spaghetti and meatballs.

Prices range from $6 to $15. Only the packed extra large pizzas are more.

Elephant Bar Restaurant
★
$-$$
Location: 73-833 Highway 111, Palm Desert, 340-0456. **Food type:** *American grill with popular Americanized Asian dishes.* **Ambiance:** *pseudo safari.* **Bar:** *full.* **Reservations:** *accepted for parties of eight or more only.* **Hours:** *lunch and dinner daily.*

Elephant Bar Restaurant is a chain of more than 30 restaurants mostly in California. It is not bad enough to rule out entirely, and children like it. They also like the wild-animal décor: leopard-print carpeting, faux animal skin tabletops, wicker, bamboo, animal prints, and African travel posters. The long mirrored bar is a popular hangout and TGIF spot with 20-somethings.

The large, sweeping menu runs towards ribs, chicken, shrimp, combo platters, an extensive battery of burgers and sandwiches, pizzas, fish, pan-Pacific stuff (Hawaiian chicken, Chinese stir-fries, pad thai), lots of teriyaki, and even a steak or two. A large kids' menu, with burgers, tacos, spaghetti, corn dogs, and fish sticks from $3 to $4.50, will usually sate a nine-year-old. A nine-option menu of huge desserts may be the real draw for the younger set. Coupons for dinner specials ($8) are commonly had from the local newspaper. On the other hand, adults can get a beer for $0.99 (with coupon), which may improve your experience.

El Ranchito

$
Locations: 78-039 Calle Estado, La Quinta, 564-0061; 31-855 Date Palm

Dr., Cathedral City, 321-9751; 78-540 Highway 111, La Quinta, 564-0668. Food type: Mexican-American. Ambiance: pleasant coffee-shop style; La Quinta location has a nice patio. Bar: beer and wine. Reservations: accepted for parties of 15 or more only. Hours: lunch and dinner daily.

Most children who know Mexican food—at least the undemanding Mexican-American style—like it. There are hundreds of such places throughout the Coachella Valley all serving more or less an identical menu of tacos, burritos, and enchiladas with rice and beans. It is a formula. Whether upscale Las Casuelas (see Chapter 12) or more casual like Teddy's (see Chapter 15), it is mostly the same. Children and adults who do not often eat Mexican food are likely to be somewhat shocked at first. Contrary to common perception, most Mexican food is only moderately hot or spicy, but it is the salsas that pack the most punch. Cilantro is an herb common to both Mexican and Chinese food that is not commonly found in heartland cooking. This, too, can be a surprise to the uninitiated, although many are enchanted by it. There are generally one or two more interesting entrées available such as a *carne asada* (Mexican-style steak), an interesting shrimp dish (*camarónes*), or whole deep-fried fish (usually tilapia). These should take care of the adult appetite. The El Ranchito chain—two locations in La Quinta, one in Cathedral City—is a good example of this kind of restaurant. They are clean and of consistent quality, and English is spoken proficiently.

The bottom line here is, if you know Mexican food, it is a healthful and kid-friendly alternative to fast food. If you do not, try it once. It is usually inexpensive as well.

Louise's Pantry
★½
$

See full review in Chapter 15.

Murph's Gaslight
★½
$

Locations: 79-860 Avenue 42, Bermuda Dunes, 345-6242; 73-155 Highway 111, Palm Desert, 340-2012. Food type: American country cooking;

fried chicken is the specialty. **Ambiance:** *farmhouse.* **Bar:** *full; skimpy wine list.* **Reservations:** *not accepted.* **Hours:** *lunch and dinner Tuesday through Saturday; family-style dinner Sunday from 3 P.M. to 9 P.M; breakfast at Palm Desert location 8 A.M. Monday through Friday.*

Murph's Gaslight has expanded to a second location in Palm Desert. This location is much more convenient for the majority of the east valley population as well as tourists, but it is not nearly as fun. Food quality is also better at the Bermuda Dunes location.

The strange little restaurant at the old location, well off the beaten path, was founded in 1976 by Ralph Murphy. Murphy was a Southern boy well versed in the country ways of collard greens, black-eyed peas, and corn pone. During the 1930s, he worked on several ocean liners, picking up the whys and wherefores of higher-end cuisine. Whether this exposure has had any effect on the food of Gaslight is unknown, as the food is strictly down home.

The building is as cute as it is unexpected. Its location is downright bizarre, on the grounds of the Bermuda Dunes regional airport, which only serves small private planes. Murph's is on the south side of the airport and accessible only from Avenue 42. Exit Jefferson from Interstate 10 and turn right on Avenue 42. Good luck at night. Once inside, the look and feel is that of a large country kitchen. Everything is green and cream and lacy.

Fried-chicken lovers (and most children are) flock to Murph's. They love the spicy batter. They love the hot, crispy, greasy pieces of fried poultry. They love the generous supply of French fries. And parents love the prices—only $9.95 at lunch and $17.95 for a full dinner.

Gaslight claims loudly that the chicken is pan-fried. Who am I to argue? It undoubtedly is pan-fried, but in a lot of oil. The chicken pieces are uniformly cooked to a deep, dark golden brown, which indicates that they are not making contact with the cooking surface. In a pan-fry with a minimum of frying oil, darker spots occur where contact is made, then the chicken is turned over and something similar happens on the flip side. These appear to be deep-fried. They are uniformly crispy and blisteringly hot upon arrival at your table.

The chicken in a basket lunch ($9.95) consists of a drumstick, thigh, and breast. The thigh and drumstick are cooked perfectly. The meat is juicy and tender without any loss of flavor. The pieces are also identical from surface to bone. In other words, the meat around the bone is not slightly undercooked and the surface not slightly dried out. All of it is identical. The breast, as is usually the case, is dried out and lacking in flavor. This, of course, is intrinsic to the nature of chicken breast, but a reduction in cooking time would certainly help. My advice, however, is to specify when ordering that you wish to substitute thighs. The restaurant will probably be happy to oblige, as thighs are cheaper than breasts.

French fries accompany at lunch, along with some interesting coleslaw. For me, fries are the last thing I want with fried chicken—just too much grease. The coleslaw, on the other hand, is designed to cut through this surfeit of fat. There is very little sugar in this slaw, and the addition of scallions and grated bell pepper give it a clean taste and a much-needed tang.

Thursday's soup du jour is navy bean. This is simple and adequate and includes a generous portion of canned tomatoes (Hey, it comes with the chicken!). Cornbread is heavily leavened, which makes for a light texture. The very lightness, however, decreases the flavor. It is sweet but not cloying.

The family-style Sunday dinner is the way to go for those who like this kind of food. For $17.95 for adults and $8.95 for children, this all-you-can-eat banquet features a mountain of fried chicken, mashed potatoes, gravy, black-eyed peas, a vegetable, biscuits, soup, corn bread, salad, and fruit shortcake with cream.

Other menu items include chicken and dumplings, chicken-fried steak, a fish, and beef tips and noodles. There is even a daily early-bird special for $10: Swiss steak, barbecue beef ribs, and traditional turkey dinner.

I have trouble rating this restaurant because I personally do not like fried chicken. That being said, I do think that this fried chicken is very good for what it is. I therefore have to give the chicken three stars. Everything else I tasted was quite mediocre and deserves one star. The cost, however, is a major attraction, and as a kid venue, it really can't be beat.

Picanha

$$$

See full review in Chapter 12. This is quite expensive for a "Children's

Corner" restaurant. The child's tab is $11.95, but many kids dine here, and they seem to enjoy this Brazilian barbecue.

Tootie's Texas Barbecue
Barbecue: ★★½
Sides: Not recommended
$

See the full review in Chapter 13. Barbecue is another way to go with kids. Finger food is always a hit.

CHAPTER 17

Kosher and Halal Options

Kosher

During season, there are more than 10,000 Jews in the Coachella Valley. That number is growing, and the Jewish population is becoming more observant. A Reform temple, two Conservative congregations, two Chabad shuls, and one Orthodox synagogue define the religious scene. As of this writing, there is not a single kosher restaurant in the valley. What can be made of these statistics? I would certainly think there would be a market for one considering this data.

The Coffee Bean & Tea Leaf is the single exception. There is a Coffee Bean in Palm Springs, one in Palm Desert, and one in La Quinta. They are springing up inside of Ralph's markets as well. These cannot be called restaurants, but with an extensive selection of pastries, bagels, and cream cheese and a menu of trendy designer coffees, they can adequately provide a continental breakfast. The locations are 100 N. Palm Canyon, Palm Springs, 325-9402 and 73-400 El Paseo Dr., #9, Palm Desert, 674-9056. Call the individual stores for details concerning kosher certification. The cheddar-jalapeño bagel with cream cheese is my favorite.

Chabad of Rancho Mirage

This is a home-style backyard barbecue held at a synagogue. Its value is in its providing kosher food, not its competitiveness.

Price: see text

Location: 72-295 Via Marta, Rancho Mirage, 770-7785. Food type: kosher barbecue. Bar: beer and wine sometimes available; BYOB but check with the rabbi. Reservations: not accepted. Hours: Tuesday night kosher barbecue from 5:30 P.M. to 7:30 P.M.; closed during summer.

The Tuesday night kosher barbecue at Chabad Rancho Mirage is the single viable full dinner option for kosher meals in the valley. Held between 5:30 P.M. and 7:30 P.M., summers excepted, this barbecue features Rubashkin Aaron's Glatt kosher meat. What's on the menu? Steak? Rib steak only. If you have to ask, kosher you are not. Since you probably aren't, it is because the loin cuts are not kosher in this country. The butchers must remove the sciatic nerve to make it kosher, and they do not do that here. They do in Europe, but it is not cost effective here. This is a one-pounder, bone-in, and pretty darn good for $18 with the salad of the week included, not an unreasonable amount. Lest the uninitiated think that salting seriously damages the quality of the meat, you are wrong. It is perhaps not quite as juicy, but unless you were to taste kosher and non-kosher back to back, you will hardly notice the difference. Ironically, when meat is grilled, it does not have to be salted according to Jewish law, but out here in the "provinces," it all comes that way.

For $8.50 you can get a large shoulder lamb chop also served with the salad. Grilled chicken ($5.50), various burger configurations (including a Cajun burger and a veggie burger) from $3.95, and knockwurst ($4) are also on the entrée list.

Except for the salad served with the steak and the lamb, everything is a la carte. A choice of six or seven sides is available, including soup, salad, baked potato, corn on the cob, and vegetarian beans. All dressings are OU Pareve. No, you cannot have sour cream on your baked potato even if you are not having meat! That also means no butter on your corn. This barbecue is strictly non-dairy.

Bring the *kinderlach*. What is a Jewish event without the children? In addition to the burgers and dogs, desserts and ices are available: $0.50 for Tofutti Cuties, $2.50 for the pie of the week. Beer is served, but bring your own wine. (Make sure it is kosher. Check with the rabbi first.) The Baron Herzog Cabernet goes best with the rib steak. Actually the Baron Herzog Cabernet is the best kosher wine available here period. No standards are compromised in its production. Four wines from Yardin Vineyard are sold at Clarks, a health-food supermarket in Rancho Mirage. Yardin, an Israeli wine from the Golan Heights, is excellent by anyone's standards.

Chabad Rancho Mirage is in a residential neighborhood. The barbecue is around the back. Just walk down the driveway and you will see the tables, children playing, and many happy diners.

The cutest five-year-old girl in the entire world handed me a menu. "Get in line there," she said, pointing, "and tell those cooking people what you want. Then mark down what you ate." She announced this in an ever-so-precocious manner. I looked at the orange computer printout. I must have looked terribly confused because the little girl handed me a stubby little library pencil and said again, "Tell those cooking people what you want." Exasperated, she pointed again. "Then after you eat, add up all the stuff on this paper then take it, this paper, over to the money box and put in the money, which is the total that you added up. See?" She pointed to a table where a little boy of maybe 10 was making change. "That's where you pay." (I subsequently learned that she is the rabbi's second youngest, and her name is Sarah'le.)

I gave her a funny look, one that asked how reliable this system was. With hand on hip and sigh, she gave me a look that was a cross between the naiveté of a totally honest person and the suspicion that I actually may be insane and not simply dense.

A short interview with Rabbi Shimon Posner attested to his wealth of information. "While it is true that the dining-out option is basically limited to this barbecue, it is also not true that kosher food is hard to get. When staying at a hotel, motel, or resort in the Palm Springs area, stay at a facility with a kitchen. The kitchen will not be kosher, but you can always buy yourself a skillet, paper plates, and plastic tableware," he advises.

What about supermarkets? Is there any fresh meat, cheese, deli stuff? Yes, but it is all spread around town. It would be nice if at least one supermarket carried an entire line of kosher products, but no one does. Albertsons (Rancho Mirage at Monterey and Country Club) carries fresh kosher meat but it is limited to a few cuts of beef (brisket, stewing meat, steaks, hamburger) and chicken. Pavilions (Rancho Mirage at Bob Hope and Gerald Ford) has a section devoted entirely to kosher products. This includes deli meat, poultry, and cheese. The poultry is all frozen, but you can get chicken, turkey, and usually duck. Pavilions carries cheese, too: goat, cheddar, Edam, mozzarella. Ralphs in Smoke Tree Village (Palm Springs at Sunrise and Palm Canyon) carries some cheese and a whole line of deli meats, including Empire and Aaron's. Ralphs Indian Wells has Empire deli meat and some cheeses. The turkey pastrami is particularly good. Ralphs (Palm Springs at Ramon and Sunrise) carries the complete line of Empire frozen entrées as well as deli meats and cheese. Trader Joe's (Cathedral City, Palm Desert, and La Quinta) sells whole chickens, chicken parts, turkey breast, ground beef, ground turkey, and steaks, all fresh (Aaron's and David's). Nathan's has added kosher hot dogs to its line. Ralphs carries them. Empire turkey is available throughout the year and almost guaranteed between Thanksgiving and the end of the year at just about any major supermarket. All things considered, a pretty impressive selection, and do not forget whole fresh fish.

Then there is Rabbi Posner's wife, Chaya. She takes meat orders, which are delivered from Los Angeles. She has an entire list of available meats, from rack of lamb, lamb chops, lamb riblets, duck, turkey, chicken, steaks, beef short ribs, deli meats, and burgers. She has a Web site, and you can place your order online. There is no markup. This is a service to the Jewish community. Much of the meat is delivered fresh, but if it's not picked up within a certain specified time, it is frozen.

Halal

Halal, the Muslim version of kosher, is not without representation in the valley. A restaurant in Palm Desert called Kabobz serves Zabiha halal meat. As far as I have been able to determine, there are no halal-certified meats available at local market in the valley, but most cheeses made by the Cabot Co. of Vermont are halal certified. Cabot is commonly available around town. Cabot cheeses are also certified kosher for Jews.

Kabobz

$

Location: 72-695 Highway 111, #A6, Palm Desert, 862-9294. **Food type:** *Middle Eastern.* **Ambiance:** *box.* **Bar:** *beer and wine.* **Reservations:** *accepted but not necessary.* **Hours:** *lunch and dinner Tuesday through Sunday.*

They advertise themselves as halal, but they serve beer and wine. This is undoubtedly an economic decision, but the two are contradictory. Kabobz also features belly dancers on Saturday nights. The music is taped. I have no idea whether or not this is "halal" or not.

Kabobz occupies the space once home to the late and seriously lamented Hedi's Paris Café, a marvel of French/Moroccan cuisine. It has been stripped of all the French bistro trappings that made Hedi's so visually charming.

Speaking strictly about the food, the kabob is obviously the signature item and there are five varieties: chicken, beef, lamb, shrimp, and ground beef. The lamb seems to be the most representative. I order the lamb. It is advertised as "spicy" and "tender." It is not spicy, but it is tender, extremely so. It is probably leg meat cut into one-inch cubes. It has that mushy, pre-digested texture characteristic of an enzyme-based meat tenderizer like Accent. Papain, the most commonly used enzyme, is found in tropical fruits, especially papaya. The enzyme does work to tenderize meat, but it does so by breaking down the cellular structure, leaving the meat unpleasantly mushy. Only the surfaces directly exposed to the tenderizer react this way, so the meat is not tender all the way through. However, in a small chunks like these it is very effective.

Ironically, the tenderizing technique that is the most effective throughout the meat and least destructive of the meat's texture is the yogurt marinade which was invented in the Middle East. Yet they don't use it here.

The kabob is served over a big serving of rice pilaf. The Indian-style dry and fluffy basmati rice is a pleasant change from all the short-grain sticky rice found all over town. The Indian long-grain rice is beautifully fragrant and subtle. It is usually done as a simple pilaf with a bit of cumin and perhaps a pinch of cinnamon. This one does not disappoint.

A little cup of tzatziki is presented as a condiment. This is not really tzatziki as it does not have chunks of cucumber. It is more like a tzatziki-flavored dip. Yogurt and dill are the base. It does complement the lamb.

All kabobs come with one side. The possibilities are grilled veggies, lentil soup, pita bread, roasted tomato, falafel, hummus, and tzatziki. I opt for the lentil soup. In what has to be another irony, lentil soup was served at this very table by the previous tenant, Hedi Hamrouni. Hedi's was superb: thick, rustic, complex, curried, and kicked up with the hot Arabic chili paste known as harissa. The back notes of onion, carrot, garlic, celery, and tomato laced their way through Hedi's lentils. Cumin and coriander would dance through the air. Hedi's soup was a rich chocolate brown. Would that this one could be classified as being even in the same ballpark. This one has the texture of split-pea soup, and it is at least one-third filled with rice. Why? It is also a green color augmenting the split-pea comparison. There are green lentils, so there is no inherent problem with the color. On the other hand this soup has been pureed to the consistency of split-pea soup. There is none of the chunkiness one tends to associate with the rustic soup. Except, of course, for the fact that the bowl is one-third filled with rice. I do not finish the soup.

Index

Indices

Bar Menu
Bar menus are typically very inexpensive
compared with dinner menus and most
often feature half-priced appetizers taken
from the main menu. It is possible to
dine even at a very expensive restaurant
by taking advantage of the bar menu.
Most often bar menus are offered in
conjunction with happy hour.

Dancing/Live Music

Below is a list of those restaurants with both live music and a dance space, whether official dance floor or simply room for those inclined to dance. Except for Village Pub and Las Casuelas, all are adult oriented.

Cheap Eats

Most coffee shops and Chinese and Mexican restaurants fall into this category; they are not listed here. See the respective chapters for those specific cuisines. See also Bar Menus.

Gay Friendly/Gay Oriented

All restaurants are "gay friendly," but a number of restaurants cater to gay taste in terms of both ambiance and menu. It is most uncommon for any of these restaurants to shun a straight couple, but it is possible that some tourists may feel uncomfortable in the more excessive of these establishments.

* Denotes author's preferences. Although I may have given an exceptionally high grade to a restaurant, it does not automatically signify that I dine there. I, for example, do not feel comfortable at formal establishments. I prefer alfresco dining (a good view I like too). Cost is also a factor. I also like an adventurous chef. This implies an owner/chef type of restaurant.

† Denotes author's lunch preferences

‡ Denotes author's breakfast preferences. Not listed in the above indices are Teddy's and Coffee Bean (Palm Desert only; continental breakfast).